VIKING

NOT MANY, BUT ONE VOLUME 1

G.K. Sasidharan has held positions in educational institutions as lecturer, postgraduate professor, principal, pro-vice-chancellor and vice-chancellor. He has published many papers on cosmology and astrophysics, and is a regular writer on scientific topics in journals and periodicals. He is the architect of the astronomical observatory on the Calicut University campus and was instrumental in the introduction of compulsory social service (CSS) as part of the curriculum in university and colleges.

Sasidharan visited colleges in various states in the country as chairman of the National Assessment and Accreditation Council (NAAC) peer team. He is the founder president of the All Kerala Astrosciences Society (AKAS). He has also authored widely accepted bestsellers. His books have been translated into many languages by eminent academicians and he is also the recipient of many awards.

ADVANCE PRAISE FOR THE BOOK

'*Not Many, But One* is a rare but precious kind of book by an eminent scientist and philosopher, Professor G.K. Sasidharan. The book combines knowledge from two separate streams to tackle some fundamental scientific and philosophical issues. The two streams considered in this book are, on the one hand, the Advaita philosophy propounded by Adi Sankaracharya and further clarified and popularized by Narayana Gurudev and, on the other, the latest findings of modern physics, astrophysics and life sciences. The issues dealt with in this book relate to the questions of the origin, structure and functioning of the Universe and the related problems of the parameters . . . Space–Time, Matter, Energy and Laws of Nature and all the important questions of the modality of creation and the identity of the creator. Of course, to this has to be added the equally important and more mysterious and puzzling questions regarding the animate part of the universe . . . the origin of life, consciousness, death, rebirth and so on.

'Professor Sasidharan has brought out very effectively how Narayana Gurudev, a Kerala sage who lived a hundred years ago (1855–1928), revived the Advaita philosophy through his own composition of hymns in Sanskrit, Malayalam and Tamil.

'The author being a physicist himself has added in the appropriate places the latest developments in physics and astrophysics relevant to the theme of the book. Thus one finds in the book many subtle aspects of quantum theory, special and general theories of relativity, the standard model of particle physics, the Higgs boson discovery and its relevance to the question of mass of particles, the Big Bang theory of creation and the recent discoveries of dark matter and dark energy. The clarifications that these developments have given on some of the earlier difficulties as well as the new complications to the earlier concepts are also brought out. Most scientists believe that the current developments point to the ultimate reality behind all that is experienced as part of the universe is "quantum vacuum", which is constructed of quantum fields endowed with potential properties for giving rise to the different particles, like electron, quark, etc., their specific properties like charge, mass, spin and so on.'

Dr B.V. Sreekantan
(Former director, Tata Institute of Fundamental Research)

'We know that for a seed to sprout and grow into the form of a plant, earth, water and air are indispensable. Similarly, to mould a good book, intuition, deep knowledge and thought have to meet in reciprocity. The light from their meeting is called the "vision". It is the vision that gives the greatness of creativity to any book. When I write about this book of Prof. G.K. Sasidharan, I cannot do it without such an introduction; because, I have not seen any literary work in contemporary literature in which all the three qualities mentioned above are blended so beautifully and harmoniously to this extent. I perceive that

Prof. G.K. Sasidharan who has achieved knowledge in science and Vedanta through his deep meditation and thought wrote this great book with that strength. I see the presence of Gurudev's divine spirit and his blessing spread throughout this book.'

Prof. M.K. Sanu
(Winner, Kendra Sahitya Academy Award)

Sree Narayana Gurudev

NOT MANY, BUT ONE

SREE NARAYANA GURU'S PHILOSOPHY *of* UNIVERSAL ONENESS

VOLUME 1

G.K. SASIDHARAN

PENGUIN
VIKING
An imprint of Penguin Random House

VIKING

USA | Canada | UK | Ireland | Australia
New Zealand | India | South Africa | China

Viking is part of the Penguin Random House group of companies
whose addresses can be found at global.penguinrandomhouse.com

Published by Penguin Random House India Pvt. Ltd.
4th Floor, Capital Tower 1, MG Road,
Gurugram 122 002, Haryana, India

Penguin
Random House
India

First published in Viking by Penguin Random House India 2020

10 9 8 7 6 5 4 3

ISBN 9780670093991

For sale in the Indian Subcontinent only

Typeset in Adobe Caslon Pro by Manipal Digital Systems, Manipal
Printed at Replika Press Pvt. Ltd, India

www.penguin.co.in

FSC
www.fsc.org
MIX
Paper from
responsible sources
FSC® C016779

To
The memory of my beloved parents
Manjippuzha Gopalan and Kettungasseril Kamalakshi

CONTENTS

ACKNOWLEDGEMENTS

At the outset of my thanksgiving occasion, in the name of Sree Narayana Gurudev, I put on record my high indebtedness to Sri Ratan Tata, Chairman, Tata Trusts and to M/s 'Sir Dorabji Tata Trust', who enabled me to make this venture a success.

I am incredibly indebted to Sri R.K. Krishna Kumar (Trustee, Tata Trusts); but for his constant encouragement and persistent discussions, this book would not have materialized to this extent. I extend my heartiest gratitude for the valuable suggestions and advice he gave for making my effort in writing this book more compelling. I am grateful to him for agreeing to bless the book by writing its foreword.

My sincere thanks go to Dr B.V. Sreekantan (renowned physicist) and Prof. M.K. Sanu (famous writer in Malayalam) for blessing the book by writing the advance praise.

I am grateful to Penguin Books, an imprint of Penguin Random House, especially to Ms Manasi Subramaniam, Ms Aparna Kumar, Ms Rachna Pratap, Mr Shantanu Ray Chaudhuri, Ms Devangana Dash, Shreya Punj, Afeefa Baig and Mr Vijesh Kumar, for their sincere effort and cooperation and admirable skill in publishing this book.

I extend my sincere gratitude to Dr C.K. Ramachandran, Dr N. Pankajakshan, Dr B. Ashok, Dr S. Sreenivasan, Adv. V. Sugathan, Dr N. Viswarajan and the late Sri Kalyanaraman for the valuable discussions about various topics in the book.

Mrs Armaity R. Sastri, Sri Vineet Jain, Ms Amrita Patvardhan, Parvathy Sajith (all of Tata Trusts), Sajeendran (Unni), Arunima, Vidhya, Vijayalekshmy, Sarath, Shreya, Sreelakshmi, Akshay, Rohit and Devananda deserve a special mention for their sincere assistance.

Finally, my affectionate thanks go to my wife Rugmini, for her steadfast support throughout in bringing out this book and to my children Sajith, Ajith, Renjith and Manju for their earnest assistance.

G.K. Sasidharan

FOREWORD

I am honoured to write a Foreword to the book *Not Many, But One* which is a tribute to one of the greatest personalities of the 19th and early 20th century in India, Sree Narayana Guru (1856-1928). Prof. G.K. Sasidharan, a physicist and philosopher, worked diligently over the last two to three years on translating into English the Sanskrit, Malayalam and Tamil sublime poems of Sree Narayana Guru. In my view, his dedicated work has resulted in the production of a classic two volume book which will inspire many scholars to study in detail the sweep and splendour of the ideas embedded in ancient Indian thought which are, at once, also resonating with the world-view of new science. This synthesis could not have been achieved in this book without the profound erudition and wisdom of Prof. Sasidharan. I have no hesitation in saying that Prof. Sasidharan's book is incomparable for its scale and depth of learning in Vedanta on one hand and in science on the other.

Many readers are familiar with the life and work of the Guru as a revolutionary, a radical social reformer who, at the same time, shunned violence and division in society and had a luminous vision of oneness across the universe. Prof. Sasidharan's work directs attention to the similarities in some of the philosophical concepts of the Guru with modern scientific views relating specially to cosmology and quantum physics. In doing so, Prof. Sasidharan's work brings out an outstanding comparative analysis of Vedanta along with a profound analysis of what some of the greatest scientific minds have articulated.

Not Many, But One uplifts the Guru's heritage from being a narrative of the social history of Kerala in the 19th and 20th centuries, a time that was dark and dismal, full of societal evils, a period when the leaders of the feudal classes of the region perpetrated what became some of the cruellest examples of caste and social discrimination, which deeply divided society, turning Kerala verily into a 'lunatic asylum' as described by Swami Vivekananda himself. The Guru's significant role seeking social emancipation is now an integral part of the history of India but his pre-eminence in the highest philosophical thoughts and the stunning proximity of the Guru's thoughts with contemporaneous developments in modern science has not been adequately known to the common man. For example, in the great poem *Darsanamala* in the portion dealing with the Yogadarsanam the Guru's verse No.7 translated into English reads as follows—

'The observed has no existence apart from the observer. Therefore, the observed is observer himself. One who differentiates this and takes his mind to the observer Atman is, best among the Yogis.' The following saying of Schrödinger could very well have been expressed by the Guru himself -

'Vedanta teaches that consciousness is singular, all happenings are played out in one universal consciousness and there is no multiplicity of selves.'

If you read the two deeply philosophical works of the Guru viz. *Atmopadesa Satakam* and the *Darasanamala* you will see, and experience, startling similarity with many statements of the founding fathers of quantum theory such as Niels Bohr, Heisenberg, Schrödinger, Pauli and others with what is described in Vedanta. In essence, quantum theory holds that the universe that we see around us is not real, it is covered by an inscrutable curtain which hides the true nature of ultimate reality. Maya is how Vedanta describes that same curtain. These are intricate thoughts and Prof. Sasidharan, with his knowledge of Vedanta, as espoused by the Guru, and his knowledge of physics and cosmology, has been able to synthesize a unified picture as never seen before something that he achieved through the medium of the persona of the great Guru. The reader will find detailed explanations on the subject in the book which even though is in three volumes, still has one single dominant theme viz. the oneness of the universe. It would be true to say that both in quantum physics and in Vedanta the central idea is that the universe is interconnected, indivisible and a single entity and it is pure consciousness. Schrödinger observed—'Quantum Physics rather reveals basic oneness of the universe.'

Refreshingly some of the poems uttered by the Guru reflected not only high philosophy but also the struggles, challenges and temptations that face an individual in the journey of life. The Guru, although a recluse from early in life, not expected to know of the actual travails of ordinary lives, nevertheless penetrated what ordinary human beings encountered in life. For example, in his poem Pindanandi he gives a beautiful explanation of how a foetus in the womb of one's mother begins the pilgrimage of life, the 'Prana Prayana'. The Guru's poem 'Daivadasakam' can be recited by any human being—one caste, one religion, one God. He understood that while man is continuing to swim in the flow of evolutionary debris, there is yet a way to shut out the five senses in order to experience an altogether different state of existence, full of bliss and knowledge—the core spiritual experience.

A philosophical question arises as to how the Guru, who espoused Advaita, someone who believed in the oneness of the universe, the Nirguna Brahman without attributes, could yet dedicate some of his poems to different divine deities like Shiva, Krishna, Ganesha, Devi and so on, all different manifestations of one reality. I would like to speculate that it is probably like the apparent contrast between classical physics and quantum physics each of which paints two contrasting pictures of the universe with little correspondence between the two. Quantum physics explains that reality can be in two states at once, that which is not real appears to be real, due to a phenomenon called the 'collapse of the wave function'. In this view a particle can be at multiple positions at the same time and becomes real only when observation takes place till then it is simply probabilistic. In the Guru's vision and in Vedanta the original cause is Nirguna Brahman, Brahman without attributes, which undergoes a wave function collapse and assumes different expressions which, in Vedanta, is described as Saguna Brahman. The underlying themes linking Vedanta with quantum physics may well be moving towards a fusion between lofty spiritual thoughts and the ultimate goals of science, a transcendental experience.

Those who are interested in this unique confluence will find reading *Not Many, But One* a very rich and satisfying experience. I will conclude this Foreword with a quotation from Ludwig Wittgenstein, the German philosopher—'The mystical is not what the world is, but that it is.'

LL,
R.K. KRISHNA KUMAR
TRUSTEE OF TATA TRUSTS
05 July 2018

PREFACE

Sarvam hi saccidānandam
Neha Nānāsti kincana
Ya: pasyatīha nānēva
Mrtyōr mrtyum sa gacchati.
Entity, knowledge and bliss are one
There is not even an iota of many
He who sees this as many
Happens to go from death to death.

This book '(Neha Nanasti)—'Not many, but one'—is a study of the works and teachings of Sree Narayana Gurudev from a scientific and spiritual standpoint. The chapters are science-bound, Advaita-based works that show a deep-rooted correlation between Advaita Vedanta and quantum cosmology. In an in-depth analysis of Gurudev's works, one sees the progression of Advaita philosophy explaining the missing links in modern science. The concept of the 'Uniqueness' took its origin in 'Nasadeeya Suktam' in Rig Veda and was builtup through *Sruthies* like Taitiriyopanishad which said 'The One desired', 'May I be many and propagate'; Chandogyopanishad which said 'Thou Art It', etc.; followed by the Brahmasutras, its commentary by Adi Sankara and finally accomplished in Sree Narayana Gurudev's works. In a sense, where Veda Vyasa (Badarayana) concluded his teachings, the successor Adi Sankara took over, and where Adi

Sankara ended his contributions to define and propagate Advaita, his successor Sree Narayana Gurudev took over the spirit of Advaita philosophy and brought it up to the present level, in tune with the latest developments in modern cosmology. Vyasa and Adi Sankara never had to face the challenge raised by science in giving the answers to intricate questions regarding the creation, existence and end of the universe, because science had not come to the field of cosmology during their periods. But at the time of Sree Narayana Gurudev, physics and cosmology had grown to their incredible levels, and their studies comprised cosmology in a broader sense. Hence, Gurudev had to face the challenges raised by the new scientific discoveries and the theories therein. But Gurudev's literary works at present are on a par with the developments in physics, at times, even exceeding science in some instances.

In the present context of the social, religious, intellectual, scientific scenario, Gurudev's teachings and messages are highly relevant. The world arena of social life has become so turbulent that all activities in one way or the other are linked with hatred, rivalry, violence, religious confrontations, economic treachery, political vengeance—many of which leading to murders, indiscipline, lack of brotherhood peace, and so on. Sree Narayana Gurudev provides many curative messages to overcome the curse of such evils, the most crucial being 'One caste, One religion, One God to human'. One need not say how indispensable it is in the contemporary perspective. There are many such messages he delivered to the people for their social and economic uplift in the society upholding universal brotherhood.

The biggest ever questions which remain unsolved, or the challenge that science raises with its complicated theories, experiments, logic and algorithms, are the ones like 'who am I?', 'what are all these, around?', 'from where did I come?' and 'where do I go?', etc. Most modern scientists show the courtesy to answer these questions saying, 'We are not going to get the answers to these questions now or at any time in future.' The scientists of the new generation understand their limitations in formulating theories and experiments that can lead them to the answers to the said questions or to a Theory of Everything (ToE) that can answer all the above questions.

But in spirituality, especially in Indian philosophy based on Vedanta, the answers are found in a unique 'substratum' where everything, the universes with all living and inert things, man and his mind that asks the questions, all reduce to a single point. It is known as absolute consciousness—the Brahman. One who asks the above questions also merges into that unique one.

There are two faculties of knowledge, namely spirituality and physics (cosmology) that deal with the secrets of the universe; its origin, existence, end and related phenomena. The spiritual approach to the mysteries of the universe had its beginning millennia ago in both the Eastern and the Western parts of the world, whereas the scientific / logical studies began only some centuries ago.

This book deals with both the faculties in their state-of-the-art status. Modern physics shows a tendency to be on a par with many of the Vedic expressions in the lessons of cosmology especially of the 'Maharishi Triune'—Veda Vyasa, Adi Sankara and Sree Narayana. Sree Narayana Gurudev's literary works contain many amazing concurrences in tune with the latest findings and theories in quantum physics, string theory, many-worlds concept, etc.

Sree Narayana Gurudev wrote more than sixty books; nearly forty of them are highly philosophical and cosmological at the same time, resting firmly on the doctrines of Advaita. This book *Not Many, But One* deals with forty-one of them, with translation into English (from Malayalam, Sanskrit and Tamil) and their meaning and commentary.

I was learning Puranic literature, Sruthies (Upanishads), Mahabharata, Bhagavad Gita, Brahmasutras, their commentary (Bhashya) by Adi Sankara, and the complete works of Sree Narayana Gurudev from childhood to the present time. As a teacher in college, I could teach almost all branches of physics at degree and postgraduate levels for about four decades. I had opportunities to present and speak on various topics in astrophysics, cosmology, Vedanta and Gurudev's works. What amazed me during my speeches in classrooms and on stages was the striking coincidence of the results of studies and research in physics and the divine utterances, especially in the works of the Maharishi Triune. Sree Narayana Gurudev's literary works showed a more significant correlation with lessons and discoveries in physics and modern cosmology than those of his predecessors.

This effort being a new venture, the correlation, though natural, is difficult to establish because both the domains of Vedanta and modern physics are not easily explorable. The author has tried his best to make the book an easily readable one by simplifying its contents without compromising on the depth and spirit of the work.

A brief account of the biography of Gurudev is given to show the social conditions that prevailed in the society during the time of Gurudev. The various chapters of this book deal with how Sree Narayana Gurudev revived Advaita philosophy and liberated it from the unholy curse of *chaturvarnya*—the caste system.

I hope spiritual leaders and philosophers of the East and the West, Vedanties, physicists, cosmologists, teachers, students and enthusiasts will appreciate this enterprising mission of correlating the two uncompromising schools of thought. The devotees of Sree Narayana Gurudev will find this an instrument to explore deeper into the literary works of Sree Narayana Gurudev and get a greater understanding of his greatness.

Kollam G.K. Sasidharan
August 01, 2018

1

REVIVER AND REFORMER IN ONE

Yadā yadā hi ḍarmasya glānirbhavati bhārata
Abhyuthānamadharmaṣya tadātmānām srijāmyaham
Paritrānāya sadhūnām vināśaya ca duṣkritām
Dharmasamstāpanārtāya sambhavāmi yugē yugē.

(Bhagavad Gita, Chapter 4, Slokas 7 and 8)

> Whenever there is the decay of righteousness, Oh! Bharata! And there is an exaltation of unrighteousness, then, I myself come forth: for the protection of the good, for the destruction of evil-doers.
>
> Whenever virtue subsides, and wickedness prevails, I manifest myself. To establish virtue, to destroy evil, to save the good I come from Yuga to Yuga (from time to time).

Sree Narayana Gurudev, the multifaceted genius at the same time a great maharishi, Advaiti (Monist), Brahmacharin (celibate), talented poet, scholar in many languages, merciful social reformer and one with a healing touch to patients, and above all, one of the greatest metaphysicians the world has ever seen, characterized as Patanjali in yoga, Adi Sankara in wisdom, Manu in administration, Buddha in sacrifice, Jesus in humility and Mohammed Nabi in mercy, was born in the year 1855 in a hut-like house known as 'Vayalvaram' in

Chempazhanthi, Thiruvananthapuram district. Chempazhanthi is not far from Thiruvananthapuram city.

Sree Narayana Gurudev's birth had many bewildering salient features. At delivery, though the umbilical cord was cut and other formalities were carried out as usual, the child did not cry as naturally expected, it did not want to suckle breast milk, and for a long time, it did not show any symptom of worldly actions. It was like the detachment of a yogi. But the child was healthy and beautiful.

The child was named Narayananand and used to be called 'Nanu' (an abbreviation of Narayanan in those days). He was the only male child and the eldest among the four children of Madanasan and Kuttiyamma. Nanu's father, Madanasan, was a good scholar with a stout body and intelligence. He was called '*Asan*' because he was a teacher, teaching children. He was a nobleman with many good qualities. Kuttiyamma, Nanu's mother, was the niece of Vayalvaram Kochanasan. She was a noble lady, a devotee and considerate to the poor. Nanu had two maternal uncles named Raman Vaidyar and Krishnan Vaidyar. Krishnan Vaidyar was a good scholar and a practitioner of Ayurveda. He was also a good teacher. Nanu's mother's maternal uncle (Kuttiyamma's uncle) Kochanansan was a noble-hearted and virtuous man. Because of his skill in copying books and documents on to fresh palm leaves from old ones, he was bestowed with the honorary title of Ezhuthan Kochanasan—meaning writer-teacher.

In short, Nanu inherited a great heritage of intellect and providence.

The Vayalvaram house is a small building with three rooms (the house is still preserved in its original form and is a centre of pilgrimage); the walls and the ground are of clay and mud, the roof thatched. There are only two doors. The house is so small that one can get inside only by bending the head. But it was the normal custom of entering into a house in those days in Kerala.

Childhood and Education

About Nanu's childhood, to quote from the biography of Sree Narayana Gurudev written by the great poet Kumaranasan in the then famous magazine *Vivekodayam*:

> The sweets and fruits intended for offerings to the deities in the worship at home, before being offered to the deity, were eaten by Nanu. He would say that God would be pleased if he was pleased. He could always outwit those who tried to prevent him from doing this mischief. It was an interesting pastime for the boy to spit on those who held hard and fast rules of untouchability somewhere around him, he would rush to touch the so-called untouchables and then come home and enter the kitchen without taking a bath, or touch deliberately the men and women who insisted on maintaining their purity.

A brief account of the social background that prevailed in those days in Kerala in general and the state of Travancore, in particular, would be relevant at this stage. This is because Sree Narayana Gurudev holds the highest position among the architects of the renaissance in south India. Before studying the details of Gurudev's literary works and his philosophy, one should know from where he uplifted the society to which he was born, from a very miserable state to something of a welfare state.

In the second half of the nineteenth century, though the social and cultural background in Kerala was explained as uniform throughout in a macroscopic view, on close analysis, it can be seen that there were slight differences in the matter of customs, ceremonies, education, etc. between the north, central and southern parts. Added to this was the imposed caste differentiation among people. It is this social atmosphere in Kerala that Swami Vivekananda referred to as 'the lunatic asylum'.

The people were differentiated by castes and sub-castes maintaining untouchability in its severe form as if it is done according to the Gita doctrine of chaturvarnya, though it was done by a deliberate misuse of the word. The casteism and untouchability among the communities were so severe that a peaceful life was not possible in Kerala in those days.

Although some people belonging to the lower castes of Hinduism had joined other religions to escape from the curses of casteism and untouchability imposed on them by the upper castes, most of them believed that they were destined to suffer such inferiority and did not leave Hinduism. With the arrival of the Christian missionaries, many were converted to Christianity. Unfortunately, this did not improve their condition.

Even in kindergarten (the then *kudipallikudam*), education was permitted only to the upper castes. Only the languages Sanskrit and Malayalam and professional subjects like astrology, Ayurveda, etc. were taught in the classes. Though the state government started many schools, admissions were restricted only to children from upper castes. Most of the schools had only one teacher, and the house of the teacher was the school. The students stayed at the teacher's house for their learning and hence these schools were known as kudipallikudams (*kudi* means house and *pallikudam*, the school). The teacher, who was called Asan (Master), did not accept any payments or rewards for his teaching. Even though this system of education was incapable of giving education to all, most people were satisfied with it, believing that it was their fate. It was only later the government started high schools and the missionaries the charitable schools.

Fortunately, there was no caste differentiation among physicians in the field of treatment. There were many scholars of Indian philosophy and expert physicians belonging to the Ezhava, Nampoothiri, Nair and Muslim communities. Most of them studied Vedanta, Ayurveda, astrology, black magic and witchcraft. There were many families who were teaching and did treatments as service to society. Many teachers and physicians never accepted any fees.

Chaturvarnya (the four caste system) divides society into four categories namely, Brahmana, Kshatriya, Vaishya and Sudra. Outside this caste system the exploited low castes were considered as untouchables and as people without human status. In all castes there were sub castes. The untouchability was maintained between the upper class and lower class and also between castes and sub castes. Ezhavas were kept away from the so called upper castes such as Brahmanas, Kshatriyas, Vaishyas and Sudras according to the then prevailing social rule prescribed by 'Manusmrithi'. To the oppressed class in the society namely outcastes according to Chaturvarnya rules had to suffer physically and mentally for centuries. Roads, temples, schools and even appearance in public places were forbidden to them.

In the ancient Vedic period till the time of Manu who framed the rules in his book 'Manusmrithi' there were no such division of the society. Even the statement of Lord Krishna in Gita, that 'Chaturvarnya is my own creation according to the quality (Guna) and deeds (karma)' was purposefully misinterpreted by the vested interests. The Gita statement never meant anyone comes under any of the divisions of the society by virtue of one's birth, but only by virtue of one's quality and deeds.

People belonging to the lower castes were suffering from the curse of the so-called chaturvarnya (four castes), a system which has no reference in Indian philosophical books like Vedas, Vedanta (Sruthies or Upanishads) and Smrities except the Manusmriti, which is still considered a controversial book by all sections of people and masters.

There are no parallels to Sree Narayana Gurudev in the history of Indian philosophy. As a maharishi, he accomplished the reformation of the society using methods in tune with Advaita philosophy by fighting for the rights of lower castes who were suppressed by casteism. He was the unique Advedic Hindu Sannyasin who was born in south India after Jagat Guru Adi Sankaracharya. Sree Narayana Gurudev was the Vedanti who declared to the world the real message of Advaita in a nutshell: 'One God, One Caste, One Religion for mankind'. This message of oneness is the message of equality in social, economic, cultural and educational systems and in all walks of life.

Fortunately, in spite of all these disorders in the social system of Kerala, the schools and colleges brought the people of Kerala to a higher status in social, economic and educational fields in later years. Thanks to Sree Narayana Gurudev and other social reformers, at present, Kerala holds the highest ranks in literacy, economy and health. This kind of renaissance in Kerala was made possible mainly by the social activities of Sree Narayana Gurudev in his time. He brought about a radical change in the mentality, behaviour and outlook of the people of the entire country, and Kerala and south India in particular. It was a great social revolution through peaceful, spiritual methods upholding the spirit of Advaita philosophy of which Sree Narayana Gurudev was supposed to be the successor to Veda Vyasa and Adi Sankara. Advaita is the philosophy of oneness. The word Advaita means 'not two' or not dual It is generally known as non-dualism or oneness. Advaita thought was evolved from Vyasa's Brahma Sutras. It was formulated as a philosophy by Adi Sankara and modernized and popularised by Sree Narayana Gurudev.

Veda Vyasa otherwise known as Krishna Dwaipayana (name relates to his complexion and birth in a dweep i.e., island) was born to Parasara and Satyavaty (Matsya Gandhi), a fisherwoman. He is one of the most revered figures in the Hindu traditions. Vyasa (Badarayana) authored the Brahma Sutras and many Puranas including the Mahabharata.

Sree Naryana Gurudev's call for people's self-dependence and self-improvement in those days remains relevant to all the oppressed and suppressed people in the world. Sree Narayana Gurudev was the driving force behind the renaissant call 'Change the laws or else; they will themselves change you' of the great poet Kumaran Asan.

How many of the objectives and messages of Gurudev have materialized today? The struggle of the Blacks in America after half a century was similar to the social revolution of Sree Narayana Gurudev. The strikers in the struggle led by Dr Martin Luther King wrote a simple slogan on a placard, and it was: 'I am a Man'. Hundreds of years ago, Gurudev taught Keralites the mantra: 'Whatever be the religion the man should become good.' Yes, the low castes and the poor are also human beings, and they deserve their rights as men.

There is no doubt that social differentiation was prevalent in other states, too. In a sense, Sree Narayana Gurudev was instrumental in initiating the revolution in the fields of social and spiritual activities, blending spirituality with modern scientific developments.

- It is very important to note that Gurudev was making all these changes strongly based on the principles of Sanatana Dharma. The novelty of Sanatana Dharma is its self-competency to update its doctrines in tune with the times. In short, Gurudev could wipe out all the failings and foibles that evolved in Hinduism over the last thousand years.
- 'Sanatana' means everlasting, 'Dharma' means ethics, moralities, and Sanatana Dharma is an everlasting unchanging spiritual belief originally in the Indian context. Sanatana also means imperishable, primeval, omnipresent all-pervading in time and space and eternal. There is no equivalent word for Dharma in English. Translation of Dharma as religious is misleading it is an organised system of rules, beliefs, rituals, etc. to worship god. It deals with purposeful and meaningful living. Its teachings afford wisdom for a meaningful life for all classes of individuals and professions.

In rejuvenating the Sanatana Dharma which does not care for the differentiation of religions, Sree Narayana Gurudev's role was great.

India's heritage and Dharma are immortal. It has survived the forceful invasions of other religions. Whenever India sinks into inertia, a leader seems to arise, through whose effort the Dharma becomes rejuvenated (ref. Gita, 'Njana Dharma Sanyasa Yogam', Chapter 4, verses 7–8). It happens as if it is a great wonder that such a master, who rejuvenates and develops the Sanatana Dharma, incarnates in almost every millennium. By their incarnation, every one of them removes all the deficiencies and ruins accumulated over the thousand-odd years prior to him. Two thousand five hundred years ago, when Dharma deteriorated, there came for the sake of rejuvenation Sree Buddha and Mahavira. They removed all the evils till then. Thereafter, over hundreds of years, again, the evil customs and curses arose, spoiling the social conditions of society. Veda Vyasa gave an impetus of wisdom through his great works, the Brahmasutras, Mahabharata and other Puranas, which led to an intellectual and spiritual renaissance and awareness of good and bad deeds. Though great and noble, they did not make a deserving impact on common men. Still, their stature continues as the main source of Indian thought, and they are revered as India's precious jewels. After another millennium, there came the necessity for a counter-reformation which led to the rise of Adi Sankara and others who could remove all the evils that had crept in over the last thousand-odd years and resurrect the Sanatana Dharma. Again, another millennium passed, and Dharma deteriorated in the society. Then came Sree Narayana Gurudev and others for uplifting Sanatana Dharma.

Sree Narayana Gurudev is the spiritual leader who was endowed with the responsibility of rejuvenation of Sanatana Dharma in his time. His way of spreading the messages of Vedanta philosophy to the common man was unique. Vedanta or uttara meemamsa is the most prominent among the six Astika schools of Indian philosophy. Its literal meaning is the 'end of Vedas'. It comprises of the philosophy of Upanishads and has many sub traditions ranging from dualism to non-dualism. Upanishads, Brahma Sutras and Bhagvat Gita form the 'prasthanatrayi'.

He brought the doctrines of Vedanta and Brahmasutra to the common man and the great heritage of India from the higher echelons of society to the poor and downtrodden. There are many magnificent stories illustrating Nanu's (Gurudev's) strong belief in God. One day Nanu (Gurudev) had an attack of smallpox. He went to a Devi temple and remained there alone for eighteen days. On the nineteenth day, when he became free of the disease, he went back to his own house. His parents asked him where he had been all these days; he said he had smallpox. When they asked who treated him for smallpox, he coolly answered it was the Goddess Devi.

Nanu was a brilliant boy blessed with many peculiar attributes. His parents thought of initiating his education. Nanu was taken to the scholarly man known as Chempazhanthi Moothapillai, a family head and the village officer for the rite. This teacher, Narayana Pillai, known as Kannankara Mootha Pillai, performed the initiation of the child. It is believed that Kannankara Moothapillai Asan at this time told Nanu's parents that this boy would one day become a great man who would be worshipped by all, and that at the age of sixteen, the boy would leave them to become a great wealth to the world.

Nanu learnt the preliminary lessons in Sanskrit and Siddharupa, Balaprabhodha, Amarakosha, etc. the primary books for learning Sanskrit literature, under Moothapillai Asan. He learnt the basic lessons of medicine from his father Madanasan and his maternal uncle, Krishnan Vaidyar.

When he was eighteen, a change in his life was visible from his appearance as that of a god-loving worshipper who was yet to step into the world of sannyasin. His attention turned completely towards the reading of the epics. He started travelling to many places, one after the other, and very rarely came to his own house. On these days, his parents and uncles became worried and often spoke harshly about his new way of life. But that did not make him leave this path.

Nanu had his higher education in Sanskrit and philosophy under the scholarly guidance of Kummampallil Raman Pillai Asan, the disciple of the great scholar Kailasanatha Sastri. Raman Pillai Asan was teaching in a school near his Cheruvannoor ancestral house (*Tharavadu*). Nanu studied in this school, staying in the famous Varanappally family house in Puthuppally near Kayamkulam during his period of education there.

In spite of his great erudition, very little is known about the scholarly poet Raman Pillai Asan. After the completion of yogic studies, he visited many places and temples and travelled begging and taking ascetic food from various houses. The begging of food is an essential part of ascetic life. Once he became an ascetic, Nanu's thrust was to get more scientific knowledge about Indian spirituality and philosophy. From Raman Pillai, Nanu learnt Kavya, drama, Alankara, etc.

Raman Pillai Asan imparted knowledge equally to all those who came to him for learning, irrespective of whether they were wise or foolish. It was natural that his disciples varied in their ability to grasp what was taught in class. Among his disciples, there were many intelligent ones. Nanu was certainly a diamond among them.

He grasped all the lessons given to him and proved that he had the intelligence and imaginative power to grasp much more. In fact, Nanu was not at all satisfied with the number of lessons given to him; instead, he wanted much more from his teacher.

In the beginning, Raman Pillai Asan taught Nanu two stanzas of 'Raghuvamsham' every day. But little Nanu felt that if the studies progressed at that rate, he would not be able to fulfil his mission of higher education in the length of time he had in mind, and he told this to the teacher, and the teacher permitted him to listen and learn what was being taught to the senior students as well. Nanu, after completing 'Raghuvamsham', was given another epic to learn. But to the surprise of Asan, Nanu had already learnt it by that time. Ultimately, it turned out to be the disciple clarifying some of the teacher's doubts regarding the meanings of stanzas in some of the books. Asan, being very honest and sincere, blessed his disciple and showered praises on him. Nanu's unusual power of comprehension made him a centre of adoration by all. It was said Nanu was so brilliant that he used to open the textbooks only in the classroom, showing that he could master anything in a single attempt. Many classmates had their doubts cleared by Nanu. He was assigned the moniter or *chattampi* of the class by his teacher.

During those days of learning, Nanu was not particular about what he ate, but he took only vegetarian food. He used to pluck medicinal leaves which he found on the way, chewed them and swallowed their juice. His classmates used to make comments, joking that the food he ate was not enough, and that was why he ate leaves found on the way. Nanu used to wake up before sunrise, took his morning bath and visited the temple regularly without fail. In those days, his favourite deity was Lord Krishna whose appearance in dreams was usual to him (See 'Sree Krishna Darsanam').

In the year 1881, Nanu contracted a severe intestinal infection. It worsened day by day, and one day he became unconscious. His parents were informed, and they came and took him home.

After learning for a period of two to three years under Raman Pillai, Asan Nanu felt that he had a long way to go to achieve his real goal. He started teaching in hamlet schools (kudipallikudams) in nearby places like Kadaykavoor, Anjengo, etc. The teaching profession gave him the name Nanu Asan. His spiritual thoughts and ascetic-like life started flourishing on higher levels. He wrote hymns about Lord Vishnu, Lord Subramanya and Lord Shiva. At this time, he learnt 'Gita Govindam' of Jayadeva thoroughly.

Nanu Asan's parents were very worried about his spiritual thoughts and detachment from family affairs. They decided to dissuade him and tried to make him a household man. They went to the extent of making him get married to a girl who was one of his relatives. The then prevailing custom did not insist on getting the consent or choice of the concerned bridegroom and the bride. Nanu's sisters, on his behalf, gave the ceremonial bridal dress to the bride and brought her to the bridegroom's house.

But none of these acts of parents and relatives could dissuade him from his vow to observe celibacy and asceticism. The marriage ended without the bride and the bridegroom living together. Nanu Asan told the girl, 'Everyone takes life for the fulfilment of a particular cause. You and I may have two different things to fulfil. You take your way and let me take my own path.' At the age of twenty-six, Nanu bid farewell to his house forever and entered into the life of a sannyasin.

The social conditions that existed then in Kerala and nearby states hurt Nanu's heart. It was this state of affairs that made Nanu found a philosophy in which society is seen as irrespective of caste, creed, nation, etc. He realized that for the eradication of casteism, Advaita was the most suitable instrument. Still, it remains an unsolved question as to whether Nanu studied Vedanta and applied it to social reformation or the social inequalities made him study Vedanta. To him, Vedanta and social reformation were mutually complementary. Both schools of thought had a stand against caste differentiation. They advocated devotion to God as a means of attaining salvation, and Advaita as the doctrine of unity. The first was a way to purify and take an individual to salvation, and hence it was personal—not directly related to society as a whole. Gurudev chose the second for the eradication of caste differentiation and associated evils in the society.

While moving from one place to another as an *avadhooth* (ascetic),he once came in contact with the owner of a Tamil book depot who came from Tamil Nadu. Nanu could see many Tamil books, and he was attracted to the philosophical ones. Also, he became acquainted with Tamil scholars who used to come to the book depot. He started learning Tamil and Tamil literature from the scholars. They were fond of the very young ascetic who held the promise of becoming a great man. This association or friendship with the scholars made Nanu a great scholar in Tamil, and in later years he wrote Tamil literary works like *Thevarapathikamkal.*

For a few days, Nanu Asan stayed in the house of Perunnellil Krishnan Vaidyan, one of his old classmates in the Cheruvannoor Kalari (school). There he met a great yogi, Sree Kunjan Pillai, who later became the famous Sree Chattampi Swamikal. They became very good friends and shared mutual respect. Since both of them had Vedanta, Shaiva Siddhanta and Tamil classical literature as their subjects of special interest, their interactions strengthened their mutual understanding to greater depths. Kunjan Pillai Chattampi was the disciple of Pettah Raman Pillai Asan.

Kunjan Pillai in those days was learning Hata yoga under the great yoga expert, Thaikkattu Ayyavu Swamikal. Kunjan Pillai, because of his deep friendship, took Nanu Asan to Ayyavu Swamikal. Nanu got acquainted with Ayyavu Swamikal and learn that a yoga from him.

The following is from an article written in *Vivekodayam* by Kumaranasan about Ayyavu Swamikal: 'Taikkattu Ayyavu was a great soul who had many great qualities. He was the spiritual advisor to the great men like Sree Narayana Gurudev and Chattampi Swamikal. He attained salvation on 6th Karkkidaka 1084 ME (1905 CE) in his house. Nobody was aware of his age. Ayyavu, who was nearly 80 years old, never had any disease . . . A few days prior to his death, he felt pain and swelling on the back side of his legs.

He sat fasting, saying that the time has come for his Samadhi.' Asan continues, 'A few minutes earlier to his death he said only this: "I am going." It was the end of the worldly life of a Hata Yogi who could foresee the time of his death.'

Ayyavu Swamikal was a staunch follower of the customary rites of Maha Muni Agastya. He advised such traditional practices to Nanu, and on realizing Nanu's urge and ability, inspired him to go for penance. He explained to him the facilities available in Marutwamala, a mountain near Kanyakumari, and gave him instructions for doing penance.

Nanu Asan, as an avadhooth, travelled widely in Travancore, Cochin, Malabar and throughout south India in search of the truth, directly experiencing it from the world around.

He went to mountainous forests in search of the absolute reality. He lived in forests full of wild animals and in the mountains, enduring all climatic conditions like rain, cold, etc., eating only tubers, fruits and leaves, and drinking only spring water. He lived with wild animals in peaceful companionship.

Earlier, Nanu went first to Veli Mala. Nobody knows how long he lived there. He went to Marutwamala for rigorous penance. It is said that in his travel to Marutwamala, Nanu had the companionship of Sree Kunjan Pillai Chattampi till both reached the top of the mountain. These two great men stayed there together for a few days. Realizing Nanu's ardent desire, and validating the suitability of the selected cave 'Pillathatam' and its surroundings, Kunjan Pillai Chattampi left the place, wishing all success to his beloved companion.

Pillathatam was in the midst of a thick forest, which was the dwelling place of wild animals. This cave was at the top of a giant ledge of rocks. It was comparatively spacious, convenient and suitable for living without exposure to the outside world; in short, a cave suitable for prolonged yoga, meditation and penance.

Marutwamala, by its nature, was a blessed place for performing penance. Many great ascetics elected this place for their penance. Agastya Maha Muni is believed to have performed penance in the

Pillathatam cave in Marutwamala. Perhaps this is the reason why Ayyavu Swamikal, a staunch believer in the customs and conventions of Agastya Muni, suggested the Pillathatam cave to Nanu.

There are many mystical stories about the greatness of Pillathatam, and of the miraculous life of the young saint Nanu in the cave. Two of these stories are very popular. One talks about the meaning of Pillathatam. *Pilla* means child, and *Thatam*, the mark of the foot; the foot marks of a child. It is said that on the red soil inside the cave, the footprints of a child were seen at the time of Gurudev's penance. It is believed that the child who frequently visited the cave was none other than little Krishna (Swami Geetananda and many among the disciples had visited the cave and witnessed the footprints and taken photographs). The other is a story narrated by a lady called Chettiyamma and her husband who discovered young Gurudev's seat where he did penance. They said, 'There were a tiger and snake resting on either side of the opening of the cave where Gurudev was doing penance. On our approach to the opening, on the orders of Gurudev, both the creatures went away.' The lady and her husband thereafter became Gurudev's staunch devotees.

Nanu did rigorous rites and yogic postures. In the beginning, he ate fruits from the trees and plants in the forest and also tubers and herbs. The leaves of a particular species of plant 'Kattukodi' were crushed and made into juice to form sediment which was dried into the form of a cake. He used to eat this Kattukodi cake for many months, and ultimately, he came to the state of fasting. Sometime during the rigorous penance and sadhana, he attained enlightenment. It was like Sree Buddha who attained enlightenment under the *Bodhi Vriksha* (banyan tree). The meditation and penance made Sree Narayana Gurudev cut through the veil of Maya and realize the Absolute. He experienced himself as Brahman—The Universe.

As the news spread of a sannyasin doing *tapas* (penance) in Marutwamala, many people—mostly from Tamil Nadu—started coming to see the great sannyasin. They were ready to do anything to receive his blessings. They hurried to take him to their own places and houses. Gurudev blessed all of them compassionately by going to their places. But his urge to continue penance remained. He was forced to take a hard but noble decision to shift his place of penance to the Aruvippuram Mountain, which in those days was well known for the presence of tigers and leopards.

The Aruvippuram Mountain is a branch of the mountain range Agastya Kutam. The river Neyyar that starts from there and flows through Aruvippuram was so beautiful that there were no parallels to it. Gurudev did penance and meditation in a cave near to the present Aruvippuram temple. There was another cave some 10 to 15 metres to the south-west of it. This area in those days was so dangerous that it was known as the *Pulivanku*, the den of tigers.

Gurudev again started travelling widely in places where people lived. People from many places and all walks of life came to Gurudev for his darshan and blessings. This was the birth of the philosopher-social reformer in Sree Narayana Gurudev.

After the prolonged solitary life in forests and communion with the Absolute that led to his enlightenment, Sree Narayana Gurudev appeared before the people who rushed to get his divine blessings. People sought his divine touch to cure their diseases, mental agonies, epilepsy, leprosy, possession by spirits, and so on. Those who approached him with chronic and incurable diseases got wonderful results. Gurudev was capable of reading the hidden thoughts of another without having any prior familiarity with him. People were convinced by the wonderful feats he showed: his capability to see even the most minute thing hidden somewhere, reading the mind of another; that is, divining the thoughts of another, miraculous treatment. The examples of these miraculous activities and their scientific explanations in terms of the discoveries will be given when we discuss the literary works of Sree Narayana Gurudev. In view of the developments in quantum physics, quantum cosmology and consciousness studies, none of the miraculous feats can be considered simple mythical stories.

To a person who has obtained control over the five senses and mind, these miraculous events are not mythical.

The news about Nanu Asan's penance at Marutwamala spread widely among the people. When he came down from Marutwamala, people from different walks of life rushed to get his divine darshan.

Till 1885, Aruvippuram was full of forest and wild animals as mentioned earlier. There was no habitation. But with the presence of Sree Narayana Gurudev, the conditions changed and people started believing that staying there is like staying near God. There was a continuous flow of devotees from various parts of the country. This situation resulted in the need for a temple there.

The consecration of the idol of Shiva by Sree Narayana Gurudev at Aruvippuram in 1881 on Shivratri day was a historical event. The act of a non-Brahmin consecrating an idol, and performing non-traditional and non-Brahmanical rites, was symbolic, a warning to the so-called upper castes who had denied the freedom of worship to the lower castes. Above all, it was the bringing down of the noble fruits of Vedic philosophy to the common people, protecting them from conversion to other religions due to circumstantial needs. People in large numbers gathered at Aruvippuram to witness it.

A suitable place and a big stone were selected as a pedestal for consecration of the idol. While the devotees gathered around him, Sree Narayana Gurudev came down to the river and dived into its deep end. This spot is now known as Sankaran Khuzi. The people continuously chanted the five-letter hymn 'Aum Nama Shivaya' that reverberated in the atmosphere. After a long lapse of time, Gurudev did not emerge from the water. The situation became very tense, people became perplexed, but soon many started wailing. To the people's surprise, the glorious Gurudev appeared, swimming to the shore with a piece of stone in one hand. People continued to chant even louder so that it echoed far away. Gurudev kept the shapeless stone taken from the river pressed to his chest. He remained absorbed in deep meditation. First his face, and then his entire body began to shine in divine light. The people who stood near Gurudev felt the heat radiating from him. Floods of tears flowed across his face, chest and the idol. It was a ritual anointing the idol by pouring tears from the eyes of Gurudev say, 'Bashpabhishekam'. Bashpa means tears Abhisheka means anointing.

Gurudev crossed the states of *Jagrat*, *Swapna* and *Sushupti*—wakefulness, dream and deep sleep—ultimately entering the state of *Turiya* and becoming a Brahman. Then he induced the spirit into the featureless stone, which was not touched by a sculptor. Gurudev selected the featureless stone to represent the featureless *Nirguna Brahman*—the Absolute. But the induction of the spirit into the featureless stone made it featured, and thereby the *Saguna Brahman*. In short, Gurudev was inducting the invisible Brahman to the idol of Shiva for the worship of the common people. When the induction was over, Gurudev took the idol and pressed it to the pedestal. The people around who witnessed this divine scene report that the stones—the idol and the pedestal—melted and fused at high temperature, fixing the idol firmly on the pedestal. This was the legendary consecration of Lord Shiva at Aruvippuram.

It is to be noted that this was not the traditional method adopted for the consecration. At that time, there was only a thatched shed around the sanctum sanctorum. Gurudev advised the devotees to build a place of worship or a temple around the consecrated idol of Shiva. By the effort and cooperation of devotees and the blessings of Gurudev, the proposal was materialized.

After the event of consecration, Gurudev was relaxing on a little rock some distance away. A few very haughty Namboothiries, Malayala Brahmins, approached Gurudev and asked him, 'Who gave the right to non-brahmins to do consecration of Shiva?'

Gurudev retorted smilingly and frivolously, 'Look! I have consecrated only my Shiva,' with an implication that it was not the same Shiva that was fixed on the pedestals in the temples. We will come to see the real meaning of what Gurudev said under the topic of quantum entanglement.

The Namboothiries left the place bowing to Gurudev respectfully, whether they understood his meaning or not. It was a surprise to many people who were anticipating strong repercussions from vested interests. Gurudev did the legendary consecration courageously and peacefully. It became the starting event for liberating the people from the age-old curse of chaturvarnya, ban on temple entry, denial of freedom of worship, and even the denial of freedom to walk through certain roads. This was a lesson for the whole world.

The news of consecration of the idol spread like wildfire. This brought consternation among the conservatives who raised a hue and cry. But in spite of these murmurings, the sanctity and divinity of the temple remained unquestioned. The act was praised by many leaders at the national level.

The consecration of Shiva at Aruvippuram opened a new era in the Vedic culture. It opened the eyes of the national leaders, especially in their approach to the caste differentiation and the struggle for supremacy of ideology of different religions. Conversions from one religion to another, at least in south India, gradually vanished thereafter.

After the consecration, Gurudev instructed his disciples and devotees to place a signboard with the following lines inscribed on it:

Jātibhēdam matadvēṣam
Ētumillāte sarvarum
Sōdaratvēna vāẓunna
Matṛikā stānamāṅitu.
'This is the model place
where people live in brotherhood
without any difference in caste
and animosity to religions.'

This contains the spirit of Sree Narayana Gurudev's message: 'One God, One Caste, One Religion'.

It was a period of social and spiritual reformation—the Indian Renaissance wherein social and religious leaders rose to prominence, one after the other from different parts of India. India had many masters in the transformation of the destiny of the Indian people. It is grievous to note that such a multifaceted genius like Sree Narayana

Gurudev, who radically changed people's perceptions about Vedic philosophy in the spiritual field and social conditions prevailing in south India, is sidelined from many official lists of great men of India.

There are different reasons for this situation. One is perhaps that his vision and message were not propagated to the general public outside south India through different local languages or at least in English. Though the leaders mimicked his ideas and philosophical views, many of them never mentioned whose vision they had used in their speeches and writings. Another reason is the remnants of chaturvarnya remained in the hearts, and oral tradition, for most of the speakers and writers in those days. The community into which Gurudev was born made him a communal leader and failed to recognize him as a national social leader, and they failed to spread his vision and message. Still, there are exceptions to this, like the works of Nataraja Guru, a direct disciple of Gurudev, Yeti Nitya Chaithanya a scholar Samnyasin and a few others who translated a few literary works of Gurudev into English. Both Nataraja Guru and Yati Nytya Chaitanya established hermitages in India and in foreign countries.

Before 1885, the conditions that existed at Aruvippuram were not suitable for habitation, in spite of the place being very enchanting and tempting from an aesthetic point of view. On hearing the news that Gurudev had come to Aruvippuram, people used to rush to this place because they believed that staying at Aruvippuram, blessed with the presence of Gurudev, will be a place of solution for curing their diseases and other sufferings.

Many scholars and sannyasins came to this place, and many of them became his disciples.

After the consecration, Sree Narayana Gurudev engaged a committee to look after the day-to-day affairs of the temple. In 1894 the committee was constituted with the name 'Aruvippuram Kshetra Yogam'—Aruvippuram Temple Committee. While doing so, Gurudev instructed the organizers to write the names of the members of the committee around a circle so that there was no hierarchy and status involved in looking after the temple. The sanctum sanctorum, the place of a deity, was swiftly constructed.

In the course of his life, Sree Narayana Gurudev made consecrations at sixty-two different temples in and outside Kerala, each deity carrying a novel message to the devotees. The last two among these temples were Ullala Vaikkom and Kalavamkodam Cherthala where he consecrated two mirrors imparting the great Vedantic message *Tat Twam Asi*, 'Thou Art It', as if Gurudev were telling the devotee or worshipper that 'the god whom you worship is none other than you yourself'—the great message of Oneness.

Gurudev wished to have educational institutions attached to each temple. He travelled throughout Kerala and outside. This was the period in which Gurudev was deeply exploring the social realities existing in society. He witnessed the miseries, pain, caste-wise differentiation, poverty, lack of education and cleanliness, patients with incurable diseases, etc., especially in the lower strata. Wherever he went, people gathered there, making the place of stay of their 'swami' a divine place or temple. They shared their grievances with him as if he was their master and saviour. People made many offerings in the form of bunches of flowers and fruits (especially a particular type of plantain fruit called kadhali fruit—a favourite of Gurudev's). Sree Narayana Gurudev had a great wealth of devotees and disciples; the first among them was Sivalingadasa Swamikal. In his early days, Kochappi Pillai was a boy looking after the cattle. One day he happened to see the divine appearance of Gurudev on the shore of the Neyyar river, and he was attracted to him and became the first disciple. It is he who composed the prayer 'Guruashtakam' that is chanted in the Sree Narayana Gurudev temples and the houses of devotees.

Sree Narayana Gurudev continued to travel widely. He saw grief-stricken persons' ignorance, blind believers (irrational believers), exploiters and exploited people believing in non-customary rites or rituals altogether, with a dark world around but with the appearance of the light of knowledge. At that time, he even forcefully insisted that people throw away the idols of non-traditional gods, mostly gods of evil and replace them with noble gods. He made a radical change in the lives of thousands of people and liberated them from miseries and ignorance.

In 1904, Gurudev came to Varkala and relaxed under a jackfruit tree. People came to him in large numbers to receive his darshan and blessings, and the place became a temporary resting place. There he established an ashram. After sometime, Gurudev instructed the devotees to construct a permanent building for his stay as the land was not owned by any person then. He got that land registered in his name from the government. This ashram later became the centre of operations and the most revered shrine of Sree Narayana Gurudev. In 1928, Gurudev established the Sree Narayana Dharma Sangham.

Gurudev's universal humanism is reflected in the following lines of the great poet Kumaranasan.

Annyarkku gunam ceyvatināyussu vapussum
Dhanyatwamotangāsu thapassum baliceytu
Sanyāsikalingane illilla miyannōr
Vanyāsramamērunnavarum sree Gurumūrte.

'Oh! Lord! For doing welfare to others your entire life, body and penance, all were dedicated with blessings. Oh! Gurudev, there are no such sannyasins like you who left his own house and had gone to the forest for doing penance in the forest hermitage.'

During Gurudev's travels in south India, he visited many shrines. He used to sleep anywhere and ate whatever he could get. People at large accepted him as a siddhayogi. Sri Moorkothu Kumaran, who always accompanied Gurudev as a devotee and a disciple though leading a family life (*Grihasthasrami*), wrote, 'Sree Narayana Guru was a product of pure Hinduism, who could be claimed by everyone as his own Guru, without any distinction of caste or religion. But there was a special purpose behind his birth. He was meant to improve the social and economic status of the downtrodden people of Kerala, who were condemned to sub-human existence by the traditions of the caste system. So he returned to them to take up his work, prescribed by destiny.'

Gurudev made great changes in the social customs prevailing in Kerala. He removed the harmful customs related to polyandry and polygamy and the procedure in marriages, etc. Till then, the bride and bridegroom had no freedom in the selection of their partner. Gurudev insisted that in the procedure of marriage, the bride should wholeheartedly accept the bridegroom by garlanding him on the stage at the marriage ceremony. Only then the bridegroom makes her his life partner by tying the wedding string around the neck of the bride. Through this, Gurudev established equal rights for both the boy and girl in a symbolic way.

Gurudev introduced a radical change in the mode of inheritance in Kerala. Earlier, Kerala had matriarchic inheritance or inheritance in the female line, which meant while transferring the right of the family properties to the next generation, the male children had no role in it, or there was no patriarchal line of succession. This was only a procedure based on convention. Gurudev paved the way to change the custom to the present Nair–Ezhava Succession Act of equal rights, in the manner Gurudev prescribed. He made a lot of changes in the customary rituals and rites in events like marriage. He advised people to give up pomp during family functions. He abolished child marriage. Gurudev warned people against consuming intoxicating drinks; he declared, 'Liquor is poison, do not produce it, do not consume it, do not offer it.'

His role in the social and cultural renaissance in south India was unique. The present-day social structure of Kerala is, in fact, a creation of Sree Narayana Gurudev. He did not force anybody to accept whatever he said or advised, but no one resisted him.

There were evil deities like Madan, Marutha, Yakshi (a fairy woman who charms and tempts others, seduces, sucks the blood of others and kills) and Chutalamadan (an evil deity in burial grounds). Gurudev instructed the people to remove the idols of such deities and not to worship them. These bad customs, which were mostly created and promoted by vested interests, developed as convention. These turned out to be laws that find no place in Indian philosophy. The abandoning of these evil deities was carried out by Gurudev who organized local committees to advise and make the people aware of their futility through speeches in local meetings.

On religion, morality, education and industry, Gurudev maintained a modern outlook suitable to the needs of the society and its uplifting. The blind beliefs such as animal sacrifices, etc. had to be removed through bringing awareness to the people. He spoke about the philosophy of attributed and unattributed approaches of Brahman in Hinduism and explained the methods of worship of God in its pure form. He wanted to encourage people to establish temples and hermitages wherever people wanted them. He advised the people not to find fault with other religions and not to hurt the feelings of others.

One should follow, as part of good manners, truthfulness cleanliness, fear of unrighteousness (god fearing), belief in God and unity, rejecting meaningless troublemaking traditions to the extent possible, and accept noble and timely traditions, and execute them among the people through speeches and activities bringing them to the right path.

In the field of education, he emphasized its extraordinary merits and uses, and made the people aware of the dangers without it. In backward areas which were in urgent need of schools, he encouraged the people to establish schools and libraries, and made them aware of the fact that there should not be anybody among men and women who was illiterate. He made them understand the pride of being an educated man or woman.

He advocated the development of industry, farming, trade and handicrafts, etc. and tried to inculcate the habit of savings. These were to be carried out through scholarly talks by experts from various fields. At any cost, none of the lectures should provoke people in any way, hurting their feelings. No speaker should talk on subjects that are not thoroughly known to him.

There were people in large numbers from different parts of the country to carry his messages to various regions of the world. In short, there was a flood of activities along the lines prescribed by Sree Narayana Gurudev. The social changes in Kerala stand testimony to it.

Many things related to his social reformation of the low castes, downtrodden and backward classes of the society are mentioned here only briefly because there are a large number of books written about Sree Narayana Gurudev. Some may wonder how a person who lived a century ago reveals the secrets of the universe that now appear to be perfectly in tune with the discoveries in science and cosmology. There are two ways of dealing with a problem to arrive at a result. One is the logical–physical, observational, experimental, theoretical (*Vyavaharika*) method of science and the other is the transcendental (*Atheendriya*) method of spirituality. Once the conclusion or the result in both ways is the same, then the question of which method is superior does not arise.

In Sree Narayana Gurudev's multifaceted genius, what predominates is his penchant for metaphysics, especially as a metaphysician preaching Advaita philosophy. Imbibing the full spirit of Advaita philosophy developed and enriched by the great sages (maharishis) over the ages, Gurudev delivered a new version to the modern world using every word and sentence with such precision that it surpasses even the theories of modern science, including quantum physics.

Gurudev's works basically contain the substance of Advaita philosophy that came through the Vedas, the Sruthies (Upanishads), the Brahmasutras and its Bhashya by Adi Sankara. The depth of philosophy, the fullness of meanings, the aesthetics of poetry and the simplicity of expression bring his writings deep into the hearts of people, making the works of Gurudev unique.

The blending of metaphysics with physics in his writings makes his works unparalleled. In his works, there is no line which does not have the touch of science or that its philosophy does not equate with the theories of science. In a sense, many of Gurudev's works are like sutras in Brahmasutras and abstracts of wider thoughts or intangible formulae in physics. Primarily, they require commentaries similar to Bhashya in Vedic philosophy. Though the lines look like those in ordinary poems, they are deep in meaning, multifaceted, unhindered and unblemished in their contents.

What identifies Sree Narayana Gurudev amidst Indian sages (rishis) is his fruitful effort in bringing Advaita philosophy to the common people. Though there were no authentic rules in any of the Vedas or Upanishads, learning of Advaita doctrines was forbidden to the majority of people in India, who were considered to not belong to *trivarnika*s, namely Brahmanas, Kshatriyas and Vaishyas. Gurudev increased the acceptability of Advaita philosophy manifold by bringing it to light from the closed rooms of the so-called upper castes. Its sole rights were restricted to a limited circle of some sages and some so-called scholars in their assemblies and indoor meetings. Sree Narayana Gurudev brought it to the midst of the common people and liberated it to form part of their life.

In the light of historical facts and theories in philosophy, if one analyses the life of Sree Narayana Gurudev, one can see him as a philosopher as well as a social reformer or a human rights fortifier. There were many such masters who uplifted human rights in history, but most of them were not philosophers. Similarly, there were many philosophers, but very few of them could uplift human rights. Besides, in every philosopher, there will be a human rights promoter to a certain extent, and also in every human rights promoter, there will be a little of the philosopher. But finding these two qualities, of being human rights fortifier and philosopher with equal importance united in a single person, is a very rare phenomenon. In Sree Narayana Gurudev both these qualities were equally shining splendidly.

We had Kapila, Kanata, Gautama, Jaimini, Badarayana and other such great maharishis in the forefront of philosophers in India, but how many of them advocated human rights; we do not know. The epics and Puranas (Holy Scriptures) show that the legendary characters like Sree Rama, Sree Krishna, Jina and Sree Buddha were both philosophers and human saviours. In the West, Socrates, Plato, Aristotle, Epicurus, Marcus, Aquinas, Voltaire, Kant and others were philosophers; we are not sure about their role in the protection of human rights in society.

Coming to spirituality in Indian philosophy, the oldest known text is the 'Sankhya Karika'. Some of the statements found in

'Sankhya Karika', (written by Ishwara Krishna who himself described as the successor of the disciple from the great sage Kapila) believed that salvation becomes possible to one, only when he passes through the stages like *Brahmacharya*,*Garhasthya* and *Vanaprastha*, and then accepts Sannyasa. But the 'Sankhya Karika' brought forward the idea that once knowledge is obtained in the fullest sense without any other qualities, one attains salvation. But unfortunately, it did not care for the other qualities of life. This made it clear that the philosophy spread by the Sankhyans was not for the sake of philosophy alone; it was also aimed at the welfare of human society. In short, the ultimate aim of Sankhya philosophy was to uplift the people who were wandering to find the way to salvation through controversial and complex means. The lack of belief in God affected Sankhya philosophy to a great extent.

There are three works which are variously claimed to be the oldest surviving work of the Samkhya school: Kapila's Samkhya Sutras, Kapila's Tattva Samasa, and Ishwara Krishna's Samkhya Karika. Of these three, scholars consider the Samkhya Karika to be the oldest

In the relationship between the doctrines of Samkhya and Patanjali's Yoga the concept of Purusha and Prakriti is crucial. Samkhya accepts only purusha, the individual soul and prakriti, the nature or matter as the fundamental realities and it does not accept God. The Yoga Darshana accepts all the principles of the Samkhya but it adds God to it,. The Samkhya gives primary importance to the nature of truth while the Yoga deals primarily with spiritual disciplines.

Yoga utilizes the Brahman concept that is found in the Upanishads, thus it separates from the Samkhya school by accepting concepts of Vedantic non-dualism (Advaita).

Samkhyan doctrine of the relationship between Purusha and Prakriti is crucial to Patanjali's Yoga Darshana. The Samkhya gives primary importance to tattwajnana or enquiry into the nature of truth while the Yoga deals primarily with sadhanas or spiritual disciplines.

The significant variation of the Yoga from the Samkhya is not only the incorporation of the concept of Ishvara (a personal God) into its metaphysical worldview (which the Samkhya does not) but also upholding of Ishvara as the ideal upon which to meditate.

It also utilizes the Brahman/Atman terminology and concepts that are found in the Upanishads, thus breaking from the Samkhya school by adopting concepts of Vedantic nondualism.

Yoga Susthras of Patanjali took God as something which is not affected by the miseries and activities of human life, and the nature of God was evoked as *Aumkara* (AUM). What we see here is the phenomenon of giving acceptance to the belief in god, and the god being given a logical relevance.

Vaisheshika and *Njaya* philosophies (See Ch.-'cosmology brings science closer to spirituality') were put forward to prevent the Buddhists from propagating the ideas that there is no god and the Vedas are not books of true knowledge or sacred scriptures. The controversies in the opinions of these masters—even if they are great scholars in the subject—will reduce the acceptance of each in an impartial judgement. This kind of defect exists in the case of works of masters like Kapila, Patanjali, Gautama, Jaimini, Badarayana and others. The real truth, however, cannot be hidden by differences in outlook. But the philosophers like Adi Sankara and Sree Narayana Gurudev stood strongly on the foundations of Advaita Vedanta.

When we examine the social and cultural history of India, it becomes clear that Advaita, the greatest philosophy in the world, unfortunately served only the interests of a small group of people for their studies in private and to earn their livelihood. Really it was—and still is—something that filled the soul of India with sadness and afflictions. The majority of people were destined for untouchability and kept away from the mainstream by the upper castes by way of misinterpretation of the doctrines of Advaita. Due to lack of opportunity for social relations and because of unfavourable circumstances prevailing in the society, the divine light of Advaita was like a lamp in a pot.

Basically Sree Narayana Gurudev's life is the life that was dedicated to the promotion of Advaita—the philosophy of oneness. He had no life separated from the spirit of Advaita. This can be seen in his literary works and the social activities. Though the founder of Advaita philosophy is Adi Sankara, as the successor to Sankara as the greatest propounder, Gurudev's stature in Advaita is second to none. To Sree Narayana Gurudev who proclaimed 'in Advaita I follow Sankara' the rise and fall, its causes and history are very vital to his biography. In all his literary works and social reformation activities one can see his ardent closeness with Advaita Vedanta. Hence in this chapter on Sree Narayana Gurudev's role as the 'Reviver and Reformer', great importance is given to the aspects of history and relevance of Advaita Vedanta.

Because of someone's evil deeds, Advaita philosophy, India's noblest product, remained a school of thought with negative social relevance until Sree Narayana Gurudev came to the rescue. The curse of chaturvarnya (the four varnas), a creation of some vested evil interests, had echoed for hundreds of years and remained as the voice of caste-wise division in society, resulting in hatred, animosity and disgrace among the people. One of the causes of the creation of the divisions in the social structure of the people of India was the misinterpretation of the following lines in the Bhagavad Gita when Lord Krishna tells Arjuna about the class-wise division of people.

Cāturvarṅyam mayā sṛisṭam
Guṅa karma vibhāgaśśa
Tassya kartāra mapimām
Viddhyā kartāramavyayam

The four castes (varnas), according to the differentiation of attributes (Gunas) and actions (karma), are my creation. Though I am the doer of it, know me as non-performer and immortal.

(Jnana Karma Sanyasa Yogam 13)

The misinterpretation of the above lines by distorting the basic ideas was done by the people who claimed to be the upper classes. They spoilt the real spirit of the lines for their self-interests and to praise the rulers of the time for personal gain.

The main cause that led to chaturvarnya lies in the explanation of qualifications for achieving Brahmanhood; to be more specific, the eligibility for *Brahmavidya*. The question is whether one obtains it by merely taking birth from the womb of a Brahmin lady or one attains it through noble deeds in one's life. Sruthies and Brahmasutras clarify beyond doubt that one becomes eligible for divine knowledge and Brahmanhood only through one's noble deeds in life.

A person attaining Brahmanhood by birth, of course to some extent, is a creation of the belief in rebirths (Ref. 'Viveka Chudamani', Adi Sankara). Though the theories in physical cosmology state that universes are created one by one every second, they do not agree to the idea that these universes are the reproductions of the same universe many times. If you forsake the concept of rebirths in the universe, the attainment of Brahmanhood by virtue of one's birth will become irrelevant. But the concept of rebirth in another universe according to the many-worlds concept is getting more acceptance in recent times. In quantum physics, the concept of rebirth is accepted in a different way (see string theory, EEC, and many-worlds theories in the ensuing chapters).

The history of our heritage makes it known that those who learnt Brahmavidya, the divine knowledge, and who became *Brahmajnanins* (supreme scholars in divine knowledge) were not Brahmins by virtue of their births, and also they had never been subjected to *Upanayana*. They were not born to Brahmin women. Upanayana is the ritual of initiation which is restricted to the tree upper Varnas or the social classes that marks the introduction of a male child to the life of a student Brahmacharin. The ceremony is performed between the ages of 5 and 24. The variation in the age depends upon the different educational requirements of the three upper classes namely, Brahmanas (priest and teacher), Kshatriyas (warriors and rulers) and Vaishyas (merchants and tradesman).

The boy after a ritual bath is dressed as an ascetic before his spiritual guide (Guru). He provides him with a deer skin to use as an upper garment, a staff and a sacred thread. The thread consists of a loop made up of three symbolically knotted and twisted strands of cotton cloth. It is replaced regularly so that it is worn throughout the life time. Normally it is worn over the left shoulder and diagonally across the chest to the right hip. The ceremony identifies the bearer of the thread as a Dwija, means twice born. At the time of ceremony the Guru imparts the Gayatri mantra (a sacred verse) of the Rig Veda to the student's ear. At the conclusion of the initiation ceremony the student kindles the sacrificial fire and begs for alms symbolic of his dependence on others during his Brahmacharin period. Remember, Gurudev's initiation to the ascetic life started with begging for alms in different houses (as we have mentioned earlier).

Right from Parameshti, (who might be) the sage who chanted in praise of the 'Nasadeeya Suktam' in Rig Veda; the maharishis (as no caste classification prevailed) who wrote the Upanishads; Lord Krishna who made the immortal dialogue between the soul and spirit including the earlier statement referring to chaturvarnya in Gita; Krishnadwaipayana Vyasa (Badarayana), the author of Brahmasutras; and Sree Narayana Gurudev, who rebuilt blending the spiritual and social aspects of Advaita, were not Brahmins by birth. Even Adi Sankara, who had been sentenced as an outcaste by the then so-called Brahmins, was not eligible for Brahmavidya in that sense.

Like everywhere in the world, over the years, there might have been the periodical appearance of wormholes ruining our cultural heritage in the form of *rakshipta* (unauthorized addition). To boost the acceptability and appreciation of their arguments and explanations, the writers used to bring in stories and subplots with imaginary characters as heroes and heroines on many occasions. Such adornments are natural and permissible in poetics. Many are done with a great sense of purpose. There are improbable and unnatural events for symbolic ornamentations aimed at artistic excellence which stand as escorts to the events. For example, let us take the first day of the Kurukshetra war. On both sides of the warfront stand the armies of eighteen Akshowhinies ready to commence the war. According to estimates in the Puranic records at the time of Lord Krishna dictating the eighteen chapters of complicated philosophy as Bhagavad Gita, there would have been 3,93,660 elephants, and an equal number of chariots, 11,80,980 horses and 19,68,300 infantry soldiers on both sides of the arena.

In the above description of the war arrangements, there is lot of exaggeration and embellishment. One cannot believe that thousands of years ago such a colossal arrangement of millions of elephants, chariots, horses and infantry assembled for the war. Vysa, the author, wanted to maintain an unusual magnificent atmosphere where the divine uttering of the Lord are delivered to mankind through the legendry man Arjuna. He wanted the text of the divine uttering to reach generations after generations. Even those who could not understand the complexity of sentences should learn it by heart and carry it. This idea urged Vysa to glorify the situation and disseminate the philosophy.

It is easy to guess the reality of the above description; there was a colossal military arrangement in Kurukshetra, nearly 5,000 years ago, and a long dialogue took place between Krishna and Arjuna at the time when a great war was going to begin. Evidently, Vyasa, the author of the Mahabharata, was presenting the scene of interaction between Krishna and Arjuna, with the creative talent of a poet. If the author presented the same scene in a different way as if the dialogue was between two ordinary men transacting the ideas in a different scene, the great knowledge (metaphysics) discussed in the Mahabharata would not have been regarded as a noble treasure, and earned a place in people's hearts. It should be noted that the aforesaid dialogue took place at a time when the people were not sufficiently evolved intellectually to contain such complicated ideas discussed in the dialogue and were incapable of carrying such ideas vocally over to the generations that followed. Hence many learnt by heart the slokas, taking them as divine utterances, even without understanding their meaning in many cases, carried to generations.

We have many examples in our Puranic literature showing this kind of presentation of important events with the rhetorical embellishments which have survived in the society for thousands of years. In this case, Vyasa presented the event as an interaction between Krishna, who is none other than the Brahman Himself (Narayana - God), and Arjuna, a man (Nara) who had been exalted to the status of a god, in front of the majestic background described above. In short, Vyasa's way of presenting the event gave us the great opportunity of getting the holy utterances in Bhagavad Gita without much damage even today. One has to bow one's head before Vyasa for this great feat. Mahabharata belongs to the category Smrities. In Smrities, such embellishments are permitted. But in Sruthies (Upanishads), the embellishments are seldom found. This may be the reason why the Upanishads did not achieve wide popularity among the public.

Unfortunately, many authors did the opposite of this to serve the purpose of vested interests, especially in the promotion of chaturvarnya. Some of the Smrities come under this category. There are many examples; among them, the ancient controversial book Manusmriti made the greatest blow by cunningly bringing in Vedas and Upanishads to establish its trustworthiness in the explanation of the caste system. In a deliberate attempt to establish the interest of some sections of the society, Manu the author of Manusmriti is seen inefficaciously trying to mislead people as if he were bringing in the authority of Vedas and Upanishads. His way of mixing Vedas and Upanishads, jumping abruptly from Vedas to Upanishads and then skilfully to his rules, was to establish the caste system which was in contradiction to the principles of Advaita Vedanta. Advaita rejects caste-wise differentiation. Manusmriti starts with the lines (Sloka 5, Chapter 1) explaining the creation of the universe in a manner almost in tune with those in Rig Veda, 'Nasadeeya Suktam' and continues narrating the evolution of the universe in a way almost similar to that in Taitiriyopanishad (Hymns 6 and 7, 'Brahmanandavally'). Gradually, the tone deviates from Vedic concept, especially from Advaitic thought. Manu very cunningly creates the impression that his arguments and rules have the endorsement of Vedas and Upanishads. In a way, it is like linking astrology with astronomy for its reliability. Slokas 29 and 30 of the Smriti add to the caste classification, and Slokas 88 to 92 classify the castes as if commanded by God. Manusmriti slyly paved the way for the misinterpretation of Vedic doctrines, especially the one quoted from Gita (4–13) above. In a sense, it is the biggest blow in the form of chaturvarnya that India had to its social harmony.

Like other authors, the sages also wrote books creating probable and improbable circumstances for the manifestation of great ideas, narrating puffed-up stories and glorified verses. In many cases, it is like presenting an object in a golden cover. But Vyasa did it for a noble purpose knowing the value of the contents. He presented the contents of Bhagavad Gita as if those doctrines are uttered by God Himself to Man. It is the duty of one who is curious about the truth to discern the real events from the unreal ones which the poets and the authors used as exaggerations in their artifices. It is an undisputed fact that in our philosophical works—Sruthies and Smrities—there is the possibility of having additions and amendments (*prakshipta*) to the original work by different persons after many years.

Many such changes (prakshipta) that happened afterwards have either enhanced, reduced or damaged the intrinsic value of the book, and at times, have harmed it by replacing the original ideas with opposite and contradictory ones. This may be the cause hidden behind the frantic dance of chaturvarnya which trampled upon the majority of people in India. It might have been the failure in properly analysing the meanings of words and the nature of circumstances; the chaturvarnya had its origin from a very thin and sensible border due to the deliberate misinterpretation of words in puranic books by the vested interests for example, the uttering 'Chaturvaryam maya srishtam,' Chaturvarya is my creation in Gita (4-13). The more unfortunate fact is that no inquiry or search has been done so far to find the real culprits who paved the way for such a sinful deed. The fundamental problem here is the right or eligibility for the study of divine knowledge (Brahmavidya). The question is whether the eligibility for Brahmavidya is obtained through one's good qualities and noble deeds or whether one inherits it from being the son of a Brahmin woman. The order of varna (castes) is only subsequent to the above eligibility and is a secondary phenomenon. In none of the great works such as Bhagavad Gita, Vedas, Sruthies and Brahmasutras, is there any mention of the eligibility for Brahmavidya as obtained by virtue of one's birth. On the contrary, what is mentioned in those books is just the opposite. Brahmasutras have categorically described the qualities for the eligibility for Brahmavidya. (This accursed hereditary view of castes has been condemned by all great masters and enlightened men in India. Adi Sankara, who relinquished the Brahmin caste system in which he was born, wrote: 'No birth, no death, no caste have I.' In 1916 Sree Narayana Gurudev made a similar proclamation, 'I have no caste to remove misunderstandings, if any, among his worshippers and disciples.')

In none of the great works is there any mention of the qualifications for Brahmavidya as obtained by virtue of one's birth. Those who plead Sudras are not eligible for divine knowledge, quote the sutras 34–38 known as Apasudradhikaranam in Brahmasutras and its commentaries by Adi Sankara. Those who attack Adi Sankara, the greatest philosopher ever known in the history of divine knowledge, impose the evils of chaturvarnya on him. On analysing his literary works, one can see that it is not fair that anybody imposes the responsibility of chaturvarnya on Adi Sankara. In the course of our future discussion, we will see that Sree Narayana Gurudev could contain it in full spirit, and he proclaimed as follows: 'In the case of Advaita, I follow Sankara,' and he wrote in 'Anukampadasakam', '*Saralādvaita bhāṣyakāranām guruvō ī anukampayāntava.*' (I adore my preceptor, full of compassion, the author who simplified Advaita through commentaries.)

In the lineage of Advaita philosophy, Sree Narayana Gurudev stands at the same exalted position as Vyasa (Badarayana) and Adi Sankara. Among this Maharishi Triune, one complements the other (Sree Narayana Gurudev supplemented with a cosmological view). To understand the periodical evolution that Advaita philosophy had undergone over the ages, it is most logical to consider Vyasa, Adi Sankara and Sree Narayana as contributors in succession. By distorting the meaning of utterances in Bhagavad Gita and by propagating arguments contrary to the spirit of Advaita to establish the philosophy in favour of chaturvarnya, the upper classes forcibly held the monopoly of Advaita to uphold their privileged position in society.

Sree Narayana Gurudev, who found the real greatness of Advaita, accepted it as the leading light of his social philosophy. In his works, he wrote statements in tune with the metaphysics of Advaita and framed his activities accordingly. He broke open the walls of the caste system (*Varnasramadharma*—caste-wise differentiation) and gave an impetus to Advaita philosophy. In other words, Sree Narayana Gurudev liberated Advaita philosophy from the hands of a small group of people and delivered it to all people of the world, establishing the fact that it is a common property they inherited. He resisted all futile efforts by a group with vested interests to distort the nobility and greatness of the philosophy of *Kevaladvaita*. He made it blossom so that it became part of the common man's life. Gurudev made a pincer attack to rebuild the real strength of Advaita from spiritual and social fronts, which his predecessors Vyasa and Adi Sankara could not, as they ignored or took too lightly the impact of the evils of chaturvarnya.

In its search for absolute reality, Advaita philosophy takes 'the entity of man' and his relationship with the universe as its ultimate aim. It is something that is hidden in the secrets of creation, existence and dissolution of the universe. In the works of the Maharishi Triune—Badarayana (Vyasa), Adi Sankara and Sree Narayana—and in the aphorisms in Vedas and Upanishads (Vedanta), the principal topic of discussion is the secret of the universe. Advaita philosophy establishes the relationship between God, the universe and man as different manifestations of one and the same thing such that none is foreign to the other. Badarayana's Brahmasutras made tangible the ideas evolved from the Vedas and Sruthies that the universe is the manifestation of 'The One'. Adi Sankara, in his turn, defined it in a logical manner using a question-and-answer method. He elaborated the metaphysics of Advaita, writing commentaries to Brahmasutras, and made it a full-fledged religion. Whereas Sree Narayana Gurudev rebuilt Advaita philosophy, blending it with theoretical cosmology in respect of its theoretical aspects, liberated it from the level of a topic of discussion in the secluded meetings of the so-called scholars, and brought it to the common man. The Advaita philosophy has three aspects: 1) the belief in god; 2) the spiritual outlook; 3) cosmology (the study of the secrets of the universe). The debut of Advaita thought was in the form of hymns in the Vedas. These hymns were intended to manifest prosperity on earth by praising the gods of nature. Even though the lines (utterances) in the Vedas are supposed to be superhuman, they are only hymns written by maharishis. Once the nature of belief in god paved the way for the idea of live and inert things and vacuousness at the beginning of the universe, there came the manifestation of Nirguna Brahman (*Para Brahman*—the Brahman without attributes).

The discovery that 'the Brahman is the one and the only one' seems to be the first logical step in Advaita philosophy. This first-ever logical discovery in the studies of the universe is found in the 'Nasadeeya Suktam' in Rig Veda. It says that the creation of the universes is the result of the greatness of penance of the only thing 'The One' (*thapasthan mahina jayathaikam*). The statement about the creation of the universe 'thapasthan mahina jayathaikam' is almost in tune with the findings of modern physics and cosmology. What makes Advaita philosophy so great is found in its argument that the beginning of the universe is from a void-like point. Similarly, in both schools of thought—Advaita philosophy and physics—the explanation of the evolution of the universe that followed after the creation, is almost the same. The ten incarnations of Vishnu (*Desavatharam*) in Indian mythology is only an example of the evolution of life.

The absolute vacuum, the attributelessness and the invisibility of Brahman in the beginning that Advaita philosophy explains are almost in harmony with the explanation of modern cosmology about the beginning of the universe. Later, Badarayana in Brahmasutras quantified the idea of Brahman that grew and spread to form the visible universe. In those days, this idea did not have any social relations or interaction with the day-to-day life of men. It was Adi Sankara, through his commentaries on Brahmasutras, who initiated the process of giving a human quality to Advaita philosophy for its survival. He defined it as a basic spiritual philosophy. The entire works of Adi Sankara still remain a symbol of pride of Indian civilization, except for the controversy over the curse of chaturvarnya imposed on him, especially on his commentaries on sutras 34–38 (1, 3) in Brahmasutras and the misinterpretation of lines in Viveka Chudamani. The greatness and relevance of his contributions will continue forever. Unfortunately, Adi Sankara could not take the Advaita doctrines to the common people and create enough influence in the fields of knowledge and activities (*jnana* and karma fields). Still, it is an undisputed fact that his works have widened the scope of Vedic philosophy in a major way.

In the modern world, no philosophy can survive to ignore the relevance and importance of the discoveries and inventions of science through its observations and experiments. The problems that spiritual philosophy faces now were not the same as those faced in the times of maharishis and Adi Sankara. In those days, the topic of the relation between man and the universe was dealt with only religion and spiritual teachings. During the early days, when science was at an infant level in its awareness about the vast universe, it was quite natural that its knowledge about the infinite cosmos was lacking. Therefore, science could not contradict or reject the arguments put forth about the universe by religions and spirituality.

The situation has changed. Theories in physics, with the support of mathematics and experiments in laboratories, started playing a crucial role that has an unprecedented influence on the people in their day-to-day life. In view of the fast developments in science, the ordinary man who lives in a world of dreams is boastful of its invincible power. A few decades ago, he dreamt that through progress in science, man would conquer the entire universe.

From the latter half the last century, that attitude has changed. Now scientists working in the fields of physics and cosmology are well aware of the limitations of science in dealing with the secrets of the universe. It was such an awareness that very recently led many scientists, especially cosmologists, back to the anthropic principle which has now become a subject of discussion among physicists. The anthropic principle is a branch of knowledge that links science with spiritual philosophy. Today, scientists do not claim that science is all-powerful. Unlike the scientists of early days who were opposed to the relevance of metaphysics, the scientists of today do not maintain any hostile attitude nor underestimate spiritual cosmology, the reason being evidently the latest discoveries in science about the universe. Unfortunately, this new awareness has not come to the level of common people. It results in a lack of interest and intellectual interaction among the people to learn and understand the knowledge imparted by the wise sayings in spirituality.

It is essential to be aware that metaphysics and science are only two ways to the same goal along two different paths. Fortunately, the latest trends show that the two paths of the search are coming nearer in their studies about the secrets of the universe. This trend, in fact, heightens the relevance of spiritual philosophy and mysticism. There is no doubt as to the fact that if more studies and research are conducted in the spiritual field by scientists, science also will gain a lot in their dealings with unsolved problems, mostly in cosmology. In short, till today, science has dealt with, and is still dealing with, only a minor part of the real substance of the universe that is already known to metaphysics on a macroscopic scale. Science is confined only to the study of physical phenomena and the discoveries therein which come under the limited power of comprehension of man.

Comprehension is not merely a physical phenomenon. If spirituality remains incapable of giving convincing explanations to the findings of science, especially of modern science that has obtained unprecedented progress, it will cast a shadow on its reliability. It is here that the relevance of Sree Narayana Gurudev's contributions to metaphysics and modern cosmology comes. Sree Narayana Gurudev, besides being a spiritual guru, understood the pragmatism of science and the achievements the society obtained through the development of science. He knew that its growth and merits thereof could not be ignored. He was thoroughly aware of it and foresaw the role science was going to play in the future. Keeping such a realistic view, he brought Advaita philosophy to the midst of the common people, giving it a new face. Standing on the foundations of Rig Veda, Upanishads, Brahmasutras and its commentaries by Adi Sankara, he correlated Advaita philosophy to modern physics. It is because of this Sree Narayana Gurudev stands at the same elevation as Vyasa and Adi Sankara among the Indian maharishis in spirituality and as scientists like Einstein, Niels Bohr and Schrödinger in cosmology.

The above discussions lead us to the fact that to understand Gurudev's philosophy in its full sense, the study of modern science also is inevitable, as both Advaita and science ultimately aim at the same thing, namely, 'Man's Entity'. Both schools of thought confirm that the key to man's entity is the study of the creation of the universe, its existence and dissolution. All Vedas, Upanishads, Brahmasutras, and works of Sree Narayana Gurudev comprised different views of the universe. There is not a single verse in the entire works of Sree Narayana Gurudev in which the central point is not the universe; perhaps in a hidden-and-explicit manner since, in many of the poems one cannot understand whether it contains an element of science whereas in many others touch of science can be easily understood directly. The touch of science is missing in the works of rishis and Adi Sankara, because, as a branch of knowledge, science did not start dealing with the phenomena like the creation of the universe, etc., in those days. At the time of rishies and Sankara the awareness and hence the power of comprehension of people in general, were very poor. Though the above said masters discussed cosmological phenomena in very early puranic literature of India, the people could not go deep and understand them. Nasadeeya Suktam in Rig Veda is an example. But to analyse and evaluate their greatness, the power of comprehension of the people were not sufficient: if they could understand and follow, the history of

India would have been different. The omniscient Sree Narayana Gurudev, with the skill and precision of a scientist, gave the touch of modern cosmology to all his works in spirituality. It elevates Gurudev to the status of one of the foremost spiritual masters of India. His method of reformation of the society and the messages he gave were simultaneously in tune with spiritual considerations and scientific conclusions.

Man's intense longing to know the secret of the creation of the universe is as old as human civilization. Knowing that the foundation stones of knowledge are the 'ultimate truth' of the universe, philosophers and scientists, by this time, have travelled a long way, seeking the secrets of the universe and their own entity. At last, science stands at a stage where it is unable to cross the border or the Planck Limit to reach the first moment of creation, leaving it to the domain of singularity, a stage yet to be understood. Many scientists believe that with the present theories, limitations of instruments and experiments, they can never go beyond the Planck limit, say, 10^{-43} seconds and 10^{-33} cm, beyond which all physical laws break down. Many of them are of the opinion that since the entire phenomena in the universe are not physical, metaphysics has to be brought in to solve this problem. We can see in the forthcoming chapters how far maharishis like Sree Narayana Gurudev have gone beyond the limits of science in cosmology.

It was mentioned earlier that spiritual philosophy and modern science, fortunately, show a tendency to move in the same direction. The conclusions of science are getting nearer to the findings of spirituality. Indian philosophies, in general, will be very useful to physics and cosmology, which are engaged an effort to formulate a Theory of Everything (ToE) applicable to all phenomena in the universe. Similarly, as far as the metaphysicians are concerned, science can help them to a very great extent in getting more reliability and acceptability for their doctrines; spirituality is to be linked with the observational results of science. Sree Narayana Gurudev—perhaps for this purpose—gave, in almost all his works, an interrelation of spirituality (especially Advaita philosophy) with modern cosmology.

The original sources of metaphysical theories in India are the Vedas, namely Rig Veda, Yajurveda, Samaveda and Atharvaveda. Most of the philosophers and a great number of Indians believe that Vedas are superhuman and divine. Advaita is the most important among the various philosophical doctrines, created by the sages of India. The primal seed of Advaita thought was planted in Rig Veda, which is believed to be divine and is claimed to be the first book of knowledge. This thought developed by Vedas, Upanishads, Badarayana (Vyasa) and Adi Sankara ultimately reached Sree Narayana Gurudev and obtained more similarity with the conclusions of modern science.

Aryabhatta, Varaha Mihira, Bhaskara and many other Indian astronomers using scientific methods have made many contributions to the field astronomy and cosmology. The path of progress in the field of Western cosmology that started with Nicolaus Copernicus developed through Galileo Galilee, Johannes Kepler, Isaac Newton, Albert Einstein, George Gamow, Alan Guth and Erwin Schrödinger, reached Stephen Hawking, Roger Penrose and others.

In the light of innumerable constraints of science to discover the ultimate source of the phenomenon called the universe, at least some scientists now believe that the approach of spiritual philosophy is equally relevant. The awareness that this topic still continues to be something which is beyond their reach leads them to such a belief. The limitation of science is that all its convincing theories, such as special theory of relativity, general theory of relativity, atom models, quantum gravity and superstring theory, could only bring under its studies and findings a mere 4 to 5 per cent of the entire matter and energy in the universe even at this developed stage of man's perception and power of comprehension. This means 95 to 96 per cent of the entire content of the universe (to be more specific 23 per cent in the form of dark matter and 73 per cent in the form of dark energy and dark matter) is still beyond the limits of the human power of comprehension.

It is important to note that these facts are obtained from observational results and are confirmed by scientists. Intellectual honesty is the insignia of science. That is why scientists always in their ultimate conclusions, avoid agnosticism and turn towards spiritual philosophies. Because of this, there is the touch of spirituality in the views of a good number of modern scientists. Today, we see a freestyle approach in the search of the scientists. Spirituality which has been rejected by classical physics, is not forbidden to modern physics. It recognizes that not only matter and energy but also beauty and belief are all physical realities. The greatest change in the field of science is that modern scientists do not like to fasten the universe to artificial laws. Albert Einstein himself has remarked that the physicists of the new generation are more within the walls of the influence of spiritual problems when compared to the old generation. Many discoveries that have taken place lately have brought scientists closer to spiritual philosophies. It is so because science is not an isolated branch of knowledge; it is complementary to the knowledge of self.

To find the unique value of spiritual philosophies, especially that of Advaita in the present state of affairs, the study of modern science is essential. Therefore, those who learn spiritual philosophies should learn the primary lessons of modern science. Likewise, for arranging the path for onward movement and for more discoveries, the scientists should ensure the study of spiritual philosophies. Perhaps, spirituality may find solutions to the innumerable problems which are not addressed by science due to its limitations. A compromise between physics and spirituality may be a forerunner (omen) to the ToE—the one which physics is very anxiously waiting for. There may come a time when spirituality and science complement each other in explaining the unsolved problems in physics and cosmology.

To evaluate the contemporary relevance of Advaita philosophy, especially regarding the universe, it is essential to know where science has ultimately reached with the aid of logic, theories, mathematics, algorithms and the results of experiments and observations. Science, by going back in time, reached a point very close to the moment of creation. Unfortunately, it has not yet reached the exact point—the moment of creation.

At the same time, differentiating mortals (transients) and eternal, and sacrificing the fruits of actions on earth and heaven controlling the mind and sense organs with a desire to obtain salvation, the maharishis, who have the thirst for divine knowledge through their unending meditation, saw the secrets of creation, the existence and the end of the universe which in their opinion, are only the creation of the sense organs. They knew the different states of the universe such as the Brahman without attributes (Nirguna Brahman) and that with attributes (Saguna Brahman) before and after the moment of creation of the universe. Whether it is in science or in spirituality, the process of searching for the secrets of the universe is the biggest effort that human civilization has ever seen. There are no two opinions about it. It is very promising and auspicious to note that the conclusions of modern scientists show a tendency to come closer to Advaita philosophy.

It was mentioned earlier that to understand the Vedic concept of the universe—that is seen throughout the Vedas, Sruthies, Brahmasutras, its Bhashya by Sankara and the works of Sree Narayana Gurudev—it is necessary to know the details of the conclusions arrived at through the studies carried out by physics and cosmology. For the study of the universe—either through spiritual means or through scientific means—there are no shortcuts. Therefore, the discoveries, conclusions, mistakes and corrections that were adopted by both the methods at different stages of time are to be noted with care. Besides, there should be a general awareness about how science has arrived at the present state of progress through its continued experiments and observations. One must know what view the great sages had about the secrets of the universe thousands of years ago, to compare it with modern theories and recent discoveries of science. This awareness will be very helpful in getting an idea of the similarity between the findings of modern physics and the views of the great sages, and an understanding of how Sree Narayana Gurudev interrelated Advaita philosophy with modern science.

A question naturally arises as to how is it possible that a century ago, a sage who never had the opportunity to study physics and modern cosmology could allude to the latest ideas that have been introduced in modern physics and cosmology, in his writings. Quantum mechanics addresses whether a tuned consciousness can do such miracles.

Can you imagine, one day you can live simultaneously in two separate places or even in two different planets or universes by teleportation? Do you believe that one day, your imagination will become a reality? The answer is yes. Quantum mechanics brings science closer to spirituality says that subatomic particles can do this incredible feat. The great sages of India who accomplished the power of concentrating their entire entity on a single quantum by virtue of their rigorous penance performed by inflicting pain on the body could entangle with other quanta at a distant place or even another planet or universe by the phenomenon of 'Teleportation'. The recent theories and experiments of quantum physics endorse the possibility of this feat. In quantum mechanics, this phenomenon is restricted to a subatomic level of electrons, protons, neutrons, quarks etc, as big objects do not follow the rules of quantum mechanics. But this unusual nature of quantum behavior, conspicuous in the micro world, is gradually extending to the macro world. Scientists are searching for applications that would assist us in overcoming the limits of space and time and the constraints of classical physics. Recently, Anton Zeilinger at the University of Vienna in Austria transmitted entangled photons over a distance of 90 miles and set a record. Scientists believe that in future it will help space experiments to overcome the restrictions of space, time and cost. The 'SPACEQUEST' (Quantum Entanglement Space Experiment) is only one example. It is in this context we confirm the incredible feat of Sree Narayana Gurudev's instantaneous appearance at many places. There are many instances of Gurudev's presence at many places at the same time, participating in social and spiritual programmes. The above explanation of quantum physics endorses the fact that the great sage Sree Narayana Gurudev, by virtue of his divine power (obtained through rigorous penance), could perform the act.

Sree Narayana Gurudev was a 'thought reader'. He possessed the extraordinary power of reading the thoughts of others. From the scientific point of view, it is possible only if the minds are entangled at the time of reading the thought. There are references which say that the great sages of India could transmigrate their souls to others' bodies. Gurudev had this 'yogic power' and practised it on many occasions as mentioned in almost all biographies of Gurudev. Even staunch rationalists like Sahodaran Ayyappan and M.C. Joseph had to admit it in the interviews with Prof. M.K.Sanu.

The renowned writer and teacher Prof. M.K. Sanu once asked Sahodaran Ayyappan what was his opinion about Sree Narayana Gurudev's miraculous powers. After a significant smile, Ayyappan fell into deep thought and said, 'From the beginning, I noticed an unusual thing in Swami [Gurudev] that he could read the minds of others.'

There are many such events reported by witnesses from all walks of life in south India.

Suppose that you get a letter from New Delhi. The possible routes (mathematically, infinite possibilities ranging from '0' to '1') through which the letter comes from New Delhi to where you are (say, Kollam) can be via Bengaluru or Chennai or Kolkata or even through the Moon or Mars or anywhere in the universe. Instead of the letter, let a person from New Delhi meet you at Kollam. The letter being inert is incapable of telling the route it had. Though the person is aware of his exact route, unless he tells about it, he is also like the letter so far as you are concerned. In short, both the letter and the person have their paths unknown to you. This means that they have no definite positions during the time they are between the starting point and the end point. But it does not mean that they take no path as they travel between starting and ending points.

Though the letter and the person experienced their paths, you (the observer) do not know their paths. In general, every particle (quantum) possesses its own individual history, which is known only to itself. If an observer wants to know the particle in full, he has to become one with it by quantum entanglement. Since in quantum entanglement there is no space and time consideration, that is, there is no past and future but only present, you can see the past as well as the future at the moment of observation as a present. Quantum entanglement brings oneness by quantum collapse. This means it is a unique situation where both particles become one or losing separate entity. In Advaita Vedanta the absolute one cannot have a second because there is no separation between two bodies as any second one is forbidden to the absolute one. Space and time are properties that make separation. If it is not there, then there is no separation. Then, to know the entire history, what is required is a tuned quantum mind that can entangle with a quantum of the observed object. (see ch. Cosmology brings science closer to Spirituality)

There are many incidents of Gurudev's miraculous ability to cure diseases of patients who were otherwise left as lost cases by famous physicians. Such patients were cured of their serious illness within a short period of time with a look or miraculous touch of Gurudev. More surprising was that the medicines prescribed by Gurudev were only some common fruits, tubers or leaves. When the same fruits or tubers were administered to similar patients with the same disease by other physicians, the results were disappointing. When somebody asked Gurudev about the secret of this superhuman feat, he smilingly replied: 'Those are only momentary treatments.'.

A patient and his disease have a story of infinite probabilities till the moment of observation or diagnosis; maybe from the moment of his birth to the moment of diagnosis, or that may extend to many of his past generations. An ordinary person, or even the patient himself, cannot be aware of this. But a tuned consciousness in a particular quantum state can entangle with an identical quantum state of the patient and get the entire story of the patient and his disease at the moment of observation, revealing the cause and the present state of the disease. Gurudev, who had journeyed vastly in forests and populous lands and had tasted or had even eaten almost all kinds of fruits, tubers, herbs and leaves, was aware of their chemistry and medicinal value. This knowledge made him prescribe panacea medicine. When he used the word 'momentary', he never meant an astrologically auspicious moment.

This extraordinary divine power of Gurudev gave critics, including some local physicians, an opportunity to raise the question as to why when affected by serious illness, Gurudev could not treat himself. As we have seen earlier, quantum entanglement requires two different objects. In this case, one has to be an already tuned quantum mind so that it can entangle with an identical quantum of the other (the patient). The entire soul and body, when quantized to a single point, there is no question of finding another identical quantum in his body once entanglement is done. Hence it is very clear that a self-treatment by entanglement is absolutely impossible. To those who expressed the above apprehension, Gurudev once retorted, 'It is only the inert body that feels pain, not me.'

On another occasion, a worshipper (it is said it was the great poet Ulloor S. Parameswara Iyer/Vailopalli Sreedhara Menon ,a great poet), a little surprised, asked Gurudev,'Gurudev, you have saved many patients from their agonies by your divine power, when it comes to your pain, you seem to be incapable of getting rid of it?'

Gurudev retorted, 'Where can I get in this world such a person loving me so much and who can take over all the pain from this body?' The great worshipper smiled, understanding what he meant. But many could not understand it.

It is evident from the words of Gurudev that over the years of his life, because of his mercy to suffering people, he took the agony from them and freed them from pain by entanglement with them. All such pains he received from others had accumulated and reached a climax at the fag-end of his worldly life because, in every act of treatment, Gurudev himself became the patient. But to take over this accumulated agony, there has to be another person, equally loving and capable of entanglement with him. It was only the Brahman who loved him so much who could share the pain and become 'one' with him.

Gurudev said (in a different context), in the concluding sentence of 'Chijjada Chintanam', 'How can these blockheads know the greatness of this feat?' There is another version that requires awareness of the spiritual approach of rebirths. As mentioned above, Gurudev, while treating the patient, takes over the disease from the patient, and that remains in Gurudev's inert body. When this is done for many patients, their diseases accumulate in Gurudev's inert body. Gurudev can experience the accumulated pain at any time according to his will. But, unless the pain is experienced in the present life itself, it will obstruct the way to Moksha, and that in turn, will result in another rebirth instead of merging with Brahman. This view becomes more relevant when Gurudev's momentary treatment is explained on the basis of quantum entanglement.

During his visits to the houses of devotees and in meetings, he prompted people to give education to their children as he believed that only through knowledge, can one get real freedom. He wanted them to learn science and technology. He insisted that the organizers of the Sivagiri pilgrimage convene a full-fledged convention on science and technology, inviting experts in their respective fields to deliver lectures. Remember, this was a century ago! He established many public schools. The impact of Gurudev's effort brought extraordinary results. It led to the social upliftment of the socially and economically backward classes. There arose a new generation of highly qualified individuals such as scholars, writers, etc. and professionals such as doctors, engineers, scientists, etc.

As most of Gurudev's literary works are cosmology-oriented; though his contributions to astronomy, astrophysics and cosmology were very significant they were less understood by his disciples and others. It was not made known to people around the world and hence less appreciated by them due to their unawareness. The fact that Gurudev is one of the greatest cosmologists in the world is not known to many. In this context, one cannot ignore the divine blessings behind the feat of giving new birth to Indian astronomy by the great scientist Manali Vainu Bappu whose parents were devotees of Gurudev and got his blessings for the infant.

Let us see how Gurudev's poems amaze us about his foresightedness as a spiritual leader and a cosmologist. He foresees the future of investigations regarding the secrets of the universe.

The swine pierced the earth to see your foot and the swan
Flew upward to find your head both could not find you in full
Oh! Mountain of fire you may devour me along with the senses
Adorable Shiva! Supreme Master! I bow and prostrate.

God Vishnu, taking birth as a swine, pierced the earth deeper and deeper and tried to see the foot of Shiva (the bottom end of the universe). The God Brahma on a swan flew upward to find the head of Shiva (the farther end of the universe). Both of them could not so far find either the foot or the head, and they continue their never-ending search.

('Sadāšiva Daršanam', Poem 10)

Gurudev symbolically takes the God Shiva as the universe and explains the situation of the two-faced search to find the ultimate secret of the universe.

The worshipper prays to God Shiva to take him to dissolve in Shiva (Brahman, the Universe) and end the illusion of duality.

Sree Narayana Gurudev in the above lines comments on the fate of studies about the secrets of the universe. One set of searchers go deeper and deeper into the micro world, analysing the structure of matter (standard model) and the moment of creation of the universe on their way by studying molecules, atoms, electrons, hadrons, quarks and very recently reaching the Higgs boson; yet not arriving anywhere near their target. Higgs bosons are carriers of Higgs fields that give mass to matter. Physicists are aware of their limitations. They can never reach the moment of creation where the laws of physics break down, and physics can never go beyond the Planck limit (beyond which all space and time. mass and energy reduce to a single point, the singularity). Another set of searchers go to space exploring more and more expanse of the universe to find the ultimate limit of the universe (general theory of relativity). But going beyond the planet Mars or at the most, at the boundary of our solar system, is humanly impossible. String theory, quantum cosmology and the multiverse concept, endorse this argument. We will see in the next chapters cosmology brings science closer to spirituality

Rig Veda millennia ago revealed:

Iyam visṟṣtiryatē ābhabravanadi vā datē yadi vā na I
Yō asyādhyakṣa paramē vyōmanthsō aṅga vēda yadi vāna vēda II

Whence all creation had its origin?
Whether he fashioned it or whether he did not
He, who perceives it all from heaven,
He alone knows the beginning—or maybe even he does not know.

Sree Narayana Gurudev in 'Brahmavidya Pancakam' advised,

Pṟajñanam twahamasmi tatwamasi tad-
Bṟahmāyamātmeti sam-
gāyan vipṟacara pṟaśānta mānasa
twam Bṟahma bōdhōdayat
Pṟarābdham kwa nu sancitam tava kimā-
gāmi kwa karmāpyasat
Twayyadhyastamatōf khilam twamasi
Saccinmātramēkam vibhu:

Oh! Dear, you realize the Brahman and then understand that 'I am the Supreme knowledge' (Prajnanam Brahma) and 'Thou Art It' (Tat Twam Asi). Know that this Atman (soul) is that Brahman (the universe) (*Ayamatma Brahma*). Bear this experience of realization and live in peace, as a person devoid of all dualities, love and hatred. Once you attain this, worldly worries and troubles will not affect you. The curse of previous births will all be vanished. There will not be any future deeds. Oh! Dear, deeds themselves are non-existent. While it is not in you, it is imputed to you as if it is there. Understand that everything is superposed on you. You are unique, substance and knowledge.

Sree Narayana Gurudev became one with Brahman at 3.30 p.m. on 20 September 1928. Sri Guruprasad Swamikal who was witness to the scene of the Great Samadhi narrates 'the historical event'. At the time of samadhi, Sri Vidhyananda Swamikal at the request of Gurudev was reading the *Jeevanmukta Prakaranam* in the presence of Sree Narayana Gurudev. In 'Yogavasishta', it reads as follows:

> He reached the state of mind that saw happiness everywhere. The sacrificial fires, Tapas, gifts and holy waters had no meaning to him. He was abundantly supplied with wisdom and was friendly to all. He was desireless; in his eyes, nothing was supernatural. He was indescribable, yet moved in this world like anybody else. His mind was not bound by any longings after Karma, was indifferent towards joy and pain, not bothered about good or bad results. He was content with whatever he obtained whether in the state of self-awareness or of Absolute Consciousness he was never affected by anything. He was the same whether while moving in a family or was in a solitary hermitage; grief and pleasure never affected him. He was far and near to anyone. He believed in one Reality of Atman. He was not clingy, not arrogant. He had no fear or anger to anyone. He was beyond Trishna (Thirst). He was not becoming. He did not even long for Salvation. He was content. He always transacted the present duties neither longed for things in future nor ruminated upon things of the past. He was a child amongst the children, old amongst the old, mighty amongst the mighty, youth amongst the youths, compassionate and understanding with the aggrieved, was noble, benevolent, loving and clear in intellect.

Gurudev, the great soul in deep meditation, was attaining salvation while Vidyananda Swamikal was reading that part of the book *Jeevanmukta Prakaranam* explaining the liberation from the worldly ties and becoming one with the Brahman. It was the scene Gurudev foresaw in his prose 'Atmavilasom':

'The God, who sees without an eye, hears without ears, touches without skin, smells without nose, tastes without tongue, is the supreme soul. I am the counterpart; my body is inert. God is light. Oh! I was extrovert. Now I become introvert. So far, I was in a divine mirror. This itself is my God. I never saw it any before. Now before me, there is not any veil. God and I have become One. Hereafter, I am forbidden from interactions. Oh! See! I become one with God.'

Sree Narayana Gurudev attained liberation as stated in *Jeevanmukta Prakaranam* in 'Yogavasishta'.

It was reported by the disciples and devotees who were looking after him that since two days before the samadhi there were no symptoms of urinary disease (as endorsed by the joint opinion of the famous physicians, Dr Noble of the department of defence and Dr Sommerwell, a renowned physician). Gurudev was in deep meditation closing all the senses, a state of Turiya resembling the first poem in 'Atmopadesa Satakam'. Since Gurudev entered into the state of Turiya, he was beyond the limits of space and time. In Turiya all the sense organs namely, eyes, nose, ears, tongue and skin are closed. Hence, the physical world around becomes vanished, only the all-pervading eternal Brahman exists. All concept of space and time gets vanished it is the state of oneness. Therefore, except the moment of clinical death of the illusory body, the exact moment of Gurudev's liberation from the worldly bonds is beyond our guess.

There are recent medical reports about people coming back to life even forty to fifty minutes after their clinical death marked by cardiac arrest. Similar explanations are found in *Garuda Purana* (Chapter X, 36–39). 'Then, of him who is righteous and has thus performed the rites, O Bird, the life-breaths easily pass through the higher opening. The mouth, eyes, nostrils and ears are the seven gateways through which go those of good deeds. Yogins go through an opening in the head.''When the rising and descending life-breaths, which are joined, become separate, then, becoming subtle, the life-breath departs from the inert body.'

The experience of those who went through such events (as narrated by them) and came back to life from death opens new avenues of correlating science with spirituality.

Epilogue

The people all over the world are witnessing the great relevance, the nobility of philosophy and the accelerated impact of Gurudev's messages social life and metaphysics. But many people take Gurudev merely as a social reformer mainly because they fail to understand the worth and the depth of his literary works at first sight. But to have a clear idea about his stature as a great philosopher and cosmologist, one should have a thorough knowledge of his literary works and the philosophy behind his consecration of the idols in temples. That demands a thorough reading and analysis of - the not so easy to understand - literary works numbering to more than sixty in different languages, namely, Malayalam Tamil and Sanskrit. Out of this, more than forty are highly philosophical and demand enthusiasm for deep study and thought.

Who was Sree Narayana Gurudev in his fullness? Was he a mere social reformer or a yogi by birth and a staunch Advaiti? He was both, but more than that he was a great poet, a scholar in many languages, a merciful physician with a healing touch and many other attributes. But above all these, he was one of the greatest cosmologists. To understand his personality and contributions to the field of social life especially in Kerala and neighboring states one has to learn about the social inequalities created by caste differentiation that prevailed prior to the ascent of Sree Narayana Gurudev.

Chaturvarnya—(the four-fold caste system is the perpetual blemish India had to bear due to the misinterpretation of the aphorism in Ṛig Veda that Brahman from his face (head) created the Brahmins (Scholars—men of divine knowledge), from the upper arms the Kshatriyas (warriors), from the thigh the Vaiṣyas (men of trade) and from the foot the Sudras (the working class). But what maharshies meant was Jñana Kanda (divine knowledge) as head, Karma Kanda as the feet and Upasana Kanda (worship) as the heart. The same was a view that Lord Krishna held in Jnana karma sannyasa yoga (Gita) in the classification of castes. Sree Narayana Gurudev, footing firmly on the doctrines of Advaita philosophy fought against this lingering evil and saved both the lower castes and Advaita. He wrote in *'Jatinirnayam'*, 'How cow-hood is their race (caste) to cows; manhood is their race (caste) to men. In that case castes like Brahmins etc. are not castes (that is what Advaita meant). What a pity? Nobody knows the truth. Gurudev then continues to establish this argument in biological terms in the lines that followed in*'Jatinirnayam'*.

Sree Narayana Gurudev understood that the differentiation in all forms, especially economic and social fields, arrive from the feeling of duality. Love, hatred, anger, etc., are all its creation; once that is abandoned, there comes the feeling of oneness that is non-duality. Then since there is not a second, there cannot be any differentiation between things; there will not be different castes, different religions and different gods. There will not be love even between two, but only self-happiness. There will not be anything to acquire; there will be no desire or greed. Not anybody to hate, and there is no hatred if there is no enthusiasm to get more, there is no greed.

Gurudev understood that the factor that creates the feeling of differentiation between man and man is the feeling of duality (*Dvaita*), and the only remedy to eradicate it is to believe in Advaita (non-dualism).

Pulaya (caste)was kept away from Ezhava (caste) and Ezhava from the so-called upper castes such as Sudra, Vaisya, Kshatriya and Brahmana according to the then prevailing social rule prescribed by Manusmriti. The oppressed class in the society, namely outcastes, according to chaturvarnya doctrines, had to suffer physically and mentally for centuries.

Kapila did not believe in God though Gaudapada took him as God himself. Buddhists also came up with arguments for atheism and non-acceptance of Vedas as creed or maxim. Vaiseshika and Nyaya philosophies were contradictory in their opinions. Philosophies of Kapila, Kanada, Gautama Jaimini and Badarayana had the same defect of lack of unity in their arguments.

Adi Sankara and those masters who lived before and after him, though they lived in the midst of chaturvarnya, did not try to remove casteism due to two reasons. One is that the people in general, were not intellectually developed to contain the real spirit of Vedas and Vedanta; they did not care for opposing casteism. Two, the masters of Advaita maintained the belief that Advaita is a personal experience and the only reality and all dualities, including caste differentiation in social life are unreal or Maya.

There were other reasons also. One, is that in the Vedic-period caste system was not in the picture even though some terms that can be misinterpreted were used in Vedas here and there. But they were used in the real sense and meaning which does not agree with the fabricated chaturvarnya explanation in Manusmriti. Two, the people, in general, were not aware of the basic cause and motive of the vested interests behind caste differentiation.

Those who criticize Sankara should remember that he had many limitations in this aspect. He lived only for a short period of thirty-three years and the depth of his thought and the way it was discussed could not be understood by the majority of people. He had to fortify Advaita philosophy from the attack of Buddhism by refuting their arguments. In short, Sankara, who lived 1200 years ago (788–820 CE) had a different social atmosphere around him. The vast majority of people were not aware of their own rights even about their social identity. Still, he could foresee the danger behind the social differentiation and disclosed to the generations to come, the story of how he adopted a *Chandala*, an outcaste, as his ultimate master through the lines in 'Manisha Panchakam'. In this context, remember! Even in the twentieth century, Sree Narayana Gurudev had to publish a proclamation saying, 'I have no caste. I do not belong to any particular caste.'

In fact, Sree Narayana Gurudev maintained a spiritual belief which cannot be challenged by even the most modern theories in physics and cosmology. It is clearly manifested in his message to the annual meeting of Sree Narayana Dharma Paripalana Yogam held in 1908 that 'worship of God should reach all houses and hearts'.

About Gurudev's greatness as a spiritual philosopher and social reformer, the great leaders of India made the following comments that stand testimony to the stature of Gurudev.

'I feel like the greatest privilege in my life to have a darshan of venerable sage Sree Narayana Guru. I had the fortune to stay one day in his holy ashram. Her Excellency the Regent Empress also spoke to me about the greatness of Guruswamy'—Mahatma Gandhi

'I had the good fortune to come into contact with several saints and monasteries. I have never come across one who is spiritually greater than Swami Sree Narayana Guru of Malayalam, nay a person who is on a par with him in spiritual attainment'—Rabindranath Tagore

'Where great men have lived, that place becomes a holy ground something like a temple, because of their thoughts and prayers that lie enshrined there. Sree Narayana Guru lived here and from here radiated his message—the message of one caste, no division. That message is still very much needed in these days'—Jawaharlal Nehru

'Sree Narayana Guru is considered as one of the five or ten Avatars that have appeared in India during the last hundred years. My humble respects to the memory of this great sage'—Acharya Vinoba Bhave

'He was a Jnanin of action, a great religious intellectual, who had a keen living sense of the people and of social necessities'—M. Romain Rolland

'A great Social Reformer, a staunch promoter of Hindu Religion, and a true Philosopher Sree Narayana Guru was a revolutionary yogi of Kerala'—Dr S. Radhakrishnan

'May his blessings are upon all of us, Gurudev was the personification of love as Jesus Christ and Lord Buddha'—Swami Chinmayananda

'I had a vision of God in human form; Sree Narayana Guru who was renowned in the Southern-most of India was that "Supreme Being"'—C.F. Andrews

'Sree Narayana Guru had not much to talk to me, for he was the "Mahatma" of high intellectual supremacy'—Ramana Maharshi

2

VINAYAKASHTAKAM

In 1908 Gurudev visited Kottar, a place near Nagercoil, in Tamil Nadu. In those days, people of that area took the evil deities like Malla, Chudalamada, Karinkali, etc. as their favourite deities for prayer. Gurudev removed all those idols of evil deities and constructed a temple named Pillayar Kovil and consecrated the idol of Lord Ganapathi otherwise known as Vinayaka. Many believe his poem might have been written on that occasion. This is a prayer song in praise of Lord Ganapathi. It is in simple Sanskrit and contains eight verses.

The poem reveals through these lines the method of meditating on the favourite deity to attain self-realization. Regular chanting of this in the morning and evening gives the self-confidence to lead an unhindered worldly life. Before all ritual ceremonies, the chanting of prayer songs in praise of Ganapathi is performed, as a rule.

(Original text in Sanskrit)

Namaddēvavṛuntam lasadwēdakandam
Siraṡṛī madindum ṡṛitaṡṛīmukundam
Bṛuhacārutuntam stutaṡṛīsanandam
Jaṭāhīndṛakundam bhajē fbhīṣtasandam.

One with the group of gods bowing heads around
Shines as self-shining taproot of Vedas wears
The moon on head shedding light, adored by Vishnu
Accompanied by Lakshmi, one with beautiful
Bulky stomach extolled by ascetics like Sanaka
Puts on the serpent as the garland of jasmine on matted hair
And one who blesses devotees for fulfilment
Of their desires, Oh! Vinayaka, I adore you!

2

Kiladdēvagōtṛam kanadhēmagātṛam
Sadānandamātṛam mahābhaktamitṛam
Saracandṛavaktṛam tṛayīpūtapātṛam
Samastāṛti dātṛam bhajē sakti putṛam.

One born in the lineage of gods,
With the body shining like gold,
Remains as the personification of happiness,
Friend of the devotee, one with a beautiful face
Resembling autumnal moon, home of Vedas,
Remains as sickle for cutting all miseries
Of devotees, the son of Goddess Parvathi,
Oh! Vinayaka, I meditate you!

Gaḷaddānamālam caladbhōgimālam
Gaḷāmbhōdakālam sadā dānaśīlam
Surārātikālam mahēśatmabālam
Lasatpuṇḍṛaphālam bhajē lōkamūlam

One with the flow of rutting juice wearing
Shaking chain of the serpent in the neck,
One with the colour of black clouds,
With the habit of giving favourites of devotees,
Killer of the demons the foes of gods,
One who is the son of God Shiva who

Shines with holy ashes smeared on the forehead,
Cause of the universe, Oh! Vinayaka, I worship you!

Urastārahāram saratcandṛahīram
Suraśṛīvicāram hṛutāṛtāribhāram
Kadē dānapūram jadābhōgipūram
Kalābindhutāram bhajē śaivavīram.

The one who wears a necklace of pearls on chest
Crescent Moon on the head as gilding, one always
Interested in the prosperity of the gods, who removes
The burden of the hostility of downtrodden and friend of the sick
The one who pours rutting juice on the cheek, wearing
Serpents in the bundle of matted hair, one who is
Symbol of Pranava with the mark of the stag, son of
Lord Shiva, brave one, Oh! Vinayaka, I adore you!

Karārūdamōkṣam vipadbhangadakṣam
Calatsārasākṣam parāśaktipakṣam
śṛitāmaṛtyavṛikṣam surāridṛutakṣam
Parānandapakṣam bhajē śṛīśivākṣam.

One with deliverance kept in palm, clever enough
In avoiding dangers, one with beautiful eyes
Like petals of the lotus, one who helps the mother,
Power of Shiva in the creation of the universe, its existence
And dissolution one shines as the heavenly tree to dependants
And minces demoniac trees, one who helps to experience
Universal bliss, with prosperous eyes and auspiciousness
Full to the brim, Oh! Vinayaka, I meditate you!

Sadāśam surēśam sadā pātumīśam
Nidānōdbhavam śānkarapṛēmakōśam
Dhṛutaśṛīniśēśam lasaddantakōśam
Calacūlapāśam bhajē kṛutapāśam.

The one who always remains an embodiment
Of auspiciousness, Lord of gods, strong enough to
Protect always, one who is the primordial cause
The seat of affection of Lord Shiva, one who
Wears beautiful moon on the head, one with
Shining tusks, shaking trident and bondage in hands
One who breaks the worldly bondage
Of devotees, Oh! Vinayaka, I worship you!

Tatānēkasantam sadā dānavantam
Budhaśṛīkarantam gajāsyam vibhāntam
Karātmīyadantam tṛilōkaikavṛuntam
Sumantam parantam bhajē f ham bhavantam.

The one who shines always taking different forms,
Making rutting juice flow, one who blesses nobles with
Prosperity, well known as elephant faced and shines
Taking different forms, which keeps the piece of own broken
Tusk in one hand; remains as the cause of the three worlds,
One who moves slowly, one who shines as Vedanta fame
Brahman, who exists beyond the limits of
The entire universe, Oh! Vinayaka, I meditate you!

śivapṛēmapindam param swaṛṇavaṛṇam
Lasaddantakhandam sadānandapūṛṇam
Vivaṛṇapṛabhāsyam dhṛutaswaṛṇabhāndam
Calacāruśundam bhajē dantituṇdam.

The one who is the body form of the love of Shiva,
One beyond the Maya, one with the
Shining of gold, and with a piece of shining tusk
One fully immersed in eternal bliss,
One with a face with particular colours
Mixed beautifully, who wears the golden pot
One who has a beautiful trunk and the face
Of elephant, Oh! Vinayaka, I worship you!

3

ANUKAMPADASAKAM

(Original text in Malayalam)

Orupīṭayeṟumbinum varu-
tarutennuḷḷanukambayum sadā
Karunākara! Nalkukuḷḷil nin-
tirumeyviṭṭakalāte cintayum. 2

Aruḷāl varumimbaman paka-
Nnoru nenjāl varumallalokkeyum
Iruḷanpine māṟṟumallalin-
Karuvākum karuvāmitētinum.

Aruḷanpanukampa mūnninum
Poruḷonnāṇitu jīvatārakam;
"Aruḷuḷḷavanānu jīvi" ye-
Nnuruviṭṭīṭukayī navākṣari.

Aruḷillayatenkilasthiti tōl
Sira nāṟunnoruṭambutānavan;
Maruvil pravahikkumambuva-
Ppuruṣan niṣphalagandapuṣpamām.

Varumāṛuvidham vikāravum
Varumāṛillaṛivinnitinnunēṛ;
Uruvāmuṭalviṭṭu kīrtiyā-
Muruvāṛnninanukamba vinniṭum.

Paramārthamuracu tēṛviṭum
Poruḷo? Bhūtadayākṣamābdhiyō?
Saralādwayabhāṣyakāranām-
Guruvōyīyanukambayāṇṭavan?

Puruṣākṛuti pūṇṭa daivamō?
Naradivyākṛuti pūṇṭa dhaṛmamō?
Paramēśapavitṛaputṛanō?
Karunāvān nabi muturatnamō?

Jwaramāṛi vibhūti koṇṭu mu-
Nnaritām vēlakal ceyta mūṛtiyō?
Arutāte valanju pāṭi au-
Daramām nōvukeṭuta siddanō

Haranannezuti pṛasiddamām
Maṛayonnōtiyamāmunīndranō?
Mariyātuṭalōṭu pōyora-
Pparameśwarante parāṛthyabhaktanō?

Nararūpameṭutu bhūmiyil
Perumāṛīṭinakāmadhēnuvō!
Paramātbhutadānadēvatā-
Taruvōyīyanukambayāṇṭavan? 10

Meaning and commentary

Verse 1

Always bestow compassion on me
That no torment is made by me even

To an ant, Oh! Mercy! Let the thought of
Your holy form not get away from me.

Oh! Lord the seat of mercy! Give me kindness not to do anything to cause pain even to an ant and the memory to my mind to keep your divine form in my mind without forgetting.

Karuna is mercy, and Karunakara is the embodiment of mercy. God is the embodiment of mercy. From Brahman (Saguna) to ant are living things. Among living creatures, the ant is a very small, trivial one. Even to such uncared for creatures, one should show utmost mercy. The first step to mercy is not to torment others. The poem stresses that the mercy towards fellow creatures is more important than even the memory of God. The poem is basically a message for non-violence. The devotee, therefore, prays to the God that he should be blessed with the habit of not harming any fellow creatures.

Verse 2

Due to knowledge comes pleasure
To the heart without kindness come all miseries
Ignorance destroys love and thus becomes
Cause of miseries and the seed of all perils.

Real knowledge brings in pleasure, but the mind without love brings all sorts of grief. Ignorance annihilates love, and thus, ignorance becomes the cause of grief. This becomes the seed of all dangers.

In short, it says the cause of all good qualities in one is mercy to others. Likewise, the cause of all evil deeds is hatred. This verse instructs that one should get rid of all hatred that keeps away mercy. Due to compassion for fellow creatures, one gets peace of mind and pleasure. One with a heart without love to others will face sufferings in life. Unless we show love to others, nobody will love us; we will be subject to hatred of others. Hatred is darkness, whereas love is light. When the mind is shadowed with darkness, love gets lost from the heart. It becomes the cause of all sufferings in life.

Verse 3

The content of the three, knowledge, love
And mercy is the same, and it is the
Leading star of life only 'the wise lives'
Chant these nine letter hymn again and again.

It is the same truth, which is the root cause of all the three—knowledge, love and mercy. They are the same. This truth takes the life from the ocean of worldly miseries to the other shore. Only the blessed one with knowledge lives. This hymn with nine digits should be chanted again and again.

Only he who possesses mercy is eligible to be a living creature. Once there is no mercy in one's heart, one is nothing but an inert stone. The natural instinct of a living thing is the eagerness to serve fellow creatures. The statement in the third line, namely '*Aruḷuḷḷavanāṇu jeevi*', is the core part of the poem. Always chant this nine-lettered hymn 'Arulullavananu jeevi', (which in the Malayalam language contains nine letters) meaning 'One who has mercy is the Man'. Mercy implies the other two qualities, love and blessing also. This verse gives prime importance to mercy in life.

If life ends without knowing the truth of life, it will be a total failure. Note that it will lead to more and more births for eternal miseries. Real life is one who is aware of the secrets of life. Ignorance about life is death itself. The undivided unchanging consciousness is the only real thing. Knowledge, love and mercy are the three founding stones of the same thing, the blessedness (*Arul*). One who knows the consciousness, believes and experiences it as everything, is the one with real knowledge.

The substance of blessing, affection (love) and mercy are the same. For a nobleman, they are interconnected and almost synonyms. Only such persons who have their minds blessed can have love for others. Love brings people together. It is this love that becomes the instrument to feel sympathy for others and share their empathy. Mercy, in effect, is a combination of blessing, love and mercy, and is qualified as the star of life as it can save life showing the other shore of the ocean of worldly sufferings.

Verse 4

He is only a stinking body with bones
Skin and nerves, if without knowledge
That man is only water flowing in the desert
And a useless odourless flower.

If one is without the knowledge of consciousness and the mercy that follows, then one will be the body built with bones, skin, blood, nerves, etc., excreta that emit a bad smell. He will be like water in the desert. His life becomes useless like the flower of madder plants without fruits and smell.

In the previous verse, the importance and relevance of mercy in social life were explained. In this verse, Gurudev discusses the vileness of a person who has no mercy. He says such a person will be simply bones, skin and a mix of nerves that emanate a filthy smell. He will be only a mirage creating a sense of water in the desert. That man is a useless one and a flower with a bad smell that will never become fruit. Gurudev scolds such persons in sharp words.

Verse 5

The inert body undergoes changes in
Six ways that not affect the knowledge
Separated from the inert body, stands
Mercy in the form of fame, eternally.

Be born, exist, multiply, evolve, decay and be destroyed, though such six changes happen to the inert body it does not happen to the real consciousness. Just like this, consciousness abandoning the inert body taking the form of glory, compassion will exist eternally in this world.

To the body comes six different stages, namely, take birth, exist, flourish, evolve, decay and perish. Like the six stages of life come to the body; the consciousness does not have any such stages. Whatever is different and changing is transient and not real. Consciousness is unchanging, not with a second, and is eternal. The body is transient, whereas consciousness is eternal. Therefore, even when the body is lost, consciousness prevails. To such a noble person who led a graceful life to show mercy to all, even if his five elements of the inert body are lost, his fame will prevail.

Verse 6

Is it the one who spoke the truth who rode
The chariot or the sea of mercy and endurance
Is it the teacher who taught Advaita in
Simple commentary, the man of mercy?

Is it Lord Krishna, the unique truth as charioteer told Arjuna the absolute truth or Buddha the ocean of kindness to living things and forgiveness? Or is it Sankara who wrote the simple commentary to Gita, Upanishads and Brahmasutras; the one with compassion?

From here onwards, Gurudev takes as examples the great men who were full of mercy toothers. He is narrating their lives and their contributions to the softening of human minds. The lines are written as if he is perplexed as to who is the greatest among them as the embodiment of mercy, love and blessing, and indirectly shows that all are great in one aspect or the other.

Is it Lord Krishna the merciful riding the chariot of Arjuna sitting as charioteer who consoled Arjuna who fell in deep sorrow over his fate of fighting and killing his relatives and friends on the other side of the war front, uttered the universal truth to Arjuna as if he is the symbol of all leading worldly life, or is it Sree Buddha the centre of the ocean of forgiveness! Sree Buddha who revealed that animal sacrifice is in itself a great sin is evidence of his kindness towards fellow creatures. Even those who tormented him, he pardoned taking such evil deeds as due to their ignorance. His greatness we see in his mercy.

Is it Sree Sankara the merciful who wrote in simple language commentaries to Vedas, Upanishads and Bhagavad Gita?

Here, Sree Narayana Gurudev addresses Sri Sankara as his preceptor. He takes him as one who poured knowledge of Advaita philosophy into him as his predecessor. This should be pondered in the light of Sree Narayana Gurudev's statement, 'In Advaita, I follow Sri Sankara.' In Sankaracharya, also once viewed through his writings, what dominated is his mercy to others.

Verse 7

Is it the God who took the shape of a man?
Is it the charity that appears in the form of the nobleman?
Is it the holy son of the supreme God?
Or the merciful Nabi the noblest jewel.

Is it the God himself came in the shape of man? Or is it Lord Sree Rama the symbol of morality in the form of divine man? Or is it Jesus Christ, the son of supreme God? Or is it Mohammed Nabi, the jewel of mercy?

Is it God Himself the merciful who took the shape of a man? This refers to Veda Vyasa who wrote Mahabharata, Bhagavad, Gita, Brahmasutras, etc. Through these works, the crux of Vedas (believed to be direct utterings of God himself), Upanishads, all Sruthies and Smrities in Vedic philosophy, was imparted to generations and paved the way to establish a way of life—an immortal culture. It requires a superhuman quality. An ordinary person cannot succeed in doing such a colossal work. This may be why Gurudev qualifies Vyasa as one who is God himself in disguise. Vyasa's kindness was unlimited.

Is it Sree Rama who is the embodiment of morality or virtues, one who kept the strict observance of duty? He is described as 'Ramo Vigrahavan Dharma', meaning Rama is the idol form of righteousness (Dharma). Rama had a sense of justice, honesty and determination in his style of administration. He forsakes his crown to save his father from violating the promise to his wife Kaikeyi and lived in the thick forest for fourteen years. He saved the people from demons and brought peace to the country. There are many examples that reveal Sree Rama's kindness and mercy to his subjects. In Ramayana, Sree Rama is taken to be an incarnation of Lord Vishnu.

Is it Jesus Christ, the son of God the merciful? His birth from the Virgin Mary shows that he is the son of God. He is praised as the saviour of the world. He censured the bad customs which prevailed among the Jews for the well-being of society. Jesus, who attained enlightenment through rigorous penance, performed many deeds of mercy to suffering people, using his healing touch to treat their diseases which were supposed to be incurable. Even people who committed sins were pardoned, and later, some of them have become devotees and even saints. Under the unjust verdict of the court for crucifying him, at the time of crucifixion in the last prayer what he requested was, 'Oh! God pardon these people who are ignorant of the sin they are doing.' Can anyone measure the depth of his mercy?

Is it Mohammed Nabi, the last among Nabies, the merciful! Gurudev qualifies Mohammed Nabi as the precious jewel among all human beings on earth. He removed many evil customs that then prevailed in Arabia through his exhortations as a prophet. He always showed mercy to the poor and suffering. He dedicated his entire life for the uplift of society. He mercifully endured all such evils. He uplifted the people who were sunk in the ocean of ignorance and evils, and showed the right path of truth to the world.

Verse 8

Is it the deity who removed pyrexia smearing
Ashes and did unprecedented wonders
Is it the seer when worried about pain sang hymns
In Praise removed the severe pain of stomach.

Is it the ascetic Thirujnana Sambandhar who showed many unprecedented mystical wonders and who cured the fever of Kubja

Pandyan by simply smearing ashes, or is it the ascetic Appar, who suffering severely with pain when there was no way out, cured his stomach pain by chanting hymns of the Lord?

In this poem, Gurudev presents not only the incarnations but also the founders of religions.

Thirunjana Sambandhar, who once cured the high fever of King Kubja Pandyan by smearing ashes, is referred to here. Appar, Sundara, Manikya Vachakar and Thirunjana Sambandhar were holy men with divine powers who lived in Tamil Nadu. When the king, Kubja Pandyan, was laid up, his wife along with their minister approached Jnana Sambandhar to save Kubja Pandyan from his heavy fever and save his life. Jnana Sambandhar smeared ashes on him. Immediately his fever subsided. The king was hunchbacked from his childhood. That was why he was known as Kubja (hunchback) Pandyan. Jnana Sambandhar made the king's body upright. Sambandhar wrote and sang many melodious songs. He, along with his wife, left to heaven bodily and merged into the divine light.

Thirujnana Sambandhar, with great affection, called a boy named Marulneekkiyar by a favourite name 'Appar'. From then onwards, the boy was known as Appar. He became famous. His parents died when he was only a boy. Appar was looked after by his sister. Appar gradually became a believer in Jainism. The grief-stricken sister, Thilakavathiyar, who noticed it, prayed to Lord Shiva to make his brother Appar again a devotee of Shiva. Thilakavathiyar in a dream heard from Lord Shiva that her brother will suffer due to abdominal disease and thereafter will become a devotee of Shiva. Later, Marulneekkiyar became affected by stomach disease. His sister, chanting 'Aum Nama Sivaya', smeared ashes on the abdomen of Marulneekkiyar; he was then cured of the disease. Appar is also known by the names Dharmasenan, Tirunavukkarasu Nainar, etc.

Verse 9

Is it the great Maharshi who dictated Vedas
To God Shiva himself, making him write?

Is it the noble devotee of God Shiva
Who went to the heaven bodily alive.

Is it the great ascetics who dictated the famous Vedas which Lord Shiva himself copied from what he dictated or is it the most merciful devotee of Shiva who went to heaven while living on earth with the inert body?

Manikya Vachakar and Sundara Murthi Nainar are the other two contemporary divine persons referred to in the poem.

Manikya Vachakar was a brilliant boy from his childhood. Later he became the minister of the scholarly King Arimardhanan. Manikya Vachakar, otherwise known as Vadavooran, was a great devotee of Lord Shiva. One day, while he was praying in front of the idol in the temple, an old man came to him and imparted divine knowledge. The old man was Lord Shiva himself. Thereafter, Vadavooran became an ascetic, resigning from the post of minister. He wrote many beautiful poems and chanted to the Lord. One day Lord Shiva appeared before him and told him, 'Your poems are excellent; you are a jewel (*manikyam*) among the poets. Hereafter you will be known as Manikya Vachakar.' On another occasion, another old man met Manikya Vachakar and requested him, 'I want to copy down your poems.' Manikya Vachakar sang, and the old man copied it. The next morning, when the priest opened the door of the sanctum sanctorum, he saw a letter written in dried leaf near the idol with a script: 'This is what Manikya Vachakar dictated and copied by Nataraja.' This is what Gurudev mentions as '*Haranannezhuthi prasiddhamaam mara*'.

The part mentioned from the third line is referring to Sundara Murthi Nainar, the holy man believed to have gone to heaven bodily sitting on a white elephant. Even gods, including Lord Shiva, were eager to hear the beautiful songs of Sundara Murthi Nainar. The Emperor Cheraman Perumal accepted the discipleship of Sundara Murthi Nainar. He brought Sundara Murthi Nainar to Kerala. Nainar, a devotee of Lord Shiva, while going bodily to heaven riding on a white elephant, took Cheraman Perumal also as he was attending to him. This is what Gurudev means by the words *pravarddya bhakta*. The writings of Thirunjana Sambandhar, Appar and Sundara Murthi are known as Thevara compositions in Tamil. Gurudev asks, 'Are these divine men who went to heaven bodily the merciful ones?'

Verse 10

Is it the celestial cow who transact
On earth in the form of the human being?
Or the most wonderful celestial tree of
Charity, who is the one with mercy?

Is this the divine cow Kamadhenu who took the form of a man, came to earth and dealt with our world? Or is it the most wonderful divine tree Kalpa Vriksha that gives everything magnificently on request?

Kamadhenu is a cow that delivers anything to anybody for the fulfilment of one's desire. This special attribute of Kamadhenu is applicable to all persons of mercy. Still, there are certain divine persons who deserve it in its full sense. Sibi and Pridhvi are two exemplary characters in the Puranas. Sibi is the grandson of Yayati and the son of King Usinara. Emperor Sibi, to save the life of a pigeon that sought refuge from an eagle that followed the pigeon to catch and eat, had to offer flesh from his own body equal to the weight of the pigeon (as if it is the right of the eagle to eat the pigeon as it is the prey) as compensation to the eagle. He was such a person of mercy in history.

Pridhvi was the son of Venan, a sinner and immoral king. King Venan was killed by his own subjects. Even at the time of birth, there were divine features in Pridhvi. Many saints praised him as an incarnation of Lord Vishnu. Emperor Pridhvi, seeing the miserable life due to lack of food and cloth, assumed that it was all due to the earth swallowing all the vegetation on it, and that is the reason for the severe famine. In fury, he started destroying the earth. The earth got afraid of this. She took the shape of a cow. Pridhvi told earth,'You are disobeying my orders. Why are you not giving the required things to my subjects? Whoever it be, a man or a woman or a neuter, an egoist without mercy towards living things, once the king kills it, that is not a sin'. Kamadhenu, the cow, told Pridhvi, When a matching child sucks my udder, I will yield whatever it desires'. The emperor made the mountain Meru as the child and milked the udder. It yielded herbs, jewels, etc. Thus, Pridhvi the merciful emperor served his subjects.

Paramatbhut Danadevata refers to Karna, the eldest among the Pandavas. This also indicates Ranti Deva, a king, belonging to the Bharata dynasty. He was so kind that whatever he had, he gave to the poor and became poor himself along with his family. The family lived forty-eight days without food, and at last, one day, a little gruel was available to eat. While the family was getting ready to eat, a Brahmana came to their house begging for something to eat. One half of their food was given to the Brahmana respectfully. Again, when the family got ready to eat the other half, sharing with all, another man came begging for food; the other half was given to him. As soon as that fellow left, came the third one, a hunter with dogs asking for food. The remaining food was given to the hunter and the dogs. Then came a*chandala*; seeing him, Ranti Deva said, 'I don't want anything other than the God, I want nothing else. I am ready to take over the miseries of people with the dedication of this water. Let everything be freed from the miseries of the world.' Saying thus, he gave the remaining water to the chandala. How great is his mercy!

Karna gave his life-protecting armour and the ear ornaments to Devendra who came as an old man in disguise. Knowing that it is a trap to kill him by Arjuna (Indra's son-like person) when he does not wear these, as a nobleman Karna handed them over to Indra. In fact, Karna was giving his life to Devendra. How great are his nobility and mercy! The same was the case with the Emperor Mahabali. He offered his life to Lord Vishnu who came in disguise as a dwarf Brahmana monk.

Phalasruti

Arumāmaṛayōtumaṛtavum
Guruvōtum muniyōtumaṛtavum
Oru jātiyiluḷḷatonnutān
Poruḷōṛtālakhilāgamattinum.

Result scripture -

Meaning of what the Vedas say
What the teachers teach, the ascetic means
Are all one and of the same kind.
Once thought, the content of all origins.

There is only one unique non-dual truth—the Advaita. There is no distinction between the views of Saiva sect and Vaishnava sect in this. Name forms are transient and unreal like a snake superimposed on coir. What the Holy Vedas reveal, meaning what the preceptor tells, what the yogis tell, all belong to the same category. If deeply thought, all maxims show only one content; there is only one truth.

Those who have found this truth will not get confused when many things are seen in different names and forms. Those who stick on to name forms are really blind. Those who see the duality in religions and fighting are ignorant of real truth. In fact, these fights are mere fighting with shadows. This is why Sree Narayana Gurudev makes it clear that the content of all philosophies and sciences are the same—the absolute truth. One who has realized this ultimate truth leads a peaceful life. All the great men of mercy, like those mentioned above, have realized the truth. Their mercy had no barriers of religion, caste, country, etc. but is for all humankind.

4

SADASIVA DARSANAM

This is believed to be written while Sree Narayana Gurudev was staying at Marutwamala after vigorous penance. This is a prayer song praising Lord Shiva. It contains ten verses. Gurudev prays to the idol of Shiva as the symbol of the visual universe or the Saguna Brahman. In one sense, it explains the vastness; that is, the beginning-less, endless nature of the universe. The concluding verse reflects it beautifully through an example of Lord Vishnu and Lord Brahma trying to see the foot and head (the beginning point and the end point of the universe) by going deep into the earth and to the farthest end of space, but their efforts ended in vain. This gives a lesson or indication about the futility of efforts of the scientists to arrive at both ends of the universe.

(Original text in Malayalam)

Maṇam tuṭaṅṅiyeṇṇi maṇṇiluṇṇumeṇṇamokkeya-
ṛṛiṇaṅṅinilkkumuḷkkurunnurukkinekkinakkiṭum
Guṇam niṛanja kōmaḷakkuṭatilannuminnumi-
Nniṇaṅṅaḷaṅṅumiṅṅu meṅṅumillanallamaṅaḷam.

Kaḷam karuta koṇṭaluṇṭiruṇṭakoṇṭakaṇṭeẓum
Kaḷankamuṇṭakaṇṭanenkilum kaniññukoḷḷuvān

Iḷampiṛakkoẓunnirunnu minnumunnatatala-
Kkuḷamkaviññā kōmaḷakkuṭam cumannakuñjaram.

"Aram" tiḷacupoṅṅumāṭalāẓinīntiyēṛiya-
Kkarekkaṭannu kaṇṭapōtaẓinjoẓinjuninna nī
Curannucūẓavum corinjiṭunna sūktikaṇṭuka-
ṇṭirannuninnitenmuṭikkucūṭumīsanē!

Śanairuyaṛnnuyaṛnnu vannuninnukonnutinniṭum
Dinamdinam dinēśanindhuvennuraṇṭukandhukam
Manamkavinjumāṛiyāṭumaṅṅumaṇṇoṭeṇṇumī-
Janamninakkumokkeyum jayikkumādidaivamē!

daivamē, ninakka nīyum njānumonnutanneyennu
kaivarunnatinnitenniyaṭiyanilla kāmṣitam
śaivamonnoẓiññu maṛṛumuḷḷatokkeyeṅṅumiṅṅu
māyvalaññuẓanniṭunna vaẓiyatum ninakkil nī.

Ninakkilindhucūṭanonnutanne nīyoẓinju ma-
ṛṛenikudaivamilla ponviḷakkiḷakkumāẓiye
Manamtuṭaṅṅiyeṅṅumeṅṅamokkekkinakkiṭum
Kanamkuṛanjamēniykaninjuvanna kannale.

Nilamnilamparāṛupāmpelumpoṭampiḷikkala-
Tilamviḷaṅiṭunna cenciṭakkiṭakkaṇanjiṭum
Cilankakanṭu cancalappeṭum mukhammalaṛnna pū-
Nkilakku kumpiṭumpaṭikkinikkaninjukūṛu nī.

kaninjumaṇṇumappumappuṛam kalaṛna kāṛṛoṭa-
ṅṅaṇaññuviṇṇilannuminnumonnirunnuminniṭum
maṇamkalaṛnamēniyētatinnu nī malaṛnniṭum
manikku mānamilla malliṭunnorallumillitil.

Itilkkiṭannu kēṇuvāṇu nāḷkaẓiññiṭunnini-
Kkitilparam ninakkilentu vanniṭunnu sankaṭam

Matikkoẓunnaṇiññiṭunnamannavā,kaniññumu-
Nmatikkuṭamkaviññu pāyumāṛu cūṭiyāṭu nī.

Aṭikkupannipōyi ninmuṭikkorannavumpaṛa-
Nnaṭutukaṇṭatilla ninneyinnumagniśailamē,
Eṭutu nī viẓuṅṅiyenneyindriyaṅalōṭuṭan
Naṭiciṭum namaśśivāya nayakā, ṇamō nama

Meaning and commentary

Verse 1

Counting from smell all subjects on earth one by one
Getting away from them concentrated on devotion to God
The mind full of devotion dissolving in self the beautiful form
Full of goodness without inauspiciousness is ever auspicious.

All organs of senses such as ear, eye, skin, tongue and nose getting separated severally getting rid of all grief experienced following the involvement of inert things, the mind concentrated in meditation dissolved in himself who experiences salvation, the embodiment of bliss has no inauspiciousness anywhere. It is always absolutely pure.

To get the concentration of mind, the functioning of all the sense organs through such effects as smell, taste, form, touch and sound should be stopped. One should overcome the action of nose, tongue, eye, skin and ear. Once it is accomplished, the Brahman manifests to him in the form of unattributed (Nirguna) or attributed (Saguna) aspects. The devotee here wishes to get the full realization of happiness through deep meditation.

Verse 2

The neck black as dark cloud and matted black hair are seen may
Make a feeling as if consumed impurity but the crescent moon worn as

Trichilia spinosa on the head the overflowing pond showing compassion
Lord's beautiful form looks like an insane red elephant.

The neck is black like dark clouds. Likewise, matted black hair also can be seen. Though, it will seem like neck swallowed some serious impurity, to prove that he is the embodiment of mercy wears on the head the moon Trichilia spinosa (sweet-smelling leaves), the pond filled with water of Ganga river, Lord! Your beautiful form shines like a rutting elephant.

Black colour in the neck and the matted hair are only external marks. One who looks at the Lord sharply, will see the Lord as the embodiment of mercy, wearing the moon and river Ganga on the head. Crescent moon is compared to the trunk of the tusker and water in Ganga as the oozing fluid from the rutting red-coloured elephant. Lord Shiva's body is believed to be red complexioned. Even though the Brahman is seen as containing some impurities like the universe, internally it is the real truth.

Verse 3

A spoilt sea full of hatred boiling turbulently when crossed swimming and
Once reached the other shore by chanting, Lord! When I saw you absolutely
Free of worldly relations experiencing the knowledge manifested surrounding you
I always beg with bowed head dissolve and make me merged in you completely.

Leaving the inert thoughts found the real form of the Lord, once crossed the ocean of worldly miseries which is turbulent with the curse of mutual hatred, chanting of prayer songs. Oh! Lord! Who is free of all worldly relations, repeatedly experiencing the true knowledge manifested by you, oh! Lord, I bow my head in adoration I pray! Let me be merged and dissolved in you.

The word '*Aram*' used in this verse indicates mutual hatred. The main cause of all miseries in the world is this hatred. The devotee fed with this is trying to attain self-realization through the meditation of God. Once he accomplishes self-realization, he comes to understand that in the absolute form of Brahman, the impurities of the universe have not been touched.

Verse 4

The Sun and Moon Day by day rise up repeatedly killing
Bit by bit and eat as two balls thrown up and down in play
Charmingly, thereby the entire wishes of the people buried
Be victorious the beginner of play the primordial God!

You play joyfully with the two balls, namely the Sun and moon (which seize the longevity of people moving time repeated rise and set) by throwing them up and down alternatively that rise and set day by day. Because of that, all worldly wishes of people are lost. Oh! Lord! Who did the first cosmic play, ultimately you alone survive victoriously!

Gurudev explains beautifully the role of time in the universe as a play of jugglery of the Lord. The God is the beginner of the play of throwing up and down alternately two balls, namely the Sun and the moon. When the balls move up and down, the universe loses its longevity in every event of the ball going up or down. This is why Gurudev makes the remark 'kill and eat'. The time always kills and eats everything. None of us knows about it. Hence without knowing this, many end their lives without getting any purpose. The devotee likes to avoid such a situation.

Verse 5

Oh! God! This devotee has no other wishes other than
To get the experience that you and I are one, except

Your blessing, other things are only ways to suffer
In illusory world remember! It is all your play.

Oh! God, once thought, you and this devotee are only one thing, the Brahman. I do not have any other wish other than the experience of our oneness. There are no other means to attain salvation other than the realization of absolute truth. The worldly desires like attainment of heaven, etc. are only ways to suffer the grief of births and deaths, if thought those two are your own play.

Whatever be the favourite deity, one should make certain that the deity is the symbol of Brahman, and also that the ultimate aim should be the attainment of realization that it is the deity. This is the order of meditation of a seeker of real truth. Who do not obey this rule, take the favourite deity as a separate God and do rituals and gain virtual pleasures. Those who pray for getting worldly gains, they get them. Those who desire to get heaven, they get them. But these worldly gains are only transient, or momentary. But those who wish to get the benefit will have to suffer in repeated births and deaths. That is why the devotee specifically mentions that his only aim is to get the opportunity of attaining the Lord himself.

Verse 6

Oh! One who excels the light of golden lamp if thought I have
No other God other than you, the crescent moon wearing Lord.
From mind, etc., the changing inert feelings dissolve in you one with
Slender body merciful like melting sugar candy, Oh! Lord! Save me!

Oh! Lord! Who shines like a flare of fire that excels the shining of a lamp that spreads golden light, once thought I do not have a god other than you who wears the moon on the head. One who has the form, full of peace by slowly dissolving all inert imaginations such as mind that come one after the other Oh! Lord! Like melted sugar candy come shedding mercy! Save me!

Gurudev usually uses the names of sweet material to address the Lord. Sugar candy is an example. It is used to increase the sweetness to the experience of God. The mind, etc. is meant to refer to the ego, mind and wisdom, etc., internal components of the self. The use of '*nikki nokkidum*' indicates the sweetness of the devotee's experience.

Verse 7

Ganga inside and snake, bone, gingili-sized moon all these at
The centre of the matted red hair and seeing anklet wore on it
Stood to hesitate, you raised her face by your hands blossom-like
Bunch of flowers bless me with such love to bow your tender palm.

In the inside shining with the divine Ganga, snakes, bones, gingili moon at the centre of red matted hair embellished by all these, seeing the anklet wore on it standing in hesitation, Goddess Parvathi who came to kiss on your forehead, you shifted her face with your hand like a bunch of flowers, Oh! Lord! The beautiful one, how much affection you showed then, bless me with that much affection.

There are many things like river Ganga hidden in the Lord's hair. Without knowing it, Goddess Parvathi happened to see the anklets in the hair, immediately suspecting them to be the anklets of Goddess Ganga, though she stood hesitating for a while with great affection bent her face to kiss the forehead of Lord Shiva. Realizing it, Shiva raised both his hands unfolding the fingers like the blossoming bunch of flowers. Parvathi's face and head bent affectionately to the hands shining like a blossoming bunch of flowers. The devotee prays to Lord Shiva to bless him with such affection.

Verse 8

Whoever is spread in land, water, fire, wind and entire space?
Always unchanged and bless the universe is you

> Even shining diamond is not parallel, any darkness of ignorance
> That always afflicts the universe is not found in you.

That eternal thing which is the embodiment of bliss exists and blesses pervading the earth, water, fire, wind and space without change, that itself is you oh! Lord! Even the diamond which spreads light without obstruction is not as bright as you. In your divine body, the darkness of ignorance which always tortures the world is not seen at all.

The Brahman is the self-shining unique entity. There is no ignorance or Maya. Maya is a phenomenon that is superimposed on the real entity which is characteristic of living things; so long as it is there, one cannot realize the real entity. Once it is realized and removed, there is only one thing: earth, water, air and fire, and all, including the universe, will vanish. There will be only one thing that pervades everywhere. In that unique thing, there is not a second. That is Brahman that shines brilliantly at its own.

Verse 9

> Being in it leads a life of miseries what further grief to
> Come once thought Oh! Lord! Who wears the crescent moon
> Like sweet-smelling tender leaf mercifully dance making my
> Ceremonial water pot of wisdom overflow and spread outside.

Though the Lord was there everywhere without knowing that, this devotee trapped in worldly relations always weeps and weeps in grief and lose vital power once thought what grief is yet to come greater than it? One who wears sweet-smelling leaf (Trichilia spinosa) like crescent moon! Lord! You dance mercifully making the ceremonial water pot of my wisdom worn in front of me overflow and spread outside.

Though the Brahman pervades everywhere, it is not known to the inert-oriented mind that is ignorant of it. To experience that awareness, the only way is to concentrate the mind on the Absolute. That state of wisdom is denoted by the word '*Munmati*' (the god, oriented wisdom). As the concentration of the devotee increases, his internal wisdom, the self-experience starts overflowing. Then he gets the experience of the Absolute as filling everywhere.

Verse 10

The swine pierced the earth to see your foot and the swan
Flew upward to find your head both could not find you in full
Oh! Mountain of fire you may devour me along with the senses
Adorable Shiva! Supreme Master! I bow and prostrate.

The swine went downward deeper and deeper to see your feet, and to see your head (the other end) swan flew upward. Oh! Lord who shines as volcanoes! Both swine and swan could not find your head and feet so far. I pray Oh! Lord! Without delay, dissolve me into you along with the organs of knowledge and organs of activities Oh! Cosmic Dancer! The embodiment of bliss! I pray with folded hands Oh! Lord! I prostrate! I prostrate! I prostrate!

See the story narrated in many Puranic books like Bhagavatam. Lord Vishnu once thought of seeing the feet of Lord Shiva. He incarnated the form of a swine (*Varaham*), and dug the earth deeper and deeper to see the foot of Lord Shiva whose body is believed to be of abnormal height. Likewise, Lord Brahmadev thought of seeing the head of Lord Shiva. He flew on his vehicle Swan (*Arayannam*) upward to reach the head of Shiva.

In spite of these efforts, Lord Vishnu and Lord Brahmadev could not reach the feet or head of Shiva so far.

Here in this verse, Gurudev indirectly hints at the future of the search for the secret of the universe or the absolute reality. Lord Shiva is taken to be the symbol of the visual universe.

Physics, the subject which takes the lead in the study of the universe, was carrying out its investigation through two different angles—from the subtle (micro) side and the corpulent (cosmic) side. The microscopic studies started with the analysis of matter, searching its fundamental components, and concluded that they are molecules.

Further experiments with new, precise instruments revealed that the smallest components of matter are not molecules, but they found them to be still smaller things, like atoms, then hadrons and electrons, subsequently quarks, etc., and reached the present state identifying Higgs boson. Still, we could not find the bottom point on one side and the end point at the outer limit on the other side of the universe, even with our spacecrafts and space missions to see the other end of the universe. In short, physics could not so far explore the extreme ends, namely the beginning, end and the upper end of the universe. The scientists do not hope to find it ever in future because all these are beyond human imagination and access.

5

BRAHMAVIDYAPANCHAKAM

(Original text in Sanskrit)

Poem - 1

Nityānitya vivēkatōhi nitarām
Niṛvēdamāpadya sad-
Vidwānatṛa śamādiṣtakalasita
Syānmukthikāmō bhuvi,
Paścāt brahmaviduttamam pṛaṇatisē-
Vādyai pṛasannam gurum
Pṛucēt kōf hamidam kutō jagaditi
Swāmin! Vada twam pṛabhō!

Poem - 2

Twam hi brahma na cēndriyāṇi na manō
Budhiṛ na citham vapu
Pṛāṇāhangkṛutayōf nyadapyasadavi-
Dyākalpitam swātmani
Saṛvam dṛuśyatayā jadam jagadidam
Twatta param nānyatō
Jātam na swata ēva bhāti mṛugatru-
ṣṇābham darīdṛuśyatām.

Poem - 3

Vyāptam yēna carācaram ghaṭaśarā-
Vādīva mṛutsattayā
Yasyāntasphuritam yadātmakamidam
Jātam yatō vaṛttatē
Yasmin yatpṛalayēf pi sadghanamajam
Saṛvam yadanwēti tat
Satyam vidhyamrutāya niṛmaladhiyō
Yasmy namaskuṛvatē.

Poem - 4

Sṛuṣtwēdam pṛakṛutēranupṛaviśatī
Yēyam yayā dhāryatē
Pṛāṇīti pṛavi viktabhugbahiraham
Pṛājñassuṣuptou yata
Yasyāmātmakalā sphuratyahamiti
Pṛatyantarangam janaiṛ-
Yasyai swasti samaṛthyatē pṛatipadā
Pūṛṇā śṛunu twam hi sā.

Poem - 5

Pṛajñānam twahamasmi tatwamasi tad-
Bṛahmāyamātmēti sam-
Gāyan vipṛacara pṛaśāntamānasā
Twam bṛahmabōdhōdayāt
Pṛārabdham kwa nu sancitam tava kimāgāmi
Kwa kaṛmmāpyasat
Twayyadyastamatō fkhilam twamasi
Sacinmātṛamēkam vibhu.

(See explanation and commentary in chapter.1 Vol.2)

6

SREE KRISHNA DARSANAM

In those days when Sree Narayana Gurudev was undergoing higher education under Kummampalli Raman Pillai Asan staying at Varanappally house, he was a great believer in Lord Vishnu. Lord Krishna was his favourite deity. As narrated by Sri E.K. Ayyakkuti, a retired judge, Nanu (Sree Narayana Gurudev) used to get the divine sight of Lord Krishna (Balakrishna) in wakefulness and sleep.

One night, while Nanu was sleeping, he heard an unusual sound of somebody from outside calling him to follow. Nanu found some image was moving in front of him while following, and at some point near the small canal in the compound, the image all of a sudden turned to face Nanu. Alas! It was Lord Krishna in his divine appearance. On seeing this unusual sight, Nanu fainted and fell down and remained there till the morning. His colleagues, the elders of the family and others tried to wake him up but he was still in a state of unconsciousness. At last, Raman Pillai Asan was informed about the incident; he rushed to see his beloved pupil. He sprinkled a little water on Nanu's face and asked him to wake up. Nanu woke up. Asan asked him what had happened to him that made him faint. Nanu said he saw Lord Krishna in his original divine form (*Virat*). Then Raman Pillai Asan asked Nanu to explain the details of what he had actually seen. Nanu recited the following single verse (it is told that in the early literary works of Sree Narayana Gurudev, while introducing himself as the author, he used to write, '*Iti Balaramante vasina: Narayana virachitam'* the name Balarama is another version of Raman Pilla. Pilla means child. This showed Sree Narayana Gurudev's great respect for his preceptor, Kummampalli Raman Pillai Asan). Hearing this, Raman Pillai Asan became very happy as he was relieved of his long-time desire to get the divine sight of Lord Krishna. He got the happiness of realization of his desire for which he prayed in the nearby Krishna temple for years. He felt he had the fortune of receiving the divine sight through his beloved little pupil.

(Original text in Sanskrit)

Bhūyō vṛitti nivṛittiyāybhuvanavum
Sattil tirōbhūtamāy
Pīyūṣadwani līnamāycuẓalavum
Śōbhicu dīpapṛabha
Māyāmūṭupaṭamtuṛannu maṇirangatil
Pṛakāśikkuma-

Kkāyāvin malaṛmēni koustubhamaṇi-
Gṛīvante divyōtsavam.

Scope of livelihood* vanished, the universe
Dissolved in the Absolute
The nectarous sound became latent around
What seen is the light of the unique lamp
The veil of Maya opened what remains
Shining in the gem-like mind is
The merriment of the blue-complexioned
Flowery body of Lord Krishna.

The state of continuing with livelihood has all vanished, the entire universe has dissolved in unique absolute reality, and the nectarous

* By desire, by begging or by cultivation or trade.

sound became latent, what is seen around is only the light from a unique brilliant source. The veil of Maya is opened, what shines in the gem-like mindis only the merriment of the blue-complexioned flowery body of Lord Krishna.

Livelihood is in four different ways.

One, by collecting small quantities of food to live or by going about begging; two, eating by begging or doing agriculture; three, living by doing business (a little viciousness is involved in this usually); four, living depending on somebody. Of these four, the first one is the best, second is mediocre, the third is bad, and the fourth is heinous. The fourfold livelihoods (*chaturvrities*) are also said to be food, sleep, lovemaking and play (Ref. Amarakosa, Manu and Bhagavata Purana).

7

THEVARAPATHIKAMKAL

Shree Narayana Gurudev composed his literary works with great dexterity in three languages—Malayalam, Tamil and Sanskrit. 'Thevarapathikamkal' is a prayer song Gurudev wrote it in the Tamil language, and it contains fifty poems. This collection of five *pathikams* is divided into groups of ten poems each. It is written as a prayer worshipping the Nayanar idol of Shiva. Here, Gurudev presents one of the basic principles of Advaita philosophy in the form of hymns in praise of the God Shiva. The poems the great Tamil poets wrote for worshipping their deities are known as *Tevaram*. These poems were sung by Gurudev all of a sudden without preparing the script prior to his visit to the Shiva temple, and the exact date of this visit is not known, though some consider it to be 1914.

The *Tevaram* (தேவாரம் *Tēvāram*) denotes the first seven volumes of the *Thirumurai*, the twelve-volume collection of Shiva devotional poetry. All seven volumes are dedicated to the works of the three most prominent Tamil poets of the seventh century, the Nayanars—Sambander, Thirunavukkarasar and Sundara. Sree Narayana Gurudev refers to these names in 'Anukampadasakam'. The singing of tevaram is traditionally done in Shiva temples in Tamil Nadu.

(Original text in Tamil)

Pathikam 1
Poem 1

.Jñānōtayamē jnāturuvē
Nāmāthiyilā nargatiyē
Yānō nīyō yāti param
Yatāy viṭumō pēcayē
Tēnār thillai chīratiyār
Tēṭum nāṭāmarumanūṛ
Kōnē, mānnērmiẓipākam
Kontāi nainār nāyakamē.

One who becomes known on enlightenment, one who is the embodiment of consciousness one who shines as the eternal light! Please tell me, who is the primordial reality that is going to be the ultimate truth? Is that you or me? The one who shines as the saviour of Arumanoor, where people come in search of the blissful reality, the one who keeps Parvathi with the eye of doe on your side, Oh the God of gods tell me.

The absolute reality is realized only with knowledge acquired through yoga, meditation, etc. Here Gurudev uses the word '*Njanodhayame*' to address the Brahman, the only one who has obtained and experienced everything. Once enlightenment is obtained, one can understand the absolute of himself and others. By virtue of his being the observer, *Njathuruve* is used in this context. Everything in this universe is only the name forms of the absolute one. Before the manifestation of the name forms, there was only the absolute one and the absolute consciousness devoid of names and forms. The line that follows indicates that the use of 'I' and 'you' and their feelings creates the urge to reach for the truth. Once the secret of this feeling is found, the fact that you and I are nothing but one will be manifested. Here, the last lines accept the God Shiva as the favoured god in the form of Nainar.

Poem 2

Alwaye nīyennāviyoti
Yākkaiporul mummalamutirum
Tēlwāyitayittiriyāma
Ttevē kāvāy periyōve
Nālvātantam narunarena
Nerukkintatu pārarumanur
Nālvānintātārāyo
Nāthā naināar nāyakame.

Oh! God protect me along with my prana, Oh, my Lord! This body is one that always discharges the three specks of dirt—gout, biliousness, phlegm (the three causes of illness according to Ayurveda). Oh lord, who is the asylum of everything, protect me from suffering without being inside the mouth of such a scorpion. Oh Lord! See as time goes on day after day. I suffer without refuge. Oh, the God who reigns Arumanoor, give me refuge at your foot.

The body that houses the life, along with the three filths: gout, biliousness and phlegm, these are the filth emitted along with prana. It is this body that always torments the life (spirit) like a scorpion. It is this body that makes contact with the worldly relations. Oh Lord, save me from this relation without putting me to the sufferings due to this relation. As time passes, the body without any refuge makes life subject to ageing and other miseries. This is what Gurudev refers to as *Nalvandham*. The address 'Nainar *Nayakame*' is repeated in all the poems.

Poem 3

Vānāi malaiyāy vadiyinum
Vānāl viṇāyaẓiyumunen-
Unāyuyirayudayōnay
ontāy niraiyay vārāyō
Kānāyanalāy kanaikadalāi

Kārār veliyāyarumānūr
Tānāynirkum tarparamun
Tāl tā nainār nāyakamē

Oh God of gods, be kind enough to make me experience that you and me becoming one and shining everywhere as my body, my spirit and my master before my life become useless as sky and forest fade out emaciated. Oh, Lord! Who shines as the unique ultimate cause the Brahman like roaring oceans and sky full of thunderstorm, give your feet and bless me.

In all his works, including his early poems, Sree Narayana Gurudev tried to unravel the experience of Advaita. This is a song which explains the experience of non-duality beautifully. In this poem, the universe is taken as a forest in the sky. Once immersed in that, man's life becomes futile. Before becoming so, one should turn inward to find out the ultimate reality. Then his body, prana and master will be experienced as one entity. Besides, he will realize that he himself is the absolute truth that shines everywhere. Once this stage is attained, let it be the forest or fire or the roaring ocean or the sky with thunderstorms, whatever it be, the different forms of the universe, everything will be found as the Nirguna Brahman that shines as the embodiment of salvation shining as Nirguna Brahman at Arumanoor. This itself is the experience of non-duality or salvation.

Poem 4

Uruvāyaruvāyaruvuruvā-
Yontāi palavāyuyirkkuyirāi
Terulāyarulāy teruruni
Ntidamāynadumāttiravaṭivāi
Iruḷāi veḷiyāyikaparamā-
Yintāyantāyarumānūr
Maruvāy varuvāyēnaiyālvāy
Nātā nainār nāyakamē

With form without form, with and without form, as unique, as several, as prana of prana, as light, as mercy, being a place where the wheels of Chariot move, in clear form only at the middle, as darkness, as sky, as this world and the other worlds, as the present and as the past one who dwells at Arumanoor, come near, Oh Lord of gods save me.

The Brahman seen as the transient visual universe and unattributed Nirguna Brahman experiencing the state of Turiya is interlinked in this poem. At first sight, it may look as if the ideas about the Brahman and its attributes are contradictory. In Upanishads also, we can see such contradictory explanations of Brahman. When Brahman is manifested as the universe, it is attributed to a form. The gods in temples are manifested visual forms of Brahman in its Saguna Brahman aspect. But in the state of experience of God, it is a state of trance which makes one none other than the God himself. In that state, the Brahman has no form. That means Brahman is both with form and without form. In the state of realization, the Brahman is unique or non-dual. When the Brahman is seen as the universe, it is several (numerous); when seen in the absolute, because of desire, the Brahman vibrates, and the creation of the universe begins. Hence the Brahman is prana of prana. If there is no observer to look with awareness, no inert body can become visible; then, the Brahman is the light of the universe. Since it is the embodiment of bliss, it is mercy for those who approach it. Since the universe appears and repeatedly disappears, the Brahman, who is the creator, has no beginning and end except for its transient existence sometime between its appearance and disappearance. Darkness is the indistinct state before the creation of the universe. The three states of time, namely present, past and future, are not different. The God in the Arumanoor temple is a visible form of Brahman.

Poem 5

Pūvai manamāi punarasamāi
Podiyāy muṭiyāy nediyōnāi

Tīvāyurvāy tiriciyamāy
Tēnāramutāy tikaẓintāi
Nī vā kāvāy ēnaiyālvāy
Nitta! cutta!arumānūr
Tēvā!mūvā mutal vōnē!
Tēnē nainār nayakamē

Oh Lord! You shine like a flower, as a fragrance and as honey in flower, as minute as the ultimate cause pervading everywhere as brilliance, as to form and as the observed objects to the senses and the trickling nectar. Oh Lord! Come near and protect me, oh! The eternal one, the unblemished who gracefully dwell at Arumanoor, shines as unchanging bliss, save me from grief.

Gurudev illustrates that the greatness of meditation is found in the ability to see everything around as different forms of manifestations of the Absolute. To one who can search the ultimate cause, it becomes evident through the process of search (‘*neti, neti*’), one reaches the minute, and once the cause of the minute is explored further, one sees it as nothing but the absolute consciousness. To him, who sees the god as everything, he will become the honey-trickling Lord. To him, the Lord is eternal and changeless.

Poem 6

Ariyum vitiyum teṭiyinum
Aṛiya neṛiyāyerivuruvāy
Mariya marimanidavaṭivāi
Mariyātē yini vā kāvāi
Piriyatanaiyalvaitēva-
Ppiriya periyōrarumanūṛ
Purivāṇarulīdum kovē
Pūvē! nainār nāyakamē.

As the phenomenon which could not be found even after the search of God Vishnu and God Brahma, as the self-shining eternal body who keeps the deer which is like on the left side oh lord! Come near me, keep me without undergoing death. Protect me always without leaving me away. Oh Lord! Who dwells at Arumanoor as the endeared God of gods, protect me.

The God Shiva in Arumanoor temple is taken as the symbol of the universe. In all his writings and consecration of idols in temples, Gurudev takes the three words Brahman, Shiva and the universe as synonyms of the same word. Brahman in the manifested or attributed form (Saguna Brahman) is the universe. The universe in the spiritual sense is symbolized as God Shiva, that is to say, Brahman, Shiva and universe mean the same thing but are used in the relevant context to suit spiritual aspects. The statement '*Ariyum Vidhiyum Thedinum Ariya*' has a story behind it. God Vishnu and God Brahmadeva once went in search of the foot and the head of Shiva respectively to understand the entirety (Virat) of Shiva. Vishnu dug deeper and deeper into the earth to see the foot of Shiva. While Brahmadeva on his swan rode higher and higher to see the head of Shiva, both Vishnu and Brahmadeva failed in their mission and admitted that the Brahman (Shiva) is endless (See 'Sadasiva Darsanam', Poem 10 by Gurudev).

Poem 7

Anto yinto yamatūtar
Kkantē nintāṭārāyō
Kuntē kudaiyē kotanamē
Kōvē! kāvāi kulatēvē
Anteyinteyaratiyē
Nāyē nīyē yarumānūṛ
Nintāyuntārāyō
Nata! naināṛ nāyakamē

May it be the other day or today the time to surrender before the messengers of Yama (personification of death) bless me giving your foot at that time. Save me, Oh mountainous umbrella (shelter) the wealth of cattle Oh Lord! Guardian deity all the time till now I was a staunch worshipper; I was your slave like a dog. Oh Lord! Who dwells at Arumanoor, bless me giving your feet, Oh! God of gods!

One who gets birth as a human should meditate on God. There is no life fulfilment act other than it. It is the meditation that frames the future of life in rebirth in other worlds. This poem gives the many-worlds concept as well as the Vedic concept of no death, no birth (Refer the introductory part of 'Atmopadesa Satakam' - the eternity of consciousness, in Vol. 2).

Poem 8

Nintāraticēratiyār tam-
Nintātiyalām nīkki nitam
Cantānamatāi nintālum
Cantāpamilā nan mayamē!
Vantāpamilātēn munnī
Vantāl vayeyarumanūṛ
Nintāi, nintāḍārayō
Nāta, nainār nayakamē

Oh Lord! The one who removes Maya always from the worshippers who adore your flower-like feet, oh the auspicious one, not touched by any day-to-day afflictions, come and save me from severe grief. Be, at Arumanoor and bless me giving your feet. Oh God of gods! Give me refuge.

Life is an undivided part of Brahman. It is Maya that creates the feeling that life is separated from the Brahman, the absolute reality. Only with clear awareness, Maya can be removed. Life is always affected by grief. But Nirguna Brahman, the Brahman without attributes (the absolute reality), is never affected by grief. Once Maya is removed, the worshipper gets the absolute reality manifested, and he becomes one with it.

Poem 9

Ponnē, maṇiye maratakamē
Pūvē, matuvē, pūmpodiyē
Mannē mayilē kuyilē van-
Malaiyē, cilaiyē manilamē
Ennē! yiniyālvāyniyē
Eliyēnāyēnarumānūṛ
Tannantaniyē nintāi nar-
Tata nainār nāyakamē

Oh! Lord! You are gold, jewel, emerald, flower, honey, pollen, grain, earth, peacock, cuckoo, mountain, rock, continent and everything, protect me. I am humblest of the humble ones. You shine as the Absolute at Arumanoor. Oh! Great father, the God of gods, save me.

Here Gurudev uses the many-worlds concept, touching different forms of inert things on earth to address the idol Nainar who is supposed to be the God Shiva. By comparison, Gurudev gives the indication that the idol of Shiva is a symbol of the absolute one.

Poem 10

Kallō maramō kārayamō
Kaṭenam nannencariyēn yān
Allō pakalō ninnaṭvi-
Ttalo alamāy nintaṭyēn
Collāy nallāi curutimuṭi
Collāyallāyarumanūṛ-
Nallārmani matava! kāvāi
Nātā nainār nāyakamē

Is your heart a stone wood or black iron? I cannot understand why this unkindness, tell me. As the embodiment of Bliss, as the essence of poetic doctrines of Upanishads, as unknown to others, as one who sheds light, oh Lord the lover of cowherds, husband of Goddess Lakshmi, protect this devotee during day and night if trapped in commotion, without meditating your foot directly. Oh God of gods, protect this devotee.

The use of the word Mahadeva indicates Krishna, and this is to show that God Shiva and God Krishna are one and in fact the same.

Pathikam 2

Poem 1

Enkum niṛaintaitiraṟṟimayātava
Rinpuṛu cirpūtarē
Ponkum pavakkatalirpatiyatē patikku
Nnarul purivāi
Tinkal tirumudicutti kaẓuntivya
Tēcōmayānantamē
Tankakotiyē namai taḍuttāl
Kolvāy nī karunā nitiyē

Spread everywhere widely without a parallel, one who shines as merciful to gods, oh light of the mind! Bless me giving compassionately and don't let me fall into the turbulent worldly life. One who spreads brilliance around the matted hair top that wears the crescent moon and shines as the embodiment of bliss, oh affectionate, the abode of mercy, save this devotee from the worldly passion. Oh Lord! Protect me.

Poem 2

Tīyē tiruvīṛaniyum tirumēniyi
Ttinkalolimilirum
Nīyē niraiyakkaḍalinkanimancanam
Ceyyātarul purivāy
Kāyum punalum kaniyum kanal vā-
Taivatai ninantarunti kannīr
Pāyumpati patiyir paramānantam
pēyyum paramcudarē

The splendour that burns the consequences of actions in the previous births and smeared with sacred ash on the body that shines in the moonlight, like that, Oh! one who sheds mercy on me not to make me immerse in the hell of the worldly life. Enjoying the ripe and unripe fruits and honey of the tree of worldly life always meditating the glorious God, as if drops of tear because of the love of God the ultimate cause that sheds boundless bliss. Oh Lord! Do mercy.

Poem 3

Cutarē, cutarvittolirum cutar
Cūẓtirikkum curavi cutar cūẓ
Katalē, matikankaiyaravankatanku
Kavari viricatai
Vitamunḍamutankaniyum mitar
Kanatilanai navamicai
Kutikontatinālenkōl
Kontalar konṛai yarintukūvum kuyilē

Oh! The self-shining God! Who shines as the celestial cow (Kamadhenu) that grants all wishes spreading rays of life around, one who wears the moon, the Ganga and the serpent tied in the wide matted hair! Without seeing the blue-coloured neck that swallowing poison you and served nectar to the devotees, what use is there in living on this earth? Oh Lord! Who wears flower of cassia fistula on your head or cuckoo who sings the song of happiness, what is the use of it?

The Brahman is self-shining. All the constituents of the universe shine, receiving light from it. In Bhagavad Gita it is '*Jyothisham Mapi*', Jyothi meaning 'the light of lights'; and Upanishads say, '*Thasya Bhasa Sarva Mitham Jyothi*', that is, 'using its light, everything shines'.

Poem 4

Kuyilvāṇi kurumpaimulaiyumai
Kūtinintāṭum karumaniyē
Mayilvākanan vantarulum mani-

Mantiram kolmalar mēniyanē
Kayar kanniyar kankal mūntrum
Katirtinkalumankiyumankolirum
Pūyankam punalum catayum pulanāi
Niram putiyar pulanē

Oh! Lord! Who shines as star-like diamond used to dance in the company of Parvathi with the sound of cuckoo and with breast like beautiful tender coconut, with the son Subramanya sitting on the lap, one with flower-like body and three eyes resembling the eyes of beautiful women, the shining moon, fire, snake, water and matted hair you shine manifested to the senses.

Poem 5

Pulenattupporikalattu paripūraṇa-
Pōtam pukante puttē-
Lulakattutalōtuyirullamoṭukumiṭa
Nkotumpoẓintu
Nilaipettu nirancanamām nirupātika-
Nittarankakkatalē
Alai ponkiyatankimatankiyala
Nkōlamākkātarul purivāy

Devoid of ego (I ness), devoid of senses and devoid of the universe in the God who is praised as absolute knowledge losing all desires due to the experience which makes the body and prana forgotten, and became in the state of loneliness. Oh, the waveless ocean speckles and unconditional, the waves in the visual form raised and dissolved and again rose without making the consciousness agitated. Oh! Lord! Shed mercy.

The experience of all-pervading absolute consciousness in the state of salvation is explained here. There, ego or senses, body, prana or mind are not existent. Because of that, the entire experience of universe vanishes. There the experience is like the ocean without waves. The creation and dissolution are all perceptions of the mind created by Maya. This repeated creation dissolution phenomenon produces a feeling of turbulence in consciousness. The prayer is to avoid such passions created by Maya.

Poem 6

Vāyurkkuṭamenna varampile
Vakkatalir paṭintankuminkum
Nāyikatētinum nattamtiriyā-
Tanukkirakam nalkituvāi
Pāyum mirkamum paracum patar-
Ponkaravim patamum cataiyir
cāyum ciṛupiṛaiyum caranankaḷum
Carvam caran purivām

Though trapped in the ocean of Satchidananda, the supreme soul in whom goodness, knowledge and bliss unite like in a pot without a mouth. Bless us not to wander here and there like dogs. Running deer and Parashu (The weapon of Lord Parameshwara), the raising hood of a snake, the crescent moon, your holy foot, let all become our refuge.

Poem 7

Purivāyir putaintu munnam pon-
Maliyai cilaiyāy kunittu pūtti
Puramūntumeritta pirān umpartampirān
enperumān potuvāi
puriyunnatanampuviyir pulaināinēn
amputiyittiraipōttiriyuma-
cakanmāyai cikkiterintilana-
ntō! Cemmiēniyinē

Hiding behind the fort of three demons (the traditional enemies of gods) the sons of Tarakasura converted the golden mountain 'Maru' into a bow and drawing it burnt the three forts into ashes. Oh, my God! Shiva, the God of gods! Who shines at Arumanoor, me, your servant, is suffering like the waves in the ocean coming and going not with the awareness of the secret of the relation of cosmic Maya. It is amazing, Oh, God! One with the red-coloured body, save me.

Poem 8

cemmēni civaperumān ciramālai
yaṇintu cenkōl celutti
cemāntaram vēraṛutituvōntirumantirāl
cetacayam peralām
pemmān pinakkātanentum perum
pitanentum periyōr peyari-
ttimmānita vīttilanancumuyyum vakai
yenganantōyiyampāy

God Shiva, red and beautiful, who wears skulls, strung chain saved the universe. With your name divine mystic spell liberate us from rebirths. Bless me to overcome the worldly thoughts. Oh Lord! The one who is called by the seekers of truth as the master of the world one who lives in the burial ground, a trickster tell me how can I escape from this world where I reached, tell me the way to escape from this human world where I have reached. Wonderful!

Poem 9

iyampum patamum porulumiraiyinti-
yiṛaiyōnirukkuminta
viyappum veḷivānatengen viḷaiyāta
viḷaiyum vitiyenkalo
ceyikkum vaẓiyengalcempor-
cōtiyē cenmaccerukkaṛukkum
taikkenna kaimāru ceyvēntayā
varitiyē taramittamiyēn

Oh Lord! One who pervades everywhere how is it that you have become the wonderful sky wonderfully without touching a bit of the spoken word and its purpose? How is it that without becoming it how one gets the feeling that it is there. What is the trick to winning that Maya? Oh, our reddish-gold lamp! What reward is to be given for the mercy that annihilates the miseries of birth? The sea of Mercy! I wander here as a destitute.

Poem 10

tamiyēn tapam ceytatariyēn capā-
nāyakar cannitikkētinamum
kaviyēn kaẓal kantu kaikūppikatai-
kkannīr vārtu kanintumilēn
navinmālai punaintumilēn nālvar
nāvalar cūtum tiruvatikkam-
pūvi mītenaiyē vakutāi pulaināyēn
pizhaippatengen pukalvāi

I being destitute did not do penance to know you Lord. I did not think of reaching your august presence. Oh Lord! Who presides over the court of gods every day? Seeing your feet and bowing my head did not shower tears compassionately, did not sing chants making garlands and chant. I dedicate myself to this beautiful world before you, who keep fixed in mind the four poets Appar, Sambandhar, Sundara Murthi and ManikyaVachakar, tell me how can I, your devotee escape.

Pathikam 3

Poem 1

ōmātiyil niṛkum porul nītānnulakenkum
tāmāki valarntōnkiya cāmāniyatēve!
viyōmānalapūniroliyōtāvi vilakkō-
ṭāmatanu vārayi namukkāyamitāmē

The Brahman is known through the hymn 'Aum Nama Shivaya' also became corpulent as a single body the universe. Oh Lord! I should not get that big form by attaching the five elements (space, fire, earth, water and air) to the soul. This devotee wants only that achievement or gain.

Poem 2

āmōtamumaminta makāmantiramitontum
namātu namkkintarulāyō namaiyaḷum
komānarulum konṭa kuẓām kūviyanaintā
lāmōtamumaminta makāmantiremumellām

The great hymn Aum is bliss giving. Will it not happen that the Goddess of knowledge Saraswathi bless me bestowing the great hymn. If the hymn is chanted loudly by a group of devotees who have become objects of the mercy of the Lord, that will result in great happiness. Then this great hymn will become fruitful.

Poem 3

ellā uyirum ninnurumellā utalum nī
ella ulakum ninkaliyallātavaiyillai,
pollātanavellām poticeytāntarul pūvil
pallaruyirālum paratēvē, curacōvē

All lives are your parts, all bodies are you yourself. The entire universe is your play. There is nothing other than you. Remove all the evils and bless us. Oh, God! The refuge of all living things on earth! Bless saving us.

Poem 4

kōvēru pirānē, kuriyattōnki viḷankum
muvēẓulakum mōntumeẓum mōnaviḷakke

pūvēṛu pirānum netumālumpotikānā-
tāvecarkalānāruruvārōrarivārō.

The god who rides on ox pervades all things everywhere that shines when the entire universe is waved without being found by Brahma seated on the lotus, and Lord Vishnu immersed in deep adoration of Shiva, whoever attains the death (Samadhi) of ascetic they will find your entity.

Poem 5

vārō varaiyō vārutiyō vānavarpērum-
tārō taraiyō tanmalarō tarparanē
yārō niraṛiyēnatinayēnarulvāyē
nirāṛanivōnē, nita mālvāi nimmalanē

Oh Lord! Who art thou, the Absolute? Whether the dark cloud or mountain or ocean or the dwelling place of the god or a beautiful flower, I do not know. I seek your refuge. Save me oh, the one who wears Ganga on the head, the Virtuous, save me.

Poem 6

nimalā, nittiyanē, nirpayanē, nirkunanē,
avamē puvinayēnaẓiyata nitamālvāi
namanaikkaẓalāl kāyntanatēca, namainīyē
puvimītarul vāram purivāyā perumānē

Oh Virtuous, the eternal, the fearless, the unattributed, save me always from losing the life by going after passions like worthless dogs on earth. Oh, Shiva! Who killed to death the god of death shower your mercy on this devotee on earth. Oh God! Bless me.

Poem 7

Manē maticūtummaraiyōnē cataiyāṭī
Vanōṟkal vaṇankum vativē vantarulvāyē;
Tēnē, teḷivē, tīncuvayē, tivviyaraṣamta
Ntōnē, tunaiyē tonmaṟai oraṟunaṟvōnē.

Oh the essence of Vedanta who wears the deer and crescent moon and with alluringly moving matted hair, the one worshipped by gods at your feet, come immediately and protect me. Oh, the seat of sweetness like honey and the unblemished, one who fuddles like liquor, one who gives divine bliss which is praised by the Vedas and six Vedangas, you alone are my refuge.

Poem 8

Unarvārārivārōrivayenkumilankum
Unaṟvē pōkkuvaiyē, pōtavarampintiya pūve
Punalē, puttamutē, vittakame, vantarunī-
Yanalē, veḷiyē, mārutamē, manilamē vā

Those who wake up after experience become men of knowledge. Oh, the embodiment of experience that shines as the only consciousness the one who dissolves everything in you, the flower, infinite consciousness or water or nectar the embodiment of wisdom come and bless me. Oh fire, space, wind, Earth come and bless me.

Poem 9

Vā vā caṭayirkkankai vaḷaṟkum maṇiyē, en-
Pāvāy, matiyē, pankayamē, panmaṟamīṟāy
Tēvātikal pōṟṟum teḷivē tiṇkaṭal cērum
Nāvāi enaiyālvāy, naticūdi narakārē.

Oh, the precious jewel in which Ganga makes waves in the matted hair come near immediately, one who exists as my darling, as my wisdom, oh! Lotus, one who stood at the end of Vedas long ago and protected the gods and others, the embodiment of wisdom, protect in the form of a ship to cross this worldly ocean, the destroyer of the hell who wears the river, protect me.

Poem 10

Kārēṛu kayarkkaṇṇiyar vīcum valayirppa-
Ṭṭārāraẓiyātōravamē niyaṛiyāyō
Erutēṛu pirānē etirvantemmayaṛīrum
Cārāmutamontīntaruḷayē perumanē.

Oh Lord! Who is there not falling worthlessly into the net cast by beautiful ladies with eyes like blackish fish? Do you not know this? One who travels on ox! Be kind enough to come directly to me and give me a meaningful blessing removing my illusory worldly desires. Oh Lord! Bless me.

Pathikam 4

Poem 1

Taricanam tiruṭṭirucciyankaḷattuttikam pariyāy
Ppariyatanam ceyyum paṇṭitaruḷḷam palikoṭuttu
Tturicaraccuṭṭu tattuvankalattuttani mutalāi
Kkaricanam kantakaṛaikkantaren kulatāivamē.

Removing the differentiation of the three aspects of observation or the act of looking, the observer or one who looks on, the observed or the object looked on (seen) (*jnatya*, *jnana*, *jneya*—the *triputi*) wearing the sky as dress (naked) wander offering fully the heart of the supreme knower (Brahmajnanin) removing all stains and illusory thoughts becoming embodiment of absolute bliss and found clearly the blue-necked Shiva is my guardian deity.

Poem 2

Ātaracattin paripūraṇatilacatppiṛapancam
Pātārakitam pavikkumappatcam piṭiviṭātē
Nātaparanāyi naṭu ninta nāṭṭanaẓuviyātmā-
Pōtamkeṭutu punaruttiti viṭṭatentāivamē.

The universe becomes void in the total attainment of wisdom, which is the base of all manifestations of the universe, will not remain as an obstruction to the experience. Footing firmly on that experience getting rid of the observed that was an obstruction to the experience, the absolute reality removing the manly feelings, ended all manly rebirths. This eternal Brahman is my god.

Poem 3

Vānattu mannerupparuppattu vananti cikuttamaṛṛu
Kānaṭṭukāla cakkirappiramamaṭṭukkatiroḷivāy
Jñānakkanal kariyattu jñātirkurumūlamaṭṭu
Mānankaḷattu makāmounamen kaṇmaṇittaivamē.

The sky, the earth, the fire, the water (the five elements) all vanished, forests, directions, sin too vanished, consequence of action in previous births and the feeling of time lost, the fire of knowledge extinguished, relatives, masters, ignorance all vanished as the sign of glory shining in absolute silence is my god—the absolute consciousness.

Poem 4

Muppatti mukkōṭiyattu mummūṛtikal pētamattu
Kaṛpitattoytappirapañcamām kānarkamalaṛṛu
Mupporuḷattu muppāraṭṭumuttikal mūntṛumaṭṭu
Muṛpaṭum mukkaṭkirumaṇikkōven kulataivamē

The 330 million gods vanished, the differentiation of Brahma Vishnu Maheswara triune ended the mirage of the imaginary concept of duality of the universe, the differentiation between life, earth and god, the illusion of the three qualities *Satwa, Rajas, Tamas* attributes are all ended. The fourth stage of life before salvation (this stage of seeing the god whom one used to pray direct in front of him) near to the god (Samipya), understanding the god (knowing the god) lost or the differentiation of bodies as corpulent, subtle and cause all such things to vanish and when it appears, it is my guardian deity with the three eyes.

This Shiva in the state of Nirguna Brahman is what Sree Narayana Gurudev consecrated at Aruvippuram, placing an unshaped stone untouched by the sculptor

Poem 5

Vākkumanamattuvān cutarāy vativontumattu
Nōkkumitankanarunki nōkkukoḷḷaticayamāya
Ākkumattirkkumati cukkumamāycuyam cōtiyāy
Kākkumenkāruṇṇiyacāli namakkukkulataivamē.

The word and mind left out as the light spread over the entire sky without form widely found everywhere looked like the wonderful object, indirect experience as subtler than the human spirit, the most subtle and self-shining who protect this universe is my merciful one, is our guardian deity.

Poem 6

Viṛttiyittōnti virikinte vicuvappiramamaḷaintum
Viṛtiyinuḷḷe layippittu viṛticattikalrnthu
Viṛtiya viṛtikaḷattu viṛakattericutarpōl
Catucitānandapūranaccelu vancayanamakkē

By the coming into mental activities felt as existing and multiplying becoming support of the growing and expanding universe, if the universe along with its activities dissolved introvert within, it will be supported to the ignorance which is the power of activities, in the state of salvation activities and own activities fade out like the flame shining without fuel that let us experience as Sachidanandam (body, mind and bliss) as absolute reality.

Poem 7

Paṛmacorūpam piramamkoṇṭu pētappeṭuttināl
Karumatar pirārattakarumattināl karikantatupōl
Kaṛmakkuruṭar karamkoṇṭu kaṭṭipiṭippatinō
Kaṛumicciṭunnu karunākarakatiyentavarkkō

That which is only an imaginary object because of mere illusion is seen as different. Those who live viewing the Absolute Brahman as many in the field of activities by virtue of their worldly activities will become like blind men 'seeing' the elephant. These ignorants involved in activities due to the desire to embrace this inert universe as real. Therefore they always suffer involving in activities. Oh, the merciful one, what is their fate?

Poem 8

Ellāvumavan ceyalente makkuḷḷōreḷitaruḷal
Collāmārcolliya cūkkumaccukaporuttum veḷiyil
Pallāyiramkōtyaṇṭam palikotuttappūviyir
Cellātu cenmanivartivarumo civataimamē.

Hearing my humble words that everything is Lord's play only, the light of subtle reality which can only be known by experience, oh Lord! Will I have to escape from the worldly relations of births and deaths without reaching the place of experiencing the absolute consciousness where the thousands of universes dissolve and disappear?

Poem 9

Ellāmakamakamentē kapōtamvarutiyatum
Nillātuninnil kalaṛti nīyunānumattiṭattu

Tollaiyaṟumentu tontatinirkkitentappoẓutum
Collitoẓumentuyaramoẓikka cukakkaṭlē.

Giving the feeling of 'oneness' which is the self-realization that all these things seen around are I myself, removing the feeling 'I' merging into the self-shining Brahman setting the ego completely, living in worldly relations always pray humbly that in the state of absolute consciousness remove all miseries oh the ocean of pleasure.

Poem 10

Pūranacattilacarppātamattupurātanamām
Kāraṇamattukkaruvattukkariyacankarpamattu
Tāraṇayum vittutattuvam patattu vitapporulām
Māranamkottiyatiyattarūpamen taivamē.

The obstruction by the non-existing inert things in absolute existence being vanished, the concept of old cause vanished, the feeling of effect lost as the obstruction of inert things vanished, my god is shining as 'unique' with strong experience in the sense of non-dualism as indicated by the words 'Tat' (that) and 'Asi' (you).

Pathikam 5

Poem 1

Cittenturaikkiṟ catapātakamuṇṭatai piruttu
Ccattentu collilacattumankē vantu cārntitumāl
Cittam kuḷurnta cukameniltukkamanaittumattō
Rittanmayulloru taivamentume namakkuḷḷatē.

If we say 'Chit', the mind the inert will be excluded from it. Instead of 'chit if we say Sat' (existing), the 'Asat' (non-existing) inert also will be included in the existing. If we say pure cool pleasure, it comes to the state of being devoid of all miseries. The god that exists as the pure entity and pure pleasure is my own god always.

Poem 2

Circatamattuccerintilankiccata cattumattu
Parpalakāt cittukaḷattuppantanirmmōtccamattu
Caṛkkarayin cuvaipōlanparuḷḷam kavarntu niṛku-
Mittanmayilloru taivatamentṛumemakkuḷḷatē

The comparative feeling of mind and inert being lost and the comparative feeling of existing (entity) and on existing (void) lost, the feeling of many visual things lost, the desire (longing) for getting rid of relations completely lost being as sweet as jaggery rice, one who stole the heart of the devotee is always my god.

Poem 3

Ontanti rantenum kuttam pavikkumatanti veṛum
Kunte niṛpaḷḷamum nērē viruttam kurititiṭilō
Kuntitumkuttam kuṭintamparuḷḷam kavaṛnta pincu-
Kanrentiruviḷaiyātalikkaṇṭatulakamellām.

When we hear about 'one' immediately the feeling of two follows. Besides, when we hear about a hill, we get the opposite feeling of a pit. Whatever we see as the universe is the holy dance of Paramashiva that attracts the heart of the worshipper removing the feeling of duality, which produces the experience of Advaita.

Gurudev, in a cosmological sense, explains the dual approach to the various phenomena in the universe. The human mind cannot imagine anything absolute; it is done only relatively. Without comparing with a second one, the definition of 'one' is impossible. It is difficult to comprehend also. Let us see a very good example. Imagine that you are the only person in this universe. Somebody asks you, 'Where are you standing?' You cannot give an answer if there are no other things in your neighbourhood to compare with. More precisely, imagine that you are the one and the only one (A) in this universe. Remember! There is nobody in the universe other than you (A). In that case, if somebody asks you about your location, there won't be a proper answer to it because there is no object with which your position can be compared. Now suppose there is the second person also—say your friend (B)—in this universe. Then for giving the location of your position, you have to mention how far away you are from your friend (B). You have to measure the distance between (A) and (B). Unfortunately, even after the introduction of the second person (B) (or any object), the problem is not solved since you cannot measure the distance between you (A) and your friend (B). To measure the distance between you (A) and your friend (B), there has to be a scale. It means, even at this stage, your position and the distance do not become relevant. Again, if a third person (C), another friend, is also there in this universe along with you (a total of three persons, you and your friends, that is A, B & C only), then the distance between you and your first friend can be measured taking the distance between your first friend (B) and your second friend (C) as a measuring scale. By comparison, the distance between you and your friend (A & B) might perhaps be two times the distance between your first and second friends (B & C) or else, might be half of it. It is in this manner the distances between objects are measured in metre, foot, etc. as measuring scales (units). In short, to measure the distance between two objects, the distance between two other objects is taken as the scale of measurement. In the above example, the locations of the friends (B & C) are considered as the two ends of the scale. Even though one cannot locate or define (A) in physical terms when it is the only thing in the universe, its existence is a reality. In its loneliness, that is, in the absence of things around, it appears to be non-existent. This apparent feeling is the creation of our inability to comprehend the Absolute. There are no laws in physics that enable us to tide over this problem.

No physical law will ever emerge to define the Absolute. How can physics explain the existence of an object when it is the only object in the entire universe? To physics, it is non-existent though it really exists. This, in fact, is the situation before Planck time, which Stephen Hawking considers as the situation where laws of physics collapse to 'singularity'. When the universe emerges (the big bang explosion), from singularity there arises dualism in the universe. Advaita philosophy explains it as mere perception of mind or the creation of Maya, which is an outcome of ignorance. Duality exists in dealings only. It is the comparison that brings in the feeling of duality. It is the emergence of secondary objects that hides the Absolute; relativity of dualism is the creation of the aforesaid dual approach. It is on this duality that Albert Einstein's theory of relativity is founded. The feeling of the illusory appearance of objects will continue to persist until the universe collapses into a singularity in the 'big crunch'. To get rid of dual feeling, one has to attain the absolute monistic state, which can only be imagined. To put it in terms of physics, one has to go to the state of absolute singularity. These are all things opposed to the spirit of monism, according to which everything in the universe is the magic of Sree Parameswara. But Parameswara—we have seen in Sankara Bhashya—is only the wakeful (Jagrat) aspect of the universe. In all his works, Gurudev takes Parameswara as the symbol of Brahman (universe) in its wakeful form. The ultimate aim of life is to remove the dual feelings and obtain the reality of monism.

Poem 4

Ilakkanattilirikkukaikuttametiṛkaṇattil
Mūlapporuḷillai mūntāvatil pinmutivumenkē
Kalatilonti virippuḷḷatontir kaṭum pakaiyām
Mālumayanumatiṛ patturuttiranum mayntiṭumē.

It is not wise to live in these dualistic experiences. In dualistic experience, there is no Brahman without attributes, and hence, there is no truth at all. Once, fallen into the three attributes like the '*Thrigunas*' then how can it be possible to quit. If we long for something in our life, we may be put to great betrayal. In short, it is not only the illusory universal phenomena which have beginning, existence and end but also Brahma, Vishnu and Maheswara, the different forms (aspects) of Saguna Brahman which will also dissolve into the Absolute—the Nirguna Brahman.

The poem—that starts by saying that there is not even an iota of truth in the dualist experience—takes the concept of time as its central topic of discussion. Time has three different states—the past, the present and the future. We will see later in this book that these three time considerations are not absolute but only relative. 'The present' is the time interval between the past and future. If we examine the length of this interval, we can see that it is almost '0'. For example, imagine a coin whose sides represent the past and future in time. Then the time 'present' will be the thickness of the coin between the sides. We know that even if we reduce the thickness of the coin to almost vanishing thickness, there will still be the two sides. And this duality of the coin (that it keeps two sides) will continue until its thickness becomes zero and the coin disappears. Then 'the present' will vanish and naturally the past, and the future will also vanish. It is the situation of singularity; the real state of Brahman without attributes. It is this Brahman, Sree Narayana Gurudev characterizes in his 'Daivadasakam' as 'Thou art the present, past and the future' and 'Thou art the "Word" (Pranava or Aumkara)'.

One need not say how loftily Gurudev interrelates spirituality with the ideas of modern science. What it means is that the time 'present' is a phenomenon one can only imagine, but it is not real. Later in this book, we will see that the 'present' for a person is 'past' for another, and is 'future' for a third one. The duality in consideration of time between past and present and present and future all vanished at the time of the big bang, i.e., when the entire space and time are reduced to a singularity. The assumptions based on relativistic time consideration as to what is happening (present), what happened yesterday (past) and what is going to happen tomorrow (future) are only the perceptions of the mind. We know physics endorses the fact that the 'present' of one is not the 'present' of another. This is understood from the following example; imagine that an object 'C' is there in front of two persons A and B. Suppose that C is at a distance of 5 metres from A and 2 metres from B. At first sight, both persons claim that they see the object in front of them simultaneously 'here and now'. But the claim that both A and B are seeing the object C simultaneously at the same instant, say, 'now' is not true because we see an object only when the light from it falls on the retina of our eye. The rays of light starting from the object at the same instant first reach person B who is nearer to the object than person A. Then only the light rays reach person A. In short, the information about the presence of the object C reaches persons A and B depending upon the respective distances they have from the object C. Therefore, the 'now' of person A comes only after the 'now' of person B, though both are seated in front of the object. If the persons have to get a common 'here and now', (to get rid of their duality in observation), they have to merge into one body. This is a universal phenomenon. There is no such thing as a common universal 'here and now'. If we want to have a common or universal 'here and now', all things in the universe should reduce to a single point where all dualities vanish. It really is the singularity or the state of Nirguna Brahman. This shows that all our ideas and observations based on duality are only misconceptions. Once we have arrived at this stage, there will not be any space-time differentiation of creation, existence and dissolution. By then, even Brahman, Vishnu and Maheswara, who are believed to be their presiding deities, will merge into the Brahman without attributes.

Poem 5

Mālumayanum makēcuran ruttiran catācivanum
Kālacakkirapiramattai kaṇṭu kaikūvittevvulakum-
Līlayin vaitulayippittu lingapiratiṭṭaiceytu
Mēliḷakātemeẓukiṭṭuraippittatentaivamē.

Making Vishnu, Brahma, Maheswara, Rudra and Sadashiva stand with folded hands in salutation seeing the spinning of the wheel of time giving birth to the entire universe by own play and dissolving the entire universe in himself in the minute form (linga) without any change in own form, one who stands immovable as if fixed strongly is my god.

Poem 6

Vēṛuvēṛām vitayankalverumñcatamē poṛiyir
Cērumappōtu cekamparamenkuñcerintilankum
Ceerarul cōti civacitparapānuveẓuntaruli
Kūrirul kōrikuḷittu veḷiyiṛkkulāvumatē.

The things which are seen as different are only inert ones. These things are seen spread as this world and the other world (the world of the dead) when they join the five senses. The Brahman, the heavenly glory, auspicious, consciousness and primordial cause go in a solemn way making the ignorance removed, and that itself will remain spread in the outside also. Like the rising Sun (the Brahman) removes the darkness of night (ignorance) with its rays.

Poem 7

Pāraimpulaṅṅal poṛivāyamatintuppakaṛvariya
Kāraṇa kāriyamattu karaṇakkavar katintu
Pūranacōtiyir puttappurutappuraikatīṛntu
Cīraṇamirccēkaccōtiyircintai tiṛaikotuppēn.

Ended in mind, the five elements such as earth, unexplainable torrents of cause and effect finished, the veil of desire in mind removed, the life form of the man lost as awakened to the glory of Brahman, I keep my thoughts always in the universal glory manifested in Vedas.

Poem 8

Tēkamitutittamalla tivviyanantatteḷḷamuti-
Ttākamaṛa mūẓkiccātanaccāttiyacarvoẓintu

Pōkumpatikkuppavanē kanātankaruṇai pūtta
Ppākampakaṛnta pacunkoṭiyōtinkaṇai vatentō.

This body is not perpetual, immersed in the pure nectar of divine eternal bliss until the thirst (desire) ran out, the differentiation between the cause and effect vanished so as to bring experience of non-duality, the only master of the universe full of mercy like the Kamadhenu, when will you come running towards me oh Lord!

Poem 9

Pañcappatum paṛavaikkō parampiyippāẓmanamām
Puñcaikkaḷai koitu pulamkuṭippokkiẓamām
Kañcikkuṭikko kutiyētti ni karunakaranē
Tancamtiruvatiyentu tamiyēn talarukintēn.

To protect the birds that are the senses which wander not satisfied with anything or this cruel mind involving in everything and perplexed without finding shelter or the five worldly senses that are useless weeds given reaped and wandering in this meaningless worldly life. Oh, Merciful, God! Is it for this that you gave me this human body? As a destitute, I feel and become tired, and you are the only refuge for me.

Poem 10

Entakkaṇattiletiraṛṛemanvalaiyil piṇippa-
Ttantakkaṇamakankāra minjñānappirakācamuntāi
Entakkaṇankalumattātiniṛ paracivattin
Kantakkamalamalaṛpatam rantumkati namakkē.

That moment when the net of death is spread unhindered trapping inside at the same moment the human ego gets the light of consciousness, the aspect of Brahman without being influenced by any other thoughts and while attaining the oneness, bless me rendering the fragrant foot of Shiva shining like the lotus, let that be the support of this devotee.

8

DAIVACHINTANAM II

Jīvēśwarajagatbhēdarahitādwaitatējassē
Siddavidyādharaśivaścaravē guravē nama
Aum namōnamassabradāyaparamaguravē
Jaya jaya swāmin!

(Original in Sanskrit)

The Lord of life devoid of universe differentiation,
The brilliance of Advaita Scholar realized!
Symbol of Shiva, Oh! Master! I prostrate
Aum! I prostrate! Salute traditionally oh! Supreme Master,
Oh! Lord! Be victorious! Be victorious!

(Original text in Malayalam)

Ithoru mahāvicitṛam tanne! Nirindana jyōtissāyirikkunna nintiruvadiyil marumarīcikāpṛavāham pōle prathamadṛiṣtya dṛiṣtāmāyirikkunna sakalapṛapancavum ālōcikkumbōl gaganāravindatinte stiti pōle tanne irikkunnu. Anyatajadadukharūpamāyirikkunna ith nintiruvadiyil sṛiṣtikkappettittuḷḷatumalla. Swayameva jaatamayathumalla. Nintiruvadiyaal srishtikkappettittullatanenkil nintiruvadikk karanakartrudoshamundennu parayendivarum. Nintiruvadi karanakarthrudosamillatha nirvyapariyalle? Athukond athorikkalum yuktamalla. Sudda jadatinu swayameva jatamakunnathinu nivritiyilla. Iprakaaramanirvachaneeyamayirikkuna eeprapanchavum sachitananda khanamaaya nintiruvadiyum koodi tamaprakaasangal pole sahavaasam chytukondirikkunnatutanne oratyalbhutam. Njangalude trikaranangalum pravrutikalum ellaam tegooroopamaya nintiruvadiyude neere tamomayamaaya karpoora dhooliyude avastaye prapichrikkunnu. Athukondippol nirahankarikalaya njangalum nintiruvadiyum tammil yathoru bhetavumilla. Bhedarahitanmaraya nam iruvarudeyum madyavartiyaaya bhetavyavahaaravum engineyo chiranjeeviyumayirikkunnu. Nintiruvadiyum njangalum prapanchavum ee tripadhaartavum anaadinityamaaya nintiruvadi tanne. Appol nintiruvadikk Advaita siddiyumilla. Njangalkk bandanivrutiyumilla. Ithikoodateyum nintiruvadikkum njangalkkum tammilulla sevya sevakabhavatinum haanivarunnuvenkilum nityabaddanmaarayirikkunna njangal nityamuktanaaya nintiruvadiye sevikkunnath yuktam tanne. Nityabaddarude bandhathinu nivrutiyilla athukond athu nishprayojanamaayitanne teerunnu. Prayojanamillatha pravruti cheyyunnath moudyamennatre, paravaan padullu. Ee anaadiyaya njangalude moudyavum nintiruvadiyil tanne avasanikkunnu. Inganeyulla sarvopakariyaya nintiruvadikkaykond oru vidatilum onnum upakarikkunnathinu njangalkku bhagyamillate aayallo! Daivame, ee vyasanavum nintiruvadiyilthanne nirdhooliyayirikkunnu. Ithellam pokatte! Eathu prakaramenkilum swapnatil kanda kataye jagratil prasangichu kreedikarikkunnathupole, rajasataamasavrutikalil sphooreekarich padarnnirikkunna ee anyatajadabhaadaye athisookshmamaya sudda satwika vyapakavritiprakasatil kreedichotukki, aa nischalavrutimatramaayi anubhavich aa akhandaakaravrutiyude golastanatil nilkkunna njangalkkum nintiruvadikkum tammil sooryaprakasagolangalkkullatupole yatoru vailakshanyavum illennulla anubhoodiye drudeekarich bhoogabhoktyabhogyanubhoodi vitt sareeracheshtamatra pravruthiyodu koodi yadheshtam viharikkunnathinu nintiruvadiyude anugraham undaakanam. Athinaayi kond namaskaaram, namaskaaram, namaskaaram.

Ha! This is wonderful! In you, the fuel-less (self-shining) light, the entire universe appears as a river of water in the desert at first sight, once thought to remain in the state of the flower of the sky. This, virtual inert grief form is not created in you also, and not self-created, if it were created by you, then one will be forced to say that you have knower knowledge defect. As one devoid of worldly activity, it is not at all logical. The pure inert things can never take birth by themselves. In that sense, this indefinable universe and you the embodiment of entity (existence), knowledge and bliss (Sachidanandam) as if light and dark live in coexistence is a great wonder. Our mind, word and body (the *thrikarmas*) and activities have become darkness bound dust of camphor in front of your glorious body. Hence there is no difference between you and us who are without ego. The act of differentiation between us somehow has become ever living. Your Lordship as the universe, we and these three things are the beginningless eternal Lord. Then your quality of non-duality is lost, and we lost our abandonment. Besides, though the devotee–devoted relation gets deteriorated, it is proper that we worship you the one who is eternally free from all bindings. But it is impossible to keep relation with those who are eternally free from all bindings. Therefore that becomes useless. The act of useless work can be said as only stupidity. But this beginningless stupidity of us also ends in you. We feel sorry that we could not get an opportunity to do any service in any manner, to a benefactor like you. Oh! Lord this grief also has crumbled and dissolved in you not leaving a bit.

Let it be cast aside! Somehow or other, like enjoying by narrating in wakefulness the events seen in a dream this virtual binding that shines spreading in worldly activities of love and anger, enjoying in the light of pure virtuous act experiencing as only the worldly activities remaining at the points of destination strengthening the feeling that between the lord and us, there is no difference in traits like the sunlit worlds, abandoning the feelings of enjoyer, enjoyment and object of enjoyment Lord! Bless us to live freely reconciled with only body movement. Oh! Lord, you bless us. For that, I prostrate! Prostrate! Prostrate!

9

DAIVADAŚAKAM

This, the most popular, at the same time characterized as the loftiest of hymns in Advaita philosophy, contains ten verses. There are people who qualify this collection of verses as an Upanishad. This is a prayer song which is devoid of space and time. It is believed to be acceptable to all creeds, religions and sections of people. This is one of the very rare prayer songs in which the devotee does not make any demand or request to God for giving something. On the other hand, the devotee praises God for whatever is given to him as the God's blessing. It is a poem the devotee chants in praise of the Absolute.

(Original text in Malayayam)

Daivamēkāttukoḷkaṅṅu
Kaividātiṅṅu ñaṅṅaḷe
Nāvikan nī bhavābdhikkō
Rāvivan tōṇi ninpadam

Oṇṇonnāyeṇṇiyeṇṇitto-
Ṭṭeṇṇumporuḷoṭuṅṅiyāl
Ninniṭum dṛikkupōluḷḷam
Ninnilaspandamākēṇam

Anna vastṛādi muṭṭāte
Tannurakshicu ñaṅṅaleṅ
Danyarākkunna nīyonnu
Tanne ñaṅṅalkku tamburām

Āẓiyum tirayum kāṛṛum
Āẓavum pōle ñaṅṅaḷum
Māyayum nin mahimayum
Nīyumennuḷḷilākaṇam

Nīyallō srishtiyum srashtā-
Vāyatum srishtijālavum
Nīyallō daivamē, srushti
Kkulla samgriyayatum

Nīyallō māyayum māya-
Viyum māyāvinōdanum
Nīyallō māyayē nīkki-
Ssāyūjyam nalkumāryanum

Nī satyam jñānamānandam
Nī tanne vaṛtamānavum
Bhūtavum bhāviyum vēṛa-
Llōtum moẓiyumōṛkkil nī

Akavum puṛavum tiṅṅum
Mahimāvāṛnna ninpadam
Pukaẓtunnu ñaṅṅaḷaṅṅu
Bhagavānē jayikkuka

Jayikkuka mahādēvā
Dīnavanapārāyaṇam
Jayikkuka cidāndā
Dayāsindhō jayikkuka

Āẓamēṛum nin mahassā-
Māẓiyil ñaṅṅaḷākavē
Āẓaṇam vāẓaṇam nityam
Vāẓaṇam vāẓaṇam sukham.

Meaning and commentary

Verse 1

Oh! God! Protect us not forsaking
Us as alien to you, you are
The captain and your word (Aum) is
The steamer in the ocean of worldliness.

The first four lines may fancy a sort of duality between the God and the devotees as if God is up in heaven and the devotees are here on the earth. Once both the verses 1and 2 are taken together, one can understand Gurudev's firm belief in non-duality (Advaita).

Since the word *'bhava'* has a meaning 'come into being' or originate, and *'Abdi'* has a meaning numeral 'four', instead of a sea of worldly attachments, it can be interpreted as Aumkārathe supreme soul where everything ultimately finds shelter. AUM (Aumkāra) has four syllables *A'kāra, U'kāra, Makāra* and *Amātra*. Then, the meaning of 'you are the shelter' or refuge becomes suitable. It will mean that you are the captain (cause—the last refuge) of the steamer, and the steamer is the virtual worldly attachments.

This prayer based on Advaita philosophy starts with a solicitation that the devotees be put into the state of having become one with the Brahman, without being left alien to Brahman in duality. The worshipper, who is under the illusion produced by Maya, feels that he has been separated from Brahman. He requests a place in the ship of which Brahman is the captain, to take refuge. The anti-dualistic desire of the worshippers not to desert them, making them alien to Brahman, is inherent in these lines. In the first poem itself, the Aumkara aspect of the universe and the desire of the worshipper to attain salvation are disclosed.

Verse 2

Counting repeatedly one by one
And when all countable vanish
Then what remains is the noble eye
Let me become throb less dissolving in it.

Once, the entire objects and the multifarious phenomena in the universe are counted one by one (rejecting one by one, notees are—not this, not this) and come to an end; there will shine the truth or reality like an eye. That is Brahman. To that Brahman my consciousness—the knowledge that I am—should merge in a way that the feeling there will shine the tr' (Brahman) is not left behind in me. There should come the condition of the unity of merging in you (Brahman) and have no throbbing in me different from that in you (Brahman).

The eye mentioned here is the same eye, which is characterized as 'dignified eye' in Gurudev's 'Sivasthavam' ('Creation of the Universe'). It is said that the entire universe came into being in its present form from this dignified eye. The worshipper also is a part of the newly formed things in the universe. Here, the worshipper expresses his desire to return to the primordial particle to which all worldly experiences and sights collapse. Physics so far, in the process of searching the secrets of the universe, was analysing the fundamental constituent of the universe by fragmenting its component materials one after the other. By this, it was trying to ultimately reach the primordial particle.

Verse 3

You are the only one. Oh! Lord
Who protect and bless us
Giving food and cloth unhindered
And providing all such needs.

Doubt may arise as to how the unattributed Brahman blesses the devotee giving them their day-to-day requirements. In this poem, the devotee praises God by way of gratitude for the mercy of God in giving food, clothing and such without hindrance and making their life blessed. It should be noted that here Gurudev takes Saguna Brahman as God through which we approach the Nirguna Brahman—the Absolute. An ordinary devotee can attain and experience himself as Brahman only through the attributed form of Brahman, God. In short, God is taken as the symbol of Brahman by superimposing attributes to an unattributed absolute one.

Verse 4

Like the ocean wind and depth
Are ourselves, our illusions,
You and your greatness, that
Awareness should come to my mind.

The sea, the waves produced in it, the wind that creates waves and the depth of the sea are interconnected. Likewise, the awareness of us, Māya and your greatness and you should come to my mind.

A wave is nothing but a disturbed form of water. It is created by the wind. The height of waves (or the crests and troughs) depends upon the strength of the wind and depth of the sea. As the strength of wind increases, the height of the waves (the disturbance) will increase provided the depth is suitable. If the depth is greater, the height and width (the wavelength) will be greater. The greater the speed of the wind and the depth of the sea, the greater the height and width of the waves.

The waves are not real because they are only the sea water that appears as waves. It is like the creations of Maya. Maya creates the miseries of worldly life like the seawater creates waves in it. The severity of miseries depends on the acts of good and evil deeds in previous births, like the size of the waves depends on the depth of the sea. This awareness should come to mind.

How beautifully Gurudev explains the similarity! The comparison agrees with both the principles of physics and Advaita Vedanta.

Verse 5

Oh! God! You are the creation
The creator and the multitude of creatures
Oh! God you on your own are
Instrumental to the creation.

Though these lines are written in simple language and style, they contain the entire spirit of Advaita philosophy. We will see in later chapters the role of primordial life force (consciousness) as the instrument (the cause) for the creation of the universe, keeping the net content of the entire matter and energy of the universe as void forever and also in the act of creation of the universe and the inflation in a colossal way of the universe.

Gurudev uses the word 'instrumental' *(Sāmagri)* very meaningfully. This usage manifests the idea behind *'Thapastan Mahina'*(because of the greatness of penance) and the desire of the Brahman as referred to in 'Nasadeeya Suktam' in Rig Veda, and also 'Sa: kamayata bahusyam prajāye yēti' in Taitirīyopanishad.

In short, in a very simple Vedic view, Gurudev explains in these lines as to what Brahman is and how the universe was created and also who had been the cause of creation, etc.

It is important to note that Gurudev ascertains the existence of a 'cause' for the creation of the universe through the use of the word instrumental. This view of Gurudev, namely 'for creation there needs to be a cause'- though contradictory to the belief upheld by great scientists like Stephen Hawking - has become relevant with the advent of the latest conclusions in quantum theory and spontaneous symmetry breaking.

Verse 6

Oh! God, you are illusion illusionist
And one who amuse in the illusion

You are the noble one who removes
The illusion leading us to salvation.

Oh God! You are the one who hides your real self and manifest illusory dexterity and relish showing the magic of creation, existence and dissolution. Likewise, Oh! God! You are the great master who removes all secrets of illusion and make us experience unity with you (merger with you).

Here, Gurudev mainly mentions the illusory acts of the Brahman. If we examine the physics of the stages of evolution of the universe from the moment of its creation to the present time, especially in the evolution of living things and their existence, it can be seen that all such things are not purely accidental happenings and without a preconceived notion. We will see in the anthropic principle that the universe evolved to the form we see now, and the way it became habitable for human beings, would have needed the skill of an architect in determining the universal constants just enough throughout for the formation of everything in the universe. There are many amazing, and at the same time, reliable examples. It is the magic of the magician whom Gurudev mentions. Everything is distributed in a sufficiently precise manner that the universe is evolved into the present shape. That is why we all live in it. Maya finds a proper place in the explanation of how billions of universes were created from non-existing matter and energy (absolute void) keeping its real value (in terms of mathematics) as '0'. Physicists and cosmologists agree with the argument that the universe was created from vacuum or void and exists as void and ends in the void. It is difficult to contain this argument, even though it is endorsed by both Advaita philosophy and modern cosmology. There is something (reality) beyond the power of comprehension of the human mind in the creation of the universe. It is the 'ignorance' that hides the reality. But to remove the veil of Maya (illusion), knowledge is essential. To see the real Brahman, the supreme soul, and to merge into it, ignorance should perish. In short, the worshipper prays to remove the illusory form of the universe which was created by the Brahman with his magic power. As the visible form is merely the perception of the human mind, he prays to raise the level of his self such that he and the Brahman are one and the same.

Verse 7

Thou art the truth, knowledge and bliss
Once thought you are the present.
Past and future too are not different
From you the only chanted word.

These lines sound the eternal nature of Brahman and the singularity that prevailed at the moment of creation of the universe. At the moment of creation of the universe, space and time were not separated from each other, that is, space and the three times (past, present and future) joined to form a single state called singularity as explained by the big bang theory. Similarly, Advaita philosophy makes it clear that at the moment of creation, it was nothing but Aumkara the chanted word (*mozhi*), the Brahman without attributes. This may be the zero-point energy (ZPE) or maybe the primordial quantum fluctuations in physics. On the basis of these, Gurudev says that unified space and time is nothing other than Aumkara, the Brahman without attributes.

Minkowski's space-time has four dimensions—three lengths and time. According to Einstein's general theory of relativity, time also is a length, which means it is equivalent to space. This may be the reason why Gurudev sees Aumkara (the word with four syllables), which is linked with time, as the universe (which occupies space).

Verse 8

We praise your noble
The chanted word that pervades
Inside and outside
Oh! Lord! Be victorious.

Oh, God! It is your presence that fills the entire universe; it is the glory of Aumkara. We adore (praise) the glory of your chanted word. Oh, God! Be victorious!

The usage of the words filling the inside and outside has to be interpreted as inside of our own universe and outside of it. There are arguments quoting theories such as the big bang theory that time and space were originated simultaneously and it was a minute particle that exploded by the unification of space and time, and there would not have been space prior to the big bang. In that case, it is natural that doubts may arise about where this particle was housed before the big bang. One answer is, if space also was inside the exploding particle, then the question as to what was there outside the particle does not have any relevance. We know in observations, no object can have an existence outside this particle except in the vacuum state. It is only Aumkara, the Brahman without attributes (a state of individual soul merging with the universal soul—Turiya), that is all-pervading, can maintain its presence simultaneously inside and outside the particle at that moment. In the case of a boundless all-pervading medium, no question of inside and outside of our universe arises. Poem 2 of Gurudev's 'Maya Darsanam'is worth quoting at this point.

Prāgutpattēr yadhāfbhāvo
Mṛudēva Brahmana; pṛadhak
Na vidyatē Brahma hi yā
Sā Māyāfmēyavaibhavō.(Sanskrit)

In what manner, earlier to its creation the pot does not exist but exists only as soil, in that manner, whoever is not seen as existing before the creation of the universe and whatever is Brahman itself, that itself is the Brahman power Maya the one with indescribable dexterity.

With the advent of string theory and the concept of multiverse, the conclusion that ours is not the only universe in the *Brahmandakataham* (collection of universes) and the discovery that there are billions and billions of other universes in this multiverse, Gurudev's view on the 'filling of inside and outside' becomes most relevant.

Verse 9

Be victorious Oh! The God of gods
Compassionate to the sufferers
Be victorious the blissful consciousness
Be victorious the ocean of mercy!

Oh! The God of gods! Be victorious! Oh! Lord, you are one who is always interested in the protection of the sufferers, the blissful consciousness the ocean of mercy be victorious!

The devotee in any of these verses does not ask for any material gain; he finds only the greatness in God. He is aware that the God knows the devotee's requirements and delivers everything without a request. The only request or desire he makes is to make him attain the state of realization and merge with Brahman.

Verse 10

In the deep sea of your glory
Let all of us be immersed
And live forever
Exist and live in peace.

Let us all without exception immerse in the ocean of your supreme soul that pervades everywhere and merge into it and live in bliss forever.

The word 'deep' *(azham)* may be interpreted as infinitely spread. In physics, very recently, from the discovery of the accelerated expansion of the universe, a new phenomenon that pervades the entire universe has been found to exist theoretically. It is known as the quintessence. One may take this as the fifth element from the meaning of the word quintessence, that is to say, *Akash*. Sutras and hymns from Brahmasutras and Upanishads support the above revelations of Sree Narayana Gurudev.

Sutra 41. *Artdhāntaratwa vypadēśadikaranam*of Brahmasutras says,

'Ākāśōfrtdhāntara twadi vypadēśāt'

Akash is Brahman, as pointed out as that is something else, etc.

Sutra 22 of Ākāśādhikaraṇam confirms,

'Ākāśastalingāt'

Akash is Parameswara (Brahman in Jagrat aspect) himself since his marks are there.

The word Akash means Brahman because the cause of the universe, including Akash (quintessence), is the Brahman.

In this context, Hymn 1-9-1 of Chandogyopanishad is also relevant,

Asyalōkasya kāgatyātirityākāśaitihōvācasarvāṇiha
Vā imānibhūtānyākāśādēvasamuthpādyanta ākāśam pratystam
Yantyākāśōhyēvaibhyōjyāyānākāśa parāyaṇam

To the question as to what is the refuge (support) of this universe, Pravāhanan gave the answer; it is the Akash. Whatever we see as the constituents of the universe are all produced from Akash. It merges back into it. Akash is greater than everything. Akash is the refuge.

The above explanations about Akash manifest the importance of the fifth element—Akash, the '*Panchama Bhootham*', or the quintessence.

It is the Nirguna Brahman that pervades the infinite space. From the mathematical point of view, for one which merges into infinity, it is impossible to have a return from it. This indicates that the worshippers pray that they should attain an everlasting unbroken consciousness with the Para Brahman (Nirguna Brahman) and should not have a rebirth. In short, the worshippers desire to attain eternal salvation by making their souls merge into the supreme soul.

10

MANANATHEETHAM

The year of writing the poem is not known. Some believe that it was in 1884. The meaning of the title is 'beyond the limit of thought'. The 'Ultimate Reality' is beyond the limits of realizing by pure logic and thoughts. One of the methods of finding the real truth is the practice of hatred to all visual things. *Vairagyam* (hatred) is the topic of discussion in the following lines; this poem is also known as 'Vairagya Dasakam'.

The subject of this prayer is mainly the devotee's desire to get rid of the emotional feelings and to keep hatred towards it. Once one has succeeded in practising hatred towards sensual feelings, the control of all other worldly longings will automatically vanish. One who seeks the truth should positively survive from the hold of tactile sensations. Those who read this poem will get the door opened to experience self-realization.

(Original text in Malayalam)

Karunkuẓalimāroṭukalaṛnnurukiyappū-
Nkurunnaṭipiriññaṭiyaniṅṅu kuẓayunnu
Perumkaruṇayāṛaniyumayyane maṛanni-
Tturumpaniniyentinuyirōṭu maruvunnu?

Marunnu tirunāmamaṇinīṟoṭitu mannil
Tarunnu pala nanmataṭavīṭumaṭi raṇṭum
Varunna pala cintakaḷaṟunnatinupāyā-
Lirannitu maṟannu kaḷayāyvatinaṭutēn.

Aṭutavarokkeyumetiṟtu porutīṭum
Paṭatalavimāroṭu paṭakkaṭiyanāḷō?
Eṭutarikirutiyaruḷēnaminiyum po-
Nnaṭitaliṟmaṟanniviṭeyentinalayunnu?

Alaññu mulayum talayumēntiyakatāril
Kalaṅṅiyeẓumāẓiyumaẓiññariyakaṇṇum
Viḷaṅṅiviḷayāṭinaṭakoḷḷumivarōṭi-
Mmalaṅṅaḷoẓukum kuṭililānu valayunnu.

Vaḷaññu valakeṭṭimadanappulayanuḷḷum-
Kaḷaññatilakappaṟava vīṇu valayunnu
Vaḷañña kuẓalōṭumulayunna miẓiyinnum
Viḷaññatatilentinu kiṭannu cuẓalunnu?

Cuẓannuvarumāḷukaḷeyokke vilakoṇṭi-
Ṅṅeẓunnaṇayumennoraṟivuṇṭaṭiyaninnum
Uẓannavariluḷḷamalayāṭiviṭeyonnāy-
Toẓunnu tuyarōṭiviṭe ninnaṭiyiṇakkāy

Iṇaṅṅiyirukonkayumiḷakkiyuyiruṇṇum-
Piṇaṅṅaḷoṭu pēṭi perutāyi viḷayunnu
Maṇam mutaloraṅcilumaṇaññu viḷayāṭum-
Piṇaṅṅaḷoṭu ñānoru kināvilumiṇaṅṅa!

'Iṇa'ṅṅaṇamenikkaruḷilentinu kiṭannī
Gunaṅṅaḷoẓiyum kuṭalamāroṭalayunnu
Piṇaññu puṇarum periyapēyaṭiyoṭe pōy
Maṇaṅṅaḷumaṟunnatinitā muṟayiṭunnu.

Muṛakkumuṛa minnimaṛayum miẓiyiḷakki
Teṛikkumoru penkoṭi ceṛutaṭiyilākki
Maṛutuviḷayāṭi maruvunniṭayilellām
Veṛutuvaruvaneẓuti nintiruvaṭikkāy.

Ayakkarutinicaṭulalōcanayoṭappon-
Ṡayataḷirilēntiyaṭiyōṭavaniyinmēl
Mayakkavumaṛutu manimēniyilaṇacī-
ṭayakkarutayakkurutanangaripuvē! Nī.

Meaning and commentary

Verse 1

Joining with black curly-haired beautiful women and involved
Forgetting the soft feet, this humble self suffers in this world.
Not remembering Shiva who bears on the head river of mercy Ganga
Why this decaying silly one lead miserable life wearing Prana?

Getting mingled with beautiful women of black curly hair, and immersed in its pleasure, I happened to forget your soft feet, hence this devotee, your dependent, is suffering in this world. Without remembering Shiva who wears Ganga the river of great mercy on the head, this silly fellow with the decaying body leads a miserable life wearing prana.

Verse 2

Your chant and ashes smeared on feet are medicines
To sufferings on earth and deliver many virtues
Not forgetting it is the device to get rid of many thoughts
That come unending, I come closer to Lord Shiva.

The medicine for curing the disease of worldly sufferings is the chant *Namassivaya*—the Panjakshari. The divine feet of Shiva smeared with ashes is capable of delivering many good qualities in inert life fixed in my mind. To remove different worldly feelings coming one after the other in spite of all efforts to stop, as a device the adoration of these feet through the chanting of this hymn, for not forgetting it I approached Lord Shiva.

Verse 3

Is this humble self, capable of fighting warrior-like women
Who fight against all those coming near to them?
Take me near to you and tell me why I should wander
Forgetting your golden flower-like feet.

Oh! Lord! Let this devotee shine enough to fight and win women who get acquaintance with those approaching them and requesting various desires, like warriors getting ready to war, oh! Lord! Bless me with your presence, always taking me as one in the category of devotees. Why should I stick on to this world of miseries, forgetting your golden, tender feet?

Verse 4

Women approaching with pendulous breasts and moving heads
Inside the heart turbulent with sexy feelings showing love outside
Keeping beautiful ogling and with sexy amusements
Suffer helplessly falling into their filth flowing body.

With vacillating breasts and moving heads, with hearts full of sensual desires inside and ogling with sexy gestures pretending love outside, and showing beautiful women approaching with sexy amusements, joining with such women, I suffer greatly longing for their body which are the source of many filths.

Verse 5

The hunter Cupid cast net around and the bird
Forgetting the God inside trapped inside the net
Curly hair net and vacillating eyes are capable of
Attracting what use of getting trapped and flutter?

The hunter Cupid to trap men cast a net around, the bird's heart forgetting the God which is the place of refuge inside, gets trapped in those net flutters in pain, the curly hair as nets, along with fickle eyes traps the prey and is still capable of attracting anybody. What use is there in getting trapped in this net and fluttering?

Verse 6

Even now this humble self is confident that all people
Come with grief get a solution here to face them
Not letting me see the suffering ones losing mind
I pray the unique to let me find out your feet.

This devotee still possesses the awareness that to those who approach with a variety of problems, you judge their problems and evaluate them in their favour and manage here. Seeing people suffer involved in different problems, without allowing them to lose mind make them find your feet with enthusiasm in this transient miserable world, knowing that God alone is the saviour, I adore you with folded hands.

Verse 7

Fear towards approaching women, with vacillating breasts
Pretending love to seize vital power through temptation increases.
I will not even in a dream join these lumps of flesh
That plays only with the five senses like smell, etc.

The fear of approaching women who vacillate their breasts, pretending love, these inert pieces of flesh that seize the prana (life) through the sensual gesture, goes on increasing. These inert pieces of flesh, devoid of self-awareness that interact only through the five senses: smell, sound, shape, taste and touch, I am not going with these inert ones even in a dream.

Verse 8

Given the fortune of getting blessings of God, why should I
Join harlots without noble qualities, remove all erotomania
That prompt to embrace, I humbly pray the god to destroy
All sensual temptations through senses such as smell, etc.

This devotee who desires only the blessings of God wants to get the fortune of being subject to the Lord's blessing. These harlots who do not possess any good qualities which are helpful for the search of self-realization, why should this devotee be made to suffer associating with these. The evil spirit that entices to embrace left fully, and to remove all sensual promptings. Oh! Lord! This devotee humbly begs you to save.

Verse 9

When a woman with frequently moving glittering eyes
Showing romantic gestures seduced enslaved and made relished
Without my likes and dislikes, I remembered, and I Prayed
The Lord to increase my hatred towards sensual pleasures.

Whenever a beautiful woman with intermittently oscillating eyes ogle seduce, enslave and make relished without caring for my likes and dislikes, I prayed the 'Lord' to increase my hatred towards sensual pleasures.

Verse 10

Don't send me to get on with a woman with vibrant eyes
For the entire life accepting her golden tender leaf-like palm
Ending illusory desires make me join Lord's body
Oh! Killer of Cupid do not send me to worldly miseries.

Do not send me to earth, to lead a life with a woman grasping her golden-collared tender leaf-like palm. Oh! Lord! Ending my desires on virtual things, take me to dissolve in the Lord's form. Oh! Lord! Who smashed the Cupid to ashes! Do not send me to the worldly miseries, please do not send me!

11

VĀSUDĒVĀSTAKAM

Gurudev has written two prayer songs praising Lord Krishna, namely 'Vasudevashtakam' and 'Vishnuashtakam'. In an old edition of these poems, Gurudev wrote, '*Iti Balaramante vasina Narayana virachitam*'. Here, in the way of recording the name of the author, Gurudev reminiscences his master, Kummampalli Raman Pillai Asan; the word Balarama indicates Raman Pillai (Bala means little one or Pillai in local language).

This might have been written during the days of his studies at Karuvannor Kalari—the educational centre where Gurudev had his higher studies, staying as an inmate of Varanappally house. This indicates the time of writing this as round about 1877. Gurudev in those days worshipped Lord Krishna, and it is believed that he had the rare opportunity of seeing Lord Krishna as appeared to him.

Sree Narayana Gurudev made no differentiation between Saiva and Vaishnava sects, being an ardent believer in non-duality or Advaita. He believed that the links of all favourite deities are temporary media for the experience of Brahman, in whom the whole universe exists, or who exists everywhere in the universe known as 'Vasudeva'. Here too, as Lord Vishnu pervades everywhere, the terms Vasudeva and Lord Vishnu are only synonyms of Brahman.

(Original text in Sanskrit)

Śṛī vāsudēva, sarasīruhapāñcajanya
Kowmōdakī bhayanivāraṇacakṛapāṇē
Śṛī vālsavalsa, sakalāmayamūlanāśin
Śṛībhūpatē, hara harē sakalāmayam mē.

Gōvinda, gōpasūta, gōgaṇapālalōla,
Gōpījanānga kamanīyanijāngasanga
Gōdēvivallabha, Mahēśwara mukyavandya
Śṛībhūpatē, hara harē sakalāmayam mē.

Neelalikesaparibhooshita barhibarha
Kalambudadyuti kalayakalebarabha,
Veera, swabhaktajanavalsala, neerajaksha
Śṛībhūpatē, hara harē sakalāmayam mē.

Anandaroopa, janakanakapoorvadundu
Bhyanandasagara sudhakara soukumarya
Manapamanasamamanasarajahamsa
Śṛībhūpatē, hara harē sakalāmayam mē.

Manjeeramanjumanisinjitapadapatma
Kanjayataksha, karunakara, kanjanabha
Sanjeevanoushadha sudhamaya sadhuramya
Śṛībhūpatē, hara harē sakalāmayam mē.

Kamsasuradwirakasariveera, ghora-
Vairakaramaya virodhakaraja, soure,
Hamsadiramya saraseeruhapadamoola,
Sreebhoopate, hara hare sakalamayam me.

Samsarasankadavisankadakankaya
Sarvartadaya sadayaya sanatanaya

Sachinmayaya bhavate satatam namo stu
Sreebhoopate, hara hare sakalamayam me.

Bhaktapriyayaya bhavasokavinasanaya
Muktipradaya munivrindanishevitaya
Naktandivambhagavate natirasmideeya
Sreebhoopate, hara hare sakalamayam me.

Meaning and commentary

Verse 1

Vāsudēva! Who wears in four hands Lotus Panchajanya
Kaumodaki and Chakra that removes all fears, one who
Wears Sreevalsam on the chest, one who uproots all miseries
Lord! Husband of Lakshmi and Earth! Uproot all my grief.

Oh! Lord! One born as the son of Vasudēvar! One who wears the lotus, the conch known as Panchajanya, the club (a kind of baton) known as Kaumodaki, and the wheel weapon (Chakra) that removes all fears of devotees, Oh! Lord! Who shines wearing the mark of Sreevalsam on the chest, one who eradicates all worldly desires, one who shines as the husband of Goddess Lakshmi and Goddess Earth, the one who smashes all sins, I pray to remove all my worldly desires.

Verse 2

Oh! Govinda! Son of Gopa! Who plays as a cowherd
One who embraces the body of beautiful cowgirls
The husband of goddesses Lakshmi and Earth, one
Adored by gods like Lord Shiva! Uproot all my grief.

One who born as swine to elevate the earth from the sea (Govinda), incarnated as the son of Nandagopa, one who played tending the cattle, one who enjoyed embracing the beautiful Gopikas, one shines as the husband of Goddess Earth, one who is greeted by gods like Lord Shiva, the husband of Goddess Lakshmi and Goddess Earth! One who plunders all sins, Lord! Remove all my worldly desires.

Verse 3

One with long curled bluish hair like a row of beetles and
Peacock plume, body shines like bluish ironwood flower
Brave, merciful to devotees with lotus eye, husband of
Lakshmi and Earth, Vishnu! Uproot all my grief.

Oh! Lord! one wearing peacock plume on the bundle of braided long curly hair resembling a row of blue beetles, one shines with beautiful body with the colour of ironwood flower (Memecylon tinctorium), brave, dear to the devotees, lotus-eyed, husband of Goddess Lakshmi and Goddess Earth, one who destroys all sins, let the devotee be freed from all worldly desires.

Verse 4

An embodiment of bliss who sheds moonlight on Vasudeva's
Ocean of happiness, rejoice as the king swan in Lake Manasa
In minds that see dualities pride and disgrace with equanimity
Oh, Vishnu! Husband of Lakshmi and Earth! Uproot all grief.

One who shines always as the embodiment of bliss, who sheds moonlight on the ocean of joy of father Vasudeva, one who rejoices as the king swan in the lake Manasa (mind) the highest of Sannyasin who maintains equanimity in the duality of pride and disgrace, the husband of Goddess Lakshmi and Goddess Earth, one who ruins all sins, remove all worldly sufferings of this devotee.

Verse 5

With lotus feet making jingling of diamonds in anklets,
With lotus eyes, an ocean of mercy, with the lotus in navel full
Of ambrosia giving eternal life, the seat of the joy of truth seekers
Vishnu! Husband of Lakshmi and Earth! Uproot all my grief.

One who shines with lotus feet that make the jingling sound of beautiful diamonds in the anklets, one with long lotus flower-like eyes, ocean of mercy, one with lotus at navel, one filled with nectar like medicine that makes life eternal, the seat of bliss of the seekers of truth, the husband of Goddess Lakshmi and Goddess Earth, one who destroys all sins! Oh! Lord! Remove all my worldly desires.

Verse 6

One who killed tusker like demon Kamsa as a daring lion
Who alleviates diseases as a god, descendant of Ṡūrasēna
One blessed supreme souls like Hamsa, one with lotus feet
Husband of Lakshmi and Earth! Uproot all my grief.

One who happened to be valiant lion to tusker Kamsa, one who is the moon that cures diseases which are seats of cruel hatred or enmity, one born in the family of Ṡūrasēna, one with lotus-like feet that give happiness to Brahmajnanins (supreme scholars) like Hamsa, one who destroys all sins, the husband of Goddess Lakshmi and Goddess Earth Oh! Lord! End all my worldly desires.

Verse 7

One with armour to resist the worldly grief of devotees
Accomplishes wishes of devotees, merciful, unchanging
Embodiment consciousness. Oh! Vishnu I adore you
Husband of Lakshmi and Earth! Uproot all my grief.

One who shines as strong armour to the devotees enabling them to fight the miseries of worldly life, one who delivers all desires of devotees, one who sheds mercy on those who meditate, the unchangeable, embodiment of entity and wisdom, I always adore you like the visual form of Brahman! The husband of Goddess Lakshmi and Goddess Earth, one who destroys all sins Oh! Lord! Remove all my worldly grief.

Verse 8

One who loves the devotees and destroys worldly grief
Gives salvation and always served by truth-seeking monks
Oh! Lord! Symbol of Brahman! I prostrate day and night
Oh! Vishnu, husband of Lakshmi and Earth! Uproot all my grief.

One who creates fondness in those who meditate and makes them joyful smashes all worldly sufferings, blesses giving salvation, one, always served by truth-seeking ascetics, Oh! Symbol of Brahman, this devotee's prostrations day and night! Husband of Goddess Lakshmi and Goddess Earth, one who plunders all sins, remove all the worldly desires of this devotee.

12

VISHNUASHTAKAM

This is one of the poems Gurudev composed at a young age. 'Vishnuashtakam' is believed to be written by Sree Narayana Gurudev while he was staying at Varanappally. It was during his stay at Varanappally that Gurudev wrote many of the works on Vaishnava literature.

(Original text in Sanskrit)

Viṣṇum viśālāruṇapadmanēṭṛam
Vibhāntamīśāmbujayōnipūjitam
Sanātanaṃ sanmatiśōdhitam param
Pumāmsamādyam satatam pṛapadyē.

Kalyāṇadam kāmaphalapṛadāyakam
Kāruṇyarūpam kalikalmaṣaghnam
Kalānidhim kāmatanūjamādyam
Namāmi lakṣmīśamaham mahāntam

Pītāmbaram bhṛunganibham pitāmaha-
Pṛamukhyavandyam jagadādidēvam
Kirīṭakēyūramukhai pṛaśobhitam
Srīkēśavam santatamānato fsmi

Bhujangatalpam bhuvanaikanātam
Puna puna swīkṛutakāyamādyam
Purantarādyairapi vanditam sadā
Mukundamatyantamanōharam bhajē.

Kṣīrāmburaśērabhita sphurantam
Śayānamādyantavihīnamavyayam
Satsēvitam sārasanābhamucaiṛ-
Vighōṣitam kēśiniṣūdanam bhajē.

Bhaktāṛtihantāramahaṛnniśantam
Munīndrapuṣpānjalipādapankajam
Bhavaghnamādhāramahāśṛayam param
Parāparam pankajalōcanam bhajē.

Nārāyaṇam dānavakānanānalam
Natapṛiyam nāmavihīnamavyayam
Haṛtum bhuvō bhāramanantavigṛaham
Swaswīkṛutakṣmāvaramīditō fsmi.

Namō fstu tē nātha! Varapṛadāyin!
Namō fstu tē kēśava! kinkarō fsmi
Namō fstu tē nāradapūjitāgghṛē
namō namastwacaraṇam pṛapadyē.

Phalasrithi

Viṣṇuaṣtakamidam puṇyam
Ya : patēt bhaktitō nara:
Saṛvapāpaviniṛmuktō
Viṣṇulōkam sa gacati.

Meaning and commentary

Verse 1

Oh! Lord Vishnu! One with eyes like Blossoming
Red lotus adored by Shiva and Brahmadeva, Eternal,
Manifested to nobles, the ultimate, the primordial
Who resides in bodies, I find refuge in you, always!

Oh! Lord one with beautiful eyes like the blossomed red lotus, one adored by Brahmadeva and Lord Shiva, one who never perishes, one who manifests clearly in the minds of noble people, one who is the ultimate cause of the universe, one who existed as shining soul even before the creation of the universe, one who is well known as *Purusha* since residing in inert bodies and one who pervades everywhere, I adore you!

Verse 2

One who delivers bliss and favourites, the embodiment
Of mercy who smashes sins of frenzy who keeps
Subtle tools of creation, Cupid's father Lakshmi's
Husband, the all-pervading primordial cause, I adore you.

One who blesses the devotees, delivering favourite results, one who is seen as the embodiment of mercy, one who smashes sins of the period of frenzy, one who keeps always in self the subtle components for creation, one who is the father of Cupid, the husband of Lakshmi—the Goddess of wealth and prosperity—one who pervades inside and outside of everything and the primordial cause of the universe. Oh! Lord Vishnu, I adore you.

Verse 3

Oh! Lord Vishnu! One with beetle colour, dressed in
Yellow silk adored by Brahmadeva and other gods

Shines wearing crown and bracelets as primordial
Cause of universe I adore you always bowing my head.

One who wears yellow silk cloth around the waist, one who is blue in colour as a beetle worshipped by gods like Brahmadeva, one who shines as the creator of the universe, one who shines wearing crown on head and golden bracelets on the shoulder. Oh! Lord Vishnu, I adore you.

Verse 4

One with the snake as the bed, the saviour of the universe
One who receives different bodies again and again
Adored always by gods like Indra one with the most
Attractive form Vishnu the primal cause! I adore you.

One who rests on the cot Ananda the king of snakes, one who is the only saviour of the universe, one who is the body universe, who takes different bodies (universes) in incarnations, one who is adored by all gods including the king of gods Indra, one with a body that attracts hearts of everyone. Oh! Lord Vishnu, the ultimate cause, I adore you!

Verse 5

One who lies spreading light around the sea of milk
One without beginning and end, imperishable
Meditated always by good folk, one with lotus at navel
Adored by devotees, Oh! Lord Vishnu, I meditate you.

One lying on the bed of snake (Ananda) and spreading light around the sea of milk (*palazhi*), one without beginning and end (eternal), imperishable, one meditated always by noblemen, one with lotus flower at navel, one who is prayed loudly by devotees, one who smashes ignorance, Lord Vishnu! I adore you.

Verse 6

One who alleviates the grief of devotees, one with
Lotus feet worshipped by great ascetics
One who smashes visual universe, cause and effect
Real and virtual, Oh! The lotus-eyed, I adore you.

One who alleviates all miseries of the devotees one with lotus-like feet which is adored always by great ascetics, one who removes all feelings of visual universe created by Maya (ignorance) one who stands as the primordial cause of the universe and gives shelter to all, the ultimate cause, at the same time shines as the cause and effect, one with the lotus petal-like eyes, I always find shelter in Lord Vishnu.

Verse 7

The source of Vedas! The fire that burns the forest of sins
One without name and form, infinite, imperishable
One took many incarnations to lessen miseries of the world
One with the status of master of the universe, I adore you.

One who is the source of Vedas (Narayanan) and one who is the fire to burn the forest of sinners (demons), one without any defect at any time, one who took many incarnations to reduce the miseries of the world, one who took forms of many universes repeatedly oneself self-imposed (accepted) as the master of the universe, always I adore you.

Verse 8

Oh! Lord! Who blesses giving boons, prostrations!
Oh! Vishnu I am your servant, prostrations!
Oh! One with the feet adored by Narada, I prostrate!
Oh! Lord! Prostrations! I attain refuge at your feet.

Oh! Lord who blesses the devotee giving all his desires, my prostration! Oh! Lord Vishnu, my salutation! I am your servant Oh! Lord! One whose feet adored by the sage Narada who belongs to the tribe of gods; I prostrate you! Oh! Lord! I attain your feet wholeheartedly. I bow to you.

> One born as a man if chants the eight
> Holy verses in praise of Lord Vishnu
> With devotion becomes free of all sins and
> Attains the state of experiencing Brahman.

One who is born as a human being, if chants, again and again, these eight holy verses or Ashtakam in praise of Lord Vishnu, with utmost devotion becomes free of all blemishes in heart and attains the state of experiencing the Brahman, attaining salvation.

13

NIRVRITIPANCHAKAM

This poem was written in 1916 by Sree Narayana Gurudev while visiting the saint Ramana Maharshi at Tiruvannamalai. The following verse and the five verses that follow it were written seeing the state of a maharishi experiencing the ultimate bliss. These were written in a notebook still kept in Tiruvannamalai Ashram.

(Original text in Sanskrit)

Kō nāma dēša kā jāti
Pṛavṛiti kā kiyadwaya
Ityādivādōparatiṛ-
Yasya tasyaiva niṛvṛiti

āgaca gaca mā gaca
Pṛavišya kwa nu gacasi
ityātivādōparatiṛ
Yasya tasyaiva niṛvṛiti

Kwa yāsyasi kadā fyāta
Kuta āyāsi kō fsi vy
ityātivādōparatiṛ
Yasya tasyaiva niṛvṛiti

Aham twam sō fyamantaṛhi
Bahirasti na vāsti vā
ityātivādōparatiṛ
Yasya tasyaiva niṛvṛiti

Jnjātājnjātasama swānya-
Bhēdasūnya kutō bhida
Ityāti vādōparatiṛ
Yasya tasyaiva niṛvṛiti

Meaning and commentary

Verse 1

Where is your place, which is your caste?
What is your profession, what is your age?
To whom such questions ended he only
Attains salvation or eternal peace.

What are your name, place and caste, what are you, how old are you, etc., to whomever such questions have ended, he himself is one who attains salvation.

Salvation is the last state where one gets detached from all dualities. The dualities arise depending on inert bodies in subtle and corpulent forms. The questions like, where is your place, what is your caste, etc., originate from the feeling of duality and create in one's mind the linked inert objects and phenomena, resulting in confusion and loss of peace of mind.

Verse 2

Come, go, don't go, and come near,
Where you are going in all such hue
And cry and arguments in whom such things
Ended, only he can experience the bliss.

Whoever gets the end of arguments, such as come, go, where you are going, he alone will experience salvation.

Man is born activity-bound; the cause of birth ever is activity. The activity includes the activities of mind like imagination, thinking, speaking, and the human body does all that. Unfortunately, it is the activities that hide absolute consciousness. Or, in other words, activities are only virtual feelings because no action is capable of creating or destroying something.

Verse 3

Where are you going when did you come
From where do you come, who are you?
Whoever got the end of such questions
To him, only the attainment of absolute comes.

Where are you going, when you came, from where you come? One who got the end of such questions attains the experience of salvation.

All the questions arise from the feeling of duality. Either indicating place (space) or showing the time, the question who are you, results from the feeling that the other one is different from you. Once the state of salvation is reached, these dualities vanish and the feeling of a 'second' ends.

Verse 4

Me, he, inside and outside
Whoever got the relief from all
Such arguments, he alone gets
The experience of salvation.

Me (I), he, that man and this man inside, outside and there is, and there is not, and whoever gets rid of such deliberations to him only the attainment of the Absolute comes.

There are also questions arising from the feeling of duality. To get the feeling of 'there is', there should be a second to evaluate as to whether there is or there is not. When one alone is there in the universe, then, who is there to know it, only another can experience it. But as the one (Brahman) pervades everywhere, to him where is the inside and outside.

Verse 5

Known since in full bliss and not known since
Not a second to know no distinction as me
Or the other where are the two in it
One who ended such discussions alone gets salvation.

Since full attainment of eternal peace is an experience of an indeterminable (supreme) knowledge, it is known at the same time; there is nothing else to know like something unknown. Since there is no differentiation between me and another, where are the two? One who gets retirement from such arguments and gets the silent experience, to him only there is salvation.

Full attainment of eternal peace is an indeterminable experience of supreme awareness. It appears as complete silence in a human body. It is a state of being without any attributes. Hence there is no differentiation between the known and not known. There is no distinction between me and you or anything else. In physical terms, one is non-existent when that is not known. There will not be anything existing in that sense, even a physical existence of the Absolute. In the ordinary course, it is tough to understand this. There come many arguments about the possibility. Gurudev makes it clear in the verse that only such a person who has come to the state of complete silence with the awareness gets salvation.

Arguments are the product of duality. It succeeds only in the material approach; at higher levels of investigation about the secrets of the universe, it fails. It leaves many questions unanswered (it is recognized by modern physics). Modern science now accepts the fact that many things happening in the universe raise unanswerable questions; logic, theories, hypotheses, algorithms and all cannot solve and answer such questions. There comes the relevance of Advaita; physical and mathematical solutions cannot lead us to anywhere near the absolute reality.

14

ASRAMAM

At the time of the establishment of Advaita Asramam (1913), Sree Narayana Gurudev requested some devotees (who were advocates) to prepare a by-law for its working. But they could not do it. Then saying, 'Why not I', Gurudev wrote these verses as the by-law.

Gurudev had a desire to constitute an organization of his disciples to propagate, the ideas of Advaita Vedanta to the world, based on his line of thinking. This was why Sree Narayana Gurudev established the Sree Narayana Dharma Sangham. The different stages of life were insisted as celibacy (Brahmacharya), family man (Garhasthyam), renouncement of worldly pleasures, or the life of meditation (Vanaprastham) and renunciation of all worldly relations or ascetism (*Sanyasam*). Those who belong to Sree Narayana Dharma Sangham were a group of monks who have adopted ascetism. These verses are intended for them, in particular.

(Original text in Sanskrit)

Āśṛamē fsmin guru kaści
Dwidwān munirudāradhī
Samadṛuṣti sāntagambhī
Rāśayō vijitēndṛiya

Parōpakāri syāddīna-
Dayālu satyavāk paṭu
Sadācārarata śīghṛa-
kaṛtavyakṛudatandṛita

Adhiṣṭāyāsya nēṭṛutwam
kuryātkāncit sabhām śubhām
Asyāmāyānti yē tē syu
Saṛvē sōdarabudhaya.

Yadwadatṛaiva tadwaca
Stṛīṇām pumsām pṛuthak pṛuthak
Vidyālayā diśi diśi
Kṛiyantāmāśṛamā sabhā

Ēkaikasyāmāsu nētā
Caikaika syādwicakṣaṇa
Saṛvābhiranubandō fdwai
Tāśṛamasyābhiranwaham.

Meaning and commentary

Verse 1

In the hermitage (Ashram) there should be a preceptor, with
Knowledge of real truth, who abandoned all selfish thoughts,
A universal benefactor with equanimity with a noble and
Peaceful heart, one who has conquered the sensual feelings.

To lead the Dharma Sangham, there should be a guru (master). The first verse explains the quality and qualifications of the chief of the ashram. This verse gives the essential qualities and qualifications required, in general, to be a monk in the ashram.

Basically, they are all the mentioned qualities of a real seeker of Truth. He should be one who knows about the absolute reality, should be one with knowledge and devoid of all self-interests. The guru should be a benefactor to the society and should behave with equanimity; at the same time, one with a peaceful mind, a noble heart and who has subdued all sensual feelings. He should forsake all his self-interest; he should be one who does not become emotional and show hatred. He should see things without dualities. And he should have overcome all worldly pleasures.

The qualifications required by Gurudev indicate the greatness of the position of the guru of the ashram.

Verse 2

That preceptor should be one who is alert in helping others
Considerate to the grief-stricken, one who always keeps
Honesty, and skilful, virtuous and who carries out tasks
With high speed, also one who has forsaken all laziness.

The guru should be always vigilant and do things beneficial to others. He should be compassionate to the suffering, should be honest, smart, virtuous and one who carries out his responsibilities vigorously. He should be devoid of all laziness.

This verse gives the instruction to the guru as to how he has to execute the authority as the master of the ashram.

The guru should execute all his duties as a person of nobility. He should be a benefactor to the public. He should be merciful and virtuous, should keep strict morality and be very smart in carrying out his responsibilities, he should not be lazy.

Verse 3

Remaining in the leadership, the preceptor should constitute
An organization that works for the well-being of
The people whoever are joining this organization,
All of them should keep brotherhood among them.

Being in the leadership of this ashram, the guru should organize organizations that deliver well-being to the world. Whoever is joining this organization as members, they should keep brotherhood mutually.

The differentiation by caste, religion, creed, poverty, wealth, etc. is only creations of vested interests. Such evils will obstruct the way to reach reality. Hence it should be removed. The ashram should keep the spirit of the writing on the board at Aruvippuram temple. '*This is the model institution where everyone lives in brotherhood without any barrier of differentiation of caste or religion.*'

Verse 4

In the same way, as done in headquarters
At every place, separate educational institutions,
Hermitages and organizations should
Be arranged for men and women.

How things are done at the headquarters of the organization, in the same manner, separate schools, ashrams and organizations should be constituted for men and women at every place.

Verse 5

In every one of the organizations, there should
Be a scholarly leader, attached
To all these organizations there should
Always be a branch of Advaitasramam.

In each of these bodies thus constituted, there should be a leader attached to all these bodies, and there should always be a branch of Advaita Asramam.

15

SIVASATAKAM

'Sivasatakam' is a literary work of 100 verses which enables the devotee to perform the prayer to the favourite deity Lord Shiva with more devotion and concentration. All the 100 verses are prayer songs. It was written in 1888 while Gurudev was staying at Aruvippuram after the consecration of the idol (a shapeless stone showing it as a symbol of unattributed Brahman)of Shiva. There is another version about the place at which it was written. It says, 'Gurudev himself told while discussing the content of verse 24 with one of his disciples Swami Bhaskarananda (formerly Maravoor Bhaskaran Nair) that he wrote those poems while he was in Marutwamala doing penance and it was meant for the benefit of the people.'

Sree Narayana Gurudev in all his literary works and consecrations took Lord Shiva as the symbol of Brahman. In a close analysis of the nature of the idols he consecrated and the verses he wrote, one can find that Gurudev took Shiva, Brahman and the universe as synonyms of the same word Brahman.

Most of the advaities take Shiva as their favourite deity. Like Adi Sankara, Gurudev also took Lord Shiva as the symbol of Brahman. But in symbolic representation of Brahman, he maintained the differentiation of idols. At Aruvippuram, the idol represents Nirguna Brahman. In this present work, Sivasatakam, Lord Shiva is in the attributed state (Saguna Brahman). Other examples are Shiva at Kolatukara temple, Aramanoor temple, etc.

These verses reflect the feelings or sentiments of his mind. From the contents of the poem, it seems all the verses are aimed at making the reader or the devotee attain knowledge, hatred towards worldly things and salvation. Even at a young age, Gurudev attained enlightenment, and these verses were written after his attainment of enlightenment. But it should not be considered as containing only his mental feelings. The depth of this prayer song is so great that one who reads this carefully can get the door opened to the life of a sannyasin.

(Original text in Malayalam)

Aẓakoṭubhāratayuddhamadriyinmēl
Muẓuceviyanmuṛikombukoṇṭumunnam
Eẓutiniṛaceliyōṛkkinaṅṅi nilkkum
Muẓumutalākiya mūṛti kātukolka!

Arumaṛanālumorikkalōtimunnam
Karimukilvaṛnnanu pankuceytunalki
Paramatuvalluvaṛnāvilum moẓiñña
Pparimalabhārati kātukolka nityam!

kanakamayil mukalēṛi vēlumēnti-
Kkanivoṭu kaṇṇiṇa kaṇkaṇam niṛaññu
Janimaranacuṭukāṭilāṭi veṇṇī-
Ṛanitirumēni tuṇaykkaṇam sadāmē.

Sanakasanandasanatkumārarmunpām
Munijanamoṭupadēsamōtimunnam
Kanivoṭutekkumukham thiriññukallāl-
Tanalilirunnorumūrti kāttukolka!

Siva!siva! nintirunāmamōṛtukaṇṭā-
Leviṭeyumonnumitinnu tulyamilla
Iva palatullilaṛiññirunnamī ñā-
Niviṭeyivannamalaññiṭunnu kaṣṭam!

Haribhagavānaravindasūnuvum nin-
Tiruvilayāṭalaṟiññatillayonnum;
Hara hara pinneyitāraṟiññiṭunnū
Karalilirunnu kaḷiciṭunna kōlam?

Ceṟupiṟa ceñciṭayinkalāṟumēṟum
Tiṟamiyalum phanimālayum tripundra-

Kuṟikalumammadanan dahica kaṇṇum
Purikavumenikku kāṇaṇam tē.

Dinamaṇitinkalaṇiñña kaṇṇu raṇṭum
Maṇimayakuṇṭalakaṟṇayugmavum tē,
Kanakatilakkusumam kuniñukūppi-
Dinamanusēvakal ceytiṭunnamūkkum.

Paẓavinayokkeyaṟutiṭunna toṇṭi-
Ppaẓamoṭupōriletiṟtiṭunna cuṇṭum
Kaẓukiyeṭutoru muttoṭotta pallum
Muẓumatipōle kaviltaṭaṅṅaḷum tē.

Amṟutoẓukumtiramālapōle taḷḷum
Timṟutayutatiruvākkumen cevikku
Kumaṟiyeriññukumiññeẓum manatī-
kkamṟutucoriññatupōleyuḷḷanōkkum

Kuvalayamokke viḷaṅṅiṭunna puttan
Paviẓamalakkumuḷaceẓum nilāvum
taẓuvinaveṇmaṇitārakaṅṅaḷum ni-
nnoẓivaṟe rakṣakal ceyyuvān toẓunnēn.

Aravavumellumiṭakkiṭakkaṇiññum
Karimukil kaṇṭu kuniññiṭum kaẓuttum
Varadamabhītikurangasūlapāṇi-
Tirumalaṟnālumaṇiññu kāṇaṇam tē.

Uragalasatkṛitamālamāla caṛti-
Pparilasitōrasibhūri bhūti pūsi,
Parimaḷamuṇṭu muraṇṭiṭunna vaṇṭin-
Nirakaḷoṭum tirumēniyennu kāṇām?

Oẓukiṭumambaragangatante nīril
Cuẓiyoṭutulyamudiceẓunna nābhi-

Kuẓiyileẓunna kaḷindakanyamēlō-
Ṭṭoẓukiṭumennakaṇakku rōmarāji.

Tuṭiyiṇatannilurica vāraṇatōl
Paṭayuṭayāṭayuṭutatinpuṛat
Paṭamoru kayyileṭutu Vālumāyi-
Kkadiyil muṛukkiya kāñciyennu kāṇām?

Kariyurikettiyuṭuttanantakaca-
Puramatu pūttiyalankaricu pāmpum
Parimaḷabhūti potiññu pūsiyanti-
Tiruviḷayāṭalitennu kāṇumi ñān?

Malaraṭi raṇṭilumitta pūñcilanka-
Kkulakal korutu kaḷiciṭunnanēram
Kalakalennu kiluṅṅiṭum cilambi-
Nnoli ceviraṇṭilumennu kēḷkkumī ñān?

Muṭinaṭuvādimuṭiññu mūnnumonnāy
Vaṭivoṭuninnu viḷaṅiṭum viḷakkin
Cuṭaroḷi cuttu tuṭacu sōkamākum
Kaṭalatukoṇṭu kaṭanniṭunnu kūlam

Kuvalayanāyakanaṛkkanagnihōtā-
Vavanituṭaṅṅiya bhūtiyañcuminnī
Tava maṛimāyāyamitāṛkkaṛiññiṭāvū
Kavijanakalpitakāvyamennapōle!

Matikala cūṭiya ponkuṭam matikku-
Ḷḷatimṛitukōmaḷanāṭakam naṭippān
Kotiperukunnatukondu kandatellā-
Muditamitokkeyumaṅṅucerumallō!

Bhagavatiyamma pakutu pāti vāṅṅi-
Ppakuti mukundanu naḷki munnamē nī,
Bhagavati nintirumēnitannilinnō-
Ragatiyirippatināgrahicīṭunnu.

Paśupati pāśamoẓicu pāhimāmō-
Raśubhamenikkaṇayātetakkavaṇṇam
Piśitamaśicu paruta piṇṭamō ñā-
Naśuciyitennakatārilōṛtiṭāttu?

Atisaranam vami tanne vannitinnā–
Ḷatiparidāvanaceytatokkeyum nin-
Matiyilaṛiññu maṛannu pinneyum ñān
Gatiyaṛiyāte valaññiṭunnu kaṣtam!

Malayatiluṇṭu marunnu mūnnu pāmpum
Pūliyumatinnirupāṭumuṇṭukāval
Pulayaneṭutu bhujicu pātiyinnum
Vilasati nīyumeṭutukoḷka neñcē!

Dharaṇiyiliṅṅane vāẓuvānasahyam
Maraṇavumilla namukku pārtukaṇṭāl
Taruṇamitennu dharicu tāpamellām
Smarahara tīṛteẓunnallukente munpil.

Vayaṛupatappatinuṇṭu kaṇṭatellām
Kayaṛi maṛiññu mariciṭunnatinmun
Daya tirumēni manassilōṛtu bhakti-
Kkayaṛukoṭutukarēṭṭaṇam manam mē.

Arulvaṭivāyorupōl niṛaññunilkkum
Paramasivan bhagavānaṛiññu saṛvam
Suranaditinkalaniñña daivamē! Nin
Tiruvaṭi nityamanugrahiciṭēṇam.

Muẓumatimūṭu turannu muteṭuta-
Kkuẓiyilaṭaca kurangamuṇṭu kayyil
Taẓaleriyum poẓutūṛi mūlamoḷam
Puẓayoẓukunnatu vāẓka bhūvilennum.

Janimṛitirōgamaṛuppatinnu sanjī-
Vani paramēswaranāmamenniyilla,
Punaratumokkemaṛannu, pūtukāykkum
Punakritikoṇṭu niṛaññulōkamellām.

Naraharimūrti namiciṭunna neṭṭi-
Tirumiẓitannilerica māraninnum
Varuvatinentoru kāraṇam porichī-
Derimiẓitannilitonnukūṭeyinnum.

Paṛavakal patumaṛutupaṭṭinilkkum
Kuṛikaḷoẓicu karutaṭakkiyāṭum
Ceṛumaṇicennu ceṛutu kāḷanāgam
Neṛukayilākkiyoḷiciṭunnu nityam

Siva!siva! tatwamoẓiññu saktiyum ni-
Nnavadhi paṛaññoẓiyāte nādavum nin
Savanamatinnu samitatākki hōmi-
Ppavanivanennaruḷīṭukappanē! Nī.

Ceṛumayirtōlupotiññu catupōvān
Varavumeṭutu valattuvāyuvinmēl
Carukucuẓannu paṛanniṭunnavaṇṇam
Tiriyumatiṅṅuvarāte tīyiṭēnam.

Karumana ceytukaḷicu kaḷḷamellām
Karaḷilamaṟtiyoralpanekkuṟic
Karuṇayirutiyanugrahiciṭēṇam
Karaperukikkaviyum samudramē! nī

Toẓilukaḷañcumoẓiññutōnninilkkum
Muẓumatiyāẓikaṭaññeṭutu munnam
Oẓukivarunnamṟutuṇṭumāṇṭupōkā-
Toẓuviloṭukkamudikkumaṟkkabimbam

Oruvarumilla namukku nīyoẓiññi-
Ṅṅorutuṇa tāndavamūrti pāṟtalatil
Smarahara! Sāmba! Sadāpi nī teḷiññi-
Ṅṅoru kṛipanalkukilentuvēṇṭu pinnē?

Umayoṭukūṭiyaṭutuvannuvēgam
Mama matimōhamaṟutu meykoṭut
Yamanuṭekayyilakappeṭāteyennum
Samanila tannu taḷaṟca tīrtiṭēṇam

Calamiẓimāruṭe cañcu kaṇṭu nilkkum
Nila niṭilatirunōkku vacaṟut
Pala pala līla tuṭaṟnniṭāte pāli-
Calivoṭu nin padapankajam tarēṇam.

Kaṭiyiṭayinkaloḷicirunnu kūṭum
Poṭiyiluruṇṭu viraṇṭu pōkkaṭippān
Aṭiyanu sangativannidatiruti-
Ppaṭiyaruḷīṭuka pāṟvatīsa! Poṟṟī!

Yamanoṭumallupiṭippatinnu nītā-
Nimayaḷavum piriyātirunnukolka;
Sumaśarasāyakasankadam sahippān
Nimiṣavumenneyayakkolā mahēsā!

Sukhavumorikkalumilla dukhamallā-
Tihaparalōkavumilla tellupōlum;
Sakalamtiṅane śastra sammatam ñān
Pakaliravonnumaṟiññatilla pōṟṟī!

Oru kuri nintirumēni vannu munnil-
Tirumukhamonnu tiricu nōkkiyennil
Perukina sankaṭavankaṭal kaṭati-
Taruvatinennu taram varum dayālō!

Avaniyilañcuruvappil nālumagni-
Kkivayorumūnnoru raṇṭu kāṟṟil vānil
Tava vaṭivonnu taẓaceẓunnu kāṇmā-
Neviṭeyumuṇṭu niṟaññu ninniṭunnu.

Malamakaḷuṇṭorupāṭu māṟiṭate
Mulakaḷulaññamṛutūṟi mōdamākum
Malamukaḷīnnoẓukum puẓayāẓiyen
Talavaẓiyennoẓukunnitu śankarā!

Bhasitamaṇiññupalunkoṭotuninnam-
Bhasi talayil tiramāla māla cūṭi
Śwasitamaśikkumalamkṛutīkalāpi-
Casi tirumēniyiraṅavēnamennil.

Ahamorudōṣamorutaroduceyvā-
Nakamalarinkalaṟiññiṭātavaṇṇam
Sakalamoẓicutarēṇamennumē ñān
Bhagavatanugrahapātramāy varēṇam.

Purahara, pūṟvamitentu ñān piẓaci-
Paravaśabhāvamoẓiññiṭāyvatinnu
Puramericeytatupōle janmajanmā-
Ntaravinayokkeyerikkaṇam kṣaṇam mē.

Sumaśaravēla turatiyōtti nīta-
Namaraṇamenmanatārilennumennil
Kumatikulam kolayānapōlekuti-
Timiranirakku timiṟtiṭātirippān.

Cuvayiloḷiyūṟaloẓiññu śītaraśmi-
Kkavamaticeyvatinulla ninkaṭākṣam
Bhavamriti mūṭupaṟiññu pōkumāṟi-
Ṅṅivanutarena, matinnu vandhanam tē.

Karaṇavumaṅṅukuẓaññukaṇṇuraṇṭum
Cerukiyiruṇṭu camaññu jīvanāśam
Varumaḷavennumaṟiññukoḷḷuvānum
Hara! Hara! Nintirunamamuḷḷil vēṇam.

Jaya jaya candrakalādhara! Daivamē!
Jaya jaya janmavināśana! śankara!
Jaya jaya śailanivāsa! Satām patē!
Jaya jaya pālaya māmakhilēśwara!

Jaya jitakāma! Janardhanasēvita!
Jaya siva! śankara! śarva! Sanātana!
Jaya jaya mārakaḷēbarakōmaḷa!
Jaya jaya sāmba! Sadāśiva! Pāhi mām

Kaẓaliṇakātukiṭannu viḷikkume-
Nnaẓalaviṭunnaṟiyāteyirikkayō?
Piẓapalatuṇṭivanennu ninakkayō?
Kuẓiyilirunnu karēruvatennu ñān?

Maẓamukil vaṟnnanumakṣi paṟicu nin-
Kaẓaliṇatannilorarcana ceytupōl
Kaẓi varumōyitinnaṭiyannu nin-
Miẓimuna nalkiyanugrahamēkaṇē!

Ozikazivonnu paraññoziyāte ni-
Nnazalatilitturukum mazukennapōl
Kazalinayinkalatannuvatinnu nī
Vaziyarulītuka vāmadēva,!pōrrī

Malamukalīnnuvarunnoru pārapōl
Mulakutimāriya nāl mutal mānasam
Alarśarasāyakamallupiticu nin-
Malaratiyum jagadīsa! Marannu ñān.

Kulagiripōleyuraciḷakāteyi-
Kkalimalamuḷḷilirunnu marakkayāl
Balavumenikku kuraññucamaññu ni-
Rmmalanilayennu tarunnatiyannu nī?

Kulavumakannu kudumbavumanane
Malayilirunnu mahēśwarasēvanam
Kalayatu kālamanēkabhayam bhavān
Talayil vidhicatu sammatamāy varum.

Vakayariyāte valaññitumenne nī
Bhagavatiyōtorumicezunaḷḷiva-
Nnakamurukumpati nōkkitukonnu mā-
Maghamorunēramatutuvarātini

Aruvayartannodu kūtiyōtiyāti-
Tirivatinitirinēravum ninappan
Taramanayāteyurukkiyenmanam ni-
Ntiruvatiyōtorumicu cērtitēnam.

Oru piti tanne namukku ninakkili-
Tiruvatitannilitenni marratellām
Karaḷilirunnu kaḷaññakhilam nira-
ññiriyiriyennaruḷunnariveppozum.

Karamatiluṇṭu karutumaṭakki ni-
Nnarikilirunnu kaḷippatinennumē
Varamaruḷunnatu vāridhiyennapōl
Karuṇa niṟaññu kaviññoru daivamē!

Puramorumūnumerica purātanan
Hariharamūrti jayikkaṇameppoẓum
Purijaṭa tanniloḷicukaḷiciṭum
Suranadhi tūkumorīśwara! Pahi mām.

Paramoru tunpamenikku bhavānoẓi-
ññoruvarumilla digambara! Ninpadam
Taraṇamenikkatukoṇṭaghamokkeyum
Taraṇamahankaravāṇi bhavārṇṇavam.

Miẓikaśil ninnoẓukunnamṛutatira-
Ppoẓikaḷil vīṇoẓukum paramāẓiyil
Cuẓikaḷil ninnu cuẓannu nin-
Kaẓalkaḷilvannaṇayunnatumennu ñān?

Maẓapoẓiyunnatupōl miẓiyinkal ni-
Nnoẓukiyolicurukitiruvuḷḷavum
Paẓayoru bhaktajanam bhavasāgara-
Kkuẓiyatininnu kaṭnnu kaśmalan ñān.

Vaẓiyilirunnu varunna bādhayellā-
Moẓiyaṇamennoru nēramenkilum mē
Miẓikaḷil ninnamṛitūṟiyaṟiññu nin-
Kaẓaliṇakaṇṭu kaḷippatināgraham

Piẓa palatuḷḷilirunnu palappoẓum
Cuẓalvatukoṇṭu śivāya namōstutē
Caẓivarumennu ninacurukunnu ñā-
Naẓalatiliṭṭaliyunnoru veṇṇapōl

Mizimuna koṇṭu mayakki nābhiyākum
Kuziyilurutti maṛippatinoruṅṅi
Kiziyumeṭutuvarunna mankamāṛtan
Vazikaḷiliṭṭu valakkolā mahēśā!

Talamuṭi kōti muṭiññu takkayiṭṭa-
Kkolamadayānakuluṅṅivannu kombum
Talayumuyarti viyatil nōkki nilkkum
Mulakaḷumenne valakkolā mahēśā!

Kuruvukal pōle kurutu mārviṭatil
Karaḷupaṛippatiniṅṅu kacakeṭṭi
Taramatu nōkkivarunna tīvinakki-
Nnorukuṛipōlumayakkolā mahēśā!

Kaṭalu coriññukaḷaññu kuppakuti-
Taṭamatilittu niṛacu kummi nāṛi-
Taṭamulayēntivarunna kaivalappen-
Kodiyaṭipāṛtu naṭatolā mahēśā!

kurutiniṛaññucoriññu cīyolikkum
Narakanaṭukkaṭalil bhramiyāte, nin
Caritarasāmritamennuṭe mānasē
Corivatininnu cuḷicu mizikkaṇam

Śaranamenikku bhavacaranāmbujam
Nirupamanityanirāmayamūṛtiyē!
Nirayanirakkoru nēravumenne nī
Tiriyuvatinnorunāḷumayakkolā.

Paramapāvana! Pāhi purārayē
Duritanāśana! Dhūṛjjaṭayē nama
Caraṇasārasayugmanirīkṣaṇam
Varaṇatennu valāntakavandhita!

Sarasijāyatalōcana! Sādaram
Smaraniṣūdana!māmava nī patē!
Karuṇa ninmanatāriludikkaṇam
Giriśa! Mayyanuvāsarameppoẓum.

Putiyapūvu paṟicu bhavāne ñān
Matiyilōṟtoru nēravumenkilum
Gativarum paṭi pūjakalceytati-
Llatinuṭē piẓayoyitu daivamē!

Pativatāyiyorikkalumenmanam
Kutiyaṭaṅṅiyirikkayumillayē!
Matiyuṟañña jaṭakkaṇiyunna nī-
Ratiraẓiññoẓukīṭina mēniyē!

Vidhivaracatu māṟivarān paṇi
Pratividhikkumakaṭṭarutayat
Iti paṟanjuvarunnu mahājanam
Matiyilonnadiyannaṟiyāvatō?

Stutipaṟaññiṭumenkilanāratam
Muditarākumaśēṣajanaṅṅaḷum
Atuminikkarutēṇṭatilninneẓum
Putayalum bata! Vēṇṭa dayānidhē!

Atiroẓiññu kaviññoẓukunna ni-
Nnatirasakkruṇatiramālayil
Gativarum paṭimuṅṅiyeẓunnu ni-
lpatinu nīyarulēṇamanugraham.

Kumidinitanniludicu kāluvīsi-
Ssumasarasārati sōmaninnum
Kimapi karaṅal kuṟanju kālumūni-
Tamasi layicu tapassu ceytidunnu.

Kalamuzhuvan tikayum pozhutāy varum
Vilayamitennakatāril ninakkayō!
Alarsaramūlavirōdhiyatāya nin-
Talayilirunnu tapikkarutinniyum.

Alyorukōdiyilanju varunnatum
Talayilaninju tazhacu sadāypozhum
Nilayilakāte niṛanju cidambara-
Stalamatileppozhumullavanē! nama

Malamukalēṛi vadhicu mrigaṅaltan-
Tolikaluricu tarunnatininnivan
Alamalamennu nincezhunalliyāl
Pala phalitaṅalpaṛanju cirikkumō?

Nilayanamēṛi njelinjirunnivannam
Talayanapōle tadicu tīṭṭi tinnu
Tulayanamennu puraiva bhavānumen
Talayil varacatitentoru sankadam!

Kalipuruṣan kaduvāpidippatinnāy
Malayilirunnuvarunna vāṛupōle
Kaliyugaminnitileṅumundukālum
Talayumaṛutu karastamākkuvānāy.

Malarmanamennakanakkumūnnulōka-
Tilumorupōle parannu tingivīsi
Kalasajalapratibimbanabhassupōl
Palatilumokke niṛanjarulē! Jaya!

Malajalamuṇṭorupāṭu niṛañňu mu-
Mmalamatilmuṅimuḷacuḷavākuvān
Viḷanilamaṅňu vitacu paẓutaṛu-
Tulakarbhujicalayunnu sankaṭam.

Palitajarāmaranaṅal palappoẓum
Puliyatupōle varunnu piṭikkuvān
Polivitinennuvarum bhagavānude
Kaḷiyivayokkeyanādiyatallayō!

Cila samayam śivasēva muẓukkayā-
Liḷakarutateyirunnaliyum manam
Palapoẓutum bhagavānuṭe māyayil
palakuṛiyiṅṅanetanneyirikkayō

Apajayamonnumenikkanayātini-
Tapasi nirantaramenmalamokkeyum
Sapadi dahicu sukham taruvānumen-
Japakusumatirumēni jayikkanam

Avamaticeytu taẓacakāṭu tannil
Bhavamritivitumulacu mūdumūnni
Bhuvanamatinkalirunnu mannutinnum
Śavameri tinnuvatō narikkorūṇō!

Janakaanumammayumātmasakhipriya-
Janavumaṭutayalvāsikalum vinā
Jananamedutu piriññiṭumeppoẓum
Taniyeyirippatinē taramāy varū.

Aṇayilirunnaruḷīṭumanugṛaham
Dinamaṇi cūṭiya tamburānitonnum
Aṇuvaḷavum piriyāteyirikkumen-
Maṇikal namukkuvarum piṇitīrtiṭum.

Piṇiyinikkaṇayāteyinitiru-
Ppaṇiviṭakkoru bhaktiyuṛakkaṇam
Taṇalilirunnaruḷunnatu ceñciṭa-
Kkaṇiyumambaragangayuṭe tira.

Aṇimuṭikkaṇiyum tiramālayil
Taṇiyumenvyasanaṅṅalatokkeyum
Paṇiyaṟuppatineppoẓumatiru-
Kkaṇikal kāttuka kāmavināśana!

Paniyumaphanimāla piricucēr-
Taṇiyumaciṭayāṭivarunna ni
Nnaṇimukhāmbujamakṣikalkoṇṭini-
Kkaniyaṇam karuṇākalaśambudhē!

Amaravāhiniponni varum tira-
Yikkamaramennakaṇakku paṭaṅṅaḷum
Samarasatil viricaravaṅṅaḷō-
Ṭamarumaciṭayāṭiyaṭukkaṇam.

Kuḷiṛmatikoṇṭukaḷiṛtu lōkamellā-
Moḷitiraḷunnoru vennilāvu poṅṅi
Teḷuteḷevīśiviḷaṅṅi dēvalōka-
Kkuḷamatilāmbal viriññukāṇaṇam mē.

Meaning and commentary

Verse 1

One who wrote the full story of Mahabharat War
Sitting on the great mountain with a big ear and
Broken tusk blesses the truth-seeking devotees
Oh! The manifested form of Brahman! Save us.

When Vyasa dictated the epic Mahabharata, the God Ganapathi, one with an extraordinarily big ear to hear properly and with his already broken piece of tusk, wrote the entire story sitting on the mountain. Oh! Lord! Ganapathi none other than the manifested form of Brahman himself! Bless us!

There is a story behind the composition of the great epic Mahabharata. When Vyasa thought of composing Mahabharata, which is considered to be the fifth Veda in Puranic literature, because of its vastness, he sought the assistance of someone who can write at once what he dictates. In search of such a brilliant assistant, he approached Lord Brahmadev to get his advice. Brahmadeva suggested the name of Lord Ganapathi. Then Vyasa approached Lord Ganapathi and sought his assistance. Ganapathi accepted to assist Vyasa but with the condition that Vyasa should go on dictating continuously without a break even for a moment. Vyasa accepted the condition but he, in turn, put a condition to Ganapathi that he should not write even a word without understanding the meaning of the word fully. Probably it is the reason why Sree Narayana Gurudev mentions an extraordinarily big ear to hear even the words spoken with the lowest voice and an extraordinarily big pen that is the broken piece of Ganapathi's tusk.

In the Indian tradition, after the prayer to Ganapathi, it is to Saraswathi, the Goddess of knowledge, the devotion is offered. In the second verse, Gurudev does it with the prayer to the Goddess of wisdom, Saraswathi.

Verse 2

Oh! One who shines with the fragrance of absolute
Who disclosed the four Vedas in the beginning, shared
With dark-complexioned Vyasa and then made spoken
Through the tongue of Thiruvalluvar, save me always!

One who shines with the fragrance of the Absolute who disclosed the four Vedas at the beginning shared with the dark-complexioned Krishna Dvaipayana Vyasa and then made them spoken through the tongue of Thiruvalluvar, the devotee be always saved by Goddess Saraswathi.

The words are the manifested form of Goddess Saraswathi. Vedas are supposed to be the first appearance. Saraswathi, the Goddess of letters or words, divided her manifested form into four, the Ṛig, Yajur, Sama and Atharva Vedas and imparted them to Vyasa. This is why Vyasa is believed to be the author who divided the Vedas into four, and hence he is known as Veda Vyasa. The very name of Vyasa is Krishna Dvaipayana, indicating his dark complexion. Thiruvalluvar, the great saint and poet comprising the spirit of Vedas, wrote the famous Tamil book *Tirukkural*. A part of this work has been translated into Malayalam by Sree Narayana Gurudev.

Verse 3

After chanting hymns in praise of Lord Ganapathi and Goddess Saraswathi, a devotee starts a prayer of Lord Subramanya who had been Gurudev's favourite deity during his early days.

> Mounted on the golden peacock, and holding lance
> With eyes full of tears of love and mercy
> Dancing in the graveyard of birth and death
> Smearing holy ashes, let the Lord protect me!

Lord Subramanya mounted on his golden vehicle the peacock and holding his weapon lance, pouring tears from both the eyes due to the unlimited care for the devotee dance in the burial ground like a physical universe of births and deaths as if smeared with ashes of burnt dead bodies, one who shines, let the Lord protect meal ways.

Verse 4

After offering prayer to the favourite deity as part of the introduction of this work, comes prayer to Lord Shiva in this verse.

> Giving advice to ascetics Sanaka, Sananda and
> Sanatkumara and other monks by mercifully
> Turning the head towards the south in the beginning
> Sitting in the shade of the stone platform, protect us.

Giving divine advice at the beginning of the world and looking southward to the four son-like persons (those dear to the heart and accepted as real sons, though not) Sanaka, Sananda, Sanatkumara and Sanatana of God Brahma deva and to the other ascetics resting on the stone platform, Oh! The famous Dakshinamurti (Shiva) protect me.

In the beginning, Lord Shiva was sitting in the shade of a banyan tree with his head looking to the south. It was in this position he uttered the divine advice or Brahmavidya to the saints. Hence Lord Shiva is known as Dakshinamurti. Dakshina means the south.

Verse 5

This verse reveals that continuous chanting of hymns of Shiva makes the path of activities pure and lead to the realization of Brahman.

Oh! The embodiment of auspiciousness!
Once thought nothing is equivalent to your
Holy name anywhere though knowing all these
I am wandering here like this; it is pitiable!

Oh! The embodiment of auspiciousness! Once thought about the divinity of your holy name, in the whole world there is not another, equivalent to your name. Though I am aware of many of your nobilities, because of ignorance, this devotee with worldly longings lives a miserable life in this world. What else can be said other than it is pitiable?

Verse 6

This verse says that the Lord Brahma and Lord Vishnu are not sufficiently aware of the doctrines of Lord Shiva that remain in the heart.

The god Vishnu and the one born in
Lotus flower is ignorant of any of your
Holy play, Oh! God Siva, who else know
In their hearts, about your role of play.

Oh! Lord who destroys all curses. Your play of magic is not clearly understood by any of the gods Vishnu and Brahmadeva born from the lotus navel of Vishnu. If so, who else can know about the magical play of Shiva, the embodiment of consciousness existing in the hearts of the entire creatures in the universe?

Brahman in the absolute form is unique. Being non-dual, there cannot be a second to observe his divine play and understand it, whether the observer is the Brahma or Vishnu who is only attributed forms (Saguna Brahman) of Brahman. The absolute (Nirguna) Brahman pervades everywhere and everything in the universe. Therefore, any kind of identification of it with respect to another is impossible. But a devotee grieves deeply in not knowing the secret of the divine play about which anybody else other than Brahman himself is unaware of.

Verse 7

From this verse to verse 17 the devotee prays to Lord Shiva to make available the entire form from foot to head of Shiva manifested to him.

The crescent moon wore on your head, Ganga
In your matted grey hair, chain of smart snakes
The smearing of holy ashes, the eye that burnt the Cupid
And the eyebrows that smash be manifested to me!

The crescent moon worn on your head, the river Ganga in your grey-tinted matted hair, the chain of smart snakes and the forehead smeared with ashes also with other marks, the eye at the centre of forehead that flashed the flame and burnt the god of love Cupid and the eyebrows that look ready to smash the world be made manifested to me.

Verse 8

The Sun and the Moon as the two eyes
The two ears wearing diamond rings
The golden sesame flower bow saluting
Your nose and worship every day be seen.

Both the Sun and the Moon as two eyes, both the ears wearing rings of the diamond, the golden flower of sesame bow in salutation your nose every day be seen.

Verse 9

Your lips excelling bryony fruit breaking
The consequence of actions in previous
Births the teeth like cleansed pearls
Your cheek like the full moon be seen.

Your lips that destroy the consequences of actions in previous births completely, and that exceed the beauty of bryony fruit, your teeth like the cleansed pearls that radiate beauty, and your chins that shine like a full moon be seen by me.

Verse 10

Like continuous waves in a stream of nectar
Your profound holy words in my ear
To the heart burning with roaring flame,
Your look the flow of nectar be obtained by me.

Your continued divine words like the flow of waves of nectar pour to my ear be experienced by me as if pouring nectar on the burning feeling of my heart which comes up roaring, bless me with your merciful look.

Verse 11

The lips shining as coral hills that charm the face
The smile resembling sprouting moonlight
The teeth spread and shine as stars be seen and
Protect me from the actions of previous births.

Your beautiful face resembling blossoming waterlily, the lips seen as coral hills smile as if moonlight sprouts from your lips, your teeth that shine as stars like white pearls spread from that smile be seen before me. I adore you to remove all my curses due to my worldly life in my previous births. When the moon rises the water lily blossoms like that lotus blossoms when Sun rises. The wording in the poem shows a natural aesthetic touch.

In this verse, Gurudev repeats the explanation of the beauty of the teeth and lips in a much-exaggerated manner as Gurudev thinks his explanation in the above verse is not enough. He takes the lotus flower as the symbol of the face, the chain of gems as the symbol of lips, moonlight as the symbol of the smile and the stars that shine as the symbol of teeth when smiling. This verse and its content reveal a talented poet in Sree Narayana Gurudev.

Verse 12

Wearing chains of serpents and skulls alternatively
Your blue neck to which the dark cloud bow
The body with four flower-like hands that
Bless, protect, carry deer and trident be seen.

Wearing garlands of snakes and skulls alternatively, and your blue neck makes dark cloud bow in respect, the four flower-like hands, one grants blessings, the other gives protection the third carries deer and the last holds the trident and your form be seen.

In this poem, Lord Shiva is presented as having four hands. One hand is to bless the devotees. The second one gives refuge; in the other two hands there are a deer and a trident respectively. The term *abheeti* means refuge, and there is an indication that Lord Shiva is one whose neck is blue.

Verse 13

Chest shining beautifully with chains of snakes
Adorned with garlands, smeared with holy ashes
Humming flock of beetles carrying the fragrance
Of flowers when can that holy deity be seen?

Your chest beautifully wearing the necklace of snakes and the flower garlands, smearing plenty of divine ash, when can I see your divine body surrounded by humming beetles?

Verse 14

The navel like the whirlpool in
The water from the heavenly Ganga
And as if Kalindi flows upwards
Is like your flock of body hair.

The white ash smeared on the belly pictured as the flow of Ganga and the hollow of the navel as the whirlpool, the flock of hair on the chest is compared to the river Kalindi flowing upward. The water in Kalindi is blue coloured, and the confluence of Ganga and Kalindi is famous.

Verse 15

Both thighs covered with peeled-off skin
Of elephant as armour and keep in

One hand the hood up leaving tail with
The snake girdle, when can I see them?

The peeled (when wandered as a hunter) off skin of the elephant covering both thighs worn as armour as if getting ready for war, above this armour keeping the hood of the snake in one hand and its tail tied around as your waist string leaving the tail extended, when can I see all these?

Verse 16

Dressed in skin peeled off from elephant
Fastened with loincloth of snakes and serpents
As ornaments, smeared with holy ash on
The body when can I see you dance at dusk?

You are dressed in the peeled-off skin of an elephant, fastened with the serpent as waist string, dressed up with snakes as ornaments and smeared with holy ash, when can I see your dance at dusk. Oh! Lord!

Verse 17

When you dance tied with trinkets of
Tiny bells on your flower-like legs then
The twisted trinkets make hilarious sound
When can I hear that sound in my ears?

When you dance with jingling anklets worn on both the flower-like legs, the twisted trinkets make a hilarious sound. When can this devotee hear that jingling sound in both the ears?

Thus, after the head-to-foot description of the favourite deity Shiva, through the devotion of the entire body, one can attain the state of pure consciousness and thereby cross over the sea of miseries. See the following verse.

Verse 18

After the above description of the entire body of the Lord from top to bottom, Gurudev makes it clear that his ultimate aim is to attain the state of Turiya and escape from all worldly sufferings.

The beginning middle and end went and
Became one and shone as the single supreme source
Evaporate boiling the sea of sins of earlier lives
Make the wise pass over the sea of miseries.

Losing their identity as the beginning, middle and end, the three became one and shine as the supreme source after boiling and evaporating the water of consequences of the actions in the previous births, the man of wisdom surpasses the sea of miseries.

The ultimate aim of life is to get the realization of absolute consciousness crossing the sea of worldly life. The absolute consciousness is the all-pervading eternal phenomenon that shines as the light of all lights. In the heat rays of the sun of knowledge, the sea of miseries will be evaporated, and the devotee can reach the other shore. The instincts towards worldly activities are put to an end. Only when all worldly longings are lost it becomes possible. For that, there should be the knowledge of non-duality, and that in turn requires the concentration of mind. It is for that purpose Sree Narayana Gurudev wants us to meditate Lord Shiva foot to head as the favourite deity and as the symbol of Brahman. It becomes evident through these lines that the different consecrations at various temples are meant to make the devotee understand that it is the gradual way of attaining realization of the Absolute Brahman, the state of Turiya. Turiya is the fourth state of mind beyond Jagrat, Swapna and Sushupti. Turiya is the state where the devotee gets the experience of Brahman. This concept is referred to in many of the works of Gurudev. Examples are verse 28, 'Atmopadesa Satakam' and verse 1, 'Adyaropa Darsanam', etc.

Verse 19

Moon, the lover of water lily, Sun, Fire, sacrifice
And Earth all such elements of yours is a great
Jugglery like great poets' imaginary creations
In their works, who can know this secret?

Moon the lover of waterlily, sun, fire and the priest who gives offerings of holy materials in the sacrificial fire while chanting, earth, etc. the five elements, all these are fabrications of imagination like the poets make their works through imagination.

All the verses in Sivasatakam are based on Gurudev's resolution that the Brahman, Lord Shiva and the universe are the same or synonyms of the same word. Many atheists make the remark that if you cannot show the Brahman visually, how can the logic of Brahman the Absolute sustain. The answers are: one, the Brahman is beyond the limits of logic; two, being unique—the only one—where there is no scope for a second, the observer being the second, how can the remarks of the atheists sustain? Vedanta says it is the Brahman—the Absolute that is reflected (*Vivartha*) as the eighth—or appears as the eighth—*Moorthi*. Moorthies (bodies) are the Sun, moon, sacrifice, earth, water, fire, air and space. We know nothing other than these eight in this visual universe. Gurudev takes the idol of Shiva as one with the above eight bodies and describes it with the great skill of a talented poet.

Verse 20

Beloved Shiva wearing the crescent moon
Strongly wish to act in a simple, beautiful drama
Brought all these worldly costumes to the scene
All these are surely suitable for the director of drama.

The beloved Shiva wearing the crescent moon on the head, since strongly wishes for acting in a simple and joyful drama, suitable for his wisdom. All these costumes—in the form of the universe are brought to the scene. All these are certainly suitable for the director of drama.

This poem marks the beginning of turning towards more philosophical descriptions.

Verse 21

The Goddess Ma took half of your body
You gave the other half to God Vishnu already
Oh, Mother! The bodyless Lord likes
To live resting his body on your holy body.

The Goddess Parvathi took half of your body as her share, and the other half of the body has been given to the God Vishnu by you earlier. Oh! Goddess Parvathi, the Lord who shared his body in two halves and became bodiless and one without any other means wishes to stick on to your divine body and live.

Verse 22

Let the master of Jeevas without putting me
To any distress ending all the worldly ties
Am I an obese eating flesh, save me
From the ugly thoughts coming to mind.

Let the Lord, the master of all living things, save me by not putting to any distress due to my worldly bindings. Am I a body become obese by eating flesh? You save me from evil thoughts, not coming to my mind.

Verse 23

I once burning like fire approached you
And lamented on all my excess lust

You took that in mind but forgot thereafter
Hence I suffer not knowing where to go.

Once burning like fire, I approached you and lamented on my excess sensual activities. You heard and understood it properly. After some time you forgot it, again because of that I am suffering very seriously without knowing where to go. It is pitiable!

The word *Atisaranam* means an excessive interest in lustful pleasures, and surrendering to it will result in making life a blank. The word *Vami* means fire. To abate it, the only remedy is prayer. When there is a break in the regular prayer, the flame will again be strengthened. Lust is like diarrhoea. Excess consumption of food will make this disease. When medicated, one gets relief for some time, but if the medication is not continued for the full course, it may attack again. Excess lust will lead to sufferings in life. It can be cured by constant prayer; once hindered, it repeats again. Gurudev, in the following lines, symbolically prescribes the herbal medicines available on the mountain for the complete cure of the disease due to excess lust.

Verse 24

Three herbal medicines are there on mountain
Snake and tiger stand guard on both sides there
The tribal man ate half of the herbs and you may
Take the other half that remains, Oh! Self.

There are the three medicines, namely, Sat, Chit and Ananda (being, mind and bliss) which are the components of attributed (Saguna) Brahman, and on both sides of these stand love and hatred due to worldly longings as guards like a tiger and a snake. Of the three medicines, one half was consumed by the tribal man or the great ascetic (*pulaya/pulava*) who is aware of the existence of Satchidananda in mind, and the other half was left. The word pulaya/pulava indicates a tribal man or a great ascetic or a man of great wisdom.

Here, mountain refers to the absolute consciousness and the three medicines, the components of attributed Brahman. The first half is said to be consumed by pulaya/pulava, tribal man, or the great ascetic.

But from the wording, it implies that the half that still remains is not half but full as described in Shanti mantra of Isavasyopanishad.

'Ohm pūrṇamada pūrṇamidam
Pūrṇāl pūrṇamudachyathe
Pūrṇasya pūrṇamādāya
Pūrṇameva vaśiṣhyathe.'(Sanskrit)

That (Brahman) is perfect/infinite
This (the manifested Universe) is perfect/infinite
This has sprung from that
When this (which was a part of that) is taken from that
The remainder is still perfect/infinite.

When we speak of Brahman, this is infinite, that is infinite from infinite sprouts infinite; if infinite is taken away from infinite, what remains is infinite.

Brahman, the invisible phenomenon, infinity, has a very novel property that is when infinity is added to infinity it makes only infinity; when infinity is subtracted from infinity, it again is infinity.

It is like this. Suppose there is an infinite number of rooms in a hotel occupied fully by an infinite number of persons. If one day, occupants from alternate rooms are vacated, then the people left in the hotel will be half of the infinity that is infinity itself, and those remaining in the hotel is half infinity which will still be infinite because half infinity is infinity itself.

Here, in the above verse, Gurudev brings in the vastness of Satchidananda, where Sat (being) is the experience of the pure entity, Chit (mind) is the pure awareness, and Ananda (bliss) is a property for which we cannot think of any boundary. An addition or subtraction in the size of being or the size of mind or the size of bliss is immeasurable, and the three are invisible. All these properties are infinite like the Nirguna Brahman. Hence, understand that the mentioning of an addition to or subtraction from the infinite absolute consciousness (the mountain mentioned in the poem); that is, ate one half and left the other half is only to prompt the devotee. Every devotee gets half of the medicine, leaving the remaining half (as full). Gurudev is well aware of it. In these lines, Gurudev's talent in bringing out the latest concept of physics and Vedanta is exemplary.

This verse brings to our notice the situation that existed in Marutwamala, the mountain well known in Puranic literature (Marutwan is Hanuman—Ramayana) for herbal medicines. It was where Gurudev was performing penance in Pillathatam cave. It was in this cave Gurudev attained enlightenment, in another sense, the Brahman in the form of Satchidananda manifested to him. At the entrance of the cave, there were a tiger and snake on both sides as guards at the time of Gurudev's penance. Their presence at the entrance of the cave is endorsed by many of the biographers and people who lived then. The medicines on the mountain refer to the enlightenment in the form of Satchidananda, and the scholarly ascetic pulaya/pulava (the ascetic) who ate one half mentioned symbolically in the poem refers to Gurudev himself. Many maharishis, including the great saint Agastya, did penance in the Pillathatam cave.

Verse 25

It is unbearable to live on earth like this
Once thought, we have no death too, taking
It as the opportunity one who burnt Cupid
End my grief and make your royal appearance.

It is miserable to live like this, burnt in worldly lecheries on earth. Once thought, there is no death for us. Oh! God who smashed the Cupid, understanding the present state of the devotee, take this as an opportunity to remove all my sufferings and make your royal appearance before me.

Verse 26

To satisfy the mind, there are visuals
Irregularly distributed, before death with
Mercy in your mind, Lord! Save my mind
Give me the rope of piety to climb up.

Enjoying the worldly temptations of mind and experiencing the worldly pleasures that are distributed irregularly before ending the life with an ego fall into the dilapidated well. Oh! Lord with mercy extends the coir of devotion! Save my mind disembarking me from this deep pit of worldly sufferings.

Verse 27

The auspicious God standing as the embodiment
Of grace equally pervading everywhere is
Aware of all, Lord! Who wears heavenly Ganga
And the crescent moon on the head! Bless me always.

Oh! Lord Shiva! The embodiment of mercy! Who fills equally the entire universe, one who knows everything. Oh! Lord! One who wears the divine river and crescent moon on the head, bless me every day.

Verse 28

Making the mind immersed in devotion discovering
The pearl of self-happiness the life kept in the heart is in
Your control, when the fire of grief burns flow of nectar
Prana from the brain to Sushumna be experienced on earth.

The life kept in the heart that realized self-happiness by concentrating the mind on meditation is by all means subject to your control. When the flame of grief picks up power, give the devotees in the world the opportunity to experience every day the flow of prana as the nectar of immortality begins from the top of the head down to *Sushumna*, the vital nerve at the bottom.

In Vedanta, the full moon is the symbol of mind. There is another version that moon is the mind of the Lord in his entirety (Virat). Penetration of the full moon means the mind is kept in deep meditation until the beginning point is reached, as it is at the bottom of mind the self-happiness exists. Here the pearl means happiness. It has another meaning as the diamond. Since the precious diamond is kept in safe custody underneath, only by digging sand the mind by a spade of wisdom, the treasure of self-happiness is possessed. *Kurangam* is the symbol of life. Kurangam is derived from 'running animal of the land'. Life is also the running part of the Lord on earth; the life (prana), especially the life of the devotee, is always under the Lord's control. It is well known that Lord Shiva keeps a deer in one of his hands. The life submitted to the Lord turns to the Lord for shelter whenever the fire of worldly life begins to burn it.

As the meditation begins to take strength, spreading of prana like the nectar of immortality starts from the head and makes the experience throughout the body. From then onwards the entire miseries are lost and become immersed in happiness. This is what Gurudev means by '*ūṛi mūlamōḷam puzhayozhiki*' in the third line.

Verse 29

To alleviate the disease of births and deaths
The only suitable medicine is the name of
Parameswara, people forgetting it again foster
Forests full of flowers and imaginations.

For complete destruction of the worldly life in the form of births and deaths, there is no medicine other than the divine name of Lord Shiva. But the entire world forgets the ultimate aim and the route of meditation, again and again, foster the growing forest full of flowers prompting imaginations of births and deaths.

The ultimate aim of life is to alleviate the disease (malafides) of worldly life. The flowers of the forest of worldly life are the prompting thoughts. Births and deaths are their fruits. While engaging in the day-to-day life, the prompting thoughts increase and produce more births and deaths. Therefore, while doing worldly activities, one should see that those promptings do not blossom. If not done so, this fostering forest will go on increasing in the form of more flowers and fruits.

Verse 30

The third eye in forehead saluted even by
Lord Narasimha that burnt Cupid why it
Comes back and makes me suffer, burn him
Again with your fire-spitting eye and save me.

What is the reason why the Cupid comes even now and makes the mind suffer from passionate feelings though you have burnt him to ashes with your fire shooting the third eye at the centre of your forehead that is being bowed due to fear even by Lord Narasimha Murti? There is nothing more difficult than conquering lust. One might overcome it.

Verse 31

This verse says that even if one wins over the influence of sense organs and realizes Kundalini prana, that will not be complete self-realization.

Killing bird-like senses five and avoiding
Their subjects containing the full strength
When you dance the dreadful serpent take
The tiny diamond and hide on the head every day.

The five senses of knowledge and the five organs of activities combine to form the features. Since they move rushing like birds, they are given the common name *parava* (birds); Gurudev in 'Atmopadesa Satakam' (Poem 8) explains the sense organs as birds that devour fruits such as light and so on. Sound, touch, etc. are senses of knowledge, and speak, give, take, etc., belong to the category of subjects of activity. Once one wins over the senses and mind becomes concentrated, the spreading of Kundalini prana starts. Kundalini by nature is like a serpent or string whirled up in Sushumna nerve. Kundalini yoga is a particular state of experience of mind while moving towards the attainment of self-realization.

Verse 32

This verse gives the reply to the question as to what is to be done once not satisfied, even with the experience of prana.

Auspicious Shiva! Reality, vibrations and sound
Incorporeal vanished; bless me to reach the state
That I am capable of sacrificing myself as firewood
In rituals to reach you, Lord! Do not say to postpone.

Oh! Lord! The embodiment of bliss! The awareness of reality lost, the vibrations of life force halted, sourceless sound vanished; bless me making me strong enough to do the holy sacrifice as firewood, Oh! Merciful Lord! Do not postpone it giving excuses.

It is with the introduction of the vibrations of life force that the absolute reality gets veiled. Prana and sourceless sound are two subtle forms of vibrations of the life force. When the mind of a yogi comes very close to the point of self-realization, he hears many attractive sounds. It is the sourceless sound when both vibrations of life force and the sound close the veil that hides the Absolute vanish, and the absolute reality becomes clear.

Verse 33

Here the devotee prays to give him the courage to burn the subtle body so that he can receive another body if this body is lost.

> Covered with skin full of tender hairs and fate
> To die leaning towards spirit on the right side
> Longing for pleasures like birds fly from
> Branch to branch burns it not to come again.

Like the birds covered with tiny hair-like feathers, with the natural habit of decay and perish, like the birds bend on to prana on the right side prompted by pleasures fly from one tree to another, allow me to burn the subtle body that wanders from one world to another in the fire of knowledge so that it is not repeated.

The only way to realize the absolute reality is to burn the subtle body in the fire. The subtle body is one with a mind full of sensual feelings. The burning of the subtle body means the removal of such emotions. So long as the subtle body remains, it will take corpulent bodies one after the other during births and deaths like flying birds. Skin cover refers to the corpulent body that decays and perishes. So long as the subtle body remains in the skin-covered decaying body, it will have to share the experience. The Upanishads say the wakeful state gives importance to the right side of the body.

Verse 34

In this verse, the devotee who happened to lead a life doing harm to others prays as a repenting poor simple man to bless him mercifully.

> Doing cruel deeds and involved in worldly
> Pleasures and fascinated on inert things

Believing them as real to me a mean fellow
Show mercy, save me; Oh! Overflowing ocean.

Oh! Lord! The ocean that crosses the shore and overflows! I, a silly fellow who did many wicked deeds and engaged in silly worldly pleasures misunderstanding virtual scenes as real, lived longing for them. Oh! Lord! Show mercy on me and save. Oh! Overflowing ocean.

Verse 35

The five mental states vanished and reached
The state of Brahman, earlier churning the unbroken
Ocean of wisdom drinking the flowing nectar
If went on, at the end of it Sun rises in the east.

The indivisible consciousness the ocean of milk (palazhi) when the five states of mental activity, namely, prana, *viparyaya*, *vikalpa*, *nidra* and *smriti*, subsided reached at the mental perception of Brahman getting seasoned through earlier training, even if the happiness in the flowing cold prana that spreads like ambrosia in the inside is experienced, without getting confused assuming it as real supreme reality once moved forward, at the end of the path to the fulfilment of Nirguna Brahman, the Sun, the absolute consciousness will arise.

Verse 36

I have nobody other than you on earth to
Help me, Oh! The killer of Cupid! Dancer deity
In a pleasant attitude accompanied by wife
If you show me mercy what else do I get?

Oh! Lord! Who burnt the Cupid and live with the wife! I have no one other than you in this world to help me. Lord! One who likes ecstatic dance! If you happily bestow mercy on me always, what else is there for me to achieve.

Verse 37

Come near quickly along with Uma perish
The fascination of my mind showing your figure
Without being trapped in the hands of Yama
Remove my tiredness and give me stability always.

Oh! Lord! Come near me along with Parvathi without delay and destroy the darkness of ignorance in me. Showing your original form, give me equanimity of a holistic view of God so that I am not put to grief by falling into the trap of death.

Verse 38

Break the stance of looking at lips of beauties with
Moving eyes by opening your eye that smashed Cupid
Don't make me continue in different plays in the world
Give me your lotus feet and bless me mercifully.

Oh! Lord! Break the state of standing looking lustfully at the lips of beautiful ladies by opening your eye on the forehead that burnt the Cupid to ashes. Give me your feet for adoration without making fun of me in many ways in this world.

Verse 39

Let me not hide in the loins and fall
In increasing sensual pleasures frightened
Causing death give me steps to reach you
Oh! Lord of Goddess Parvathi, the protector!

Without bringing about the condition of spoiling life by always engaging in erotic plays with women and bring up erotomania and thereby becoming spoilt. Oh! Husband of Parvathi! My saviour! Develop awareness of aim and concentration of mind in me.

Verse 40

Oh! Lord! To win over Yama in fight
You sit in protection on the inside of me
Let me not happen to get a single moment
To bear the pain of lust, Oh! Lord Shiva!

To win the struggle with death, Oh! Lord! You remain in my inside without leaving me even for a moment. Oh! Master of the universe! Save me from wandering with the infliction of passion, not even for a moment.

Only through continuous meditation of God, the fear of death can be removed. Here, the devotee prays to Lord Shiva not to leave him separated even for a moment because in his presence the devotee will not die as Shiva is killer of the killer. If one thinks that since in both this world and the other world, there are things of material pleasure, then why should one hesitate to enjoy them, remember that such pleasures will only lead to continuous miseries and are only illusions.

Verse 41

There is no happiness except miseries,
Not even a bit of this or the other world
All endorsed by science, I do not know
What is real and what is not, Oh! Lord.

In fact, I have experienced only grief and never any pleasure in this life. This world and the other world are not existent even a little. These things have been already determined in full by science. Oh!

My saviour! Being ignorant, I could not know so far what is true and what is untrue. The day is the symbol of truth, and night is that of ignorance. But I could never experience them clearly differentiated. Therefore, Oh! Lord, you are the only refuge.

Verse 42

Oh! Lord! When will I get the fortune
Of seeing your holy face turned towards
Me once and make me cross the rising
Great Ocean of grief, Oh! Merciful!

Oh! Merciful Lord! When will I get the fortune of getting your presence before me once, looking straight towards me turning your divine face glancing and take me to the other shore crossing this ocean of worldly miseries?

Verse 43

Elements in the earth are five, in water four
In fire they are three for air it is two
In space, only one your subtle sound
Found everywhere filling everything.

In the earth, there are five constituents, namely, sound, touch, shape, taste and smell. In water, there are four—sound, touch, shape and taste. In the fire, there are three—sound, touch and shape. In the air, there are only two—sound and touch. In space, there is only one which is your subtle sound 'Aum' (Pranava) that pervades everywhere.

The energy first appears in the form of sound, and its manifestation creates the feeling of space, and the sound spreads as energy in the entire space as all-pervading. This also indicates that space is not empty but with something (quintessence). Once space is the unattributed Brahman devoid of sound (primordial), the feeling of material space will be lost, and the absolute reality will become manifest. Gurudev gives a picture of the formation of various stages of matter.

This verse explains that one who viewed this seriously can experience the existence of the Absolute that spreads everywhere in the form of the sound 'Aum'.

Verse 44

On one side sits your inseparable companion Parvathi
The daughter of mountain, the nectar of joy trickles from
Her swaying breast flowing like a river from the mountain
Of happiness, when will it flow over my head, Oh! Shiva.

Oh! Lord on one side of you sits your inseparable companion the daughter of mountain (Parvathi). By the shaking of the breast of that mother trickle ambrosia and flows like the great river from the top of the hill of happiness. Oh! Lord! Sivasankara when will that river flow over my head?

The question of the devotee is as to when will the river of ambrosia that trickles from the breast of mother Parvathi from the mountain of happiness flow over his head.

This verse proves that even before attaining full salvation, the supreme power can pour the nectar of happiness through the flow of prana.

Verse 45

Smearing ash, wearing the chain of waves
Of crystal-like water and life-eating snakes
As ornaments on your holy form, the sword
To chop rioters, Lord! Show mercy on me.

The devotee prays again to see the manifested form of the Lord.

Smearing ashes on the body, wearing the chain of waves of Ganga, water that shines as crystals and decorated by killer snakes as ornaments on the body. Oh! One, who is the sword to cut the tree of worldly life, let your divine body shed words of blessings on this devotee.

Verse 46

As if not feeling to do any harm to
Anybody in mind, remove all my
Tendencies of passion and hatred forever
And is made subject to your blessings.

The devotee believes that the way to the realization of absolute truth is to tune the mind so that there is no hatred and ill will towards anybody and hence he prays for that.

Oh! Lord! Let the mind of this devotee be purified forever! Remove all affinities of love and hatred such that I do not think of doing any harm to anybody, and this devotee is made an object of your mercy.

Verse 47

Oh! Destroyer of cities, what wrong I did in
My earlier births that my worldly longings
Do not leave, destroy all consequences of my
Past life like you did smash the Tripuras.

Oh! Lord! Who destroyed the Tripuras! I, this devotee, do not know what sin I did in my earlier births so that I cannot escape completely from the worldly longings in this life. Like you burnt to ashes the Tripuras, burn all my misdeeds in earlier repeated births and liberate me.

The inherent tendencies of activities accumulated through repeated lives after births and deaths should be annihilated. To accomplish self-realization, it is highly essential. The devotee prays to the Lord to completely destroy them.

Fate is the effect of the collection of activities done during the past repeated lives. Self-realization is possible only when all such after-effects of deeds in the past lives are destroyed. The devotee prays to Lord Shiva who smashed the Tripuras to ashes, to smash all the after-effects of his evil deeds in the past.

Verse 48

In me, the multitude of evils congregated, like
Tuskers rake and accumulate not to make
My mind raked by ignorance, remove all
My lust, oh! Lord! Remain always in me.

The collective malice not to rake up and increase the darkness of ignorance in me, like the tuskers rake up and store sand, remove all lustful thoughts completely in me Oh! Lord! You always live in me.

The devotee again praises the Lord for making the experience of the presence of the Lord removing all lustful imaginations.

Once the Lord is settled in the heart of the devotee, he has only one thing to do—purify the heart of the devotee by removing all evil feelings. Even if the devotee's heart is not pure at the time of settling, the Lord himself will remove all such evils and keep the mind purified. The Lord alone is capable of doing this.

Verse 49

The red colour completely vanished, your
Merciful look excelling moonlight as if
Uprooting the world of births and deaths let fall
On me, for it, I worship you, Oh! Lord.

The red colour of the attribute of pleasure completely vanished and the look, full of attributes of nobility that excels the cool moonlight be shed upon this devotee in a manner as if the worldly life of births and deaths is uprooted. For that, Oh! Lord, I adore you.

The love of luxury is the basic cause of all evils. Once it is removed, the pure heart becomes filled with noble thoughts. To accomplish it, the devotee prays to remove the evils and to shed your blessing for noble thoughts.

The attribute of pleasure, lust, love and hatred is symbolized by red colour. This attribute leads to worldly longings; once this is removed comes the feeling of noble deeds, and that requires the Lord's merciful look at the heart. The devotee prays to the Lord to shed on him merciful look for removing the red of evil thoughts and bring in the light of noble thoughts.

Verse 50

The mind word and body tired, both eyes
Drawn back and sight lost at the brim
Of death to remember always the destroyer of evils!
Let your holy name be there in my mind.

When old age comes, the mind wears out and is exhausted; both eyes are drawn inward lose sight and stands at the brim of death, Oh! The hunter of all sins! Your name should be there inside the mind.

The devotee prays for his having remembrance of the Lord at the time of his death. Because it is at that moment, the mind feels the nature of future life. But to have the reminiscence of the Lord, one should keep the same throughout his early life. At these moments of departure, everything happens in a natural way. To bring the memory of God all of a sudden will not be easy. If one deeply reminisces on God at the time of death, even though he is going to another birth, it will lead him to the attainment of God.

Verse 51

Be victorious! Oh! God! The bearer of crescent!
Be victorious! Oh! Siva, the destroyer of births and deaths
Be victorious! One who lives on Kailas! Protector of nobles!
Be victorious, the supreme! Bless me protecting!

This and the following verse are prayer songs hailing the Lord to show the devotee's excitement.

Oh! Lord who wears crescent moon on the head! Be victorious! Oh! Sankara who ruins the grief of births and deaths! Be victorious! Oh! The saviour of nobles who reside at Kailas be victorious! Oh! The master of the universe! Who protects me be victorious!

Verse 52

Be victorious! One who won the Cupid! One worshipped by Vishnu!
Be victorious! Oh! Shiva! One in a fury and immortal
Be victorious! Handsome like Cupid!
Be victorious one with the Goddess! Siva! Protect me!

Oh! Lord who smashed Cupid! Adored even by Lord Vishnu, be victorious! Be victorious! The embodiment of bliss who blesses us, the deity in a fury, one who is eternal (never changing) be victorious! Be victorious! One who stays with the Goddess Parvathi Oh! The deity of auspiciousness! Be Victorious! Be victorious! Protect me.

Verse 53

Are you not seeing my grief desirous
Of seeing your feet praying sadly
Do you think I have many mistakes?
When I escape from this world of miseries?

Lord! Do you not know my grief in spite of my prayer lamenting to see your feet! Do you think this poor devotee has many misdeeds? Oh! Lord! When am I going to escape from this pond of worldly life?

In this poem, the devotee doubts as to why, 'In spite of my prayers to this extent, I wonder why you are delaying to bless me mercifully.'

Verse 54

Heard that once the black-complexioned
Lord Vishnu scooped out his eye and
Dedicated at your feet can this silly man
Do it, protect me giving your holy look.

Here the devotee doubts as to whether it is because his dedication is less than what is expected that the Lord does not seem to be happy.

I have heard that the rain cloud-coloured Lord Vishnu once plucked off one of his eyes and offered at your feet in adoration. Will it be possible to this devotee who is suffering from the bodily longings? Oh! Lord! Protect me shedding merciful look at me.

Once Lord Vishnu was performing dedication at the foot of Shiva with petals of lotus, at last, he found that there is a discrepancy of one petal. As compensation, he scooped out one of his own eyes and offered it at the foot of Lord Shiva.

Verse 55

Oh! Lord of loftiness! Protector! Without postponing
Saying objections like candle melts and vanish
Let me vanish in the fire of desire to see you
Show me the way to vanish melting at your feet.

The devotee feels that his sufferings will vanish only if Lord Shiva blesses him to obtain bliss.

Oh! Lord! Who shines as merciful Saviour! Without postponing on excuses to show me the way to dissolve in your feet and disappear like wax melt and disappear put me in the fire of my desire to see you.

It is the ego of the individual soul that hinders the opportunity to dissolve in the absolute reality and attain salvation. The devotee prays to make his ego vanish, melting in the fire of desire to see you as the candle melts in the fire. Oh! Lord! Do not postpone it on one or the other context. Lord! Show me the way to do it.

Verse 56

From the days of infancy like a rock
From the top of a mountain was under
Constant attack of the arrows of Cupid
I forgot your feet, Oh! Lord of the universe!

Again the devotee complains that the lust as big rubble stands as an obstruction.

From the time of my infancy, throughout my life so far like big rubble falling from the top of a steep mountain, my mind was subject to attack by the Cupid's arrow of lust. To show the severity of the attack of the feeling of lust, Gurudev compares it to the fall of hard rubble down the steep mountain valley.

Verse 57

Like the Kulagiri mountain, the filth of lust
Greed and hatred remain unchanged in heart
And hides the real self, hence my strength
Reduces, when will you give me purity?

Here the devotee asks the Lord as to when he gets the blessing to obtain purity.

Since the Atman, the embodiment of bliss is hidden by the evil spirits such as lust, anger and greed that resulted in frenzy entangled and precipitated in mind like the unchanging set of mountains. This devotee's strength seems to be reducing. Oh! Lord! Are you going to bless me giving sufficient purity required for experiencing the self?

Verse 58

Clan, likewise the family left and sitting
Alone in mountain praying Shivà
Whatever fear of time creates what you
Impose as coming; I am ready to accept.

The devotee now takes a firm decision that whatever may come of this, to do meditation sitting alone.

Staying in solitude on a mountain, I was continuing the worship of Lord Shiva, forgetting my clan (heritage) and my family. Whatever be the fear that it imposes on me let it do it. Whatever you have decided as my fate, Oh! Lord! I am prepared to experience it according to your will.

Gurudev, in this verse, explains the mental state of a lonely devotee. A lonely devotee always finds full refuge in the Lord. He never fears the running of time. Whatever be the consequence of his own deeds that may come as past activities, he does his work. Whatever be the result, he takes them as the gift of God.

Verse 59

Oh, Lord! Come along with the Goddess and
Look mercifully on me melting the mind
Of this devotee destroyed in differentiating
Between what is the real and what is unreal.

The devotee prays to shed mercy on him that no sins touch him.

Oh! Lord! Be kind enough to come in a solemn way near me along with Goddess Parvathi, this devotee who is afflicted by being unable to differentiate between which is true and which is untrue, bless me looking at me mercifully until my heart melts due to my devotion so that no sin touches me ever.

Verse 60

Lord! Keeps my mind not going after women
And wander with sensual thoughts and acts
Not for a moment, Oh! Lord, make my mind
Unite with your holy self with devotion.

The devotee prays to fill his mind with the devotion of the Lord, removing all sensual feelings such as lust.

Oh! Lord! My mind be dissolved in devotion and merged in you to become one with you so that not even for a moment desire to wander behind women sticking on to them and show lustful acts.

My mind be made united with yourself devotionally without letting me even a moment showing gestures of lustful acts going after women.

Verse 61

Once thought our only refuge is your
Holy self except that removing all other
Things and seeing the real truth filling
In and out remain peacefully, says wisdom.

The devotee believes from his worldly experience that life can be made blessed only by holding firmly on to the Lord.

Once thought about the general nature of prompting of this world, the only protection to us who wander in the worldly sufferings is the string of attachment to the Lord of the universe. The available knowledge about the universe instigates us to abandon all worldly imaginations from the mind and to see the absolute reality in full inside and outside and remain in peace.

The one who clearly understood the prompting of wisdom, cannot find anything else here other than sufferings. The reason for the turbulence of mind is due to fear of after-effects of the past activities. This turbulence of mind is the same as a wealthy, to a poorly educated and an illiterate. Because of temptations, one cannot live without acting. In other words, everyone is prompted do work and live in tranquillity.

Verse 62

To play the drama of life always
Sitting beside you leaving all ego
I am in your hands, God! Your blessing
Is like overflowing ocean of mercy.

The view of the devotee is that his life is in the hands of the Lord.

Always enjoying your presence to act the worldly drama, the life of the devotee who has forsaken all egos is always under your control. Oh! Lord! With overflowing mercy! Your blessing of this devotee is as vast as the boundless sea.

The Lord blesses everyone without the consideration of caste, religion, wealth or position without any differentiation. But before the blessing, he makes us act in the worldly drama a little. Therefore noble men doing good deeds lead their life peacefully.

Verse 63

Be victorious! Oh! The embodiment of Vishnu and
Shiva who smashed the cities of Tripuras
Oh! Lord! One who set afloat river Ganga
And kept it hidden in matted hair, protect me.

The devotee prays to the Lord who smashed the three cities (puras) and makes the flow of the heavenly river Ganga. Be victorious and bless.

Oh! Lord! One who burnt to ashes the cities of Tripuras! The ever known combined form of Lord Vishnu and Lord Shiva! Be victorious always! Oh! Lord! Who causes to flow the divine river (Ganga) hidden without the knowledge of any in the middle of the matted hair on your head to bless the devotees, Lord! Save me.

Verse 64

Clad in directions! I am in great grief
And no one to depend other than you
Your foot is my boat in which
I will cross over the sea of sins.

The devotee explains how to cross the ocean of worldly life as 'the only boat is the foot of the Lord'.

This devotee has excessive grief. Oh! Lord! One who has made directions as robes! I have no other protector than you. Your foot is my boat. In that boat, I will ferry across the sea of sins.

Verse 65

Tears of pathos flowing from the eyes
Breaking the wall between life and sea of soul
And reaching the absolute falling in whirlings
Of happiness, when am I approach your foot.

The devotee full of devotion shedding fears of sadness inquires as to when he can reach the feet of the Lord.

The waves rising from the flow of tears produced from the melting of mind in devotion breaking the bank of bodily happiness that separates the living from the sea of Brahman and mixed up repeatedly in the whirlpools in it. Oh! Lord! When can this devotee reach your feet?

Verse 66

Like fall of rain, tears of devotion flowed from
Eyes when reaching the heart where you exist melt and
Dissolve in you, can this sinner devotee feel as
Landed from the bottom of the sea of worldly grief?

The tears of happiness like torrential rain flowing from the eye melt the heart where you exist, Oh! Lord! When this sinner who lived as your devotee for long can join you? When can I believe that I have escaped shoring from the bottom of the ocean of worldly life?

Verse 67

Every day once at least think of removing
Troubles in my journey of life, when
Tears of bliss drip from eyes clearing the mind
Desires to dance with joy seeing your feet directly.

The devotee, though, cannot shed tears of happiness thinking about the Lord, desires to make it possible at least one time a day.

Taking all domestic worries as only the creations of own worldly activities in this course of life, this devotee wishes that these should be removed at least once a day shedding tears from the eyes of this devotee, understanding you by purifying the mind and to dance in bliss seeing your feet directly.

Verse 68

Instincts of previous births inside frequently
Make me suffer, my prostrations! To you
Oh! The embodiment of bliss! Thinking of
The possible danger I burn like butter melts in heat.

So long as the instincts of past deeds remain in mind, repeated reminiscence and worship of God should be continued.

This verse also contains adoration and self-dedication, which are explained in this work at relevant places.

Since temptations of many worldly longings come overcrowded to the mind and create troubles, let there be my prostration to you. Oh! Lord! The embodiment of bliss! I fear that I may without discernment fall into the dangers. I burn as if butter burns in heat.

It should be noted that all the nine methods of religious rites—hearing hymn in prayer, adulation adoring, reminiscence, sycophancy, worshipping, servitude, alliance and self-dedication—are referred to in different contexts.

Verse 69

Attracting with an enticing look of eye and throwing
Into navel ready to upset life upside down
Women with breasts like money bag & put me
Not in their way and trouble me, oh! Lord Shiva.

The devotee prays again, as the biggest instinct of evil deeds is the lust that should be destroyed.

Oh! Lord! Do not trap me in the lustful games of the woman who attracts with enticing look and putting into thoughts of carnal pleasures, who gets ready to upset the entire life upside down coming with money bag like breast and do not put me to grief.

Verse 70

Oh! Lord Shiva! With well-combed hair
Wearing earrings like rutting elephants
Come trembling raising husks and head,
Such breasts looking at sky let not disturb me.

Oh! God of gods! Women with their hair combed made shining and braided wearing ear ornaments with breasts making the impression of rutting elephants come excited raising their tusks and head as if looking to the sky should not get an opportunity to infatuate (prompt) me.

Verse 71

Like sparrows sprout on breast women
Ready to attack the hearts of men with that
And wait for an opportunity let me not
Trapped in that fire like danger, even once.

On breast sprouting as sparrows and pecking like birds women ready with tied of the bodice to peck the hearts of men are waiting for an opportunity to approach Oh! Lord! Let me not be seduced even once in this life by women with such breasts, the symbols of great danger.

Verse 72

Like water from ocean poured out, dung put
As if amassed with rubbish stuff vulva stinks
Beautiful young women come with obese breasts
Let me not turn to them, oh! Shiva!

Like different waste material scooped and collected on the shore (like urine poured out), the vulva filled with different filths around emit an evil odour. Oh! Lord! Do not let me wander behind beautiful young women who approach with tightly packed breasts.

Verse 73

Filled with blood overflowed and trickling rotten
Not be fascinated to fall into that ocean hell
Look at me sharply and shed to my mind
The nectar of happiness on hearing your stories.

Oh! Lord! Do not let me fall into the vagina of women as if falling into the middle of the sea of hell and roam about. Let me hear your story that shed ambrosia of happiness in my mind. Let your eyes be directed straight to me and look.

The piety of hearing is mentioned here. First pondering about the filthy body, one should become free from bodily pleasures. Thereafter, getting interested in hearing stories about the Lord, the mind gradually becomes devoid of emotions and evil thoughts and becomes pure. When good qualities grow in mind, one becomes eligible for experiencing the Brahman.

Verse 74

Oh! Lord! The embodiment of the unequalled,
The Imperishable, the unaffected form! To this
Devotee your lotus foot is the only refuge,
Let me not be pushed to the row of hells.

Oh! Lord! Unequal, unchanging and devoid of grief! To this devotee, your lotus foot alone is the refuge. Never put this destitute who has no other refuge, at any time, at any moment to be caught in the series of hell.

The devotee takes the favourite God as the symbol of Brahman. Brahman is the ultimate cause of the entire universe. Therefore, there cannot be a second to it. This is why Gurudev describes Brahman as '*Nirupaman*'. The ultimate cannot be produced from another so also decaying after some time. Therefore, it is *Nitya*, eternal. Brahman is bliss compactified, and it is '*Niramaya*'.

Verse 75

Oh! Destroyer of Tripuras who bears matted hair
Destroyer of miseries, invincible, most sacred,
Worshipped by Indra, save me! When can I get
Opportunity to see your lotus feet and worship?

Oh! Lord! One who smashed Tripuras! One who wears the crown of matted hair! I adore you. Bless me, Oh! Invincible one who destroys all sins! When am I going to get the good fortune of seeing and reaching your lotus feet which are adored even by Indra?

The devotee who has accepted attainment of Brahman as the ultimate cause will always be anxious about the moment of getting such fortune, the way to reach the ultimate is to pray again and again.

Verse 76

One with eyes widened like a lotus! Protect me!
And give acceptance as devotee Oh! Master
One who smashed Cupid! Oh! Lord
Have always mercy in your mind about me.

Oh! Lord! One with eyes like a blossomed lotus! One who burnt Cupid! Lord! Protect me also giving recognition among devotees. Oh! The Lord of mountain Kailas, be kind enough to keep me in your mind on all days and always.

Verse 77

Plucking fresh flowers and keeping you
In mind, Oh! Lord not even once with
Purified mind I could make offerings to you
Is this the punishment for my lapse?

Collecting newly blossomed flowers, this devotee not even once worshipped you, meditating you in mind for protection. Oh! Master of the universe is this suffering punishment for my lapse?

Verse 78

Oh! Lord! With the body on which overflows
Water from Ganga hidden in your matted hair

My mind does not rest leaving vacillating
Imaginations even once a day, fixed on you.

Oh! Lord! One with the figure of overflowing water of Ganga wore in the matted hair on the head in which the moon exists frozen. I do not see my mind get free from the rising imaginations at least once in a day concentrating the mind on meditation.

Verse 79

The written fate is not possible to change
It cannot be changed by any atonement
The great men used to say so
How can this devotee understand all these?

Depending on one's deeds, whatever one has to experience as reward or punishment by fate cannot be avoided. There is no remedy for the consequences of actions in previous births. I learn that the great seekers of truth have stated so. This devotee cannot understand it. You yourself should save me!

The collected domestic worries (bindings of present life) that have not been started experiencing exists as a propensity (*Sanchitham*). The possible future act is *Agami*. These two will vanish once the realization of wisdom comes. But the one who took the present life is to experience it, even the men of wisdom with their inert body. There is no remedy for it; this is fate. But when men of wisdom experience the fate, they do not feel sad. But others grieve. This is the difference between men of wisdom and worldly men.

Verse 80

If the words of praise are said always
All people become happy that too not
Possible any more I don't want its related
Attachments, but your mercy only, Oh! Lord!

Always people feel happy when they are praised telling unreal, fabricated stories about them. That too is impossible hereafter. Oh! Merciful Lord! It is a pity. Therefore I do not want the attaching relations of love. I want only your mercy.

With slandering and fictitious praising stories, people make others happy. This type of activities will ruin the minds of their own and of others leading to evil tendencies and will strengthen the worldly longings. The devotee feels that he does not want such things to happen. He wants only the mercy of God.

Verse 81

Your mercy that pours the nectar of bliss
Overflows beyond the limits of
Its waves of mercy! Bless me that
I can join you and live happily.

In the pushing forward (like waves) of your overflowing mercy, you give ambrosia of happiness. Bless me to immerse in such a way that I can join you and live in satisfaction.

Verse 82

The moon is widely known as the charioteer
Of Cupid rises and spread rays on
The pond of lilies lose brightness and
Fall in darkness does lonely penance.

The moon well known as the charioteer of Cupid coming up from the pond of waterlily arise shedding rays losing some of its phases and falling into darkness and doing lonely penance.

Symbolically, the mind coming up and falling in love with women desirous of pleasure, losing some of the vigours and suffering from grief tries to keep the memory of God in mind.

It can be explained as the mind the symbol of moon rises and, putting the rays a woman going after worldly pleasures and falling in love with her, lose brightness and fall in darkness (ignorance) does single-mindedly penance.

Verse 83

When the moon gets all its lost phases back
Then the only merger is that in your mind?
Must not suffer however sitting on your head
One hostile to flower arrows of lust!

When the moon recouped all its phases and became full or when the mind becomes normal and satisfied with all desires, do you think only then you give salvation merging with you? In any case, hereafter do not make it happen to grieve sitting on your head. Oh! Lord who can approve all lustful imaginations.

If it is the lust that creates the grief in the moon and the mind, the devotee feels that the Lord also is responsible for it, because the moon is suffering sitting on the head of the Lord, who burnt the Cupid who produces lust. Then why is the moon not given salvation? The mind grieves sticking on to the Lord. Then, why is the mind not given liberation from the lustful thoughts? Oh! Lord, it is only your mercy the ultimate remedy.

Verse 84

Wearing on the head the billions of roaring waves
Coming and always with definite form, unchanged
And all-pervading, existing at the temple
At Chidambaram, Oh! Lord, I adore you!

The river Ganga coming with innumerable waves rush roaring and shedding on the head of the devotee Lord taking discrete form always without any change made the heart of the devotee. Oh! Lord who stays in the famous temple of Chidambaram I adore you.

Symbolically, shedding the life-bearing cold stream on the devotee making subject to wisdom always existing as all-pervading in space where consciousness is spread. Oh! The Absolute! I adore you.

Verse 85

If you come considering me as capable
Of climbing on mountains killing animals
Stripingoff their skins and give it to you
will you Laugh cracking jokes of my inability?

Oh! Lord! If you come near me thinking that this devotee is capable of entering into the mountain places, kill wild animals and strip off their skin to offer to the Lord for wearing, when seeing my inability will it happen to ridicule me saying jokes?

Symbolically, entering into the subtle parts of the mind reducing the strength of love, lust and anger, etc. make the Lord happy that this devotee is capable of doing it. If you come near, will it happen to ridicule by seeing the inability of this devotee saying jokes?

Verse 86

Like what I am doing today sitting home
With ego eat and become fat like pillows
And perish is the fate you wrote on
My head, how severe is my grief.

Your decision made even much earlier as to this devotee to sit in house trapped in arrogant egoist feeling of 'I', 'me', etc. to eat and grow fat and spoil the life, Oh Lord! How pitiable is it?

Verse 87

Like a cruel tiger coming out of
The forest to catch and eat life
Everywhere in this world to cut hands
And the head, Kaliyuga is seen ready to act.

Like the ferocious tiger come from forest to domestic land to catch prey and eat, like that the era of frenzy (Kaliyuga) gets ready to cut life everywhere in this world into pieces.

Dualities, love, hatred and rivalry are seen everywhere in the world. People are running after physical pleasure; diseases and natural calamities are increasing and there is no peace of mind. Those who seek absolute reality are very rare. These are the characteristics of this frenzied period (Kaliyuga).

Verse 88

Like the fragrance of flower spread and
Filled the three worlds uniformly like the sky
Reflected in water in the pot Oh! Merciful!
Who shines as many lives, be victorious!

Oh! Merciful Lord! While spreading over the three worlds, earth, heaven and hell, thickly and uniformly like the fragrance of the flower, at the same time like the sky reflected seen as different things in water in the pot, you shine in the forms of different lives, Oh! Lord, be victorious!

The Brahman is all-pervading; it fills the inside and outside of all at the same time, it shines in all things seen as different in the form of life in living things. Like the sky reflects in the water in the pot and water in the lake, the Brahman reflects in everything. Similarly, in all worlds, the Brahman exists inside and outside like the fragrance of a flower.

Verse 89

A lot of filthy water full of lust, anger
And greed plunged in that to sprout
Sowed in farm to ripe and reap
People eat and suffer, really pitiable.

The water of worldly activities flowing out from the forest of worldly relations full of filth such as lust, anger and greed is there around. It is a pity that people fill the farm, the heart where ripens happiness, filled with the flood, sowing the seeds of promptings to grow and harvest the consequences of deeds in early births and experience grief thereof. It is pitiable.

The heart is the farm from which the happiness ripens. The three filths: water of lust, anger and promptings hide the farm of happiness. This is why Gurudev says that the heart, the farm of happiness, is filled with the water of the three filths.

Verse 90

Greyness old age and death now and then
Come like a frightening tiger to catch and eat
Oh! Lord! When it comes to an end
Your worldly play is said to be eternal.

Now and then the signals of ageing, such as grey hairs, fatigue and death come like cheetah creating the fear to catch and swallow. When is it going to an end? It is well known that your worldly play continues as unending Oh! Lord!

The births and deaths are only the play of magic of Maya. Therefore it is transient. This play of magic will go on continuing; realize that there is only one thing. Ending the feeling of many is the attainment of salvation.

Verse 91

At times due to continuous meditation of Shiva
The mind concentrates on the Lord and melts
Into bliss, most time his magic play confounds
On many, will this continue forever?

At times due to prayer to Shiva, the mind fixing strongly on the Lord himself and dissolve in bliss, most of the time prompted by Maya confuse seeing many things. Will it happen that it will continue like this till death?

Verse 92

Without any failure to me hereafter who
Always concentrate the mind on you burns my stains
In the fire of meditation to give the pleasure of salvation
Be victorious! One shines with the beauty of flowers!

Oh! Lord! Bless this devotee who has taken you as the only refuge, hereafter without any obstruction in the middle; I will always be concentrated and meditating. Lord! Burn the filth such as lust, anger and greed in my mind in the fire of meditation and give happiness of salvation. Oh! Beautiful One, whose body shines with the colour of hibiscus flower, be victorious!

Verse 93

In the thick forest of ignorance grown in disgrace
As the seed of fate births and deaths footed strongly on
Ego remains in this world whether this inert body
Be eaten by fire or animals ease their hunger?

One who grew up in the forest of ignorance misunderstanding the unreal as real, the temptations of worldly activities, which is the seed of worldly life of births and deaths sprout is rooted strongly. This inert body that spends days doing activities develops inert feelings, whether it will become food to fire or will the animals eat to subdue their hunger?

Verse 94

Father, mother bosom friends dear ones and
Close relations and neighbours all leave
Continuously born and dead, to make the life
Gratified one should himself work hard.

Father, mother, wife, dear ones and loving neighbours, all without being together for long, always depart taking births and deaths leaving you alone. If one wants to make, this life blessed, one has to try himself.

In spite of anyone being there at the time of death, father, mother, son, daughter, relative, neighbour, the inert body will decay and vanish. Therefore, along with the association of friends and relatives, seek the ultimate reality and get the blessings of the Lord.

Verse 95

The Lord wearing our non-departing Sun
On the head sitting inside me without
Leaving even a short while sheds blessings
We get virtues, and our sufferings vanished.

In this verse, the devotee declares that since everything in the universe is transient, he finds refuge in the Lord.

Lord Shiva the symbol of Brahman and one who wears the Sun on the head, not leaving me a short while rest inside me and sheds blessings. Virtues will come to us. All miseries will end (vanish).

Lord Shiva is usually known as one who wears the moon. But here it is a different context to the yogis: the realization of the supreme soul that shines in the form of Sun in the lotus with a thousand petals (*Sahasrara padmam*) is of prime importance. It is located at the top of the head. It is why Gurudev uses the words *'Dinamani choodiya thampuran'* meaning one who wears the Sun in lotus with a thousand petals.

Verse 96

Hereafter let me get enough devotion to live
Without afflictions obeying the commands
Lord, I understand what is hidden in
Your matted red hair is the wave of Ganga.

The devotee prays to give him enough strength to live in devotion and to drink the ambrosia of Ganga.

Hereafter I must get sufficient devotion to lead my life according to the commands of the Lord so that I do not get any grief. I understand what is hidden in your head is the wave of divine Ganga river that decorates the matted red hair.

Verse 97

In the waves of Ganga hidden in your
Beautiful matted hair all my miseries vanish
One who burnt Cupid! To break worldly
Relations show me your divine sight.

The devotee desires to see and enjoy the divine face of the Lord, who comes dancing as the embodiment of bliss.

All my worldly sufferings will immerse and disappear in the waves of divine Ganga that is hidden in the Lord's beautiful matted hair. Oh! Lord who burnt the Cupid to ashes or one who destroys all lust! To cut the consequences of earlier activities, always show me such divine sights of your beautiful appearance.

Verse 98

Oh Lord! Who shines as an ocean of mercy!
Your matted red hair fastened with snakes with
Bowing hoods swinging in dance your beautiful
Face shining like lotus be seen by my eyes.

Oh! Lord! Who shines as a milky ocean of mercy! Who comes nearer wearing the swinging chain of snakes that bow lowering the hood in tune with your dance, let this devotee get an opportunity to fix your face that shines like a lotus in heart be seen by my outer eyes.

In short, the devotee desires to see the Lord as filling both inside and outside.

Verse 99

Like the stern to break the waves of
Divine Ganga, seen as surrounded by snakes
Spreading hoods uniformly your sight wearing
Matted hair be seen dancing. Oh! Lord!

Like the stern of the ship that stops the water of divine river Ganga, the top surrounded by the snakes uniformly spreading the hoods, divine form of the Lord wearing matted hair come dancing, be seen.

If divine Ganga is considered as flow of cold prana and the snakes as nerve system, one gets the philosophical picture as when the cold streams of prana spreads all over the body to obstruct the movement like the stern of the ship, the mind in the same form is surrounded by the nervous system like *Ida*, *Pingala* and Sushumna, let this devotee get the fortune of seeing the divine body covered with matted hair come near and perform the cosmic dance (see 'Kundalini Pattu').

Verse 100

Through the experience of eternal bliss felt the
Entire universe as filled with glittering moonlight
Of peace spread making the universe the heaven
Let my heart the lily blossom in that pond.

The hundredth verse concludes with a prayer to the Lord meditating on Him repeatedly, and at last, attaining the state of experiencing non-duality, the devotee's heart the waterlily blossomed, the Lord be seen full of bliss.

Though indivisibility of absolute reality is experienced as spread throughout the entire universe and filled with ultimate bliss, the moonlight of peace shining brilliantly, spread everywhere, the waves raised glittering made this world a heaven. Oh! Lord! My body is a small pond in that heaven; let me have the fortune of seeing my heart blossom like the water lily in that pond.

The moon that emits cool rays as if making all the worlds cooled at high altitudes shines, glitters and spreads light everywhere. Oh! Lord! Let me have the fortune of seeing water lily blossoming in the heavenly pond due to the fall of moonlight.

My heart, the waterlily, should blossom, as the moon is the lover of water lily. The water lily blossoms only with the touch of the moon. The word *Kulirmati* means both awareness of absolute truth, and non-dual experience. The non-dual experience in the realization of everything is one without a second. Once one begins to experience it, to him, the entire universe will be felt as full of light and peace.

Let us now bow our head at the foot of Sree Narayana Gurudev for giving us this gift of literary work, full of philosophy, devotion and an eye-opener to the seekers of the real truth of the universe in metaphysics and modern science.

AUM.

16

SWANUBHAVAGITI

Sree Narayana Gurudev wrote 'Swanubhavagiti' in the year 1884 while he was staying at Aruvippuram. These verses are said to be dictated to Sree Karuva Krishnan Asan, one of Gurudev's ardent devotees. Its second edition was published in 1928 by Krishnan Asan. There were 100 verses in this work. Out of the 100 verses, forty are missing. The first ten verses are known as 'Anubhuti Dasakam', the next ten as 'Prapanchasuddhi Dasakam', and the third ten as 'Paramasivachinta Dasakam'. The remaining part is known as 'Vibhudarsanam'. It is in the latter part that the forty verses are missing. Krishnan Asan, in his introduction to this work 'Swanubhavagiti', says,'These poems were dictated to me by Sree Narayana Gurudev and I copied it myself and kept them. When I requested Gurudev to dictate the missing poems, he retorted, "Its author is no more." I don't feel that he will come back to this body. If somebody else writes it will not suit this.'

The above is a famous statement for which the devotees furnish different versions. Everyone knew that the entire works of Gurudev were copied down by his devotees while Gurudev was either walking or relaxing somewhere. At the time of dictating, he never used any reference book or note. It was all off-hand dictation through transcendence or intuition. Therefore, while dictating continuously the verses one after the other, if some disciple requested Gurudev to repeat any, he stopped dictation abruptly and used to tell the disciples,'That man who dictated so far is gone.'

Sree Narayana Gurudev was a pro lific writer who dictated poems instantaneously as if it came through intuition. Therefore, the repetition of the missed lines in tune with the existing was not possible.

Rao Bahadur Sundaram Pillai in his preface to the book praised 'Swanubhavagiti' as 'Thiruvasakam' of Malayalam language. This work was eulogized as *Amritatarangini* (divine utterings).

'Swanubhavagiti' has been discussed in various assemblies of learned folk.

One who attained self-realization sees the Brahman as the entire universe. Sree Narayana Gurudev was one such great soul. He explains in a beautiful, sweet language his experience. Gurudev in this work shows the talent of a great poet.

(Original text in Malayalam)

Mangalamenmēlaruḷum
Taṅṅaḷilonnicirunna saṛvajñan
Sangamamonnilumillā-
Tangajaripuvil teḷiññu kaṇkānum.

Kāṇum kaṇṇilaṭaṅṅi-
Kkāṇunnillī nirantaram sakalam
Kwāṇam ceviyilaṭaṅṅu-
Nnōṇam twakkil tulanjumaṛṛatupōm.

Pōmitu pōle tuṭaṅi-
Ppōmaṛurasamappuṛatu nāvatilum
Pōmitupōle tuṭaṅi-
Ppōmitu vāymutaleẓunnorindriyamām.

Indriyamāyiṭumannā-
Ḷindriyavum keṭumatannu kūriruḷām
Manniluruṇṭuvīẓumbōl
Tannila kaiviṭṭu teṛṛi vaṭamaṛṛāl

Aṟṟāliruḷilirikku-
Nnuṟṟōnivanennuraykkilallalaṟum
Cuṟṟum katiriṭuvōn tan-
cuṟṟāyi maṟṟoriruṭṭu vilaśiṭumō?

Vilaśiṭuvōnilanennā
Lalasata tānē kaṭannupiṭikūṭum
Nilayitu tanne namukkī-
Nilayanamēṟumbozāṇorānandam

Ānandakkaṭal poṅṅi-
Tānē pāyunnitā parannorupōl
Jñānam koṇṭitilēṟi-
Ppānamceyyunnu paramahaṁśajanam

Janmitukaṇṭu teḷiññāl
Janimṛitikaiviṭṭirikkumannilayil
Mantaḷironnu kalarnnā-
Lanavaratam saukhyamannutannevarum.

Varumitilonnu ninakkil
Karaḷilaziññozukīṭumimbamaṟum
Karutarutonnumitenna-
Loruporuḷāyīṭumannutanneyavan

Avanivanennu ninakku-
Nnavanoru patiyennirikkilum paśuvam
Avikalamāgrahamaṟṟa-
Lavakalitanandaveḷḷamōṭivarum

Ōṭivannoru kūṭṭm
Pēṭikaḷoḷikaṇṭoziññupōmuṭanē
Mūṭumorirulvannatu pi-
Nnīṭum veḷivāywarunnu tēnveḷḷam

Veḷḷam, tī mutalāy ni-
Nnuḷḷum veḷiyum niṟaññu vilasīṭum
Kaḷḷam kaṇṭu piṭicā-
Luḷḷam kaikaṇṭanellitan kaniyām.

Kaniyāmonnilirunni-
Kkanakādambaramatiṅu kāṇunnu
Panimati cūḍumatinmun
Panikatiroḷikaṇṭiṭunnapōl veḷiyām.

Veḷiyāmatuvannenmun-
Velivāyellām viẓuṅṅi veṟuveḷiyāy
Veḷimutalancilumonnāy
Viḷayāṭīṭunnatānu tirunaṭanam.

Naṭanam darśanamāyā-
Luṭanētaniṅirunnu naṭnilayām
Naṭunilatannilirikkum
Neḷunaḷonnāyavannu saukhyam tān.

Saukhyam tanneyitellā-
Mōṟkkuntoṟum niṟañña saundaryam
Pāṟkkil pāraḷṭipaṟṟi-
Pāṟkkunnōnin pakaṟnna pañjaramām.

Pañjaramāmuṭal mutalām
Paññiyilaṟivāyiṭunna tīyitilum
Maññukaṇaṅal kaṇakki-
Mmañjuḷaveyilkoṇṭapāyamaṭayunnu.

Adiyannindriyavāyī-
Naṭipeṭumitukaṇṭoẓiññu maṟṟellam
Adiyaṟṟīṭum taṭiva-
Nnaṭiyil taniye maṟiññu vīẓumbōl.

Vīẓumbōẓivayellām
Pāẓil taniyē paranna tūveḷiyām
Āẓikkeṭṭilavantān
Vīẓunnōnallitanu kaivalyam.

Kaivalyakkaṭalonnāy
Vaimalyam pūṇṭiṭunnatoruvaẓiyām
Jīvatwam keṭumennē
Śaivalamakalunnitannu paragatiyām.

Paragatiyaruḷīṭuka nī
Purahara! Bhagavānitānu kartavyam
Hara! Hara! śivaperumānē!
Hara hara veḷiyunniṟañña kūriruḷum.

Iruḷum veḷiyumitonnum
Puraḷātoḷiyāy niṟañña pūmaẓayē,
Aruḷīṭukakoṇṭaṟiya-
Taruḷīṭunnēnitinnu varamaruḷē.

Aruḷē! Ninkaḷiyaruḷā-
Laruḷīṭunnīyenikkorarumaṟayē!
Iruḷē! Veḷiyē naṭuvā-
Maruḷē! Karaḷil kaḷikkumoru poruḷē!

Poruḷē! Parimaḷamiyalum
Poruḷētanō niṟañña niṟaporuḷē!
Aruḷē! Aruḷīṭuka tē-
Ruruḷēṟāyvanenikkitiha paranē!

Paranē! Parayām tirayil-
Pparanētāvāyiṭunna paśupatiyē!
Haranēyarikil viḷicī-
Ṭorunēravuminnirutukarutarute.

Arutē paṟavānuyirō-
ṭoruperuveḷiyāya ninte mahātmyam;
Ceṟutum ninkṛipayenyē
Verutē njāniṅirikkumō śivanē!

Śivanē! Ninnilirunnī-
Cevimizhimutalāyiṟaṅimēyunnu
Ivanōṭukūṭivarumma-
Ṛṟavakaḷumellāmitentu maṟimāyam?

Maṟimāyappoṭiyaṟuma-
Maṟavāl mūṭappeṭunna paraveḷiyē!
Ceṟutonnonnumatonnā-
Maṟavotiḷakippukañña pukayum nī.

Pukayē! poṭiyē! Puramē-
Yakamē! Veḷiyē! Niṟañña putumaẓayē!
Ihamē! Paramē! Iṭayē!
Sukhamēkanamēkaniññu nīyakamē.

Akavum puṟavumoẓiññen-
Bhagavānē! Nī niṟaññu vāẓunnu;
Pukaḷpoṅṅina ninmiẓiyil
Pukayē, ikkaṇṭatokkeyum pakayē.

Pakayāmitu neyyurukum-
Nikarāy nīrāykkiṭunna narahariyē!
Pakaceyvatumiṅṅinimēl
Pukayāy vānil cuẓaṟṟiviṭumeriyē!

Erinīroṭu nilamuruki-
Pperukippuẓayāy muẓaṅṅivarumoliyē!
Arumaṟa tirayunnoru nī-
Ntiruvaṭiyuṭe pūñcilankayuṭe viḷiyē!

Viḷiyē! Vilapeṛumorumaṇi-
Yoḷiyē! Viḷiyēpaṛannuvarumaḷiyē!
Iḷakumparimaḷamoṭucuva-
Yoḷiyum poṭiyayvarutiyorunilayē!

Nilayillāte koṭunkā-
ṛṛalayunnatu pōynivaṛnnu varumiruḷō!
Alayum talayilaniñña-
Ṅṅalayunnitu tān putakkumoru toliyō!

Toliyumeṭutitu putacā-
Kkaliyekkaẓalalaẓukkumoru kaliyē!
Kaliyum kālāltulayum!
Nilayēyellā nilakkumoru talayē!

Oru talayiruḷum veḷiyum
Varavumorarumakkoṭikku surataruvē!
Arutarutarimakaḷeṛivati-
Narivararaṛumipṛasangamoru śariyē!

Śari paṛavatinum mati nin-
Caritamoṭitukoṇṭitinnu nikarituvē
Aruḷappeṭumoru poruḷē-
Taṛivālaṛiyappeṭāta niṛaporuḷē!

Poruḷum padavumoẓiñña-
Ṅṅaruḷum parayum kaṭannu varumalayē!
Varaḷum nāvu nanacā-
Laruḷpoṅṅum vāridhikkatoru kuṛayō!

Kuṛayennonnu kuṛikkum-
Maṛayōteṭunnatinu maṛukarayē!
Niṛavillayyō! Bhagavā-
Naṛiyunnillī rahaśyamitu sakalam.

Sakalam kēvalamoṭu pō-
Yakalumbōẓaṅṅudikkumoruvaẓiyē!
Sahasanakādikaḷoṭu pōy
Tikavāyīṭum viḷikkumorumoẓiyē!

Onnumaṟiññīlayyō!
Ninnuṭe līlāviśeṣamitu valutē
Ponninkoṭiyoru bhāgam-
Tannil cuṟṟippaṭaṟnna tanimaramē!

Tanimaramē! Taṇaliniyī nin-
Kani kaẓaliṇayentalakku pūvaṇiyē
Kanakakkoṭi koṇṭāṭum
Tanimāmalayōyitentu kaṇmāya?

Kaṇmāyaṅṅaḷitellām
Kanmūnnuṇṭāyirunnu kaṇṭīla!
Veṇmaticūṭi viḷaṅṅum
Kaṇmaṇiyē!pūkaẓalkku kaitoẓunnēn

Kaitoẓumaṭiyane nīyi-
Kaitavanilayinneṭutu ninnaṭiyil
Kaitaẓaviceṟkkaṇamē nin
Paitalitennōṟtu ninbharamē.

Ninbharamallātonni-
llambiḷi cūṭumnilimbanayakamē!
Vanpeẓumimmalamāya-
Kkombatinonnāy vilakkunalkarutē!

Nalkanamaṭiyanu nin pū-
Painkaẓaliṇa nīraṇiñña veṇmalayē!
Kūkum pūnkuyilēṟi-
Ppōkum ponninkoṭikku putumaramē!

Putumaramē pūnkoṭi va-
Nnatumitumokkepparannaninkṛipayē
Padamalariṇayen talayil
Patiyaṇamenmey kalaṛnnukoḷḷaṇamē!

Koḷḷaṇamenneyaṭikkāy-
Taḷḷarutēninkṛipakku kuṛayarutē
Eḷḷalavum kanivillā-
Tuḷḷuvanennōṛtoẓiññupōkarutē!

Pōkarutini ninnaṭiyil
Cakanamallennirikkilivaninnum
Vēkumiruḷkkaṭalil vī-
Ṇākulamuṇṭāmatinnu paṛayaṇamō?

Paṛayaṇamennillallō
Aṛivāmaṭiyanmuṭikku cūṭanamē!
Aṛivaṛṛonnāy varume-
Nnaṛiyātonnayirunnu vēdiyanē!

Vēdiyarōtum vēdam
Kātilaṭaṅṅunnivaṇṇamiva palatum
Ādiyoṭantavumillā-
Tētinōṭonnāy varunnatatu nīyē!

Atu nīyennālivanō-
ṭudiyātonnāyirikkumarumutalē!
Gatiyillayyō! Ninmeyy
Patiyetannen paśutwamaṛu patiyē!

Patiyennaṛiyāten-
Patiyē ninnetiraññu palarumitā!
Matikeṭṭonnilumilla-
Tativādam koṇṭoẓiññupōkunnu.

Pōkum maṇṇoṭu tī nī-
Rōharipōlē marutinoṭuveḷiyum
Nākamoṭoru narakam pō-
Yēkamatāy hā! Viẓuṅṅiyaṭiyane nī!

Aṭiyoṭumuṭi naṭuvaṟṟen-
Piṭiyilaṭaṅṅātirunnu pala poruḷum
Vaṭivākkikkoṇṭanna-
Nnaṭiyōṭonniccoẓiññvarumonnē.

Onnennum raṇṭennum
Ninnivanennum paṟaññu pataṟarute
Innikkanṭavayellām
Ninnōṭonnāy varunnu kaḷavallē.

Allennum pakalennum
Collum poruḷum kaṭanna sundharamē!
Kollennōṭuyirēkko-
ṇṭalle nī kaivilakkutanayyō!

Ayyō! Niyennuḷḷum
Poyyē! Puṟavum potiññu pōkunnu
Meyyāṟānāy vannēn
Kaiyyēntikkoṇṭoẓiññu pōkunnu

Kunnummalayumitellā-
Monnonnāy ponnaṭikku kūṭṭakki
Ninnappōḷaṭiyōṭen-
Ponnin koṭikoṇṭamaẓnnatentayyō!

Entayyō! Nīyennum
Cintakkaṇayunnoẓiñña cinmayamē!
Ventaṟṟīṭumahanta-
Kkantippiṟayēyaṇiñña kōmaḷamē!

Meaning and commentary

Verse 1

Oh! Lord! Who shines in all senses equally
The knower of all will shed virtues on me
By that my eye of knowledge will become
Manifested to you, the rival of Cupid!

The Lord who knows everything shines in all experiences of senses will shed good virtues on me. Then my eye of wisdom will shine before the Lord, who is the destroyer of Cupid without any feeling of, it is my own in any worldly things.

Verse 2

The eye that can see only sights
Not all become experienced
The ear experiences only the sound
Like that, the skin experiences the touch only.

The eye is capable of seeing only forms, but not all other subjects of experience come to it always. Like only the sound is experienced by the ear, the skin experiences only the feeling of touch.

Verse 3

Like that subjects of vision will vanish in the eye
The remaining taste will vanish in the tongue
Likewise, the smell will vanish in the nose and
All senses of observation from sound will vanish.

As explained above about form, sound, touch, etc., the other subjects will also become contained in other sense organs and vanish. The taste which is experienced by the tongue will contain in the tongue and vanish. Likewise, the smell will vanish in the nose. From tongue to all senses of action will make the experience in concerned senses and vanish.

From the eye to the nose are the sense organs and from sound to smell, etc. are their subjects,the hand, leg, sex organ; the words are organs of action. Take, walk, talk, make happy, and discharge are their subjects. The sense organs which contain the subjects and organs of action act accordingly. All organs are to act on their subjects as per rules. No doubt in all these subjects it is all one that experiences the entire things because it is me who only do and experience all these. As it is I that makes all these components work for me, there is no doubt that I am different from them. And also if the instruments are not there, I won't have the experience of my existence or existence of 'I'. Therefore, when these instruments mentioned above are removed, what remains will be I in absolute (unattributed) form. Attaining of this experience is the experience of salvation. This is what Gurudev very explicitly tells in Poem 1, 'Atmopadesa Satakam'.

Verse 4

In wakefulness the sense organs have experience
In deep sleep, the senses become not working
The experience becomes stark darkness; it is like
One who walks on rope falls when it breaks.

In the wakeful state, the eye, nose, etc. senses, that experience subjects will act as instruments of mind, but in deep sleep, these senses will become not working. At that state, all experience of senses will become stark darkness. The passing of wakeful state leaving subjects of experience to the state of deep sleep is like one travelling on rope falls down when the rope breaks and his condition changes from the walk on the rope to lie on earth after falling.

Wakefulness is a state where the sense organs spread outside and observe things. Each sense organ understands its respective subject. But it is 'I' that experiences all the subjects, depending on what 'I' experiences as forms or shapes, sound, and so on. The concept of 'I' is not a real entity as it is the creation of the experience through senses. When all the experiences of subjects are lost, there comes the third stage called deep sleep (Sushupti).In this state, all experience of things vanished into the darkness. The player on a rope depends on the rope for his play. Once the rope breaks, he falls down. It is like this: the activities during wakefulness depend on the senses. Once the senses are left, the life will return to its state of Brahman. The sense of deep sleep is the self's state of Brahman, but as it can come back when awake, it is not the attainment of salvation, the merger with Brahman himself. This may be why Gurudev advises to prostrate again and again. This change of senses is temporary and not permanent.

Verse 5

When the sensual experience vanishes and if one realizes
That this life is the real bliss covered with darkness
All miseries will get vanished then what
Other darkness exists hiding the self-shining Sun.

As subjects of sense, organs are removed and realizes that life is the real bliss and that it is hidden by the veil of Maya (ignorance)all miseries get vanished. Once the veil of darkness is removed, what other darkness (veil) can exist hiding the self-shining Sun (the absolute consciousness)?

Deep sleep is a wonderful experience. At that stage, there are no sense organs and their subjects that make us feel happiness or sorrow. When awoken, except a feeling that we slept peacefully for some time, nothing can be remembered about what happened during the deep sleep. This experience clearly manifests three important points. One is that during deep sleep, life remains as the symbol of happiness. In that state, what is experienced cannot be from something different. The other is that it was the full unawareness about anything else that gave happiness. Here, happiness is due to the full ignorance about any other thing. It makes us understand that belief and miseries are due to the awareness of our surroundings. And the third is that it is covered with a dark veil so that even the happiness felt during that time could not be experienced (Ref: lucid dream, etc., Verse 1, 'Darsanamala'). Hence deep sleep is the state of non-duality that there is no 'I' and the surroundings. Only the real Atman and a veil covering it exist. This is what Gurudev means by the line '*irulilirikkunnutton*' (The Atman sitting in darkness). Those who seek the truth through chanting and meditation are trying for the attainment of this state. They found that if in the wakeful state itself, they practise detachment from worldly desires, the world during sleep can also be removed and if done, one can attain salvation. Those who get detached from the feeling of worldly attachment and practise meditation and penance during wakefulness can remove the cover of ignorance: to them comes the feeling of being one with the Brahman. Gurudev, who obtained salvation through the said practice, indicates this in the line '*chuttum kathiriduvon*', etc.

Verse 6

If one becomes enjoyed in worldly pleasures
He will be trapped automatically by indolence.
We are still Brahman with body form
This bliss will be experienced only by removing passion.

If this life becomes only that which enjoys sensual subjects, then comes ignorance in the form of self-forgetfulness and creates the veil. For humans, even then their original form is Brahman himself. This experience of bliss is attained only when the longing for pleasures is removed and self-realized.

The experience of worldly attachment is due to the creation of the virtual cover called Maya. Any virtual feeling superimposed on a real thing does not make any change on the real thing. For example, the image of the Sun on the surface of the water, once disturbed, does not make any corresponding change in the Sun.

The absolute reality or Brahman is the real object, and all worldly scenes are imposed on it. So whatever changes happen to the Atman do not have any effect on Brahman. Other examples are the snake and coir, and mirage (water) in the desert. All that is experienced by the human senses have no influence over the real things on which their virtual image is superimposed. This is what Gurudev mentions by saying '*Nilayanamēṛumbōẓānorānandam*'.

Verse 7

The sea of bliss becomes spread and
Overflows by itself men of wisdom
Getting into that sea and drink it
Enjoy the experience of this bliss.

An ocean of bliss spreads uniformly and overflows by itself. Through their strong experience, those who have found the real wisdom that there is only one thing, get into this ocean of bliss and enjoy drinking it.

Once the self discovers its own entity, it comes to attain the state of salvation. It is this entity that pervades the entire universe as the Absolute or Brahman. Then one comes to know that the universe is only a virtual creation of Maya. Once attained, the experience of the ocean of bliss comes to it. This phenomenon cannot be explained philosophically or logically but can only be experienced.

Obstruction to this experience is the feeling of duality. Therefore, the great saints live immersed in this blissful stage always leaving all thoughts of duality. These great saints (*Paramahamsa*s) are those who got detached from the worldly life and attained salvation. Wisdom is the ship in which they travel in the sea of this blissfulness. The awareness of non-duality that there is only one, not a second, is real wisdom.

Verse 8

If the mind of people brighten on
Seeing this will escape from births and deaths

If the pure mind is subjected to
Brahman the eternal bliss will come.

If the human mind becomes brightened seeing this ocean of bliss and dissolve in it, then it gets detached from the worldly longings due to births and deaths. If the pure mind at least once is made subject to the feeling of the ultimate Brahman, then comes the everlasting bliss.

Everybody aims at getting pleasure. People wander in various worldly activities to get more and more pleasure as the worldly pleasures are transient. Worldly life and pleasure depend on other things. When the other things are not in favour, then it leads to loss of pleasure. Therefore, without depending on such another, if an ocean of pleasure that does not confine to him is found, then one need not say the life has become blessed. It is that blessing one gets by the realization of Brahman in him. The only reality is Brahman. All other things are virtual things which are superimposed on it. Since Brahman is eternal, once it is realized it will never get detached. This is the greatness of real wisdom. So long as there is only one, what relevance is there for a second? Then who is born and who is dead? This state of attainment of detachment from all other things is called salvation (Moksha).

Verse 9

If the thought is concentrated on
The bliss, the overflowing ego in mind stops
If nothing is considered as of mine
On that day he becomes Brahman himself.

If one concentrates on Brahman through meditation, the ego that tempts the mind to the feeling of 'my own' will completely vanish. One should not long for anything as if it is his own. If such attachments are removed, he becomes the Brahman himself at the same instant.

The poem establishes the fact that the longings and desires tempt one to ego (one's self) that it is mine. This can be removed through concentration of the mind on the absolute reality—the Brahman. One should never keep the feeling of worldly things as his own because such things are illusory things created by Maya, giving the feeling that they are real. The real thing can be seen only when the virtual cover of Maya is removed. The virtual things, in turn, are created by the temptation of mind in the form of ego. One should never become prey to such longings and desires that create the illusory world. Once such longings for the worldly things are removed, the existence of the worldly attachment vanishes and he becomes merged with the absolute one, the Brahman.

Verse 10

One who feels himself and me even if
He is an emperor is an animal
With the feeling of oneness, the mind leaving
Longings then come overflowing essence of bliss.

One who thinks that fellow is different from me, this fellow is different from that fellow,as if there are many, is an animal-like one, even if he is an emperor. When the mind is purified with the feeling of oneness and leaves all longings of pleasure, then he can immediately experience the bliss of Brahman that fills the entire universe.

Brahman is the only real thing, and there is not a second to it. Wisdom and thinking nature of men are meant to clearly understand this, whereas the animals are not blessed with this ability. One who does not make use of this differentiating power but goes after many things as if they are also real is an animal even if he is an emperor. The animals are incapable of finding reality by differentiation as they are not blessed with the wisdom of men. They live according to their timely temptations. But man is different; he has wisdom. A man with his intelligence should understand that even if he tries his best, he can never keep his inert body and other things as his own forever since he has to leave even his own body ultimately. He should understand in advance that he has to throw away the feeling that it is my own. Seeing these and feeling it is this fellow, that is the other fellow, etc. should be removed, and instead maintain the feeling that it is all Brahman and Brahman only, and abstain from the temptations to transient pleasures. Once such a state is reached, he can experience that he is one with the Brahman, the unique.

Verse 11

A set of fears that come running will
Immediately break away seeing your knowledge
Then darkness will come and hide it
Again appears as the flow of honey knowledge.

The scene of many things and miseries of friend and foe feeling come up rushing to the mind, and that will vanish once it sees the blissful state that has been attained through thinking and meditation. But this joyful state of mind will fade out due to its being hidden by a dark veil. Similarly, this blessed state will again appear as the flow of honey.

If reality is the only one, then wandering in love and hatred are only artificial (not real). A seeker of real truth with his body performs his duties, making the mind free of love and hatred. If this effort gets satisfied even to some extent, a sweet blessedness will be experienced in the mind; this state of mind is mentioned as '*oli*' (light) in the poem. Once this blessed state is attained, all diversities and temptations will vanish. A devotee who is aware of the fact that it is the feeling of diversities and temptation that makes this joyful state lost, will never care about such things. Still, there comes a feeling that something comes and hides this joyful state now and then. This is the cover of ignorance that hides the Atman. In a worldly man, the veil of ignorance, and the diverse scenes thereof, continues to exist. In a seeker of truth, the rise of this joyful state is experienced now and then in the beginning. This state of joy marks the beginning of salvation (ref. Gita,Poem 15, etc.). At that state, Lord Krishna says, 'All miseries set here.' Experience of blissfulness is said to be due to great penance. Gurudev refers to this state of bliss as the flow of honey from his own experience.

Verse 12

In the forms of water fire and so on
The truth shines filling inside and outside
Once the untruth that hides is found
It is gooseberry fruit in the palm.

The absolute truth taking the form of water, fire, etc. that shine filling inside and outside and that which is veiled by the cover of Maya, once found in the joyful mind through self-experience, then the secret of life will appear as a gooseberry on the palm.

In the state of salvation, the pleasant mind finds the secret of self. Then comes the experience of one's own self (Atman) that appears as the universe. Whatever is seen as different components of the universe are only pictures seen in the self. Once these things are experienced and the mind purified, the secret of life will appear as a gooseberry in the palm (Ref. 'Atmopadesa Satakam'. 78, 79, 80).

Verse 13

This universe is seen as the golden robe
Worn by the beautiful, unique consciousness
As earlier to the moonrise moonlight spreads
Bliss is the light of the full realization of absolute reality.

This wonderful system of the universe is seen as an external manifestation of the real one. The blissfulness of the mind is like the cool light that appears before the rise of the moon in the east. The blissfulness of mind is the light before the rise of the full realization of the real object.

The Brahman (Atman) is all-pervading, and hence, it exists in every living and nonliving thing in the universe. It is only the dirty feelings and emotions that hide the self-experience. All worship and the practice of religious rites are for the purification of mind. A seeker of truth should train the mind to leave all dualities and believe that everything is Brahman himself. To test whether the mind has become purified, one has to see whether the mind has reached a joyful state beyond the surrounding material world. This is the forerunner of the forthcoming enlightenment of Atman. Like the cool light spreading in the east before the rising of the moon, arrives the blessedness of mind in advance of the enlightenment.Then this wonderful universe will be found as only a fake manifestation of the only one as clear as the shining Sun.

Verse 14

That light which is the light of mind came and
Devoured all my earlier dual feelings and what
Shines as the self-shining light experienced in all
Five elements, like space, are the unique divine magic play.

That blessedness of mind which shines as a light in all those things which were thought to be many scenes are removed and transmuted into absolute knowledge (awareness) that experience as shining intensely in all the five elements such as space making the unique is your divine play of magic.

The wise used to explain the universe as the cosmic dance of Brahman (ref. *The Tao of Physics*, Fritjof Capra). The dance of Shiva (*Sivathantavam*) in the burial ground is well known. To one looking from outside, the universe will look like the burial ground where the dead bodies are burnt. But person who has attained mental blessedness will see in the burial ground only the dancing Shiva. Throughout the universe, with all its elements, the experience of the presence of uniqueness is his divine dance.

Verse 15

Immediately on experiencing the presence of Brahman
The self united with Brahman becomes witness to worldly life
The seekers of truth who unite with Brahman
Obtain the opportunity to experience bliss eternally.

Once the experience that it is the Lord's divine dance that took the forms of the universe and the outer place, the life in it immediately finds a place in the divine dance will stand sternly united with Brahman as a witness. Such seekers of truth united will get eternal bliss.

As one gains the vision of Brahman, throughout this universe, the self that gives life to one's own body and Brahman that gives life to the universe will be experienced as one.

Then he comes to know that all things in the universe are only creations of Maya and also are destroyed by it, and one's ownself has nothing to do with it. He understands that he is only observing the universe. Without interfering with anything directly but observing with presence as a witness-like Sun stands as a witness to all activities in the world. Those in the world can perform activities only with his heat and light by his presence. But Sun has no direct connection with the deeds of men, either good or evil. This is the experience ofthe person who has attained the realization of Brahman. Maya creates and destroys many inert things. It is with his presence she does all these things. But man has no relation to the activities of Maya. The seeker of truth attains the state of realization. One who reaches this state of witness experiences eternal bliss.

Verse 16

Once thought all these are all happiness
Everywhere is seen as full of beauty
Once thought all these inert forms are
Abodes formed out of the supreme soul.

The Lord's presence as the witness and the divine dance once thought are all happy. It feels like beauty pervades everywhere. Once thought, all inert things are formed from the divine entity, the prime cause. These inert things can be seen as a place of existence of life force.

After their mind becomes joyful, those, who could see the Atman, the life force, inside them can see in all these inert things the spirit of Brahman. The universe thus becomes full of beauty and happiness. They experience all inert scenes as the place of existence of life force. To those who do not know the Atman, this universe is only inert and full of miseries.

Verse 17

The body, like the cage of Atman the mind
And so on that burns as cotton in the fireof
Knowledge and ignorance like the morning
Sunlight fall on dew drops create many dangers.

The body, like the nest for containing the Atman, the mind, etc. like cotton wool materials that easily burn in the fire of knowledge and the fire of awareness as if in dew drops when tender sunlight of desires strike, undergoes dissolution (undergoes danger).

To those who have seen the absolute truth, the body is the nest of self. Once the awareness of self is awakened, the inertness of that nest burns in the fire of knowledge. As far as a worldly man is concerned, things such as body, mind, etc. are like cotton, and the conscious self is the spark of fire hidden in it. If, by the advice of the teacher and union with God, this spark is triggered when the body and mind will burn in it and merge into it, and as a result, the entire inertness of universe is cleared and becomes pure. To those who do not kindle the fire of knowledge to them, only the worldly desires (ignorance) will remain, and then their experience will be like the dews melted in tender sunlight. The ignorance of such men takes their Atman and body into danger. Because of worldly desires, the Atman is fully eclipsed, and their body and mind decay and perish. Therefore, those who wish to purify the universe avoiding this disaster should seek the Atman deeply. In short, getting rid of worldly desires (ignorance) is the most important factor in the search for reality.

Verse 18

Withdrawing from subjects and introvert
Concentrating on senses and escaped from
All other bindings like the broken tree fall
All longings will vanish by themselves.

Once withdrawn from sense organs, concentrated introvert and refrain from worldly matters, the mind becomes joyful. Through that, seeing Atman leaving all worldly thoughts, the entire inert scenes will retreat like a tree with broken roots and fall by itself on the ground.

We saw above that the knowledge will fade away as the dews melt when the tender sunlight of worldly desires strike. But when the worldly desires have forsaken the senses, joining with the mind will result in the joyfulness of mind withdrawing from the senses; thereby joining with the Atman, the solidified form of happiness and beauty will be manifested. By that, the worldly thoughts will leave the mind. It is the worldly thoughts that confuse, showing inert things outside. Once the realization of self is obtained, the outside also will be experienced as filled with the self. Whatever is there in the mind will be experienced as existing outside also. When worldly desires are removed from inside, the inert scenes will disappear like the tree with broken roots, and self-happiness and beauty will be experienced in their entirety.

Verse 19

When all these things left as useless comes
The awareness of self-shining light
Thus one who became pure consciousness will
Never fall in the whirlpool in the ocean of worldly life.

When all inert scenes around get away without any use, then comes the experience of absolute consciousness that fills thickly everywhere shining by itself. Then one who has attained by himself the state of absolute consciousness will never fall in the whirlpool of life. This is self-realization or salvation.

The word absolute means 'one'. Salvation is an aspect of the Absolute. Absolute is the state of leaving all thoughts of dualities. It is the experience of oneness in the universe, and that itself is salvation. In consciousness, its own power Maya creates the feeling of many. Whatever forms are found in all those, what really shines is only the consciousness, like only gold is there in all golden ornaments. This experience is the experience of non-duality. To attain self-realization, the consciousness which shines as Atman in one should be purified, and then only it becomes possible to get the absolute form of the universe, the non-duality. Once the entire universe is experienced as the absolute consciousness, then the feeling of many worlds and many things goes away and also the feeling of births and deaths, because if there is only one thing, then who is born and who is dead? Salvation is that realization of non-duality in the present life.

Verse 20

The entire universe then becomes a single ocean of
Pure consciousness and non-dual is known as salvation
When the awareness of inert body vanishes
Then this death will be experienced as salvation.

The entire inert universe becoming a single ocean of absolute consciousness and attaining the state of non-duality is known as salvation. Whenever the awareness of the body is completely gone, and the concept of life completely lost, then this salvation will be experienced as an escape to a different world.

In salvation, the concept of life may remain. But that concept of the body never becomes the cause of miseries. Even if one sees a mirage, he will not think of drinking that water in a mirage. The awareness of life also being completely gone and the disappearance of the cause of life is an escape to the other world. Even without the departure from the body, this escape from life can be experienced, because even if the body is there in the state of non-duality, there will not be the feeling of the body. The *Brahmavidwairishta*s, for most of the time leaving the feeling of body, experience the state of bodiless escape.

One finding the secret of one's existencewhile in this universe is the aim of life. First, realize one's own secret,and then experience that the secret of the entire universe is nothing other than the truth that is hidden in him. This is the order—one's own secret will become clear only if the wavering mind that wanders outside is concentrated introvert. For that, as a symbol of the supreme soul worship some or other favourite god and thereby become trained to get concentration. Or else, from a master hearing about Brahmanas pervading everywhere through the method of meditation, the mind can be concentrated. Here, Gurudev beautifully blends both these ways of meditation. God Shiva is the symbol of Brahman the Absolute.

Verse 21

Oh! Lord! Destroyer of Tripuras! Give me
Attainment of Brahman as it is your duty
One who destroys all evils and removes all
Dualities of Light and the stark darkness.

Oh! Lord who burnt the Tripuras, bless me with the attainment of the Absolute—the salvation. You are bound to do this favour to the devotees. One who is capable of destroying all sins, Oh! Lord! Remove all good instincts in the form of knowledge and bad instincts that come to mind as ignorance and make the mind pure, free of all.

The ultimate aim of life is the attainment of the supreme consciousness. It should be achieved while living in this world. The way to achieve this is to remove all instincts of worldly activities through concentrated meditations of God. It is not easily done. Therefore, as the first step, develop good instincts like mercy, donation, shelter, etc., and remove or discourage bad instincts like lust, anger, fraud, etc.; then, teaching the mind that everything is divine based, remove the aforesaid good instincts ultimately also. To one who believes that there is only one, the good instincts also are obstructions. If the evil instinct is an iron chain, then the good instinct is a golden chain. It is only a difference in the material of chains, but both are chains that bind one to worldly life. The God is bound to do the favour of making one attain the supreme soul, to those who consider everything in the universe as filled with the Absolute. This capability has been established by the Tripuras. Here, the Tripuras indicate three stages of mind, namely, wakefulness, dream and deep sleep, and the feelings they create are the three causes: corpulent, minute and cause.

Tripuras (demons) are three demons, namely, Vidwunmali, Tarakachakshuss and Kamalakshan. They are the three sons of Tarakasura. They did penance praising Shiva, made him satisfied and got three boons to have three never-destroying cities. Tripuras (three cities) are heaven, space and earth. The architect Mayan constructed three cities with gold, silver and iron for these demons. Later, these three demons were killed by Lord Shiva.

Verse 22

Without the adherence of evil instincts and divine
Thoughts the self-shining light since blessed
With the knowledge about you bless me
I adore you without the experience, bless me, Oh! Lord!

Without the touch of bad instincts and good instincts standing beyond, ignorance and knowledge, oh! The experience of self-shining bliss! Being blessed with the knowledge about you, I pray without knowing the experience. Oh! Lord! Bless me to experience this.

It is known very well that the substance that shines beyond ignorance and knowledge without characteristics is the Brahman, the embodiment of entity, mind and bliss. It is the mercy of the Lord that helped to know this. It is this mercy that is mentioned in the above poem. Though the devotee could understand theoretically what the substance is, he could not attain the attributed state of bliss through experience. By the portion 'without knowing', Gurudev indicates whether it is from Shiva, the king of Kailas, or Shiva as Brahman that the devotee prays that the non-dual experience of Brahman be given to him. In both cases, the devotee wants the experience of the unique Brahman.

Verse 23

Oh! Mercy! By your magic you made me
Ignorant of truth one which appears like a veil
Who becomes light of truth give refuge to
Both who shine in mind is all your game.

Oh! Merciful Lord! Since you have made a divine veil around me, this devotee is not able to know the real truth due to ignorance. Lord! Who exists as the veil to hide the real truth and also the light that enshrines the truth giving shelter to both and stand as the embodiment of mercy, one who shines in my heart, all these are your game.

The Brahman, which is the real truth, shines in all living things. But by sitting inside, you create in living things a veil of ignorance. To those who have removed the veil of ignorance and submit before you, you give light so that he can see his self. You are the embodiment of mercy; then why do you sit inside the animals and act in different ways? What else can be said about it other than it is all your game?

Verse 24

Oh! The Absolute! Whichever truth that
Spreads fragrance and fills everywhere

That truth, Oh! Merciful bless me not to
Ride and trapped in the wheel of time.

Oh! The supreme cause and the merciful! Bless me with the awareness of non-duality so that I am not trapped in the wheel of time and becoming subject to births and deaths or to continue the inert life.

The worldly life, the life of births and deaths and the flow of time are confined to the inert world. It is impossible to escape from the relation with inert things without the experience of non-duality. Here, the devotee prays to the Lord to bless him with the knowledge of non-duality.

Verse 25

Oh! Supreme! Who controls waves of rising visuals
Unbound saviour of lives destroyer of sins
Call me near! Let me not sink
Even for a moment in the ocean of miseries.

Oh! Lord who prevails as the ultimate cause of the universe and Maya your magic power that comes up creating waves as scenes of universe Oh! Saviour of life who does not link with them but controls them, one who destroys all sins! Bless me giving the sense of truth without immersing in the waves of worldly life. Don't permit me to live in this ocean of worldly life not even for a moment! Don't permit Lord!

Maya, the magic power of the ultimate cause, comes up like waves and creates a sense of the universe in it. Brahman, the cause of the Maya power without having any link with the universe-like waves by keeping away, controls them. This is what the seekers of truth have found. Gurudev indicates this in the second line as '*paranetavayeedunna pasupatiye*'. Pashupati is the protector of lives. The word *pasu* (cow) means living thing. The address '*harane*' (destroyer) indicates that to get the real truth, the sins have to be destroyed. Here it is to show the life on earth is miserable and to hint the devotee's desire to take him from this miserable place.

Verse 26

Oh! Shiva! It is impossible to explain
Your greatness by words one that shines
Without getting your mercy a little
Will I waste my life, Lord Shiva?

Oh! Lord the auspicious one, it is difficult to explain your greatness in words and the one who shines by self in the form of the ultimate cause. Will I waste my life without getting at least a little of your mercy?

The soul is the throbbing (fluctuations) of the Absolute Brahman. And life is that which reflects on the prana the soul (breath). This reflected consciousness joined with the breath creates the five elements, Sun, planets and all living things. Absolute Brahman shines by self as the embodiment of bliss behind without any emotion, though through throbbing, all the components of the universe were created; this has been known by experience, and anybody can know it through experience. These things are beyond ordinary logic, and hence, unexplainable. It is possible, either by experience or by throwing away ego, with dedication to gain the mercy of God. To those who cannot gain the mercy of God, their life will remain useless. Here the devotee takes an oath that he will not make his life fruitless.

Verse 27

Oh! Lord Shiva! Being inside you the ear
Eye and so on come out and grace and seek
Their subjects, along with them come
All other things, what magic is this!

Oh! Lord the symbol of pure consciousness! Since it exists in you the ear, eye, etc. senses of knowledge and senses of action experience the sound, etc. subjects outside. All other imaginations, along with the ego, the characteristics of life, are sitting inside the mind and observe things outside. This type of observation of things outside sitting inside the mind. About this, what else can be said except that it is all your magic.

Born from the mind, existing in mind and vanishing in mind are the senses and the mental thoughts. Without the escort of mind, they cannot have existed and cannot do activities. Even though it always existed as their base, they s earch (seek) not the mind but the inert. It is wonderful how they become thankless. They always seek the inert and suffer always. On the other hand, if they sought inside the pure blissful mind, they could have enjoyed unlimited happiness. They are not doing it. What jiggling is this? If the senses and imaginations, instead of seeking the inert scenes outside,were concentrated in introversion, the real truth could have been found.

Verse 28

Oh! Supreme light! Hidden by the veil of ignorance
Everything is seen little by little separately that covers
Completely the ignorance and the smouldering smoke
Once known as nothing but you all magic will disappear.

Oh! Absolute Brahman who is hidden by the veil of ignorance! Everything is seen little by little separately as minute things along with the veil of ignorance covering all things and the imaginary smoke of emotion once known as nothing but you; this magic of senses and mind that go around inert things outside will fade out completely. Once thought and analysed as to what this phenomenon seen as the universe is, and realized that it is all Brahman, the veil of ignorance will completely vanish. The feeling that there are so many things in the universe is really the ignorance. It is the reason for the smoke in the form of imaginary emotion. So long as this illusion of duality exists, the senses and mind will go on seeking inert things and discharging smoke. Once the truth that these are all one is realized, then their hastiness will end. The burning of mind will cease and will attain the ultimate peace and happiness.

Verse 29

Seen as smoke inside,as small things outside
As sky separating inside and outside shining as
Light experienced as bliss that separates Earth
And heaven the primordial subtle one, Bless me!

Oh! Lord who shines as imagination implicitly and as inert things explicitly! One who appears as minute things separately one by one, one who appears as the sky that separates inside and outside, one who shines as brilliance, one who is experienced as happiness inside, and one who has become this world and other worlds (the earth and heaven). In the middle of the worldly experience, one who shines as a subtle body, Lord! Shed mercy on me, making the awareness of non-duality brighten the happiness inside me!

In all living things, you exist as a symbol of happiness. The only resisting force that blocks this experience of non-duality is ignorance. The remedial medicine for this sickness of ignorance is the concept of non-duality everywhere. All those things seen as minute, subtle things separately are all one and is the Brahman. The sky which is seen as inside and outside and the shining brilliance is only one, the Brahman. What is referred to as the widely spread rain is the happiness filled in mind,and that too is Brahman. Both this world and the other world (earth and heaven) are only Brahman. The subtle life seen in between this world and the other world is also Brahman. This is the concept of non-duality. This concept of non-duality removes the distinction between the manifest and the Brahman, which is the symbol of happiness.

Verse 30

Irrespective of inside and outside
Oh! Lord! You exist filling everywhere
In your famous eye, all these seen in
Different forms are the only show of magic.

Oh! My Lord, the symbolic form of the supreme consciousness! You pervade everywhere irrespective of inside and outside. In the eye of the famous experience of non-duality, all these dualities in different forms are all mere shadows, only a show of magic.

In this poem, the use of the words 'in your eye' means in the eye of one who attains salvation. One who escaped from worldly life in the state of deep meditation without dualities realizes the unique Brahman and becomes one with itself. There is no feeling of the world (earth). But when it reaches the state of wakefulness from deep meditation, it links with the body, the inert instrument. Then there is a feeling of inertness. But for the one who has realized the real truth, this link with the body and feeling of worldly experience is only the shadow in the consciousness. He experiences it as only a show of Maya. In the desert, where there is not even a drop of water, even if the feeling of the water is existing there, he will never believe it is real water. It is to indicate this, Gurudev used the word '*pukalpongina*' (the famous). To one who has attained salvation, Brahman will be experienced as fully filling the inside and outside.

Verse 31

One who melts the ignorance like melting
The ghee one who plunders all sins and makes
Experience of breath spread in the atmosphere
Oh! One who shines as the fire of knowledge!

Oh! Lord who blesses the man, who dilutes the prompting experience of inert scenes like the ghee dilutes in heat, destroying all his sins, taking the form of Lord Narasimha. Hereafter make this experience into the form of breath spread in the atmosphere Oh! Lord who shines as the fire of knowledge, I adore you.

The seeker of truth at the first stage finds that the breath alone is the truth, and all inert scenes are only deceptive virtual Maya scenes. The word '*paka*' (revengeful attitude)indicates this Maya. Then the seeker of truth, for the full realization of breath and to experience it, learns to keep a detached attitude towards inert scenes. Removing the feeling of 'my own'(ego) about things, including body and love and hatred in mind, also left from the mind, then mind becomes filled with joy. Once it happens, comes the experience of a cool flow as if the inert feelings are melting. It is the beginning of the experience of samadhi. This is what Gurudev mentions as '*neyyurukum nikarāy nīrākidunna*'. Following that as the voluntary samadhi, he experiences the beginning of spreading of Kundalini prana. Then, the feeling of the cool flow of prana filling inside and outside gives an experience of blissful consciousness. It is this realization of prana, Gurudev indicates by saying '*Inimēl pukayāy vānilchuzhatti vidumeriyē*'.

Prana is that which evolves from awareness. Smoke evolves from the fire. Once the smoke is fully gone, fire shines clearly. Like that, once the throbbing prana stops, in the state of salvation, the pure consciousness shines brightly.

Verse 32

All inert feelings dissolved joined with the fire of
Knowledge bloated and echoed the sound Aum
Oh! Lord! What the four Vedas search always
In the divine sound is there in your anklet bells.

Oh! Lord in the form of unidentified sound form heard in Kundalini prana that overflows as cold water flow comes joined with the fire of knowledge and all inert imaginations dissolved, Lord! You are the idol entity, mind and bliss united that the four

Vedas search always manifests through the sound of your beautiful anklet, I adore you.

The experience of unidentified sound is produced with the spreading of prana. When prana enters from the spinal cord in the mind, the yogi begins to hear different types of sound. But from where it comes and what these sounds are, is not known. It is why this sound is known as the unidentified one. This unknown sound whose source is not known, when heard, indicates the arrival time just prior to reaching the Brahman. Here Gurudev takes the sound of the anklet as the indication of the Lord's royal visit. Once the unknown sound is felt as heard, the mind forgets all other worldly imaginations and dissolves into it. Since the mind is dissolved, the sound also gets dissolved in it. Then the consciousness will get manifested as self-shining.

Verse 33

Lord! Sourceless sound! Precious jewel! Shines
As the light in mind! One who destroys worldly instincts!
The beetles come after its sound with fragrance
And pollen, one who shines at salvation! I adore you.

Oh! Lord! One who experiences the unknown sound, Oh! Lord who shines as a valuable diamond in mind. Oh! Lord who reaches flying as beetle after sound! Destroying the red colour of tendency for worldly activities that come along with waves of happiness sits self-shining in the state of salvation! I adore you.

The spreading of prana and the experience of unidentified (*savikalpa*) sound pave the way to a lot of feelings. It will be experienced as in the uncertain (savikalpa) state of salvation among the unknown sounds. The consciousness shines brilliantly as a light of the diamond in mind. In the uncertain state of salvation still, a part of Thrigunas remains. But the certain (*nirvikalpa*—unchangeable) state of salvation is the state when all such influence of Thrigunas are removed, and the blissful indivisible consciousness becomes manifested. Gurudev explains this condition in '*iḷakum parimaḷamodu chuvayoḷiyum podiyāy varuttiyorunilaye*'. To know more about the certain and uncertain states of salvation, please refer to 'Yoga Darsanam' in 'Darsanamala'.

Verse 34

Like the unending storm makes turbulence
When abated in its darkness ignorance spreading
Wearing rippling Ganga on the head, you dance
Is it not the skin of darkness you wear? Oh! Lord!

Is it the veil of ignorance coming up that is experienced as darkness when the turbulent gale of worldly imaginations is ended? Is it the veil of Maya that Brahman wraps over it for the creation of the universe or is it the dark skin of elephant that is worn by Shiva who appears here wearing the cold stream of prana that overflows.

The one who is training the religious rites comes to experience many wonderful feelings. At times it may be the experience of overcast vacuums. What is this experience of overcast Maya that vibrates in the mind for creation? At first, that creates a veil around the object. It is over this cover the imaginations of objects in the universe are projected. This projection contains the images of objects and the worldly scenes. For one who tries to train meditation, the first thing he has to do is to remove this projection. Gurudev indicates this, in the line '*nilayillate kodumkāttalayunnatupoy*'. Once the projections have faded out naturally, the dark veil will appear, and this is mentioned by Gurudev as '*nivaṛnnu varumiruḷo*'. Only if this cover is broken, the real truth will appear in full. The veil is the creation of collected past worldly activities, and it is the cover of ignorance of human wisdom. Attaining detachment and removing the worldly temptations, one comes to experience the real truth. It is this cover of Maya on human wisdom, which is symbolically described as the skin of an elephant worn by Shiva.

Verse 35

Wrapped in skin kicking out frenzies full of
Worldly whirlings flaws and strife of devotees
Oh! The fire of knowledge! Who heads and
Abides by the prime cause of everything!

Oh! Lord in the form of knowledge! Who givesyour feet as shelter to those who seek to remove miseries of worldly life, full of anger and heat hiding in the cover of Maya. Oh! Lord the embodiment of truth who makes the timely adversities vanished to those who serve your feet! Oh! Lord who exists as the ultimate cause pervading the entire universe. I adore you.

Brahman is the ultimate cause of the entire universe. The real cause of all worldly relations is due to the knowledge of things as many and diverse instead of seeing the actual truthin full. To get rid of this concept of worldly things, leave all that and see the same God as filling everywhere and approach him, whether thatGod is in the form of SagunaBrahman or Nirguna Brahman. Pray to him considering that all those gods are only different forms of Him so also all those things seen in the universe. Then believe that you and your body are all the properties of that God. This is the surrender of everything; this is seeking shelter at the foot of the God. All worldly miseries and timely adversities of those who seek shelter will be kicked out by that God. To achieve the removal of the veil of Maya, only this total surrender is the way. Other than that, there is nothing else.

Verse 36

On one side darkness and light come and go
You remain divine tree to the vine of breath to
Twineand creep, nobody understands your
Wonderful play! Realizing youis the only truth!

Oh! Lord! Who shines as the divine, all-granting celestial plant to wrap around the vine of breath (life) that gives happiness whose one side is light and darkness that goes on alternating. Nobody is capable of understanding your wonderful plays. This experience of realization is really one in which the opponents' love and hatred fade out.

To know the principle of divinity, there is no way other than realizing it by oneself. Its novelty is that it cannot be explained by any logic. During meditation, when the spreading of breath (prana) in Kundalini begins, many feelings go on changing like light and darkness. But its cause, the absolute reality, also is felt there, and this ultimate reality will be felt like the divine all-granting plant on which the Kundalini spirit is wrapped around. It is compared to the absolute reality because the divine plant shows happiness and the experience of attainment at that stage. Even at the stage of realization, all love and hatred will get away. All the senses will become under control. The worldly plays of the absolute reality experienced at this stage cannot be explained by logic. The questions like how Maya came into existence and why this universe created, get answers only when one attains realization. It means the reality is one that can be understood only by realization, not by any other methods.

Verse 37

Along with your divine play telling the unparalleled
Truth becomes possible only by your realization
What explainable by words need not be the truth
Oh! The absolute truth not known from outside!

Oh! Lord! To understand your plays and to get the real meaning of truth, one has to attain it by realization. There is no parallel to the truth; anything which can be explained to somebody cannot be the truth. And the knowledge about it from outside also cannot be the real truth. But Oh! Lord, you are the one who shines as the perfect truth, I adore you.

To self-realization, there are no parallels as it is unique, and there is not a second to it in this universe. To understand the explanations of God's plays in full by men of wisdom is possible only when one who seeks it also follows that truth. The explanation that the universe is Maya, and that the divine plays in different incarnations, could be understood only when one follows the way to this experience. But the full meaning and purpose of those explanations can be understood only when that experience is obtained. This truth cannot be understood in fullby observing from outside. How can the bubble or a wave contain an ocean as a whole? To contain the ocean, the bubble or wave has to dissolve in it. Likewise, to know the ultimate reality, the mind has to dissolve in the ultimate. Such an experience cannot be explained in words. Whatever the words can explain is only the names and forms of things. But for an explanation by words, there is not a second in the universe to compare with. Since the ultimate reality is the 'only one', one cannot confirm the truth by measurement or logic by comparison.

Verse 38

Lord! Names and forms left and gone beyond the veil of
Ignorance come manifest in the soul as Consciousness
Will, the ocean of mercy, lose a bit if my parched tongue
Incapable of explaining your greatness is watered.

Oh! Lord the embodiment of truth who stands to leave forms and names and to exist beyond the veil of Maya who appears in the spread of breath as consciousness, if you fill with experience of happiness so that the tongue being incapable of explaining your real form, Oh! Lord the ocean of divine wisdom! In doing so, you are not losing anything.

The secret of Brahman cannot be understood only by the mind and senses observing from outside. Still, in the state of uncertain attainment, the mind keeping away becomes fully capable of experiencing the self in full. With the spreading of Kundalini breath, this experience of uncertain attainment becomes possible. When the mind departs from the names and forms, scenes outside and fixed strongly in meditation, the spreading of Kundalini prana starts, the mind that is concentrated experiences the departure of the dark veil. When the spreading of prana starts, the blissful awareness comes to the experience. This is what Gurudev indicates by '*parayum kadannu varumala*'. The tongue is the symbol of the mind that is concentrated in introversion.

Verse 39

Is not the awareness that the Lord has no deficiency
A creation of ignorance? Lord who exists as
The last step of discovering absolute truth is
Still unsatisfied. Alas! Lord! You know the secret.

Is it not the statement that the Lord is not losing anything a creation of ignorance. Oh! Lord, who exists as the last step of discovering the real truth, is still not satisfied even when whatever is gained, what else can be said other than it is pitiable. Oh! Merciful Lord, you know in full the secret of dissatisfaction of life, is it not?

The absolute truth is blissful in itself. It does not lose anything ever. That means it is eternal and full in entirety always. But the knowledge about things created by Maya is transient and is a virtual creation in mind. The inference that there is at least something missing in the all-pervading Brahman, itself is part of ignorance. Ignorance is the only cause of all discontents. Oh! Lord, you are aware of this. Hence give me contentment removing ignorance.

Verse 40

When all things with ego left and vanished in the Absolute
The self-shining absolute truth arose and merged always
With four elements and becoming unique One shines
As the divine sound that brings to Brahman, we adore you.

When all things (*samashti*) along with ego left and dissolved in the Absolute, the one appeared as the self-shining light, Oh! Absolute truth! The rising unique (*vrishti*) self-shining light, merging jointly with the components of the soul, the mind, self-wisdom and ego become the shining Brahman, the unidentified sound! I adore you!

If one wishes to get blessedness leaving all dissatisfactions, one has to realize the entirety of absolute reality. When all worldly feelings, along with ego depart knowingly, then rises the experience of pure consciousness; it is the complete realization of absolute reality. The experience of hearing the unknown sound that comes prior to salvation; many beautiful sounds are heard. By then the mind, thought, wisdom, ego, the four components of awareness dissolve and the sound also disappears, only the indivisible bliss—the absolute reality—remains. This is the state of complete realization. In the poem, the Sanakas are taken as symbols of awareness. Sanakas are the son-like children of God Brahma—Sanaka, Sanatkumara, Sananta and Sanatana, and they symbolize the four components of sound mentioned above. This is discussed by Gurudev in 'Atmopadesa Satakam'.

Verse 41

Your cosmic play is great nothing is known
To us clearly on one part of you
Golden vine of life creep up around,
Lord! Stand support for it we adore you!

The celestial play of the Lord is very great. It is wonderful! Nothing is known to us about it. Oh! Lord, this is a part of you that stands strongly fixed like a tree, for the Maya created the brilliant leaf of prana to wrap around.

To one who looks at this universe from outside, it seems indefinable, and nothing can be said about it; it looks wonderful! This multiverse consisting of billions and billions of universes whirling in perfect order is only your play; what else one can say about it? But for the experience of real truth, these things do not come as obstructions. The real truth can be understood only by looking into one's inner self. When the mind is concentrated on meditation in search of truth, the experience of spreading of prana comes to mind. So also, it will become evident that it is only in the awareness, like the tree on which the vine wraps, thatprana spreads. By then, it becomes clear that it is in the unchanging awareness; the vibration in the self makes the formation of the form of prana that creates and dissolves is the universal play (also becomes clear). Oh! Lord! You are the unmoving form of awareness; I adore you.

Verse 42

Oh! The unique tree! Henceforth
Your loving foot of mercy is my support
The flowers to wear on the head is the mountain
Where golden vine spreads what magic is this?

Oh! Lord the embodiment of truth who stands as the unique tree to me suffering from the heat of worldly life, your feet full of mercy is the only shelter my head covering with flowers is it the unmoving mountain the truth on which the leaf of prana grow widely and spreads. What wonderful scene is this!

In the realization of Kundalini prana, the truth clearly becomes manifested. It is in the indivisible consciousness that the prana is spreading. The happiness in the awareness is experienced as completely filled in the prana breath; then the indivisible consciousness, which is unmoving like a mountain, the prana, happily spreads everywhere like a golden vine inside it. The manifestation of these is the peculiarity of Kundalini yoga. So also as at this stage of experience, the universe will be seen as full of happiness. It is because of this Gurudev makes a comment '*taṇaliniyī nin Kani kaẓaliṇa*'. It is only when the spreading of prana also fades out that the experience of pure indivisible consciousness comes.

Verse 43

All these are Lord's magic
Don't you know there were three eyes?
One who shines wearing the moon on the head
I adore at your flower-like feet.

Oh! Lord these are all your magical plays. Is it not true that you had three eyes? Oh! Lord! The embodiment of bliss, one shines wearing the moon on the head, I adore at your flower-like beautiful feet.

How can one understand that all these universal plays are the magical play of your Lordship? Is it not well known that Lord Shiva had three eyes? If so, is it not necessary that the 'life' (Jeeva) which is part of the Lord also had three eyes? This means one of the eyes of Jeeva is closed with Maya by the Lord. We know the magic show is a play of closing the eyes. Once the magician removes the cover, we see the real things. If the third eye of Jeeva is opened, the absolute reality (truth) will become clear, getting rid of all worldly desires. The opening of the third eye is really the experience of awareness that there is only one thing, not a second, in the universe. What all things saw as diverse and many, are only virtual things. Then the experience of virtual things appearing as real in the universe will get removed.

Verse 44

This devotee who adores with folded hands
Be saved from the state of deceit
And make my hands embrace your feet
Be responsible! Remembering I am your child.

Oh! Lord! This humble devotee who bows down at your feet be saved from the drowsiness of magic and take my hands close to your feet and make me merge in you. Consider me as your own child, if so, remember, it is your responsibility.

It is not possible to escape from the crazy magic of worldly life using magic. To remove the magical events, the magician himself should try. Therefore, for this, the onlooker is forced to approach the magician himself. This means for the attainment of self-realization, the only simple way is to dedicate everything, including own inert body along with the ego, at the feet of the Lord and get rid of the feeling of 'I'. Feel everything is of God and everything is the God. One, who does so, will be taken care of by the Lord and will be taken safely to the other shore of the ocean of worldly life, and thereafter the Lord will make you merge in him. The devotee reminds the God that it is the duty of the God since the devotee is the son of God himself.

Verse 45

Oh! God of gods! Who wears crescent
The moon on the head there is nothing beyond
Your control, do not sell me wholly
To the branch of the bloated filthy body.

Oh! God of gods who wear crescent moon! Nothing happens in this world beyond your control! Be merciful! Do not destroy me, making completely a slave to the bloated body which is like a branch of a tree in the forest of worldly life.

The universe full of inert scenes is like a thick forest. The human body is like a small branch in it. Sitting in that branch if looked around, the virtual universe will appear as full of darkness like a thick forest. It so happens because observation done through the senses makes me believe that I am the body. On the other hand, if the mind is concentrated in introversion on consciousness, one gets the awareness that he himself is the consciousness. Once this awareness is obtained, he gets convinced that the entire universe is he himself. It is the Maya that creates this crazy feeling of the universe. The belief that I am the body can be removed only by the all-pervading, all-powerful god. For that, the devotee has to pray to the God for his mercy.

Verse 46

Wearing Ganga on the head and sitting on the mountain
Bless me giving your flower-like feet for adoration
Be support as an evergreen tree to a golden vine
On which warbling cuckoo vacillate, Oh! Lord!

Oh! Lord! Resident of snowy bright mountain, wearing Ganga on head, bless me giving your pair of beautiful feet for worship like a tree around which the vine wrap, to the vine of prana that produces the beautiful unknown sound like the sound of cuckoo that spread through the spinal nerve, Lord, you stand firmly as an evergreen tree. I adore you. Oh! Lord.

As the prana stands to get into the spinal nerve and spreads, sweet unknown sounds come to be heard. Spreading of prana starts with the production of sound; '*Kūkum pūnkuyilēṟippōkum*' is to indicate this. It also comes to the experience that sound and spreading of prana are taking place inside the core of awareness. It is this core of awareness that is considered as the new tree. Gurudev repeatedly explains this to reveal the importance of the abundance of happiness and the state of truth in experience.

Verse 47

Oh! Evergreen tree! It is your mercy
The golden vine spreads like this and that
Bless me putting your flower-like feet on
My head lets me become one with you.

Oh! Lord! The absolute reality! Who shines as a firmly rooted tree! It is your manifestations of mercy that creates the experience of prana spreading like a vine; full of flowers wraps the tree. Bless me putting your beautiful flower-like feet on my head and thereby let me become one with you.

Spreading of prana and realization of the alleviating experience of the unique consciousness is the experience of absolute reality. The spreading of prana before that state is the source of many such experiences. This is the experience that comes changing one by one when spreading prana passes through the fine hole situated at the centre (top) of the skull and reaches the lotus with a thousand petals and alleviate and get the experiences of many colours, sounds and smells (Ref. 'Kundalini Pattu').

Verse 48

Oh! Lord! Accept me at your feet
Do not forsake and lessen your mercy
Do not evade me from your beneficence
Take me as one uncompassionate to others.

Oh! Lord! Accept this destitute devotee at your feet. Do not abandon one! Do not make any lessening of your mercy. Do not abandon me, thinking that I am a person without any devotion.

A man by himself is incomplete. Therefore, he cannot do anything by being a man, especially in the search for truth for attaining the state of surpassing the mind. A devotee may have many occasions where he wanders due to his inability. On all such occasions, there is no way other than total submission and finding shelter at the foot of the Lord. The truth of this is identified by all seekers of truth.

Verse 49

Your compassion must not lose ever from me
But dissolve me at your feet if not
I will immerse in the boiling ocean
Of miseries, you know it without say.

Oh! Lord your mercy should not be allowed to abandon me; I should merge and become one with you at your feet. If that does not happen, this unfortunate one will continue to suffer immersed in the ocean of ignorance. Am I to say that, particularly?

There are only two options for life. Either due to ignorance leading a life of births and deaths in this ocean of worldly life or by removing all worldly longings find the real self and merge with the Absolute Brahman. If that merger is not possible, then the only possibility left is to wander in grief with deaths and births.

Verse 50

It need not be spelt. Oh! Omniscient one!
Shine inside the head of my humble self
Oh! The substance of Vedas! I lived not knowing that
Diversity will be gone, and non-duality comes.

I need not remind you, Oh! The all-knowing Lord! Shines brightly in the head of this devotee who is an indivisible part of men without knowing your realm of consciousness, Oh! Lord unaware of the fact that once the concept of many is lost, there will come an indivisible consciousness, which is the essence of Vedas I lived so far thinking that I am different from you.

It is due to the unawareness that the Brahman and I are one, life maintains the view 'I', 'I' and stand separated from you. It is Maya that creates the feeling of many and, with that confusion, self could not understand its real self. Once the feeling of many is removed, the self can understand that it and Brahman are one.

Verse 51

The principles of Vedas taught by Vedic scholars
Immediately lost once heard, likewise come
Many things devoid of beginning and end
You come merged with them as unique.

The doctrines of Vedas explained by those who have learnt Vedic texts become forgotten immediately after hearing. Many of the experiences in life come and go. Whatever remains is that which eternally pervading everywhere the experience of a merger with that is the realization of Truth.

The attainment of the Absolute Brahman is not possible through prediction or intelligence or by hearing a lot about it. Whoever dissolves in that accept that truth by him, only he can experience that truth. People used to hear many things. To them, the miserable experiences of life come and go, there are births and deaths. But who cares ever to search the secret of it. Even people who do worship God get involved in worldly pleasures. But the ultimate truth is realized only by one who throws away all worldly longings and becomes detached and gains the capability of merging into consciousness.

Verse 52

Oh! Absolute truth! If the experience of
Self is known you will remain one with me
Alas! There is no other refuge cut my
Worldly life making me as one with you.

If I can realize that my entity is only the experience of that unification, Oh! Absolute reality! You will remain as one with me without getting separated. It is pitiable! There are no other means other than this. Oh! Lord who shines as the saviour of humanity, destroy my worldly life and bless me with the state of Brahman.

Lord Shiva is the saviour of human life as if he is the cowherd of cows. The cows are human lives. Like cattle, they wander about grazing the field outside. The Lord as the cowherd controls the cattle by tying them with the rope of worldly imaginations. To escape from this binding, there is only one way (means); submit everything at the feet of the Lord and become one with him. Once that is fulfilled, then one can always remain as the absolute truth. The devotee prays to bless him to merge with the Lord.

Verse 53

Without knowing the Lord is there inside
Many search you here with a wavering mind
And not seeing you spoil life involving
Logic and argument, oh! Lord!

Oh! Lord, my Master! Without understanding that you are very much inside them, many wandered about in this world searching to find you. Worried at not seeing you and becoming incapable of concentrating the mind on anything, life is spoiltengaging in logical thoughts and arguments.

The absolute consciousness always shines in everybody. Unfortunately, everybody creates an artificial veil and hides in it. Only when that veil is removed by oneself and experiences the absolute truth, one can get his doubts cleared completely. But with logic alone, it cannot be carried out. Many without trying to get that experience of theAbsolute, try to prove the real truth through logic and arguments. They become incapable of fixing the mind on anything. Whatever is believed to be true by one's logic, in another's logic will be untrue. In short, logic changes according to individual intelligence. Therefore, whoever does not follow the path of experience of Absolute; to them, the real truth will never be manifest.

Verse 54

Like sand fire water wind and sky
Separated by a partition and all vanished
The heaven and hell all gone away
You swallow me to become one, Wonderful!

Earth, fire, water, air and sky in self-view will look as if disappear taking their shares. Heaven and hell will get away. Lord! The ultimate consciousness (Brahman)! Being dissolved this devotee who stood separately as a human self in you changed everything to only one thing—the supreme reality.

In the beginning stages of the search for reality, there comes the misimpression that there are two separate things as inert and live. It is due to the supposed virtual relation the inert body has with the absolute consciousness. Once life is imposed on the inert body, all experiences of heaven and hell and worldly miseries come up. Once the experience of salvation is realized, all components of inert things, including body will be experienced as only magical scenes of Maya. Then all heaven, earth and hell will vanish like a mirage in a desert. Even the fear arising from the feeling of two will dissolve, and the unique consciousness (the only absolute consciousness) will remain.

Verse 55

In many things indistinguishable as to the beginning, middle
And end existed away from my knowledge
But showing that everything is as absolute consciousness
Seen separated along with their ignorance and appeared as one.

Many things seen outside remained beyond my knowledge about their beginning, middle and end. But demonstrating that all such things are only one thing, the absolute consciousness then and there, leaving all along with their basic root, the Maya, a unique thing appeared shining in their place.

The secret of many things seen outside cannot be understood from outside. We know the search outside is based on space and time. But can anybody find out the beginning and end of space and time looking to outside? If that is impossible, how can we determine the beginning and end of space and time? But one who has realized Brahman can do it. He understands that everything in this universe, including space and time, is only the Brahman himself, the only one. In non-duality, where is the scope for a second that as the beginning or end?

Verse 56

Do not get perplexed seeing 'this one'
'That one' separately so also 'you' and
'He' all these seen as existing today
Merge into you it is not falsehood.

There should not be confusion as to differentiation like 'this is one', the other is two, you, he and so on. What is seen as this one, that one, you, he, etc. seen differentiated are all the seekers of Truth himself? This is an eternal truth known traditionally.

Once the absolute consciousness is found inside, it becomes evident that whatever is seen as different things are all the different forms of virtual images of the same thing. It is the same thing seen as 'this one' 'that one', you, he and so on due to ignorance. Once the veil of ignorance is removed, it becomes manifested as only one. One cannot believe this until one gets convinced from his own experience. But those who had realized the truth through meditation and penance experienced it traditionally.

Verse 57

Going beyond the time that surpasses the day
And night, Oh! God the blissful truth! Stop
My worldly life, is it not you only borrowed
And made prana vibrate, pitiable!

Oh! The embodiment of the truth that survives beyond the time that divides as day and night! Annihilate the state of life. Is it not that you simply borrowed ignorance and made prana vibrate? It is pitiable!

The superconsciousness is an eternal reality beyond the limit of time. Time is only a virtual phenomenon. It is believed to be there due to the action of Maya. If searched in sufficient depth, one can get convinced that there is nothing called time as existing and it is not anything more than imagination. The virtual feeling of life and time begin when the consciousness forgets about its blissful nature beyond the limits of time-projected imaginations. Once this imagination is removed, life will end, and the Brahmanhood will remain. Here, Gurudev says that life is an experience that Brahman borrows from ignorance or imaginations. In fact, life is only the vibration of prana induced virtually. The devotee prays to remove the induced vibration and to manifest the original entity.

Verse 58

Lord! You cover my inside and outside
Destroying my virtual body but the feeling of
The body does not vanish, still sticking on to you
I go away imagining I am different from you.

It is wonderful. Oh! Lord, you fill densely destroying my inside and outside. Still, my awareness of the body does not fully vanish. Sticking on to Lord, I get away imagining that I am different.

The experience of Brahman exists in two different forms—as attributed (Saguna) Brahman and unattributed (Nirguna) Brahman. The experience of Nirguna Brahman is the supreme, ultimate experience. An attributed Brahman (Saguna) experience is a state before coming to Nirguna (unattributed) state. In the unattributed state of experience of Brahman, the entire concept of life ends. Experience of all worldly longings departs so also the feeling of a second. All dualities vanish, the feeling created by ignorance 'I' will totally vanish. It is the state of attainment of salvation.

Verse 59

Making one by one the entire hills and
Mountains as steps for your feet movements
When I wrapped as a golden vine and spread
On you, why did you comply with yourself? Wonderful!

When I thought and confirmed all imaginations rising and falling together are the Lord's own entity and dissolved in salvation came manifested my dearest Lord's form, crushing all imaginations in him. How wonderful it is!

The experience of Nirguna state is the state of the vanishing of all imaginations that rise and fall as in the attributed state and manifestation of the undivided blissful consciousness. In the state of experience of unattributed Brahman, the awareness of life as existing separated from Brahman also vanishes. This is what is meant by the word *Atiyode*. At this state, only the awareness of the absolute reality exists. Now Gurudev concludes.

Verse 60

How wonderful! Oh! Absolute Truth! You always
Reflect on worldly feelings and imaginations
To the burning self in miseries, I adore
The charming Lord wearing—shining crescent moon.

How wonderful! Pure consciousness that fades away when awakens from salvation. Even in the state of living, you always reflect in thoughts. Oh! The embodiment of blissful absolute truth! Who adorns the life burning in worldly miseries with the shining crescent moon, I always adore you!

To a Yogi who has realized the absolute truth in the state of experience of unattributed Brahman, to him, there is no other truth other than the ultimate truth. In the wakeful state, when he involves in worldly affairs, he experiences the life and the inert universe as he did earlier. But he experiences them as things without substance in the unattributed state. The ego of such a man of wisdom will remain as bright and cool light. Grief will never touch his life.

'Swanubhavagiti' is a great literary work of Sree Narayana Gurudev. It explains the spiritual experience of the truth seekers. Let us bow our heads in respect before the divine feet of the great maharishi who wrote this poem to bless the seekers of truth.

17

ARIVU

Most of the literary works of Sree Narayana Gurudev are based on Vedanta philosophy and metaphysics. It is only with self-realization one attains the state of the 'absolute one'—the Brahman. Sat (being) Chit (knowledge) and Ananda (bliss) are different manifestations of consciousness. This work of Sree Narayana Gurudev containing fifteen poems in Malayalam is a modern Vedantic work of an Advaiti. Its depth of philosophical and scientific content is unparalleled. Only if the crux of Vedanta is understood, the greatness of the work is conceived in full; otherwise, it will look most obscure.

Arivu in the ordinary sense means the knowledge (awareness) obtained through the five sense organs, or the knowledge obtained through concentrated meditation and logical analysis. 'Arivu', in this poem, refers to something beyond the ordinary awareness or knowledge obtained through the inert sense organs. It is made explicitly clear through the first verse itself. The verses that follow it also assume the same view.

Sree Narayana Gurudev in 'The Prayer in Prose' says, 'Oh! God what is seen by the eyes is not eternal; the body too is transient like a bubble of water. Nothing else can be said other than everything is like a dream. I am not the inert body; I am the consciousness (Arivu)—the Brahman. Before the creation of the body, I, the consciousness (Arivu) was there. Hereafter even when all these have vanished "I" (consciousness—Arivu) will continue to shine like this.'

This means 'Arivu' is nothing other than consciousness to Gurudev.

(Original text in Malayalam)

Aṛiyappeṭumitu vēṛa
Llaṛivāyīṭum tiraññiṭunnēram
Aṛivitilonnāyatuko-
Ṇṭaṛivallāteṅumilla vēṛonnum.

Aṛivillennālillī-
Yaṛiyappeṭumennatuṇṭitennālum
Aṛivonnillennālī-
Yaṛivētaṛivinnatillaṛinjīṭām

Aṛivinnaḷavillātē-
Taṛiyāmaṛivāyatum viḷaṅṅunnu
Aṛivileẓunna kināvi-
Ṅṅaṛivāyīṭunnavaṇṇamaṅṅellām.

Aṛivinu niṛavuṇṭennā-
Laṛivallātuḷḷateṅṅirunnīṭum?
Aṛivētenniṅatupō-
Yaṛiyunnaṅṅenniteṅṅirunnīṭum?

Aṛivilirunnu keṭunnī-
Laṛivāmennāliteṅṅiṛaṅṅīṭum?
Aṛivineyaṛiyunnīli-
Ṅṅaṛiyum nēratu raṇṭumonnāyi.

Aṛiyum munpētennā-
Laṛivillātonnumiṅṅirippīla;
Aṛivaṛṛatitetiru-
Ṇṭaṛivennālonnumiṅṅukāṇmīla.

Aṛiyunnuṇṭillenni-
Ṅṅaṛiyunnīlētilētezunnīṭum
Aṛiyappeṭumenkiluma-
Llaṛivallenniṅu namme nōkkīṭil

Aṛivennanṅēyitumu-
Ṇṭaṛivundennāliteṅu ninnīṭum
Aṛivonnennam vēṛi-
Llaṛivallātenkilentirikkunnu?

Aṛivinnidamonnuṇṭi-
Llaṛiyappedumennatinnu vērāyi
Aṛivennālaṅṅetī-
Yaṛiyappeṭumennatēṛumeṇṇīṭil

Aṛiyunnīlannonnī-
Yaṛiyappeṭumennatuṇṭu pōyīṭum
Aṛivilitētaṛiyunnī-
Laṛivennāleṅuninnu vannīṭum?

Aṛivinnaṛivāy ninnē-
Taṛiyikkunniṅu nāmatāyīṭum;
Aṛivētinameṅaneyī-
Yaṛiyappeṭumennatētitōtīṭil.

Aṛivennatu nīyatu ni-
Nnaṛiviṭṭaṛiyappeṭunnatennāyi
Aṛiyappeṭumitu raṇṭo-
Nnaṛiyunnuṇṭennumonnatillennum

Aṛivumatinvaṇṇam ce-
Nnaṛiyunnavanil pakaṛnnu pinnīṭum
Aṛiyappeṭumitilonnī-
Yaṛivinporivīnu cīntiyañcāyi.

Aṛiyunnavanennaṛiya-
Maṛivennaṛiyunnavannumennākil
Aṛivonnaṛiyunnavano-
Nnaṛiyunnatilāṛiteṭṭumāyīṭum

Aṛiyappeṭumitinotī-
Yaṛivēẓonniṅṅutānumeṭṭāyi
Aṛiviṅane vevvēṛa-
Yaṛiyappeṭumennatum viṭuṛtīṭil.

Meaning and commentary

Verse 1

If analysed the observed universe is not
Different from consciousness, since
Consciousness is unique; there is nothing
Other than consciousness—anywhere.

If the ultimate secret of the consciousness and observed objects are analysed, it will become evident that this observed universe is nothing other than consciousness itself. Since in the experience of this universe, unique consciousness continues without any change at any time or any place, there is no other thing anywhere other than the consciousness inside and outside.

The uniqueness of consciousness should be explained. One should not misunderstand that, since there is diversity in the known things in the universe, the consciousness also is diverse and many. We know under certain conditions, space is felt as different like space in a pot or space in a room, etc. Once the pot and the room are broken, it will become evident that it is all one space. Similarly, there are not many consciousnesses in different bodies, but it is only one. In the early half of this verse, Gurudev says the observed (known) is not different from consciousness (observer). The first verse establishes uniqueness and non-duality.

One who searches the secret of the universe, at the first stage will understand that there are two factors in its experience. The knowledge (consciousness) that knows and the inert that is known are the two factors. Gurudev in this work uses the word Arivu in the place of consciousness because he considers Arivu and consciousness as synonyms. If both these factors are further analysed in all places of experience, the consciousness continues without any changes, whereas the observed inert continues to appear and disappear. Arivu the consciousness is the observer, and the inert is observed.

Consciousness is that which knows its self and experiences the being of inert bodies, which means the consciousness experiences its own self and is aware of the fact that there are inert things. Inert things are those who cannot have knowledge about their existences. This means once the consciousness is lost, all inert bodies become vanished. All things seen as inert things are like water in the desert. In short, if there is consciousness, there is experience; if there is no consciousness, there is no experience. If there is gold, there are golden ornaments; therefore, gold in its natural form and the fabricated gold ornaments are only gold. The relation between consciousness (observer) and the visual things around are like the Sun and its image on reflecting surfaces. Any change in the reflected image of the Sun does not make any change in the Sun.

Of the two, the knower and the known, knower alone is real. Once the known is unreal, why not the knower also unreal. This doubt is discussed in the following verse. Here the knower is the consciousness, and the known is observed.

Verse 2

If consciousness is not there, observed is not there
Still felt as existing, know that the consciousness is
Not there what observed is there if thought the observed
Is not seen anywhere else than in consciousness.

If the consciousness is not there these inert things which are seemed to be known are not existent. On the other hand, if anybody thinks that they are there, can their existence be experienced somewhere other than the consciousness? Once thought, one could easily understand that things cannot be seen anywhere else.

It is a different way of observer–observed relation Gurudev takes in many of his works in a different context. Examples are 'Chijjada Chintanam', 'VedantaSutram' and 'Darsanamala', etc. Many ask the question if an object is not in the experience, will it lose its experience? Gurudev gives an answer to this question in the above-mentioned examples (Ref. classical physics of objective reality; the saint who first expounded the subjective reality as part of knowledge is Sree Narayana Gurudev. Thus argument after more than half a century is found in quantum physics. See Copenhagen interpretations, Chapter 2, and Feynman's double-slit experiment).

Existence or entity is an experience. The universe is a combination of existence and non-existence (entity and illusion). Hence the visual universe is only an experience. It is the experience of consciousness. Experience is an exclusive characteristic of consciousness which the inert bodies lack. Therefore, when the consciousness is not there, all observed (known) things become vanished. The known things (observed) are inert things; they exist when the consciousness experiences it. Then the question is if an inert thing is not in the experience of an observer, why does it not come to the experience of another observer. For the answer, refer to Gurudev's 'Chijjada Chintanam' or 'Advaita Deepika'. This discussion requires detailed knowledge of observer–observed relation and objective reality and subjective reality.

Unless you experience in your consciousness, how can you decide its existence? Again it raises another question; if the observed is not experienced by one, why not that be experienced by somebody else? It can be experienced by another. But the other person also will experience it in his consciousness. Therefore, it is only when consciousness experience, the question of observed comes. If there is consciousness, there is the experience. This is what Gurudev indicates in the early part of the verse. In the following lines, Gurudev gives the answer to the question: though one is not experiencing, another one is experiencing. The argument is that the second one also experiences through his consciousness.

Verse 3

The consciousness that shines as immeasurable
Knows by itself as pure knowledge and hence
The entire observed inert things are like
Only dreams that occur in consciousness.

The consciousness leaving the state of shining now and then little by little in individuals knows by itself as that it can exist at the state of filling everywhere without a beginning or end. That can remain shining by itself as pure consciousness without the touch of inert things. Therefore, the entire things known in the universe as observed things, are only scenes in a dream in consciousness.

The inert by itself cannot experience its state of being as it has no ability to experience others' being. Now the question is, can the consciousness exist without the touch of inert things by the experience in its own being or entity. The great maharishis, including Sree Narayana Gurudev, after their own search, found the answer to this very important question. They made the consciousness pure (absolute) by rejecting inert imaginations (inert things), and to them without things being connected, consciousness can exist. In that state, the consciousness becomes unending and all-pervading. Then what happens to the visual things of the universe seen till then? It is like a dreamer dreaming lots of scenes with persons and events. When he wakes up, he realizes that whatever he saw in the dream has vanished and that he alone remains. To the yogis, it is clear that once they forget about all worldly things, including the body, the unending consciousness gets manifested. This is what Gurudev indicates in the first two lines of this verse.

Verse 4

If the consciousness is the absolute fullness
Where can a body other than consciousness exist?
How can it happen that the consciousness go and
Experience as to what is consciousness.

Once we decide that the consciousness is a complete all-pervading phenomenon, then where can another thing other than consciousness exist? How can it happen that this all-pervading consciousness goes and searches about consciousness and experience?

We have seen that in the experience of the universe, the consciousness is the all-pervading phenomenon. If so, where can another find a place to exist? It is not logical to infer when once agreeing to the fact that consciousness is all-pervading and something other than it existing in it. Still, why do we get a feeling that there are other things? The other things are only the Vivartha (apparent illusory forms—Maya created).

Verse 5

As knowledge never leaves consciousness
Then where can it vanish: once absolute consciousness
Is realized, knowing from outside becomes irrelevant
As the knower and known have become one.

If the absolute (all-pervading) consciousness does not ever perish, where can it disappear? Once this absolute consciousness is realized, there is no need for knowing it from outside as another since both the knowledge (consciousness—Brahman) and known (observed) become one.

Sree Narayana Gurudev explains about the secret manifested when the experience of absolute consciousness is realized. The illusory personal feeling 'I', 'I', once rejected, becomes aware of the absolute consciousness. When the illusory 'I' feeling is lost, the entire thing become void. The answer is that it can be experimented only if the 'I' awareness is rejected. The illusory feeling that a person is different from the consciousness, Gurudev says, will end when it takes the same condition of non-vibrating consciousness (in Poem 2, 'Daivadasakam', and also Poem 97, 'Atmopadesa Satakam'). Gurudev says that the silly illusory feeling of 'I am' will ultimately dissolve in the absolute consciousness while shining fully in him. The state of shining of the absolute consciousness cannot be attained without experiencing its realization.

Verse 6

Before knowing what it was, other than
Consciousness there was nothing else
What is left unknown to consciousness?
If consciousness has an end, nothing will remain.

This universe, before being known like this, what was it? To that question, one has to understand that without consciousness, nothing can exist. That is, this universe being known this way it was the only pure consciousness that was known. It means there were no objects not known to consciousness. If consciousness has an end, then there will not exist anything.

The question here is as to whether there is an object which is not known to consciousness. If you say it is there, then we have to explain where we experience the state of being of that object.

Consciousness is knowledge. Other than it, the existence of any objects is not experienced anywhere. This means if the consciousness is not there, we will have to assume that it has an end. Then it follows that the condition will be the non-existence of knowledge of the entire things. That is, if there is no consciousness, there are no inert objects. But the universal law states that from such a void state, nothing can come up and disappear.

Bhagavad Gita says,

Na sato vidyate bhavo
Nabhavo vidyate sata:

Nothing is either created nor destroyed. (Law of conservation of matter and energy.)

If the question is, before the universe being known like this, what was it? The answer is there was nothing else other than the consciousness: that is, before the universe being known like this, it was only pure consciousness. If the question is what object is not known to consciousness; the answer is there was nothing which was not known to consciousness. If consciousness has an end, what will happen? Then nothing will have existence.

It is that realization Gurudev explains in this poem. Chandogyopanishad also explains the realization of the Absolute in this way. It says this universe, before being observed, was only an absolute entity that is the pure consciousness. It never had an experience of duality. But the Absolute desired that it be different things, and thus the universe was created (Ref. Taitiriyopanishad). This fact can be verified by removing the illusory part and realizing the Absolute. Therefore, the names and forms are only unreal things imagined (superimposed) on the real consciousness. It is only the absolute consciousness that is real.

Verse 7

When looked inward we experience 'there is' and
Never 'there is not' if so, whether observed comes
From consciousness or consciousness comes from
Observed though, the observed is not the observer.

One who searches inwardly as to who am I clearly understands that I am there, he never experiences that I am not there. If so, is it from the consciousness the known things come or else, is it from the known the consciousness comes. Though the constituents of the universe are known in the experience of the universe, it is not an experience that comes from darkness. This can be known through a search into it.

The universe is an experience, and it is the consciousness; therefore, the universe is an experience in consciousness. This means the experience of the universe begins from consciousness. Being an entity with self-awareness, consciousness is a real entity and not darkness. So also, as starting from the consciousness which is self-shining it is real and cannot be darkness. The known inert things being started from consciousness and exist in it is not an experience starting from the darkness. The meaning of the word '*Allu*' in the verse, denotes darkness. Darkness is a symbol of ignorance. The knowledge arising from darkness is not knowledge. Since the known inert things arise from consciousness, it is not the knowledge, neither raised from darkness nor from ignorance. It can only be known by one who tries to know himself introverted. We know all awareness begins from one who knows, and also that the centre of the entire experience is 'I' who experience it. Who is this 'I'? I am the consciousness to one who experiences consciousness. In consciousness, it is only the experience that I am there. But it is impossible to experience that I am not there.

Verse 8

Consciousness is without a beginning; therefore, the universe which is observed also is without a beginning. Once the consciousness is fully understood, it can be seen that the universe is nothing other than the consciousness. Consciousness is the same everywhere. There are no different consciousnesses. If so, where is the scope of any other thing? It is the lack of understanding that creates the feeling of the known visual universe. See the following verse.

Ever since the time of existence of an observer
The observed also is existent when consciousness

Is unique where can the known exist, being only one
What else can be there other than the knowledge?

The knowledge about the universe was there since the time of existence of consciousness. Consciousness is unique everywhere; there are no different consciousnesses, if so, what else can be there? Once the consciousness is fully manifested, then where is the scope for the existence of this universe? There is no existence.

Consciousness is all-pervading and eternal. It is unique and without a second. If the universe was there right from the beginning of consciousness, where can the universe, which is a second to the unique consciousness, exist? Here Gurudev confirms his strong view of singularity (uniqueness) of consciousness (Brahman). The coexistence of consciousness and the universe is only a relation like the Sun and its reflected image on a reflecting surface. It should be understood that it was after the human mind was evolved the feeling of coexistence of Brahman (consciousness) and the differentiation in the form of the universe was felt. That feeling is a creation of the mind. The mind, in turn, was evolved as part of the evolution of living organisms.

Verse 9

Consciousness has absolute existence known has not
Which is the real knowledge, consciousness or known?
Known can never be absolute as it's
The number goes on ever increasing on counting.

The consciousness has a space of existence and is filling everywhere as the universe which is known has no space of its own for existence. Which one is the real knowledge, consciousness or the known universe? The known things being many and as their number will go on increasing when counted, they never become complete or full.

Consciousness, as everybody knows, is eternal and all-pervading. So it has the space for existence, whereas the universe has no space of its own because the entire space is occupied by consciousness. Besides, the known things such as names and forms of the universe are different, and their number goes on increasing as more and more when counted. Therefore, the known universe never becomes complete and full.

The *santipat* of Isavasyopanishad says, 'The consciousness is infinite and no addition or subtraction from it will keep the infinite nature irrespective of addition or subtraction.' This ultimately leads to the conclusion that it is meaningless to think of anything else other than it, having existence. Gurudev shows that consciousness is ultimate, and to it, there is not a second in real existence.

Verse 10

The knowledge does not know the known
All time one by one they all vanish, what known
Is not experienced by this all-knowing knowledge
From what else this all-knowing knowledge comes?

If the consciousness does not know the things which appear as known, then all such known things become perished. In consciousness, which of the known or unknown is not experienced? From what else the all-knowing consciousness can come? It means not from anything else.

The poem again confirms the uniqueness of consciousness. Consciousness shines by itself without the involvement of inert things. There cannot be a second thing to the consciousness; therefore, by comparison, consciousness need not think of its beginning and the end because it is eternal. The question of duality arises when there are the beginning and end, that is to say, only if there is more than one, the question of beginning and end comes. Therefore, where can it come from and where can it go? The inert thing whose number goes on changing becomes irrelevant unless there is something to know them. If somebody doubts that even in the absence of the knower (consciousness), it is not possible the inert things can exist.

We know unless there is something to witness and endorse their existence who will say they exist. In short, the known inert things are experienced only in consciousness. It is evident that the unique consciousness cannot come out from a second.

Verse 11

What existing as super knowledge of whatever is
Made known, know we are all parts of super knowledge.
What is the experience of realizing how is it gained
Once pondered what experience for the known things?

Existing as the supreme knowledge above all illusory knowledge which manifests the full awareness, we are all that truth. How can this truth be realized, once that is known through meditation where does the separate existence of the inert universe come?

Gurudev in the above poem differentiates between ordinary illusory knowledge and the knowledge above everything, which is the supreme knowledge. He says that we are all that supreme knowledge but how can we realize that we are the absolute supreme knowledge as Brahman. Gurudev advises, to find the absolute reality or knowledge, one has to meditate and realize it through contemplation once it is understood that we are the ultimate knowledge as Brahman himself where is the relevance of a separate existence of the inert universe.

This reminds us of 'Tat Twam Asi' (Thou Art It), the doctrine advice by Uddalaka to his son Swetaketu in Chandogyopanishad. In short, Gurudev once again confirms the principle of Advaita.

Verse 12

What is known as knowledge are you yourself
That knowledge from its own part became known
The knowledge then became two, of them
One is known as existent and the other non-existent.

You are the consciousness or the Brahman himself. That Brahman from a part of his body became known as visible (Saguna) Brahman, then God divided that visible form into two. Of the two, one is known as existent, and the other is known as non-existent.

The consciousness which is beyond the *Tripudi* (the knower, knowledge and known) is you. You are the consciousness. Consciousness is not different from you. There is only one thing that is consciousness; nothing can be different from it. We know in 'Prenjanam Brahma' (Rig Veda), the great *Drik*, the Brahman, is indicated as consciousness. Similarly, 'Ayam Atma Brahma' (Atharvaveda) also indicates that you are the Brahman. To describe who asked the question as to what he is; the answer was *Twam he Brahma*, that is, you are the Brahman or consciousness.

The illusory *jeevatman* (known existent phenomenon) and the *paramatman* (the Absolute) are not two different forms of Brahman, but both are the same. It is a fact that is established by the above doctrines of Vedas, which give us the awareness that Brahman in the form of the visible universe and the individual who seeks entity are one and the same. But in the state of ignorance, we differentiate the consciousness (knower) and the known (visual universe) as two different entities. The known has no separate entity as per the above hymns. If the consciousness or the supreme soul is considered as a great ocean, on the inside and outside of one will shine like the water in the ocean and that too like in a lake separated by a dam. When the damper of the dam is lifted, the entire water becomes the same inside and outside the damper (the cosmic space and space in a pot). (Ref. the conversation between Adi Sankara and the chandala.)

Gurudev then explains the duality of the known. The known is divided into two, and the known, we know, is the universe. The universe itself is divided into two categories, namely, the live and inert. Of the two, life knows about its existence or entity, whereas the inert is incapable of knowing its existence, but this differentiation of living and inert becomes relevant since the inert is illuminated by life.

(Ref. 'Atmopadesa Satakam', verses 41 and 42.)

Verse 13

The knowledge, likewise the feeling
Of known created in the seeker who searches
Then a spark of knowledge fell on the known
That broke it and spread as the five.

The absolute consciousness (knowledge) on one side created the vision of the known, likewise on the other side produced the feeling of the knower. Thereafter, on the side felt to be known a spark of this consciousness (knowledge) fell and split into five.

The known things known to the knower are the five elements such as space; the knowledge (consciousness) in the knower is not of the self. It is only the Vivartha, the reflected image of the absolute knowledge (absolute consciousness). When the spark of absolute knowledge fell on the aggregate of known, it split into five components, namely, sound, touch sight, taste and smell and their subjects, space, air, fire, earth and water respectively. One has to understand that the known are all inert, and the spark of consciousness that fell on them is the light of the Sun falling on the reflecting object. There is no relation between the known and the absolute consciousness (Ref. 'Darsanamala', 'Jnana Darsanam', Poem 9.)

aham mameti jñanam ya
didam taditi yacca tat
jīvajñānam tadapara
mindriya jñānam isyate

Consciousness is real. Both the knower and the known are only the Vivartha of consciousness. At the state of salvation or enlightenment, all the three components of the Tripudi, namely the knower, the knowledge and the known become one.

Verse14

If one who knows knowledge knows that
He himself is the knower
The knowledge is one the knower is another
Thus separates into six and eight.

The self who is the knower has the awareness that he is one who knows. It is knowledge. If so, the knowledge is one and the knower is another, this knowledge gets separated into six and eight.

The one who knows that he is the knowledge can understand that he is the knower himself. The knowledge is self-centred. With the knowledge of great doctrines, one can ultimately understand that knowledge is consciousness (absolute). Even to such people who attain realization, the universe, when observed externally, comes to the awareness that he knows them. This is known as the human self—referred to as human consciousness (*Jeevajnanam*). Thus, the absolute consciousness and human self (consciousness) become two. One, *Nirvikalpajnanam* (absolute knowledge) is the knowledge not conceived through the senses as there is not anything second to it. It is called the pure knowledge, eternal, unchangeable, not conceived by unattributed; and two, *Vikalpajnanam*, the knowledge obtained through the five senses, which is transient, changeable and virtual.

The absolute awareness of self-like *Aham Brahmasmi* is the absolute consciousness. Whereas the awareness that I know the subject of senses like sound, etc. indicates that the known things are the Tripudi if there is discrimination; thus along with these two joining with the known six, it becomes eight.

But when absolute knowledge (consciousness) is obtained, of the eight, only the first—the consciousness—will remain (being eternal), and all the others as they appear and disappear (transient), are unreal or illusory. That is what is discussed in these poems by Gurudev.

Verse 15

Added to the known seven
The self makes the knowledge eight
If differentiated thus the knowledge
Will be known as different ones.

Adding the aforesaid knowledge to the known makes seven, then with the self, it becomes eight altogether. Once tried to view them as different the knowledge (consciousness) itself will be felt as different.

Until the absolute consciousness got separated from the other illusory components, the self was believed to be the knower and mind, and other senses as the known. Once the knowledge is separated from the others, the self (ego) being shining in the knowledge becomes known, and thus, the number of known things becomes seven. In a deep analysis, it can be seen that the self is an experience known through knowledge. On realization, the pure knowledge (absolute consciousness), the self (ego) disappears into consciousness. This is why the self is said to be a part of consciousness; it is identified as one among the known things. When all the known things vanish and disappear, the consciousness becomes seen as absolutely unchangeable, eternal experience. This is salvation. Gurudev, experiencing this state himself, declared that it is all the consciousness that remains, all other things (known things) are illusory.

This work 'Arivu' is a supplement or say, a work that supersedes the great 'Jnana Darsanam'.

18

PRAPANCHASRISHTI—CREATION OF THE UNIVERSE (SIVASTHAVAM)

The great poem 'Prapanchasrishti' ('Creation of the Universe') otherwise known as 'Sivasthavam' is one among Sree Narayana Gurudev's songs of prayer to God Shiva. It exceeds other contemporary poems in its nature of wording, the beauty of presentation, simplicity and depth of content. He wrote this work of ten poems in 1911. The very title of the poem, namely, 'Creation of the Universe' is an indicator of the content of the work. It gives the Vedic concept of the universe from the viewpoint of an Advaiti in respect of the creation, being and dissolution of the universe. The verses reveal how the universe came into existence from the subtle form of consciousness to the illusory corpulent form by the magic of Maya power of the absolute consciousness.

This poem 'Creation of the Universe' also opens the door to a comparative study of the secrets of the universe in Vedanta and modern cosmology. This may be the first testimonial regarding the creation of the universe in spirituality on a scientific footing ever written in Eastern and Western philosophies. It contains the spirit of the creation of the universe according to Vedic philosophy from 'Nasadeeya Suktam' of Rig Veda (the first-ever statement about the creation of the universe) through various Upanishads, Brahmasutras, Gita and later commentaries of Adi Sankara and Sree Narayana

Gurudev. It contains the spirit of big bang theory and other developments in modern cosmology.

(Original text in Malayalam)

Cevi mutalancumiṅu citaṟāte mayaṅi maṟi-
Njaviṭeyirunnu kaṇṭariya kaṇṇilaṇanjazhiyum
Ivakaḷileṅumeṇṇavumaṭaṅi niṟanju puṟam
Kaviyumatētatinte kaḷi kaṇṭaruḷīṭakamē!

Akamuṭalinnumindriyamoṭuḷḷamazhinjezhumī-
Ppakaliravinnumādiyilirunnaṟiyunnaṟivām
Nakayilitokkeyum cuzhalavum teḷiyunna namu-
Kkakuṭilavaibhavaṅaḷilaṭaṅiyirunnaruḷām

Aruḷilaṇanjirultira muzhaṅiyezhunna kuḷur-
Nnurumizhi nāvilammaṇamuṇaṟnnatoṭum piriyum
Ara nimiṣatiliṅitilirunnu tikanju varum
Duritasamudra, minbamitileṅu namukku śivā?

Śiva! śiva! Mātrayil palataram citaṟunnu veḷi-
Kkivakaḷileṅumiṅitamaṟinju niṟanjaruḷum
Śiva! Bhagavāneyum citaṟumāṟu tikanju varu-
Nnivaruṭe pōrininniyarutē karunālayamē!

Alayumitokkeyum kapaṭanāṭakamennaṟiyum
Nilayilirunnaṟinjazhivatinnu ninakkuka nī
Talayilezhum taranganira taḷḷi niṟanju maṟa-
njalaṟsaravairi, ninnuṭe padaṅaḷilenniniyām?

Iniyalayāte nintiruvaṭikkaṭiyan dinavum
Manamalariṭṭu kumbiṭumitiṅaṟiyunnatu nī;
Jananameṭutu njānitukaḷil palatāyi vala-
njaniśamenikkivaṇṇamoru vēdanayilla param.

Aparamitokkeyum paricayikkumatiliru-
Nnapajayamāyananjatitu kaṇṭaṛi nī manamē;
Japapaṭamangamāmitilirunnu japikkukili-
Ṅṅuparati vannu cērumakatārilorimbamatām.

Atumitumennumunnuka nimitamitinkalezhum
Pati pasu pāsamitiṅu parambarayāyazhiyum
Mati katiroṭu maṇṇoḷi viyatanilan jalavum
Patiyuṭe rūpamenniha namicu padam paniyām.

Paṇi palatāy varunna kanakatilirunnatupō-
Laṇimizhikoṇṭu niṛmmitamitokkeyumadbhutamām!
Aṇiyaṇamenne nintiruvaṭikkaṭiyan malarā-
Maṇiyaṇiyāy nirannu tirayaṛṛuyarum kaṭalē!

Kaṭalileẓum taranganira pōle kalaṅi varu-
Nnuṭanuṭanuḷḷaẓiññu palapaṛṛoẓiyunnatupōl
Khaṭapaṭamennetutiha toṭutu vaẓakkiṭumī
Kuṭamuṭayunnatinakameṭutaruḷīṭanamē!

Meaning and commentary

Verse 1

Before scattering, the five senses ear and so on in tranquillity,
Introverted concentrated on the self and experiencing the Atman
Dissolved in the noble eye of knowledge, removed senses and subjects
Overflows the self in bliss see the divine play and be happy.

The five sense organs such as the ear, eye, nose, tongue and skin before spreading and reaching their respective subjects such as sound, sight, smell, taste and touch all were concentrated into a noble eye like a subtle object. In these senses and their respective subjects, the feeling of many was lost and the all-pervading in that which appears in this universe filled with objects. Oh! The inner self sees the play of those objects and experiences the bliss.

The reality, in fact, is that which pervades everywhere and is the consciousness. To see or experience consciousness, the feeling of many things should be abolished. Even though the sense organs experience things as many by way of their subjects, sound, etc., one has to believe that they are all manifestations of the same thing from the point of view of Vedanta. To avoid such diversity and experience the Absolute, one should come to realize this factor. Everything seen as diverse is all virtual projections of the said noble eye, and also all such diverse things alternately dissolve into this noble eye. In short, Gurudev's lines above indicate the fact that before this universe becoming so spread and diverse, everything was contained in a subtle life form, and that as compared to the third eye showing that it was so hot and pungent, capable of exploding and withdrawing the entire universe back into itself on desire which hints at the big crunch.

Let us now come to Sree Narayana Gurudev's scientific view based on Vedanta. Gurudev, one of the great masters of spirituality, has written this poem from the point of view of a cosmologist. Though this elegant work 'Sivasthavam' or 'Creation of the Universe' is created on the foundation of Advaita philosophy, he makes the reader understand that the same is true from the cosmological point of view as mentioned earlier. Gurudev, in all his works, takes Shiva as the symbol of Brahman. He deliberately put the title in two different ways; one is 'Sivasthavam' in the spiritual view, and 'Creation of the Universe' from the physical view. Gurudev's explanations in the poem are beautifully in tune with the theories of the creation of the universe in modern physics. The subtle *Ariyakannu* is identical with the primordial particle or quantum in modern cosmology. The third eye of God Shiva and the primordial particle are made identical here, very logically.

It should be remembered that this poem was written in 1911 by Gurudev; whereas Gamow's big bang theory was published in 1948 after a lapse of thirty-seven years. Later, we will see the details of the big bang, as explained by Lemaître (1927) and George Gamow, and also the singularity of the dignified eye of Shiva. It is evident that the eye mentioned by Gurudev and the primordial particle in big bang theory are not two different things. The similarity becomes so logical that the primordial particle was super-hot (10^{32} K), and in the state of singularity, and the dignified eye of God Shiva in the poem was also singular and super-hot by the Puranic concept. The dignified third eye can expand into the shape of the universe, exist and dissolve back into it like the explosion (big bang) and dissolution (big crunch). The fact that the wonders of the magic of the dignified eye go beyond the varied universal phenomena and exist there gives the indication of having many universes (multiverse) that are contained in a *Brahmandakadaham.* Remember, physics has come to the idea of many universes only very recently, that is, only within the last two or three decades.

Verse 2

Consciousness and the body along with the indiscriminating
Feeling of day and night of the senses, to the seekers of truth
Look and experience everything as contained in the jewel
Of consciousness live and do things without the torment of Maya.

Acting as the centre of illusory feeling without difference of day and night that is created in mind and external body by infatuation of mind the seekers of truth who know that all these were contained in the jewel of consciousness from the very beginning will not become subject to illusory feelings and can live a peaceful life involved in noble activities.

The three states, corpulent, subtle and cause, are indicated here. We know Jagrat (wakefulness), Swapna (dream) and Sushupti (deep sleep) are the three stages which are associated with the above.

The worldly experience confines to the inert self, inert body and the sense organs, and they, in turn, are confined to wakefulness, dream and deep sleep. Similarly, during day and night, Jagrat is the experience of the worldly things through the sense organs. Swapna is believed to be the creation of the mind during sleep. But with the advent of quantum physics and the many-worlds concept, the new belief of manyscientists is that as the sense organs are only partially opened and partly closed, the opened part gets the glimpses of other universes.The boundary of functioning and consciousness that fills inside and outside gets rid of any space-time barrier, which becomes semi-transparent to the boundary between consciousness (absolute) and the inner self. In deep sleep, as all the sense organs are fully closed, the inner awareness gets its boundary fully opened, and the inner self gets access to all universes without the limits of space and time. It should be remembered that all these feelings are in a physical sense. But in spirituality, the sequence does not end with these. There is a further stage beyond theJagrat, Swapna and Sushuptistages known as Turiya, the state of absolute consciousness. We have seen already that the consciousness has nothing to do with the above three stages as it is unique and non-dual.

Verse 3

Oh Shiva, the roaring waves of darkness falling on bliss
The pleasant inert feelings increase the urge for worldly pleasure
Leave after a moment from there, where is the pleasure to
The wise in the sea of worldly sufferings. Oh! Auspicious Lord!

The intense inert observations that look as if pleasurable that comes up turbulently as waves of ignorance on the absolute blissful reality increases the desire for worldly pleasures and in a while go away. With that desire in the form of a propensity and the worldly sufferings coming up, oh! Lord!Where is peace to the people of wisdom?

In this world of births and deaths, everything the wise feels as real is the blissful consciousness. It is the unawareness of this fact that gives the opportunity to different inert things in vision. In this whirling vision of inert things, people feel that there is a pleasure and go behind it. The result is that, without obtaining any sort of this lasting pleasure, experience only miseries throughout life in the world. It is the desire that gives rise to the visual universe of births and deaths. Once trapped in the effects of deeds in earlier births (*Karmavasana*) and birth and death circle, one has to go with it. To the wise who knows the blissful Lord, what else can be seen other than the miseries in the continued whirling. Therefore, the wise without increasing the longing towards worldly pleasures desires to dissolve himself in the blissful Lord.

Verse 4

Oh, Shiva! In sensual pleasures, the mind scatters out
In this mind senses and subjects in and out overcrowding
With own desires, seem to scatter you too into many
To those sensual subjects, Oh! Mercy! I am not able to resist.

Oh! Lord because of the functioning of sense organs the mind scatters as many outside. In this mind, sense organs and their subjects, inside and outside, according to their respective desires, seem to scatter your absolute form too. To fight these subjects of sense organs, Oh! Merciful! Know that this one has no more strength.

It is when the mind comes out through the sense organs the experience of worldly pleasure is felt. This makes the mind vacillate. We know the vacillated mind will always suffer, whereas the concentrated mind will experience self-satisfaction; it is the rule. Once the mind is involved in the feeling of worldly pleasures and scattered, the blissful reality that pervades everywhere will also be hidden and seen as different. The only remedial step to avoid this is to withdraw the sense organs from their subjects outside and concentrate the mind on the Absolute. But it is not an easy task. It requires a lot of training and the blessings of the Lord. Therefore, one who wants to win over the mind should keep awakened to get the blessings of the Lord, reduce the ego step by step, and go nearer and nearer to the Lord.

Verse 5

Oh, merciful! Bless me taking to the level of understanding
That all these transients are the fake drama of God
The waves you bear on head spreading the body and vanish
Oh! Killer of Cupid, when can I fall at your feet?

Oh! Lord bless compassionately making me know that all these visual universes seen around that go on changing continuously are only hypocrisy (Maya) and concentrate on that knowledge to realize the self. The body immersed in waves of Ganga water and getting rid of vision of inert things, when can I get the fortune of falling at your divine feet, Oh! One who burnt the God of love and passion?

The universe and its contents in the form of life and forms are continuously changing phenomena. It comes into existence and disappears repeatedly. The same is the case with human life, born, live and die in between various stages of life like a child, youth, mature, old, etc. with their corresponding experiences depending upon the age and health. All these create a feeling of continuous change. This continuous change can be compared to the happenings in a drama. The actor takes different costumes and a role in the drama with scenes of miseries, happiness and passion. But a wise man knows that all these changes are superfluous and never affect the actor.

The one from which the entire things are believed to be created takes the role of the actor in the drama. To the one, it is immaterial whether there is life, birth and death, sorrow or happiness. In these lines, the devotee prays to the one who is aware of the hypocrisy in the changes and happenings in the worldly life and waits for the opportunity of falling at the foot of the one—the Lord.

Verse 6

Not wandering anymore, this servant concentrate
The mind that will prostrate you, this you know

Though born as man till now I suffer always
Seeing many, I don't have sorrow severe than this.

Hereafter, this devotee without wandering by engaging in sense organs and their subjects will keep the mind concentrated at your feet and prostrate. You are aware of this. Though born as a man, so far, I was suffering seeing many things through the sense organs and their subjects. I have no other misery more severe than this.

The sense organs create many visuals in the mind. When such visuals come to the mind, one has to offer such sights to the Lord. That is, to keep in mind that everything seen is the vision of the Lord. To be more specific, whatever is seen is the form of the Lord, whatever is heard is the hymn of the Lord, whatever is done is the act of the Lord. This kind of unification of things felt in mind is mentioned in the words '*Malarittu kumpidal*', that is offering flower at the foot and prostrate. The same kind of adoration by putting flower is used by Gurudev in 'Atmopadesa Satakam'.

Verse 7

Oh, Mind! Failings from other unreal experiences
You approached the feet of the Lord Remember!
If meditated from this body the seat of prayer
Always you experience the bliss in your mind.

Oh! Wavering mind that always acts according to the feelings created by sense organs, remember it is after the failure from other experiences misunderstood as real that you arrived at the feet of the God. The human body is the seat of prayer to God. Sitting in this seat if prayed to God, your mind would attain self-realization devoid of sensual feelings. This is what gives full gratification.

The mind never gets full satisfaction or happiness, whatever sensual experiences are obtained. Besides, the transient, momentary sensual pleasures will result in continuous miseries.

Usually, people are fed up with this; their minds are withdrawn from such sensual feelings and come to offer their prayers at the foot of God. But still the dualities of such feelings of pleasure will continue and the corresponding miseries to their lives. One should understand that human bodies are not made for sensual pleasures only, like in the other animals. The human body with the mind is capable of seeing the spirit of God in him. What he has to do is to reduce the sensual longings of the body and concentrate the mind on the devotion to God.

The mind that concentrates at the foot of the Lord wins over the sensual feelings (*Uparati*). Once such a situation is attained, the mind realizes that there is no greater pleasure in this world than it, and he feels full gratification.

Verse 8

'This', 'that' and such thoughts make attachment to them
And worldly relations come and go, knowledge, wisdom
'I', Lord, earth, sky, air, fire and water, knowing
Are different forms the Lord, adore the foot of Him.

Since it always continues with the thought of me, you, relatives, wealth, etc., the human life becomes bound to the worldly matters like grazing the cow's crave for pasture becomes its tie, the affinity and longings become the bondage. Their life on Earth continues to come, go and change. One has to realize that the wisdom, ego and the five elements such as air, fire, earth, etc. are only different manifestations of God. Understand this and bow at the foot of the Lord.

The Lord (Pasupati) life, Jeeva, the bondage to the visual universe (*Pasam*) is the order of the universe. Here as grazing on worldly matters, the life gets the characteristics of cows. In fact, life is only part of God. Only because of this, part of it gets bound to worldly things. It becomes the cow with bondage; so long as the cow is there, life continues with its bondage to many. It will be subject to births and deaths to remove this. There is only one way. That is, all these five elements and their mixed form of the universe are to be considered as different manifestations of God himself. Unless it is understood logically and experienced through meditation by surrendering at the foot of the Lord, one can never get relieved from the cyclic life in the universe.

Verse 9

Like gold shines in different ornaments
The creation of illusory things by your magic look
Is wonderful! Wear my humble self as flower dedicated
Oh, the static sea of consciousness that manifests and dissolves.

Like gold shines in gold ornaments made in different forms as the real material all these things in the universe being felt as if the Lord himself is wonderful. Oh! Sea of consciousness that manifests everything array after array in this universe without an iota of self-movement, this devotee offers himself at your feet in the form of a flower of worship. Bless me!

Consciousness is indivisible and immovable. It manifests in different forms without any change in itself. But in the case of gold, while it becomes different forms of ornaments, it loses its form identity. Then how is it that the consciousness, without undergoing any change in its shape or attribute, becomes different things? It is by the Maya power that it does so. Once created, the created things are like the water in the desert by virtue of mirage. This is why Gurudev puts it as created by the magic look in the above verse. To remove this illusory feeling of Maya superimposed on the only one is the complete submission before the Lord.

Verse 10

Like the rows of waves come up in the Sea, come
Sensual thoughts shaking the mind, then and there

Removing the confusion showing pots, dress and such
Attachment, I dedicate, bless me before this pot is broken.

Like waves come one after another in the ocean shaking the mind, rush worldly feelings. On all such occasions, the wavering of mind removes many attachments. Showing many things as this is a pot, this is cloth, etc. relating to them in this life. Before leaving this inert body that creates attachments, let me be offered at your feet accepted and blessed.

Even if a devotee tries his best, unless he has the mercy of God, he cannot win over the sensual feelings of the mind and mercy of God. It requires a complete submission before God. In mind, the feeling of the ego 'I' and the attachment that it is 'mine' and 'it is mine' has to be reduced.

And finally submits meditating with the awareness that it is all God in everything. It is the self-attachment that leads to the attachment to many things. Therefore, the first attachment is to be got rid of by submitting oneself wholly to God. Then he gets the feeling of one that is, the God alone is there without a second to it. Once the feeling of none other than the God is there in the universe, then the desire and attachment to the others will vanish. Eternal happiness will be felt inside and outside forever. The feeling that there is not a second in the universe other than himself will remove all fear of the devotee. He comes nearer to the ultimate and attains the eternal bliss. Those who experience this in full are all known as *Jeevanmukta*s. There are people like Sree Narayana Gurudev who have attained the state of eternal bliss while living in this material universe.

19

JATINIRNAYAM

One of the most important missions of Sree Narayana Gurudev was the eradication of the caste system. It was very unfortunate that in a country where Advaita philosophy was considered as most sacred and divine from the time of Vedas and Upanishads, the caste system in its devilish form caught hold of the entire society. Ignorance and vested interests were the primary causes of this unfortunate situation. From the time of Sree Buddha, the efforts to eradicate its cause and effect went on strongly. Even though a few great men tried to eradicate such evils from time to time, all ended fruitlessly.

Though this poem is short in its number of words, it was with a great intention; Gurudev wrote this to uproot the curse of caste rule.

Living things are categorized into men, animals, birds, and so on depending upon their features.

Gurudev at the outset reveals that the categorization of a species with their identical characteristics being considered as different castes is highly illogical and unscientific.

Even otherwise, these, on the whole, reflect the notion that what we see as many names and forms are only the different forms of a unique one which is believed to be the ultimate truth or the absolute reality. To great men who understood this, even the differentiation of castes in humanity is only the illusion of the mind. Then, what is the scope for a caste-wise differentiation between Brahmana and

Paraya, etc.? The caste differentiation is only an artificial creation either of ignorance or of vested interests.

Through these lines, Gurudev played a great role in the social revolution in south India, where the caste system and its associated social inequalities were at their peak.

Manuṣyāṇām manuṣyatwam
Jātiṛgōtwam gavām yatā
Na brahmanādirasyaivam
Hā! Tatwam vēti kō pina. (Original in Sanskrit)

(Original text in Malayalam)

Oru jāti oru matam oru daivam manuṣyanu
Oru yōniyorākāramorubhēdavumillatil
Oru jātiyil ninnallo piṛannīṭunnu santati
Nara jātiyitōrkkumbōẓoru jātiyiluḷḷatām

Narajātiyil ninnatrē piṛannīṭunnu vipṛanum
Paṛayāntānumentuḷḷatantaram narajātiyil?

Paṛaciyil ninnu paṇṭu parāśaramahāmuni
Piṛannu maṛasōtṛica muni kaivaṛtakanyayil

Illajātiyilonnundovallatum bhetamōrkkukil
Collēṛum vyaktibhāgatilalle bhētamirunniṭū.

Meaning and commentary

Verse 1

How do animals are with animosity
Likewise, man is with manhood.
Brahmin hood, etc. by birth is not logical
Alas! Nobody knows the real fact.

How is it we say for the creatures belonging to the category of animals, animalism is their caste, as concluded by logic, like that, for humankind, humanness is their caste? Castes like Brahmana by virtue of birth are not logical. Pity! Nobody knows the truth.

Verse 2

One caste one religion one God is to man
One womb one form no difference therein.

The man has only one caste, only one religion, only one God, only one womb and one shape, in the category of humankind, no difference at all.

Verse 3

It is from the same species the offspring is born
If analysed, all men belong to the same caste.

It is only from the category of humankind series of offspring of human beings come. Once thought about, it could be concluded clearly that the entire humankind belongs to the same caste.

Verse 4

Brahmin and Paraya are born from human species
What difference is there in caste in the human race?

The Brahmana (upper caste) and Paraya (low caste) are born from the category of human beings. In that sense, what difference is there in the human category?

Verse 5

Once, the great ascetic Parasara was born to a Paraya woman
The Maharshi who formulated Vedas was born to a virgin fisherman girl.

In ancient times, Maharshi Parasara, the father of Veda Vyasa, was born to a Paraya woman named Adrisyanti, and Veda Vyasa, who formulated the Vedas and authored Brahmasutras was born to a virgin fisher girl named Matsyagandhi.

Verse 6

Once thought, there is no caste with any difference
The difference exists only in the individual nature.

Once thought, is there any relevance to any kind of differentiation inside the caste? It is well known that it is only when there are differences in the content of individual characteristics, there is scope for any differentiation. The following biological details establish Gurudev's statement about the necessity of a pair of male and female belonging to the same category or species to have a child born from the womb.

Interspecies pregnancy

Pregnancy between two different species is called interspecies pregnancy (xenopregnancy). It is the pregnancy involving an embryo or fetus belonging to another species other than that of the carrier (surrogate mother). This possibility is recently studied extensively and ruled out totally. But it excludes the condition where the fetus is a hybrid of the carrier and another species to exclude the probability that the carrier is the biological mother of the offspring. Interspecies pregnancy excludes endoparasitism (a parasite that resides in the internal organ of the host) where the parasite offspring grow inside the body of other species but not in the womb. But it never occurs naturally. It can be achieved artificially by transfer of embryos of one species into the womb of another female.

But it is an ethically controversial alternative to the surrogate mothers or artificial uteri for mothers with damaged uteri, or the couples who do not like to take the risk of childbirth. It may also provide a sober, drug-free and non-smoking carrier (other living things) that is cheaper than human surrogates. Even then, one has to assure another such surrogate womb can preserve the child, rendering all biographical needs of the fetus of another species when it affects the features and other characteristics for the normal human child. But for animals, it could be a valuable tool in preservation programmes of endangered species, providing a method of ex-situ conservation. It could also avail for there-creation of extinct species.

Immunologically, an embryo or fetus of an interspecies pregnancy would be equivalent to xenografts (graft of tissues transplanted between animals of different species), rather than allografts (one on behalf of another), putting a higher demand on immune tolerance in order to avoid an immune reaction towards the fetus.

In short, one can take a womb on rent and get a child fostered in that womb. The surrogate female is limited only to the service as a foster mother at a very premature stage. The child will only be of the donors of sperm and ovum (gametes).

The argument of Sree Narayana Gurudev about the determination of caste raises the question as to the reality of legendary interspecies characters in belief and literature of the East and West. It may appear to contradict the arguments in Gurudev's work,'Daivachintanam', where he proposes different shapes and features of men in different worlds.

Like different species of billions of living things live in this world, there are other worlds where innumerable living things with different smell, heat and cold, live for example, in the *Vayuloka* (space). The indication of this is evidenced by the unidentified, magical events like the throwing of stones from unidentified sources, some wonderful plays practised by some magicians, acts of men of divine powers acquired from some idols of worship, etc. Besides the belief that there are people in other worlds who appear before certain devotees of God, and give them some boons, even now such people come before the worshippers of certain idols, and still there are men with such magical powers living in the world, and this is accepted by many. This requires more investigation in cosmology. (Ref. 'Daivachintanam', 'Life on Other Worlds', etc.)

Therefore, the fact that there are people in other worlds like those in our world is an established fact without difference of opinion, since they have the speed of the wind, and do hard work being invisible. When some of them come near, feel the heat; in some others, their presence feels cold; still to some with good smell; to some others with bad odour and so on. This is why such people are called in short men from Vayuloka.

But once analysed, there is no contradiction between the two. For example, if in one world, multispecies characters like the sphinx, etc. live like men on earth; their parents will also have the same characteristics as the offspring.

20

JATILAKSHANAM

This work was written in 1914 by Sree Narayana Gurudev while he was staying at Aluva Advaita Asramam on the request of Sahodaran Ayyappan, a family devotee and a rationalist. These lines prove beyond doubt the ardent awareness of Advaita philosophy and scientific thought. This poem relieves the reader from the curse of casteism and brings him to the experience of happiness.

The cruellest curse that India had been subjected to is casteism, or the practice of chaturvarnya as dictated by the so-called upper castes in the society. The number of sufferings of people and the damage it caused to the Advaita doctrines is beyond the limits of explanations. You have already seen in the first chapter the social condition to which Sree Narayana Gurudev was born, and his divine mission to eradicate the curse of chaturvarnya and casteism, based strongly on the platform of Advaita.

(Original text in Malayalam)

Puṇaṛnnu peṛumellāmo-
Rinamām puṇarātat
Inamallinamāmiṅṅo-
Riṇayārnnotu kāṇmatum.

Ōrō inatinum meyyu-
Mōrō mātiriyocayum
Maṇavum cuvayumcōdum
Taṇuvum nōkkumōṛkkaṇam

Tuṭaṛnnoronnilum vevvē-
Ṛaṭayālamirikkayāl
Aṛinjīṭunnu vevvēre
Piricōrōnnumiñu nām.

Pērōrutoẓilīmūnum
Pōrumāyatu kelkkuka!
Āru nīyennu kēlkkēṇṭa
Nēru mey tanne colkayāl.

Inamārnnuṭaltān tante-
Yinamētennu colkayāl
Inamētennu kēlkkilla
Ninavum kaṇṇumuḷḷavaṛ.

Poḷicollunninam colva-
Tiẓivennu ninakkayl
Iẓivillinamonnāṇu
Poḷicollarutārumē.

Āṇum peṇṇum vēṛtiricu
Kāṇum vaṇṇaminateyum
Kāṇaṇam kurikoṇṭimma-
ṭṭāṇu nāmaṛiyēṇṭat.

Aṛivāmāẓiyil ninnu
Varumellāvuṭambinum
Karuvāṇinamī nīrin-
Niratān vērumāyīdum.

Aṛivām karuvān ceyta
Karuvāṇinamōṛkkukil
Karuvārnniniyum māṛi
Varumī vannatokkeyum

Inamennitinecollu
Nninnatennaṛiyikkayāl
Inamillenkilillonnu-
Minnatennullatūẓiyil

Meaning and commentary

Verse 1

Those embrace mutually and procreate
All belong to the same breed
Those not embrace not belong to human species
Those unite to reproduce belong to one breed.

Acts of embracing mutually and reproducing belong to the same category. Those creatures that reproduce without embracing are not human beings. In this world, creatures that join to mate are considered as belonging to a particular category.

Verse 2

Remember! Every species has its
Particular form, sound, smell, taste
Warmth and cold of body and look
As their individual feature.

It should be known by noting the shape of the body, the particular style of producing sound, a different type of odour, the taste of food, the body warmth, cold and the style of looking of different categories.

Verse 3

Besides, in every creed, there are
Separate characteristic marks
We identify them as separate
Species by differentiation.

Since for every category, there are different characteristic marks, people in this world naturally identify them separately as belonging to different categories.

Verse 4

Ask only the name, place
And work these three
Do not ask what caste as
The individual body itself tells it.

It is enough that when one meets, ask only the three questions: what is your name, to which place you belong, and what are you doing, by way of introduction. Do not ask what your caste is because the very shape of the body will reveal that he is a human being.

Verse 5

As the body of the individual
Itself manifests his clan hence
One with the power of thought and sight
Never ask caste of others.

Since the body discloses the category of one's caste, no one with the power of thought and sight ever asks anybody about caste.

Verse 6

People who speak and hear tell-tale
About caste are known to become subject
To downfall knowing it is only one, should
Not tell lies making tell-tales about castes.

As realized after deep thought that those who speak of caste artificially created and heard will result in their downfall knowing that there is only one caste, one should avoid the downfall creating artificial assumptions, and no one should lie.

Verse 7

As male and female are seen
Identified separately on the mere sight
We should also identify the caste
By their specific features.

As men and women are identified by their features without others' help, like that whatever can be differentiated with features that are the caste. The caste is identified by the specific features.

Verse 8

The creed is the embryo of
All bodies rising up from the ocean
Of absolute knowledge likewise, it is
The basic cause of all waves seen around.

The essence of all visuals comes up from the ocean of consciousness, which is the primordial cause of creation, is what is known as a category or separate section. Like water in the ocean is the cause of waves and bubbles, it is the consciousness that remains as the primordial cause of everything.

Verse 9

Once thought caste is the creation of
Absolute knowledge as an architect
All these castes (creeds) that appear now
Will take different forms and continue to come.

Once thought, the caste is the category created by the consciousness as the architect by changing its own form into diverse things. All these categories seen now on earth, taking different forms, will continue to come.

Verse 10

Since seen separated as different in worldly life
This diversity in form is called caste
Once this variety of breeds vanish, it is
Not possible to have activities on earth.

Since shown separated into diversity for the sake of worldly activities, this diversity in form is called class or category. Once there is no differentiation, the worldly transaction will become impossible.

21

JEEVAKARUNYAPANCHAKAM

Sree Narayana Gurudev in 1914 wrote these five verses when he visited Cherai. It is believed that these verses were dictated to Sree Achan Bava, a devotee.

Mercy to others is an inevitable quality that is to be practised to discover the self-entity of everyone. The non-violence is one with which one shows mercy or kindness to other living things, either men or animals.

(Original text in Malayalam)

Ellāvarumātmasahōdare-
Nnalle paṛayēṇṭatitōṛkkukil nām
Kollunnatumeṅane jīvikaḷe-
Tellum kṛipayaṛṛu bhujikkayatum.

Kollāvṛatamutamamāmatilum
Tinnāvṛatametṛayumutamamām
Ellāmatasāravumōṛkkilite
Nnallē parayēṅṭatu dhārmikarē!

Kollunnatu tankal varil pṛiyamā-
Mallīvidhiyāṛkku hitapṛadamām?

Collēṅṭatu dhaṛmyamitārilumo-
Talla maruvēṅṭatu sūrikaḷē!

Kollunnavanilla bhujippatinā-
ḷillenkilaśikkukatanne dridam
Kollikkukakoṇṭu bhujikkukayām
Kollunnatilninnu muratoṛagham.

Kollāykilivan gunamuḷḷa pumā-
Nallāykil mṛugatoṭu tulyanavan
Kollunnavanilla śaranyata ma-
ṛṛellāvaka nanmayumāṛnniṭilum.

Meaning and commentary

Verse 1

Is it not we must say all are
Bosom brothers, if thought,
How is it possible to kill living ones?
How can we eat them without mercy!

Since all living things are part of the absolute one, they are our brothers and sisters. If this awareness is there, how can one kill one of them? How can one eat the flesh of another living thing?

The habit of killing and eating fellow creatures is due to the duality and ego. Such people will never come to understand the real truth and will have to suffer immersed in the ocean of worldly miseries. This is why Gurudev demands that everyone practises non-violence.

Verse 2

The practice of non-violence is the best
Better than that is the fasting without eating it

Are these not what we must say?
Once the gist of all religions is remembered.

The practice of non-violence is a good virtue, and the practice of rejection of the meat as food is a much greater virtue. Those who want to discover the real truth should know that the content of all religious teachings is this non-violence.

The deed that helps man to attain self-realization is the noble deed or Dharma, and the highest among the noble deeds is the non-violence. Non-violence does not mean only the non-killing. Even abusing another is violence. Such habits arise from the duality of thinking the other man is different from you. Because it is from the duality, the fear and enmity arise.

This non-violence does not mean tolerance to any act of violence. Those who lead to some kind of danger to the society and to noble ones, violence to resist such harmful acts, as a last resort, a suitable violent act saving the virtues can be adopted.

The advice in the form of a statement given to Yudishtira by the monk Markandeya is relevant here. He told Yudhishtira:

'Na īśē balasyēti carēt Adharmam' (if cannot master the evil acts of another do violence)—in Mahabharata by Vyasa.

The meaning is, 'if there are no other means to achieve a noble cause, adopt violence' as a last resort. This is what Markandeya told Dharmaputra when he was staying in the forest losing everything, including the pledging of his wife in gambling with the Kauravas. Many people visited him and shared sorrow with him. But when Markandeya visited him, he scolded Dharmaputra, saying, 'Look, Yudishtira, under cover of non-violence you avoided a fight with the Kauravas but lost everything. Remember! For that, you did a lot of misdeeds like playing gambling and pledging all brothers and the poor wife, is that non-violence? Look! For the purpose of avoiding single violence, you did so many acts of violence, Boy! I tell you again,"Na īśē balasyēti carēt Adharmam".'

There are so many such instances in history like Lord Krishna advising Arjuna to fight against the Kauravas, without lamenting on their deaths.

The above explanation makes one feel that there is some disparity between what Gurudev advised and what Markandeya and Lord Krishna advised. But when the above lines are thoroughly analysed, one can easily understand that they contain the spirit of both, Advaita doctrines of Krishna and contextual utterings of Markandeya.

Verse 3

If the killer is the self it is pleasing to him, is it?
But fate is not always according to his liking
When you advise what is good it should
Abide by everyone equally, oh! Virtuous one!

If the killer is the self, that will be pleasing, is it? But the fate is not always according to his liking, which means at any time he can be killed. It is this law of truth that the virtuous ones have to teach and they themselves should live accordingly.

Verse 4

If no one to eat then no one to kill
Hence eating is surely greater violence
As prompting to kill, eating is
A greater sin than killing one.

If there is nobody to eat, surely, there will not be anybody to kill. Therefore, eating the flesh of prey is greater violence than killing. Since eating prompts to kill, evidently, it is the greater sin. We know the general law is that the one who prompts to do the crime is a greater sinner than one who does the crime.

Verse 5

If not kill, he is a virtuous protector
If not, he is not different from animals
One who kills never gets a place of refuge
Even if he possesses all other virtues.

One who does not kill the fellow creatures is the one with wisdom. There is no distinction between an unwise and an animal. One who kills will never get a place of refuge, even if he possesses all other virtues. Removing all dualities and attaining self-realization is the ultimate aim of life.

22

KUNDALINI PATTU—THE COSMIC DANCE OF KUNDALINI

The date of writing this poem is not known precisely as there is no specific evidence. But some people believe it to be about 1887. The poem clearly manifests Gurudev's deep knowledge of Yoga Sastra and his own experience in it. He was a fully trained yogi, and his works are mostly based on jnana yoga. He discusses the secrets of yoga in many poems. 'Kundalini Pattu' is one of the works which is based on yoga. This contains most of the secrets of the experience of yoga. The universe is created and maintained by the flow of prana that is formed where the Brahma power begins to vibrate or fluctuate. When the yogi reaches a particular stage after performing his religious rights and starts practice, the prana power in subtle form, enters the body and spreads throughout and becomes subject to experience. This kind of prana power which is experienced in one's body is known as Kundalini.

We know that Pranava (AUM) has four *mora*s or *matra*s (time for uttering a short syllable), namely, *A'kara* (Jagrat), *U'kara* (Swapna), *Makara* (Sushupti) and *Amathra* (Turiya—moralless). These matras are also known as *Vaiswanara*, *Thaijasa*, *Prajna* and Turiya of the supreme soul respectively. Turiya is the Amathra (time independent) among them. If we closely examine the time duration for the utterance of Pranava and the time taken by the universe for its expansion until it becomes transparent to neutrinos, the intervals are almost equal in the light of Gamow's theory of the creation of the universe (the big bang theory) and Alan Guth's cosmic inflation theory. It is a wonderful coincidence! Both the time intervals for uttering Aum and for the universe becoming visible are equal; this cannot be an accidental coincidence. Though the methods of science and Advaita philosophy are different, the similarity is amazing. At this juncture, the sutra under 'Kampanadhikaranam' in Braḥmasutra deserves special attention. That reads as 'Kampanal'.

Braḥmasutrasays,

'Kampanāt' (Because of its vibration)

Depending on the Brahman, the entire universe vibrates—from the beginning to the present moment. (Chapter 1, Pada 3, 'Kampanādhikaranam', Sūtra 39)

George Gamow's big bang theory described the origin of the universe as the explosion of a super-hot, super-dense subtle particle and its expansion to the form of the present universe. Once string theory and its supplementary, and theories such as thermodynamics, uncertainty principle and quantum theory were introduced, Gamow's concept of a 'primordial particle' in the big bang theory had to be replaced by a primordial 'string of Planck length'. Since then, there came the belief that the primordial energy in the universe was produced through the vibration of the primordial string of Planck length (10^{-33}cm).

Adi Sankara, quoting verse 2 of valli 6 of Katōpaniṣad, explains as follows:

Yadidam kinca jagatsarvam
Prāna ējathi ni: sritham
Mahatbhayam vajramudyatham
Ya ēthavithuramrithāsthē bhavanti.

Everything whatever is, the whole universe,
Lives in Prana (vital breath) from which
It arose it is a great terror,
A veritable quivering flash of lightning.

Whatever there is, the whole universe when gone forth (from the Brahman) vibrates in its windless breath. According to the commentator Adi Sankara, it is the highest Brahman. That Brahman is a great reverential fear, like a drawn sword. Those who know it become immortal.

The entire manifested universe vibrates in prana. Prana is Brahman. According to the meaning of '*ējya*' the verb, vibrate, the entire universe depends on the Brahman (prana).

Kundalini literally means, 'coiled'; in yoga, a corporeal, unconscious, instinctive or libidinal force (*Sakti*), lies coiled in the base of the spine. It is envisaged as a Goddess or a sleeping serpent.

Great Indian philosophers like Sree Narayana Gurudev believed that the blissful consciousness is the source (basic factor) of the existence of everything in the universe. Inside this imperishable source is a force that acts in a way rising and setting eternally. This rises in the form of vibrational energy; once this energy is stopped, the force disappears, and only the absolute consciousness remains forever.

Swami Vivekananda described Kundalini as follows:

According to the Yogi, there are two nerve currents in the spinal column called Pingala and Ida and a hollow canal called Sushumna running through the spinal cord. At the lower end of the hollow canal is what the Yogis call 'Lotus of the Kundalini'. They described it as triangular in the form in which, in the symbolical language of the yogis, there is a power called the Kundalini, coiled up. When that Kundalini awakes, it tries to force a passage through the hollow canal, and as it rises step by step, as it were, layer after layer of the mind becomes open, and all the different visions and wonderful powers come to the Yogi. When it reaches the brain, the yogi is perfectly detached from the body and mind; the Soul finds itself free.

The hollow canal, which runs through the centre of the spinal cord is the Sushumna. Where the spinal cord ends, in some of the lumbar vertebrae, a fine fibre issues downwards and the canal runs up even within that fibre, only much finer. The canal is closed at the lower end which is situated near what is called the sacral plexus. The different plexuses that have their centres in the spinal cord can very well stand for the different 'Lotuses' of the Yogi. When *Kundalini Sakti* is conceived as a goddess, then, when it rises to the head, it unites itself with the Supreme Being (Lord Shiva). Then, the aspirant becomes engrossed in deep meditation and infinite bliss.

'Kundalini Pattu' is a great composition taking the vibrations of the universe symbolically as the swinging dance of the snake worn by God Shiva. According to string theory, a branch of modern cosmology, the creation of the universe is from the vibrations of a fundamental string of Planck length. The universe exists and performs on the basis of that vibration even today. This vibration of the universe is at times characterized as the dance of the God Shiva (Shivathantavam). Kundalini is the life force which can experience the minute form of the primordial vibration as radiating from its own body. It is really the Brahman which is hidden in the human body in a minute string form. In fact, it lies huddled in the body, curled up in a compact form. There is an equivalent of this in physics called 'the string of Fermi dimension'. This is a six-dimensional phenomenon, curled up in every point in the four-dimensional space-time (Kaluza–Klein compactification).

In almost all explanations of the cosmic dance, it is pictured as the dance of Nataraja—the God Shiva. Fritj of Capra, in his famous book *The Tao of Physics* (1975), wrote, 'Modern physics has shown that the rhythm of creation and destruction is not only manifest in the turn of the seasons and in the birth and death of all living creatures, but is also the very existence of inorganic matter', and that, 'For the modern physicists, then, Shiva's dance is the dance of subatomic matter.'

The above, in the opinion of many quantum physicists, do not reflect the entire picture of the cosmic vibration of the universe. Sree Narayana Gurudev, more than a century ago, (~1887) had gone much deeper into this topic in 'Kundalini Pattu' considering the cosmic dance of the universe as the dance of Kundalini, the curled-up serpent. Gurudev's view is in perfect tune with the principles of quantum mechanics and string theory.

Sree Narayana Gurudev wrote these lines of 'Kundalini Pattu' as if he tells his mind (consciousness) to perform the dance of bliss, knowing that the greatness of this miniature form and the attributes of the colossal (infinite) form of Brahman are brought to experience by the Maya created by Sree Parameswarain his Jagrat (wakeful) or Vaiswanara aspect by his own desire.

The Braḥmasutra in 'Kampanadhikaranam' (Sutra 39) says that, 'Since that vibrates, prana is Brahman or depending on Brahman the universe is vibrating.' As discussed earlier, this vibration at the fundamental level of the universe might be the cause behind the creation, being and the end of the universe in a rhythmic way. In short, it is the sound produced by the vibration of the primordial string *'Nada Brahman'* 'AUM' that makes the universe vibrant or excited.

How beautifully, by using simple words, Gurudev brings forth the idea spiritually and cosmologically that the entire creations we see around us in the universe are derived from the primordial sound Aum (Nada Brahman) or the primordial atom or string, and also that the net content of the entire matter and energy in the universe is ever void. Creations of the world are only illusions (Maya).

Badarayana (Vyasa) in Brahmasutra ('Kampanal'—because it vibrates) and Sree Narayana Gurudev, in 'Kundalini Pattu' (and in many of his other poems), describe the universe as the creation of a primordial vibration (of Brahman). Later, quantum mechanics through experiments, established that the universe is not made out of a particle or an object; rather, it is created out of probability waves. Hence, it is essential that the reader has a basic knowledge of quantum physics.

(Original text in Malayalam)

Āṭupāmpē, punamtēṭupāmpē, yaru-
Ḷānandakkūtukaṇṭāṭu pāmpē!

Tinkaḷum konnayum cūṭumīsanpada-
Pankajam cēṟnnu ninnāṭu pāmpē!

Veṇṇēṛaṇiññu viḷaṅṅum tirumēni
Kaṇṇīroẓukakkaṇṭāṭu pāmpē!

Āyiram kōṭi anantan nī ānana-
Māyiravum tuṛannāṭu pāmpē!

Aumennutoṭṭoru kōṭi mandṛapporul
Nāmennaṛiññu koṇṭāṭu pāmpē!

Piḷḷippulitōl putakkum pūmēniye-
Nnuḷḷil kaḷikkumennāṭu pāmpē!

Pēyum piṇavum piṛakkum cuṭukāṭu-
Mēyum param poruḷāṭu pāmpē!

Pūmaṇakkum kuẓalāḷakam pūkumā
Kōmaḷamēni kaṇṭāṭu pāmpē!

Nādatiluṇṭām namaśśivāyapporu-
Ḷādiyāyuḷḷatennāṭu pāmpē!

Pūmalarōnum tirumālumārum pon
Pūmēni kaṇṭillennāṭu pāmpē!

Kāmanecuṭṭa kannuḷḷa kālaritan-
Nāmam nukaṛnnu ninnāṭu pāmpē!

Veḷḷimalayil viḷaṅum vēdapporu-
Ḷuḷḷil kaḷikkumennāṭu pāmpē!

Āṭaravamaṇiññīṭumavanoru
Nāṭāyvarum nāmennāṭu pāmpē!

Ellāmiṛakkiyeṭukkumēkanpada-
Pallavam paṛṛininnāṭu pāmpē!

Ellāyaṛivum viẓuṅṅi veṛum veḷi-
Yellayilēṛi ninnāṭu pāmpē!

Ellām viẓuṅṅiyetiraṟṟeẓunnoru
Colleṅṅumuṇṭaṛinjāṭu pāmpē!

Collellāmuṇṭu cuṭarāyezhum poru-
Ḷellayilēṛi ninnāṭu pāmpē!

Dēham nijamalla dēhiyoruvanī-
Dēhatiluṇṭaṛiññīṭu pāmpē!

Nāṭum nagaravumonnāyi nāvil ni-
Nnāṭu ninnāmamōtīṭu pāmpē!

Dēhavum dēhiyumonnāy viẓuṅīṭu
Mēkanumuṇṭaṛiññīṭu pāmpē!

Pērinkalninnu peruveḷiyennalla
Pārādi tōnniyennāṭu pāmpē!

Cēṛnnu nilkkumporuḷellām
Centāroṭunēṛnnu pōmmāṛu ninnāṭu pāmpē!

Meaning and Commentary

Verse 1

Oh! Kundalini you dance and seek the burrow
You dance, seeing the bliss of blessing.

In the form of a serpent spreading the hood Oh! Kundalini you continue your dance aiming at the vital nerves. You move forward experiencing the waves of self-happiness blessed by the mercy of the Lord.

The burrow of the Kundalini serpent is the vital nerve. When Kundalini enters into the mind of the yogi and as it moves forward, it experiences more and more happiness in the awareness of absolute reality. This is called Kundalini yoga.

Every living thing wishes to have a stable state of lowest energy for its stability. Here Kundalini, when it vibrates and spreads with higher and higher frequencies, develops a tendency to go back to the minimum state of energy or lowest frequencies. It is a universal phenomenon in which steadiness and peace come only when its extent of excitation is at a minimum. Here, because of the vibrations, the entire diverse things and various phenomena due to the feeling of excitedness come into existence. But we know from the knowledge of physics as well as of Vedanta that the original condition of the universe was in a state of unattributedness. So everything in the universe by its own instinct tries to go back to the primordial situation, in short, to become the Absolute or Nirguna Brahman.

Sree Narayana Gurudev advises the Kundalini to go back to the original attributelessness as that alone can take one to salvation. This means all the creations from the vibrations of Kundalini are to be left out one by one and take the mind to such a situation as advised in 'Atmopadesa Satakam' (Poem 1), that is to shut down the five sense organs such as ear, eye, skin, nose and tongue, to avoid the mystical creations of the vibrations of Kundalini.

When the Kundalini wakes up and spreads throughout the inert body, the wonderful experience and sights come up. It is when it starts spreading in Kundalini, and when it enters into Ida then into Pingala, and then spreading throughout, gradually subsiding, and enters the vital nerves. Then the absolute bliss starts frightening.

Verse 2

You dance in concurrence with the lotus feet of Lord
Who wears crescent moon and flower of Indian laburnum.

Here, Gurudev takes the dancing Shiva as the Brahman who vibrates (dances) with the cosmic wavelengths and frequencies incessantly, and he tells the Kundalini to vibrate in tune with the steps of dancing Shiva (keeping resonance or harmony). This means the vibrations have to be eternal because when the vibration is halted with zero frequency (and amplitude), the entire systems become void, and everything ends there. The law of conservation of matter and energy states that nothing can be created out of nothing, and nothing can be destroyed (ref. Bhagavad Gita, Chapter 2, Poem 16). Also, from Heisenberg's uncertainty principle, the vibration of Kundalini can never come to have zero frequency or zero energy (ref. principles of thermodynamics). This leads to the concept of repeated creations and dissolutions of the universe. According to Indian philosophy, the cosmic dance of Shiva is never-ending, and the creation and resolution corresponding to the rhythmic variations are in unison with the steps of the dance. (Also ref. Duane and Hunt, limit in wavelength-intensity curve of X-ray spectra), ($eV = h\upsilon max = hc/\lambda min$, where λmin can never be zero as that will make energy infinite.)

Verse 3

Seeing the divine body shining with white ash smeared
Oh! Kundalini you dance till tears flow from his eyes.

The Kundalini that rises from the vital nerve moves towards the *Ājna* cycle and spreads. It breaks and crosses the cycles called *Swadistam, Manipurakam, Anahatam* and *Visuddi*. The power components such as Satwa Rajas Tamas properties producing bundles of promptings are the basic cycles. These are known as Brahma gland, Vishnu gland and Rudra gland. In short, these three gods of creation (Brahma), sustenance (Vishnu) and dissolution (Maheswara) are all there in a person.

When Kundalini rises from the bottom of the spinal cord (Sushumna), the bundle of worldly desires and action or the Brahma gland gets crossed. When it reaches the Anahata (near the heart), the bundle of good virtues or the Vishnu gland gets crossed, and then, reaching the Ajna cycle, the bundle of worldly pleasures breaks the Rudra gland. The last one to break is the cover of darkness—the veil of Maya. This is fully accomplished only when one reaches the Ajna cycle.

The ambrosia-like streams of prana filling the inside of the body and then the streams of prana which are supposed to be carriers of pleasures fill the Kundalini power in the body nerves. Here Sree Narayana Gurudev brings out the concept of the Absolute which is filled with the bliss produced by the streams of prana.

This refers to the dissolution stage of the universe (Saguna Brahman). Brahman smeared with white ashes on the body means the eternal Brahman covered with the remnants of the dissolved visual universe with its innumerable constituents. Even at that stage, the eternal consciousness (Nirguna Brahman) shines. This is why the Kundalini, which is still acting at the lowest level of energy, is advised to vibrate seeing the eternal beauty of Brahman until bliss is obtained.

Verse 4

Oh! Kundalini you dance spreading all your
Billions of hoods like the rise of thousands of snakes jointly.

Oh! Kundalini, you are capable of becoming billions and billions of universal objects and innumerable physical phenomena. Continue the dance (vibrations). You dance spreading your hundred billion hoods like the snake *Ananthan* who has a hundred billion hoods.

Once Kundalini wakes up and spreads, the yogi comes to see directly many things that make one wonder about the subtle body inside. In all these writings about the level of heart, we have seen above that once Kundalini wakes up breaking the nerves in the vital nerve system, every base cycle is in the form of a lotus to the yogi. That's why it is called basic lotus. Along with the flow of Kundalini in every basic cycle, the yoga nerves, like a petal, get more and more liveliness in becoming subject to the experience of the yogi.

Kundalini, you being the primordial source, your vibrations create billions of visual universes. Kundalini is requested to continue its vibration manifesting all the billions of universes. This gives the indication of the awakening of Kundalini raising the frequency of vibrations that is a big bang after a big crunch.

Verse5

Oh! Kundalini you dance knowing that the essence
Of billions of hymns from Aum is me.

Experiencing the truth manifested by the billions of hymns as only the Kundalini power and the all-pervading consciousness Oh! Kundalini you dance.

Remember that the content of billions of hymns from Pranava (Aum)(in theories, observations and experiments) are all of this minute form—the Kundalini.

Pranava (Nada Brahman), including those in the form of theories, observations and experiments, are all the derived forms of this Kundalini which are being filled with absolute consciousness, knowing this clearly, Oh! Kundalini you dance.

Verse 6

You dance knowing the soft-skinned body wearing
The skin of spotted skinned panther will play in my mind.

Oh! Kundalini you dance giving me the feeling that Brahman who wears the colourful veil of Maya like something precious is covered with the striped skin of a tiger. It indicates that the absolute consciousness (Brahman) is veiled with colourful virtual worldly phenomena of dualities such as love and hatred, happiness and sorrow, etc.

Verse 7

The burial ground from where ghosts and evil spirits arise
Is grazed by Lord Shiva! Oh! Kundalini you dance.

Knowing that it is the ultimate cause (Brahman) that wanders about in the burial ground from where the ghosts (ignorance) and corpse (inert bodies) arise, you dance Kundalini.

Verse 8

You dance seeing the beautiful body into which enter
The beauty of the black-haired spread the fragrance of flowers.

Understanding that the Maya that creates the feeling of the visual universe dissolves into the blissful form Oh! Kundalini you perform your dance.

Seeing directly the blissful form of Shiva (Brahman) into whom the feeling of the visual universe dissolves, oh! Kundalini you perform your dance.

Here, Shiva is taken as the Brahman, and Goddess Parvathi as Maya. Parvathi with the tuft of hair spreading the fragrance of flowers dissolves in the soft skin body, Shiva.

In the commentary of Brahmasutras (Sutra 1.3.19), Adi Sankara argues that ignorance and Maya are the same. The cause of the universe is ignorance, and that it is the power of the prime source and therefore, *Avyakta* (invisible), *Akshara* (undestroyable) and Maya are synonyms. He continues to say 'Maya' is named form and such name forms are superposed on Brahman (see Gurudev's 'Adyaropa Darsanam', 'Darsanamala'). Maya is the collection of name forms. Since the name forms are inert, *Prakriti* is said to be no different from Maya. It is the same Maya described in association with Brahman. In Advaita Vedanta, the Nirguna Brahman is considered as different from the Saguna Brahman—the God. As Nirguna Brahman is attributeless, the Maya-bounded Saguna Brahman is taken as the cause of the universe.

Verse 9

> Oh! Kundalini you dance knowing that the essence of 'Nama Shivaya'
> Produced from sound, was there before the creation of the universe.

Oh, snake! Perform your dance of bliss. Know that the Namassivaya mantra has been evolved from the Nada Brahman (the Brahman in the form of sound); whatever the hymn manifest as the real truth, it is the primordial reality—the Nirguna Brahman.

Before the creation of the universe from the sourceless sound Aum (Nada Brahman), the Brahman (Nirguna) was existent. Knowing that Kundalini you continue to perform your cosmic dance.

Because zero-point energy can never be zero that was present in an all-pervading phenomenon in the form of primordial fluctuations (quantum fluctuations), and as nothing can be created out of nothing, the primordial cause could have been existent in the form of quantum fluctuations without any specific source.

The statement that the sourceless sound in the form of Nada Brahman was existent before the creation of the universe requires further explanation. Since there was a lot of apprehension among the public in general and controversies being discussed among scientists in particular about what was there before the creation of our universe, when did the universe came into existence, whether the universe had a beginning, etc., the question of what was there before the creation of the universe had always been a topic of debate among cosmologists in Vedanta and physics. For example, the great physicist Stephen Hawking argues that the universe had a beginning, so also the time. In his opinion, the universe has not existed forever. He says the universe and the time had their beginning in the big bang and that too as early as only 15 billion years ago. The beginning of real-time could have been at a state of singularity where the laws of physics would have broken down. He argues that the beginning of the universe would have been determined by the laws of physics if the universe satisfied the no-boundary condition. In the imaginary time direction of space, time is finite in extent but does not have any boundary or edge. The prediction of the no-boundary condition seems to agree with observation. The no-boundary hypothesis also predicts the universe will eventually collapse again. The contradicting phase will not have the opposite arrow of time to the expanding phase. Therefore, we will keep on getting the order, and we won't return to our youth because time is not going to go backwards.

The above argument, in fact, holds good only to our universe. But in view of the latest developments in quantum theory and cosmology, we cannot forget the fact that there are billions of universes, which Hawking himself refers to as bubble universes in his book. Each universe because of decoherence is independent by itself. Hence, one cannot predict as to what happens in other universes or even what physical laws are governing them.

When it comes to the boundary conditions, how one can know the boundary conditions and the extents without having any idea of things and phenomena in other universes outside our universe.

Coming to Gurudev's argument in the above poem that 'the content of "Nama Sivaya" in the form of Aum, which according to Vedanta is believed to be the primordial sourceless sound Nada Brahman, existed even before the creation of the universe as eternal' gives a more logical base. According to the many-universes concept, the universes are created like bubbles in boiling water. These bubble universes have the same fate as that of our universe in creation, expansion and dissolution. In the formation of all these universes, for each, there is a beginning and an end. Therefore, each universe evolves and ends with its own boundary conditions and extent of time. But when it comes to the billions, rather, a countless number of universes go on evolving and ending, where do you fix the beginning of time, where you can fix the boundary? In short, in the infinite, all-pervading space (we may call it quintessence), there should be a hidden cause (there are scientists who refuse to accept the role of cause) behind, it can only be eternal.

In support of the above argument, there are many theories and hypotheses explaining the many-universes concepts. For example, Paul Steinhardt, the Princeton University physicist, and Neil Turok of Perimeter Institute, propose a model cyclic universe. In that model, there is neither a single big bang nor a single beginning. Instead, the universe continually goes on through the oscillating cycle of expansion, contraction, collapse and again expansion. It is essential to note here, the creation, expansion, etc. of the universe attracts the relevance of the second law of thermodynamics which says that the entropy (disorder) of a closed system will inevitably increase over time.

Verse 10

Knowing that no one from Brahma, Vishnu and Shiva has seen
The beautiful self-shining Brahman Kundalini! Proceed with your dance.

Oh! Kundalini, know that no one including the lotus-born Brahma, Vishnu and Maheswara, has seen the blissful form of self-shining Brahman, you proceed with the dance.

Gurudev narrates the above situation that Brahman and Vishnu could never see the Absolute Brahman in the form of Lord Shiva in 'Sadasiva Darsanam' (Poem 10).

Aṭikkupannipōyi ninmuṭikkorannavumpaṟa-
Nnaṭutukaṇṭatilla ninneyinnumagniṡailamē,
Eṭutu nī viẓuṅṅiyenneyindriyaṅalōṭuṭan
Naṭiciṭum namaṡṡivāya nayakā, namō nama

The swine pierced the earth to see your foot the swan flew
Upward to find your head both could not find you in full
Oh! Mountain of fire you may devour me along with the senses
Adorable Shiva! Supreme Master! I bow and prostrate.

God Vishnu taking incarnation as a swine pierced the earth deeper and deeper and tried to see the foot of Shiva (the bottom end of the universe). The God Brahma on a swan flew upward to find the head of Shiva (the farther end of the universe). Both of them could not so far find either the foot or the head (the origin and the extreme end of the universe), and they (Brahma and Vishnu are, in the other sense, cosmologists studying micro and mega universes) continue their never-ending search.

Verse 11

Chanting the hymns of Shiva, the killer of Yama having the powerful eye
That burnt Cupid, Oh! Kundalini you continue to vibrate (dance).

Remembering the rival of sensual experience (Cupid) and rival of time (Yama) is beyond space and time, alleviating all sensual desires due to ignorance and drinking the non-dual ambrosia of Brahman, full of wisdom and beyond space and time. Oh! Kundalini you dance.

For more information on Kamari (the killer of sensual desires), refer to the following story:

Once, Lord Shiva was doing intense penance. Cupid came to obstruct the penance. He made use of beautiful Parvathi, the daughter of the mountain Himalaya (Himavan), to achieve the purpose. But Shiva, on seeing this craftiness, burnt Cupid to ashes. This is why Shiva is known as Kamari (the rival of Cupid). The story behind Kalari (the rival of killer Yama) is as follows. Once, to save Markandeya, an ardent devotee of Lord Shiva, from the rope of killer Yama, that is to save him from death, Lord Shiva had to fight killer Yama and kill him.

Verse 12

Knowing the truth resident of Mount whitened is the essence of Vedanta
Experience in mind, Kundalini! Perform your dance.
Lord Shiva is Brahman, and Brahman, as you know, is the essence of Vedanta.

In the poem, Lord Shiva is taken as the absolute consciousness about which Vedanta discusses throughout the doctrines and hymns. Also this Absolute is residing at the Himalaya, the mount whitened. The Kundalini is requested to continue its dance, knowing that the Absolute will ultimately become manifested clearly in the minds of everyone.

The deliberate use of the word 'essence' of Vedas for the Absolute is to indicate that the study of Vedanta leads one to know the Brahman. The mountain Himalaya is an indirect hint to show that attainment of the Absolute is not an easy task. It requires a lot of effort to climb to such heights as the top of the Himalayas where Kailas is located at the highest point in the world.

For doing penance, the monks usually select the top of the mountain because it requires a lot of bodily effort. Reaching the top of the mountain gives the monk an experience to keep the mind ready to undergo rigorous mental effort to reach the state of Turiya (this means physical effort in reaching the top of the mountain is compared to the hardest of the mental activities to Turiya) that is to become one with the Brahman or to realize enlightenment.

Remember, Sree Narayana Gurudev did penance at the top of Marutwamala (Pillathatam cave), a mountain, like Lord Shiva as Dakshinamurti is believed to have done penance at Kailas, the top of Himalaya.

Verse 13

Knowing that to the one who comes wearing the dancing snake
my mind
Becomes the place of lodging, Oh! Kundalini you dance.

Here the one who wears the dancing snake is Lord Shiva, and the devotee says that his mind is the seat of the Lord. The indication is that the visual form of Brahman, the God Shiva as Parameswara mentioned in 'Darsanamala' ('Adyaropa Darsanam', Poem 1), to him the devotee in his states of wakefulness, dream and deep sleep takes his mind as the seat of Shiva. Remember that this is something related to Shiva as Saguna Brahman.

Verse 14

Experiencing the blissful presence of unique Brahman that shines
by itself
Removing all inert visual things, you dance, Oh! Kundalini.

Oh, Serpent! You perform the dance of bliss together in tune with the tender feet of Sree Parameswara, the only reality and seen as the unique form who creates the entire universes from himself by own desire and dissolve everything back to Him.

The picture of Para Brahman (Nirguna Brahman) who performs the entire process of explosion, inflation and dissolution as described in physics by own desire also is manifested here.

Here, Gurudev indicates the dance of Kundalini and the cosmic dance of Lord Shiva as two different phenomena. One is the dance of mind prompted by the worldly desires based on the inert visual series of things. The other is the dance of the subtle, unique absolute consciousness. If the steps of the dance of both mind and the cosmic dance are out of phase, the absolute bliss cannot be attained. Therefore, the dance of the human mind should be made to maintain resonance with that of Kundalini. That is possible only if the desire prompting inert visual things should be expelled from the mind. This recalls Poem 2 of 'Daivadasakam', as if, to become unique (*ēkam*), removing all observed one by one in a 'neti, neti' manner until the observer alone remains. On becoming the unique observer, there is no phase difference in the steps of dance because then the observer himself becomes the absolute consciousness. Gurudev wants the unique drik to dissolve into the Absolute and become one with it.

Verse 15

Pushing out all inert visual series that appear and vanish sticking on
The graceful feet, Oh! Kundalini! Proceed with your dance.

Giving up all transient information (awareness) and reaching the absolute reality you perform your cosmic vibration, Oh! Kundalini.

The meaning of this poem can be understood as the knowledge or awareness as in wakefulness (Jagrat), in the dream (Swapna) and the deep sleep (Sushupti) being the creation of human mind due to ignorance (Maya) are to be rejected and attain the state of absolute knowledge or absolute consciousness.

Gurudev makes the same argument in another context in 'Atmopadesa Satakam', verse 2.

The mind, the senses, the body the manifold
Known worlds, if we think of them,
Is all the sacred body of the Sun rising?
In the sky of knowledge, absolute, search and find it.

The mind which is known as the self and the collection of the senses joined with own body, and the universe with its innumerable visuals, subjects to experience all these once thought are only the divine form of the ultimate Sun shining inside the ultimate cause—the absolute knowledge. Remember! This ultimate reality, which is the cause is beyond the wisdom.

A philosopher like Sree Narayana Gurudev only makes such a statement from his own experience, in tune with the hymn '*Sarvam Khalwidam Brahma*'—'the entire things in the universe is Brahman'.

Verse 16

Knowing that there is a unique infinite universal principle that fills everywhere
Rejecting all smatterings Oh! Kundalini you proceed with your dance!

The entire transient visual information received through the five senses, once given up, comes the experience of the absolute one which fills the entire universe. The five senses are alive fully or partly in the wakeful and dream states though, in the deep sleep, the senses are all closed fully but not continuing permanently and not pervading throughout. Once the border is crossed, the experience of the real Absolute comes. For crossing the border between the deep sleep and Turiya, yogic practice and penance are essential. Once one achieves them, to him, everything in the universe is Brahman himself, knowing that Oh! Kundalini you vibrate.

The moment when one realizes that the entire things seen diversely in the universe is basically only one unique thing and it is that the entire components spread out. At that moment he attains the Brahman.

At times those who realized Brahman may engage in worldly activities, at times they may keep silent for a period, still in both ways, experience the brilliant, noble Brahman beyond all worldly phenomena. It is not possible to measure the depth of their unity from the measurement of properties of their inert body.

Verse 17

Controlling all sound waves, sticking on to the self-shining
Atman like Fire, Oh! Kundalini you vibrate.

The source of all sound waves is the absolute truth. Therefore, when all the sound waves subside, that is, when the veil of Maya that produces the action of senses is removed, the Brahman becomes manifested brilliantly. In the ultimate form of Brahman, the vibrations begin only in the form of echo in Brahman. As its speed increases and crosses, different stages become audible sound ultimately.

Gurudev explains the process of creation of the universe when the sound (vibration) begins and the dissolution of the universe when the sound subsides in 'Atmopadesa Satakam' (Poem 52).

dhvani mayamāy gagman jvalikkūmannā-
ḷaṇayumatiṅkal aśeṣa dṛsya jālam;
Punar aviṭe tripuṭikku pūrttinalkum-
Svanavumaṭaṅṅumiṭam svayam prakāśam.

Filled with the primal echoing sound, the sky will glow
As a radiant blaze, all the constituents of the visible universe
Become extinct in that: then the sound that completes
The threefold awareness becomes silent, and self-radiance prevails.

As sound and the sky first appear, then all the constituents of the universe will join that sky. Thereafter, there comes a stage where the three aspects of knowledge, namely 'the knowledge', 'the knower' and 'the known' are separated. The self-shining absolute truth is the indivisible consciousness where all the components of the universe and the sound come shining and fade out.

In the explanation of knowledge in quantum physics, only knower and the known are taken as the aspects of awareness, ignoring the third aspect, the knowledge or the Brahman. This may be because it is invisible and beyond the limits of measurements, theories and algorithms of physics. Knowledge cannot be observed; it can only be experienced. The method of experience is explained in the first poem of 'Atmopadesa Satakam' by Gurudev.

Verse 18

The corpulent subtle material bodies are not eternal, know that
There is an eternal spirit in the body, Oh! Kundalini you vibrate.

For every living thing, there are three different bodies, namely, one, made by the combinations of the five elements called the corpulent body. Two, one formed by the combination of the five senses such as sound, touch, smell, taste, sight, etc. joining with an inert body formed by the five elements called the subtle body or mind. The third is that formed by dissolution of five inert elements called the ignorance or the body of cause. It is when the spirit (Atman) gets its experience of the visual universe. This is the state of wakefulness (Jagrat). When the Atman is withdrawn from the corpulent body and depends partly or relatively on the subtle body, the mind comes to the state of dream (Swapna), and when the Atman withdraws from both subtle and corpulent bodies and depends only on the body of cause alone, the mind comes to the state of deep sleep (Sushupti).

The phenomena of Atman accepting and rejecting the corpulent body are called birth and death. Atman knowingly giving up the subtle body and body of cause is known as salvation (Moksha). The phenomenon of the same spirit (Atman) alternatively receiving different corpulent bodies, itself shows that the inert body is only an instrument of Atman. At any time, the Atman can leave an inert body. As the inert bodies are only instruments, once they are rejected, the experience of the visual universe will vanish. Then the Atman will remain as an ever free, eternal phenomenon. To experience this, one should understand whether there is the ever-free eternal Atman present in the body.

For this, Gurudev says that one should engage in the training of Kundalini yoga, make differentiation of transient and eternal things, and concentrate the mind on meditation.

Verse 19

Viewing village and city with equality and
Chanting your prayer, Oh! Kundalini you dance.

Gurudev in the above lines refers to all differentiations of high and low in the words 'villages' and 'cities'. Life is a mix of peace and grief. The mind which is put in this turbulence of life is incapable of awakening 'Kundalini' or if at all awakened, leads it to the level of searching the Absolute. Therefore, a devotee who wishes to see the absolute reality should learn to keep the balanced mind in his way of meditation. Taking these as only the virtual projections of God, one should give up all feelings of high and low. (Ref. Gita, 2–48)

Oh! Arjuna, does your activities giving up the feeling of 'I', 'I' 'mine' and exercising yoga (Karma). Yoga means the keeping of a balanced mind in victory and failure. The approach that nothing is mine, everything is God is the real sacrifice.

Verse 20

Knowing that there is a unique supreme soul that swallow
Both the body and Atman, Oh! Kundalini you go on vibrating.

The inert bodies are produced when the vibrations start in the Brahman—the absolute consciousness. Life is the combination of these vibrations and the awareness that reflects on it. The vibration is the body, and the life is the awareness that reflects on vibration indicating the Vivartha.

Verse 21

Knowing that the feeling of the existence of not only space, all constituents
Including earth is from the sound, Oh! Kundalini you vibrate.

Oh, Kundalini! You perform the dance of bliss knowing that from Aumkara, it is not only Akash but also all constituents of the universe, including the earth are created.

We have seen from the introductory part of this chapter, the prior importance of sound and primordial vibration in the creation of the universe. (Please ref. 'Is the Universe the Nada Brahman' in *Kanikaprapancham, The Particle Universe* by the author). Latest developments in string theory endorse the argument that the universe is sound-based.

Verse 22

Oh! Kundalini vibrating in such a way that whole
Varied experiences go united in the flower like the heart.

The ultimate aim of life is to realize the self as Brahman. The awareness of 'I' is the part of Brahman with attributes in a human being. This part of Brahman (with attributes) is like the reflected image of the Absolute Brahman (without attributes) known as Nirguna Brahman, like the image of the Sun on the surface of the water. The image being illusory, it has no direct contact with the real Sun except that it is a virtual image. Similarly, the Saguna Brahman, of which human Atman is a part, is only a virtual image of the real Brahman. The relation between Absolute Brahman and Brahman with attributes is called Vivartha, which means the familiar Saguna Brahman is only a virtual projection of Nirguna Brahman.

If one wants to get salvation, he has to become one with Nirguna Brahman. For that one has to give up all worldly longings. (See also Poem 5, 'Brahmavidyapanchakam')

23

PINDANANDI

'Pindanandi' is a comparatively small literary work of Sree Narayana Gurudev believed to be written sometime around 1885 while he was staying at Aruvippuram.

'Pindam' means mass that is, inert body. Nandi means thanks. The verses are thanksgiving songs addressed to Brahman, who protects the inert body. This is why the title of the poem is 'Pindanandi'. There are nine verses in this work. These poems are written as prayer songs of a newborn child at the time of its birth. It is in the context of his grief on seeing his beloved mother wailing with terrific delivery pain. To the memory of the child comes the severe experience during its growth in the womb of the mother from the time of conception to the time of delivery.

In the probability of survival of a zygote and then to form the fetus, there are many deciding factors. And those factors themselves depend on a set of probabilities in a physical sense. In the complexity of these probabilities, the chance of survival of the inert body (zygote) overcoming all dangers during the early periods is almost nil, especially till the end of the first five months after conception. Gurudev, in the first seven verses, explains how these obstructions to survival are overcome. The eighth verse refers to the newborn baby's helplessness in consoling the mother who delivered him with terrible pain. She wails like a tigress, thinking about the newborn baby. The ninth verse makes a request to the all-knowing Brahman to protect him from all miseries, and if it is refused, nobody else is there to help him.

(Original text in Malayalam)

Gaṛbhatilvacu bhagavānaṭiyante pinṭa-
Meppērumanpoṭuvaḷaṛta kṛipaluvallī?
Kalpicapōlevarumennu ninacukanṭi-
ṭṭaṛpiciṭunnaṭiyanokkeyumaṅṅu śambhō!

Maṇṇum jalamkanalumambaramōṭu kāṛṛu-
Meṇṇippiṭicaṛayiliṭṭeriyum koḷuti
Dandappeṭutumoru dēvatayinkalninnen-
Pindatinannamṛitu nalkivaḷaṛta śambhō!

Kallinnakatu kuṭivāẓumoralppajantu-
Vonnalla ninte kṛipayinnaṛyiciṭunnu!
Allikkuṭatilamarunnamarēndranum ma-
ṛṛellārumiṅṅitilirunnu vaḷaṛnniṭunnu.

Bandukkaḷilla balavum dhanavum ninakki-
Lentonnukoṇṭitu vaḷaṛnnataho! Viciṭṛam
Entampurānte kaḷiyokkeyitennaṛinjā-
Landatwamillatinu nīyaruḷīṭu śambhō!

Nālancumāsamorupōl nayanaṅalvacu
Kālantekayyilaṇayāte vaḷaṛti nīye
Kālam kazhinju karuvinkalirunnunjāna-
Kkālam ninacu karayunnitu kēlkka śambhō!

Rētassutanneyitu raktamoṭum kalaṛnnu
Nādam tiraṇṭuruvatāy naṭuvilkiṭannēn
Mātāvumillaviṭeyannu pitāvumillen-
Tātan vaḷaṛtiyavanāṇivaninnu śambhō!

Annuḷḷavēdana maṛannatu nannuṇaṛnnā-
Linniṅutanneriyil vīṇu marikkumayyō!
Ponnappanannu poṛivātilorancumiṭṭu
Tanniṭṭutanneyituminnaṛiyunnu śambhō!

Entaḷḷayakamē cumaṭāykiṭati
Ventuḷḷazhinju veṛute neṭuvīṛppumiṭṭu
Nontiṅupeṛṛu naripōlekiṭannu kūvu-
Nnentāvatiṅaṭiyanonnaruḷīṭu śambhō!

Ellāmaṛinju bhagavānivaninneṭutu
Collēṇamō duritamokkeyakaṛṛanē nī
Illāruminnaṭiyanaṅoẓiyunnuvenki-
Lellām kaḷanjerutilēṛivarunna śambhō!

Meaning and Commentary

Verse 1

Oh! Lord are you not the merciful one
Who carefully fostered my body while in the womb?
Knowing that things happen only on your will
This devotee dedicates the entire body at your feet.

Oh! Blissful Lord! Is it not you who protected mercifully the inert body of this newborn infant, which is inevitable for worldly life throughout the period of pregnancy by all means? Therefore, this devotee dedicates the entire things, including the body at your feet, knowing that things can happen only according to your will.

There are lots of probabilities of miscarriage in the survival of the zygote and the blastocyst, especially during the period from the conception to the formation of the fetus. Through such obstructions throughout the period of pregnancy from the process of conception—the union of sperm and ovum—takes place only under a number of favourable conditions. The chance of getting each of these favourable conditions is meagre and indeterminable.

Gurudev in the above poem uses the words '*kalpichapole*' (as decided by you) to stress the desire (influence) of the eternal power that controls everything related with life from the moment of conception to the end of life. The probability that the spermatozoon unites with an ovum still remains indeterminable to science.

Gurudev mentions the vulnerability to damage like the miscarriage of the embryo during the first trimester (of the three trimesters of duration one to thirty-seven weeks). Here it is relevant to have a brief explanation of what happens from the moment of conception to the moment of delivery of a child. See the following sequence of events.

Almost all adult males produce billions of spermatozoa every second. Each spermatozoon produced has half the number of human DNA—twenty-three out of forty-six. Some spermatozoon will have an X sex chromosome, and others have Y sex chromosome. The length of each spermatozoon comes to nearly one-billionth of a centimetre, or 500 of them lined up in a row will make a total of 1 inch. Spermatozoa take a month or so to travel from a testicle through a long tube, vas deferens, inside the prostate gland. Semen that is the mixture of spermatozoa and various fluids is formed here. Each spermatozoon contains DNA but with twenty-three chromosomes instead of the normal human DNA numbering forty-six. The movements of spermatozoa, though they appear as that of a living organism, it is not true; instead, the movements are due to chemical reactions.

From the female side, the woman ovulates and produces one mature ovum. Like the spermatozoon, it will also contain twenty-three chromosomes; one of them is always an X sex chromosome. The ovum travels down through one of the fallopian tubes towards the uterus. In size, the diameter of the ovum is five times the length of each spermatozoon, and it is visible to the naked eye.

During the process of conception, one very lucky sperm out of billions ejaculated by the man may penetrate the outside layer of the ovum. This happens when it is at the upper third of the woman's fallopian tube. To the surface of the ovum, there comes changes in its electrical characteristics, and this prevents the entry of additional sperm. This genetically unique entity formed by the sperm and ovum is called a zygote. Some people often refer to this as the moment of conception or instant of conception as if the process takes place momentarily. But conception is a process that extends over hours.

Even though the zygote contains twenty-three chromosomes from the father and twenty-three chromosomes from the mother forming a natural human DNA of forty-six chromosomes, its DNA structure is different from the DNA structure of the father and the DNA structure of the mother, and it also differs from the DNA structure of any siblings. These differences give the child a reproductive advantage later in its life in comparison with other children in the family and in society. This is what Charles Darwin took as the driving force in his theory of evolution. His use of the statement 'survival of the fittest' means the comparative ability of a baby to survive and later produce offspring.

The zygote will contain an X sex chromosome donated by the ovum and either an X or Y sex chromosome from the spermatozoon. If the union ends with XX chromosomes, the zygote is a female; if it ends with XY chromosomes, the zygote is male. In rare cases, a zygote will be formed with XY chromosomes, producing a boy that develops into a fetus with male sexual organs visible at birth though registered as a male, yet with the female structure in its brain. This will cause them to identify its gender as female later in life and discover that it is a transgender and female. Similarly, in very rare cases, a zygote with XX chromosomes develops into a fetus that is female at birth yet having a male brain structure. Later in life, they will identify as female to a male transgender person.

Verse 2

With Earth, water, fire, air and space in the required proportion
You made my body and put in the womb and lighted
The fire of miseries Oh! Shiva, then you saved my body
From the torturing deity, giving me ambrosia of relief.

The body created using the fundamental elements such as earth, water, fire, air and sky in correct proportion and this infant devotee while inside the womb the Lord ignited the fire of life force and protected me from the Goddess of worldly activities that made me suffer. Lord gave Atman the ambrosia of life to my body. Oh! Lord! The embodiment of bliss! You are the only refuge.

The body is the creation of a precise combination of fundamental elements. The five elements are combined in a certain proportion to make the body, fixing the chemistry and physical structure of the body. It is a very complex phenomenon. The choice of suitable components from innumerable probabilities to make a male or female offspring and all characteristics remain throughout as natural instinct, the formation of features, the selection of Y sex chromosomes of the parents, even the exact time of conception with respect to the sex act and ovulation, all these indeterminate phenomena ultimately result in the birth of a child with a predetermined fate.

Verse 3

It is not only one, but many are in the hidden
Transient lives that let know your mercy
The king of gods who endures in the pot of
Ambrosia and all others are grown inside this.

Oh! Lord! Due to your mercy, not only the microorganisms living in deep depths of huge stones but also everyone including the king of heaven Devendra who depend on the pot of ambrosia for existence had their life grown from here in this womb of the mother.

The indication in the above poem is that the child overcomes all the obstructions resisting the growth from the time of inception to the delivery of the child is basically due to the mercy of God. We have seen above the complexity of body formation, ignition of life force to a body, etc. on the journey of a child going to the visual universe around. It also shows the equality in the process of childbirth in the case of all living things with the dependence on the mother without any likes or dislikes among the devotees, whether the king or the subject. That is why Gurudev says the entire living organisms carry out their lives in the same way from the same type of crucible—the womb of the mother (See 'Jatinirnayam').

Verse 4

Once thought there are no relations force and wealth
It is wonderful that with whose help that grew
Once it is known that all these are the play of God
Then there is no blindness you tell, Oh! God!

Once thought, there were no relatives including the father and mother, there were no external forces, and there was no means of support (resources) like those things required for maintenance of the unborn child's existence other than the Lord. Gurudev mentions this to show that at the preliminary stage of growing up to four to five months of the fetus (first trimester), there was no substantial interaction through the placenta and umbilical cord. Once thought, it seems wonderful how the fetus grew in such a condition where there was no help or connection with other things other than the Brahman himself. Once realized that it is all ignorance and the play of the Lord, I can escape without falling into the veil of ignorance (Maya). Oh! Lord! Bless this infant devotee to attain the state of realization.

Verse 5

Four to five months you looked after me in
The same way without letting fall into the hands of Yama
After that time sitting in the womb, I weep in gratitude
Thinking of that time, Hear me! Oh! Lord!

Until the end of the four or five months, the inert fetus was looked after very carefully by the Brahman without leaving it to abortion. Now it is all past experience. The infant devotee remembers that period of its miseries and loneliness in the womb. Oh! Lord Shiva, you hear me.

At this juncture, it is important to see the depth of Gurudev's thinking about the situation in view of the gynaecological analysis in the growth of a zygote from its conception date to the state of a normal child at delivery. The following is the sequence of growth of the embryo.

By the end of the four weeks all major system and organs begin to form. Neural tubes, digestive system, heart and circulatory system begins to form. The beginning of eyes, ears, arms, legs and the heartbeat begins. At the end of eight weeks the embryo takes human shape with large head in proportion to the body. Develops tooth budds. Eyes, nose and ears become distinct organs and bones, nose and jaws develops. The embryo is in constant motion. After 12 weeks the external genital organs develop.

The fetus or the embryo is most vulnerable during the first twelve weeks. During this period all the major organs and body systems are only in the formation level and hence can be damaged if the fetus is exposed to drugs, infectious agents, radiation, certain medications and toxic substances. Though the organs and body are fully formed by the end of three months, the fetus is still incapable of surviving independently.

The following is the sequence of growth of a child in the womb after the first trimester. The baby continues to develop into more visual levels.

After 16 weeks musculoskeletal system continues to form, the skin begins to form and then the intestine develops. After 20 weeks the baby is more active, can hear and swallow. After 24 weeks the bone marrow begins to make blood cells, taste buds form on its tongue, lungs formed hair grow and gets regular sleep. At 29 to 40 weeks (delivery weeks) bones are fully formed, movements and kicking increase, eyes can open and close, starts breathing. At 36 weeks a waxy coating of protection form, body fat increases, baby become bigger and less space to move. Body weight comes to 2.7 to 2.95 kgs. Finally in 37 to 40 weeks baby completes its full form. The organ functioning on their own. The baby will be turn in to head-down position for birth. The weight of the baby is then between 2.8 to 4.2 kgs and height 58 to 64 cms. Healthy babies come in many different weights and heights.

Verse 6

The sperm uniting with the mother's ovum joined with soul formed
The fetus I lay inside the womb in that state
And till delivery, there was not my mother and father Blissful Lord!
It was you, my father, oh! Make me grow.

The subtle spermatozoan uniting with the blood (ovum) of the mother along with the soul, takes the form of a baby stayed in the womb of the mother in between conception and delivery. During that period, there was not my mother or father for my protection. In that sense, it was you, Oh! Lord! My father, the embodiment of bliss! It was yourself who nurtured me. Gurudev uses this verse to show the child's helplessness while in the womb. In the earlier poems, Gurudev elaborated on the helplessness of the baby from its zygote–fetus to the full-fledged state of the newborn child. Hence, the indication is that the role of the parents and the surroundings is much less than the fate of the child, which is predetermined by the Brahman.

Ultimately, this results in the birth of a child with a predetermined fate.

The placenta, the supporting system, also plays an inevitable role in the growth and survival of the fetus.

The placenta, otherwise known as afterbirth, is an organ that connects the growing fetus to the wall of the uterus to allow nutrients uptake, thermal regulation, waste elimination and gas exchange via the mother's blood supply, defence against internal infection and production of hormones to support the pregnancy. The growing fetus gets oxygen and nutrients from the placenta, and it removes waste products from the fetus's blood. The placenta attaches to the wall of the uterus, and the fetus's umbilical cord develops from the placenta. These organs connect the mother and the fetus.

The placenta is a fetomaternal organ with two components, namely, the fetal placenta and the maternal placenta. The placenta develops from the same blastocyst that forms the fetus, and the maternal placenta develops from the mother's uterine tissue. This metabolizes a number of substances and can release metabolic products into maternal or fetal circulations.

The average length of it is 22cm and its thickness is 2 to 2.5 cm, with a thick centre and thin edges. It weighs approximately 500 gms. Its colour is dark reddish blue or crimson. It is connected to the fetus by an umbilical cord of an approximate length of 55–60 cm that contains two umbilical arteries and one umbilical vein. The umbilical cord is inserted into the chronic plate vessels, which branch out over the surface of the placenta, and further divide to form a network covered by a thin layer of cells forming villous tree structures. On the mother's side, these villous tree structures are grouped into lobules called cotyledons. The human placenta has a disc shape.

The placenta starts developing upon implantation of the blastocyst (embryo) into the maternal endometrium. The outer layer of the blastocyst then becomes the trophoblast which forms the outer layer of the placenta and is divided into two further layers—the underlying cytotrophoblast layer and the over syncytiotrophoblast layer. The latter is a multinucleated continuous cell layer that covers the surface of the placenta. It is formed as a result of the differentiation and fusion of the underlying cytotrophoblast cells.

It is a process that continues throughout placenta development. The syncytiotrophoblast contributes to the barrier function of the placenta.

The placenta grows throughout pregnancy. The development of the maternal blood supply to the placenta is complete by the end of the first trimester of pregnancy (approximately 12–13 weeks).

Further details of maternal placental circulation and the fetoplacental circulation, etc. are not elaborated, though they play a very important role in the growth of the fetus to the level of a newborn baby. As mentioned in verses 4, 5 and 6 above, till the functioning of the maternal and fetoplacental circulations, there were no physical contacts between the fetus and the mother. Really it was in a helpless state. The mother, father or any helping hand was not there giving protection to the child except the mother carrying it up to four or five months, and the fetus was in the hands of fate. This is what Gurudev refers to as the period of the first '*nālañcumāsam*' (four or five months), the period purely dependent on fate, say, the God.

The placental expulsion begins as a physiological separation from the wall of the uterus. The time between the moment of childbirth and the expulsion of the placenta is called third-stage labour. The expulsion happens within 15–30 minutes of birth. The placenta and the fetus are regarded as foreign allograft inside the mother and thus must evade attack by the mother's immune system. For that, the placenta makes use of many mechanisms.

Verse 7

It is good that I do not remember the grief I experienced
In the womb, if I remember I will burn in the fire of memory.
Blissful Lord because you gave me five sense organs for
The entry of light to see your skilfully created universe.

It is good that I do not remember the grief I experienced while lying in the womb. If I remember, I will be burnt to ashes in the fire of that memory. This devotee knows about this universe today because you, the embodiment of bliss and mercy, gave me great affection by way of rendering this devotee the five sense organs (the five tiny doors) which give light for getting the awareness of various phenomena and events in this universe.

Verse 8

My mother carrying me in her womb suffering very severely
Burnt her mind with long sighs delivered me helplessly and
Like a tigress wailing throughout day and night worried about me
Oh! Blissful Lord, what can this infant devotee do? Tell me.

My mother, carrying me in her womb during the period of pregnancy with burnt mind and long sighs, gave birth to me with a terrible pang of labour and then helplessly wailed like a tigress during day and night. Oh! Lord! The merciful one! What can this helpless infant devotee do to console her? Oh! Lord! You yourself tell me.

Verse 9

Lord! As you are omniscient, there is no need I take up
One by one to you one detached from all worldly luxuries
Who rides on ox I pray to remove all my worldly miseries
If you leave me, I do not have anybody else as my relative.

Oh! The all-knowing Lord! You know everything. This newborn devotee need not explain them one by one. Oh! The embodiment of bliss who ride on old ox! One who detached from all worldly pleasures! Bless me removing all worldly miseries. If you refuse to do so, remember! I have no other relative.

The indication is that the all-knowing, all-pervading Lord clearly knows who wants what. In that sense, is there any meaning in explaining specific things? It is because of the ignorance of the devotee that he makes such a request. Here the devotee praises the Lord who protected him during the entire period in the womb from the moment of inception to the present. To remove ignorance, practise the habit of meditation. It is well known that the ox is the vehicle of Lord Shiva.

24

ATMAVILASAM

(The Self-Lustre)

This is a note in prose written by Sree Narayana Gurudev collected from the notebook of his first disciple, Brahmasree Sivalingadasa Swamikal.

Atmavilasam means the manifestation of Brahman (consciousness) in different forms. It gives the divine Vedantic thought like an Upanishad. Gurudev expounds that the universe is only a reflected image (shadow)—Vivartha of Brahman (consciousness), and that becomes known through the experience of self-realization. Gurudev explains this fact using a series of the observer–observed phenomena starting with the eye. The eye is the collection of the sensitive organs (the five senses), and it is the self. Through the observer–observed argument, Gurudev establishes that the ultimate eye (the self) is the Brahman, which is the absolute consciousness. The ultimate factor is God (Brahman), which is the all-pervading indivisible consciousness. This all-pervading consciousness in its pure form fills the illusory (Maya creation) objects like the all-pervading space fills the vessels like pots. This indivisible consciousness is the self. This self, though some refer to it as self-consciousness, is not a separate entity like a drop of water in the ocean. It is an imagined fraction of a real entirety. Says Bhagavad Gita in Poem 7 ('Purushotama Yogam') the jeevatman, known as 'Jeeva' (life) is part of immortal me, it takes, the six sense organs including the mind to everywhere it goes. It is not possible to have a part of the indivisible Brahman (consciousness). Therefore, these are not part of Brahman (Nirguna). All these cannot be originated from a minute particle because such particles are not real in indivisible consciousness. Therefore, it can only be an illusory feeling—say, *Vartha*. But feeling cannot undergo evolution. All these cannot be considered as something else because, being unique (Brahman—consciousness) and all-pervading, it cannot permit a second in it. This is what makes Brahman (the ultimate consciousness) indefinable.

(Original text in Malayalam)

Aum ithokkeyum nammude munpil kannadiyil kanunna nizhal pole thanneyirikkunnu. Athbhutham! Ellattineyum kanunna kannine kannu kanunnilla. Kanninte munpil kayyiloru kannadiyeduthupidikkumbol kannu aa kannadiyil nizhalikkunnu. Appol kannu kannadiyeyum nizhalineyum kanunnu.nizhal jadamakunnu. Athinu kannine kanunnathinu sakthiyilla kanninu kannine ethirittu nokkunnathinu kazhiyunnilla. Ingane kannum kanninte nizhalum kannil kanatheyirikkumbol, avide kannine kanunnath namakunnu. Ithupole ee kannine kanunna name nam kanunnilla. Nammude munpil oru kannadiye sankalpikkumbol nam aa kannadiyil nizhalikkunnu. Appol aa nizhalinu nammekkanunnathinu sakthiyilla. Nizhal jadamakunnu. Namukku name ethirttunokkunnathinu kazhiyunnilla. Nam nammil kalpithamayirikkunna kannadiyeyum aa kannadiyude ullil nilkkunna nizhalineyum thane kanunnullu. Appol nammekkanunnath nammude mukalil nilkkunna daivamakunnu. Churukkam kalpithamayirikkunna kannadi, athinullil nilkkunna nammude nizhal, kannu, kayyilirikkunna kannnadi, aa kannadiyude ullil nilkkunna kanninte nizhal ithanjum nammude keezhadangi nilkkunnu. Ithine kanunna kannu namakunnu—kannu kanninte nizhalineyum kannadiyeyum thane kanunnullu. Nam, nammude nizhal, kannadi, kannu, kanninte nizhal, kayyilirikkunna kannadi itharum daivathinte keezhadangi nilkkunnu. Ithine kanunna kannudaivamakunnu. Oh! Ithuoruvaliyaascharyamakunnu. Namennalla nammal kanappedunnathokkeyum ingane nizhalikkunnathinu daivam idam koduthirikkunnu. Ithukoodathe ithineyokkeyum daivam thane kanukayum cheyyunnu. Appol daivam oru divyamaya kannadiyum kannumayirikkunnu. Oh! Itha oru divyamayirikkunna kannadiyil oru puthiya malaye kanunnu. Appuram itha oru padam kanunnu. Ithu nam pandu kandittullathanennu thanne thonnunnu. Oh! Itha marunnumamalayum kanyakumariyum madhurayum kasiyum chidambaravum nammude ullil aduthaduthu kanunnu. Oh! Ithethrayo doorathilirikkunnu. Nam ivide nilkkunnu. Oh! Itha oranayodikkunnu. Nam pedichu malayude mukalilerunnu. Ivideyirikkunna yogeeswaranod nam upadesam kettu yogagniyil dahikkunnu. Oh! Itha ingane kinavu kandkond unarnnu nishkambamayirunnu nudumoochuvidunnu. Chithram! Itha nam mayangi ezhunnettirunnukond onnumariyathe sukhamayurangi enningane nammude munpil nilkkunna peruveliyil orajnanatheyum ahankaratheyum veruthe kalpichu vyavaharikkunnu. Oh! Itha kilivathililkoodi varunna sooryakiranathil kidannu marayunnu dhoolipole andakodikal mariyunnu. Oh! Itha Ithaithokkeyum nammiladangi nam nammude mukalil nilkkunna divyamaya kannadiyil marayunnu. Ee kannadi nammude dhaivamakunnu. Oh! Itha pinneyum kanalilninnu vellam pongi varunnathu pole ithokkeyum daivathil ninnu pongi varunnu. Ennal daivamsamaya nammude ullil ithineyokkeyum velippeduthiyirikkunnu ennu thalparyam. Oh! Itha ithokkeyum nammodukoodi dhaivam thante divyamayirikkunna vyapakadarppanathil eduthvirich vistharamulla kannukond nokkunnu.pinneyum kanniladakkunnu. Marupadiyum kannil ninnu velippeduthunnu. Ith daivathinu oru kaliyakunnu.ith daivamsamakunnu. Alla—daivam amsamillathathakunnu. Ithukondu daivamsamennu paranjukooda. Pinne valla paramanuvil ninnu parinamichatho? Ennal, athumalla. Enthukondennal paramanukkal daivathil vivarthangalakunnu. Vivarthamennal ivide nizhalakunnu. Nizhalinu veronnayi marunnathinu kazhiyunnilla. Mattonninum dhaivathil irikkunnathinu daivamahathmyam idam kodukkunnilla. Athukond ithine veronninte amsamonnum paranjukooda. Appol ee kanappedunnathokkeyum anirvachaneeyamakunnu. Ithokkeyum anjanakkarante mashiyil theliyunna devatha poleyirikkunnu.

Ithinte bimbam daivathilirikkunnu. Ith nizhalakunnu. Ippol ee kanappedunnathum daivavum namum ayirikkunna ithokkeyum daivathiladangumbol daivam thanneyayirikkunnu. Ith daivathinte vyapakathaye keduthunnilla. Nizhalinu yathonninteyum vyapakathaye bhedikkunnathinu kazhiyunnilla. Ennuthanneyalla, nizhalineyathoru vyapakathayum kalayunnilla. Oh! Itha ithokkeyum manovegamulla oru ghadeeyanthram pole adhyanthamillathe karangunnu. Vismayam. nam nammude kannine kanunnu. Name daivam kanunnu. Nam nammude sruthiye sravikkunnu. Daivam namme sravikkunnu. Nam thwakkine sparsikkunnu. Name daivam sparsikkunnu. Nam nammude navine rasikkunnu. Name daivam rasikkunnu. Nam nammude mookine manakkunnu. Namme daivam manakkunnu. Nam vakkine thallividunnu. Name vakku thallividunnilla. Dhaivam thallividunnu. Nam kayye aadhanam cheyyikkunnu. Name kai aadhanam cheyyikkunnilla—daivam aadhanam cheyyikkunnu. Nam kaline nadathunnu; name kalu nadathunnilla. Daivam nadathunnu; nam daivathe nadathunnilla. Nam gudathe visarjanam cheyyikkunnu; name gudam visarjanam cheyyikkunnilla. Daivam visarjanam cheyyikkunnu; nam daivathe visarjanam cheyyikkunnilla. Nam upasthathe anandhippikkunnu; name upastham aanandhippikkunnilla. Daivam anandhippikkunnu; nam daivathe anandhippikkunnilla. Oh!itha, daivathil purushalakshanam kanunnu. Daivam kannillathe kanukayum cheviyillathe kelkkukayum thwakkillathe sparsikkukayum mookkillathe manakkukayum navillathe ruchikkukayum cheyyunna oru chitpurushanakunnu. Nam daivathinteprathipurushanakunnu. Nammude sareeram jadamakunnu. Pazhuthirikkunna ayogolam thejomayamayirikkunnathupole nam kannu thurannunokkumbol nammude sareeram thejomayamayirikkunnu. Oh! Itha, ippol kanappedunnathokkeyum ithupole thejomayamayirikkunnu. Oh! Nammudedaivamjyothirmayamayirikkunnorudivyasamudramakunnu. Ithokkeyum aa nistharangasamudrathinte tharangamakunnu. Oh! Ithokkeyum kanalilninnu kaviyunna vellamakunnu. Daivam kanalakunnu. Oh! Nam ithuvareyum bahirmukhanayirikkunnu. Ini andharmukhathodukoodiyavanayitheerunnu. Aa! Ivide ethryo divyamayirikkunnu. Nam ithuvareyum ninnirunnath oru divyamayirikkunna kannadiyilakunnu. Ithuthanneyanu nammude dhaivam. Ithine nam ithinumunpil kandirunnilla. Ippol namukkividam yathoru maravum kanunnilla namum daivavum onnayirikkunnu. Ini namukku vyavaharikkunnathinu padilla. Oh! Itha nam daivathinod onnayippokunnu.

Let us see the details in Gurudev's own words. 'Aum.'

'All these things are like images in a mirror. Wonderful! The eye that sees everything does not see the eye. When a mirror is placed before the eye, it makes an image of it in the mirror. Then the eye sees the mirror and the image. The image is inert. That is incapable of seeing the eye. The eye cannot see the eye directly. In this way, the eye, the image of the eye when not seen by the eye then, the eye is seen by the self. Similarly, the self that sees the eye does not see the self. When a mirror is placed before the self, the self reflects on the mirror. Then that reflected image is incapable of seeing the self. The image is inert. Self cannot see the self directly. The self sees only the mirror superimposed on the self and the image in the mirror. Then the self is seen by God above the self. In short, the superposed mirror, the image of the self in it, the eye, the mirror in hand and the image of the eye in the mirror, all these five remain under the control of the self. The self is the eye that sees this. The eye sees only the image of the eye and the mirror. The self, the image of the self, the mirror, the eye, the image of the eye, the mirror in hand all these six exist under the control of the God. The eye that sees this is God.

' Oh! How wonderful it is! Not only the self but everything is seen by the self is given space by God to reflect. Besides, all these are seen by God. Then God is a divine mirror and the eye. Oh! Here is a divine mirror a new mountain is seen, beyond that a picture is seen. It seems that it was seen by the self earlier. The mountain Marutwamala, Kanyakumari, Madhura, Kasi and Chidambaram are seen closer and closer inside the self. Oh! How far away they are. Self remains here. Oh! Here, an elephant makes the self-run. Self-fearing it climbs to the top of the mountain. Hearing the advice of Yogishwar and sitting here, the self burns in the fire of Yoga. Oh! Dreaming thus wakes up without shivering, sighs.

'Wonderful! Here the self naps and then waking up and sleeping without knowing anything and so on in the front of the self-deal in vain, the unending space (open place) superimposing an ignorance and ego. Lo! Here like dust particles roll in the rays of the Sun entering through the birds' entry hole *billions of universes roll like minute particles. Here all these dissolve in the self and disappear in the divine mirror above the self. Oh! This mirror is the God of self. Oh! Again, like water rises from the fire, all these things come up (rise) from God. The meaning is that all these are manifested in the self, being part of God. Oh! Here all these along with the self are spread in the all-pervading mirror of the God see with the wide eye. Again enclose in the eye and again disclosed (revealed) from the eye. This is a play of God. This is a part of God—no! God is indivisible. Therefore one should not say it forms a part of God. Then, is it something evolved from an atom (or minute particle)? No, it also is not, because the particles are only virtual images (Vivartha) of God. Vivartha here means image (Shadow). The image (Shadow) cannot become changed into another. The uniqueness of God does not allow a second to exist in it. Therefore, it cannot be considered as part of anything else. Then all these things are seen become indefinable. All these look like the goddess seen in the fortune teller's ink using a magic stone, the *Anjanam* [Anjanam—a kind of black substance].

'Its idol is of God. This is a shadow. Now, all these visible things, God and self—when dissolve in God, becomes God himself. It does not obstruct the all-pervading nature of God; the image (shadow) cannot break the pervading nature of anything. Not only that, any pervading phenomenon does not damage the shadow. Oh! Here all these rotate like a pulley-like mechanism that rotates with the speed of mind eternally. Wonderful, the self sees its eye, the God sees the self. The self hears the sound, the God hears the self. Self touches its skin, the God touches the self. The self tastes its tongue, and God tastes the self. The self smells the nose, and God smells the self. The self pushes forward the word; the word does not push the self. God pushes forward. The self holds the hand. The hand does not hold the self. God holds the self. The self makes the leg walk, the leg does not make the self walk. God does. But the self does not make God do. The self makes anus discharge, it does not make the self discharge, the God makes the self discharge, the self does not make the God discharge, the self makes the sex organ delighted, the sex organ does not make the self delighted, the God make self delighted. The self does not make God delighted. Look! In God, the attribute of man is seen. The God, who sees without an eye, hears without ears, touches without skin, smells without a nose, tastes without tongue is the supreme soul. The self is the counterpart[1], its body is inert, how the red-hot iron glob is brilliant when the self opened eye the self's body seems to be brilliant. Look! Here whatever is seen now is brilliant like this. Oh! Our God is a brilliant divine ocean. All these are waves of that waveless ocean. Look! All these are water overflowing from the fire. God is fire. Oh! I (self) was extrovert so far. Now I (self) become introvert. Look! How divine is here. So far, I (self) was in a divine mirror. This itself is my (self's) God. I (self) never saw it any before. Now before me (self), there is not any veil. God and I (self) have become one. Hereafter the I (self) am forbidden from interactions. Oh! See! I (self) become one with God.'

[1]Note: An example of Vivartha—the absolute consciousness and the visual universe are related as the Sun and its images on reflecting surfaces.

* It manifests Gurudev's many-universes (multiverse) concept.

25

MUNICHARYAPANCHAKAM

This is a work of five poems in Sanskrit written by Sree Narayana Gurudev. It is a magnificent noble work in Vedanta. The extraordinary linguistic style and the fullness of vocabulary are beautifully blended in this work. It is a work that reveals the greatness of Gurudev's asceticism and universality. The lines give a general picture of an ascetic who has become a Jeevanmukta. About the occasion of writing these verses, there are different versions. In 1911 Sree Sivalingadasa Swamikal, Gurudev's first direct disciple, wrote and published an explanation of these verses.

An ascetic is one who has realized the Absolute and one who has crossed the limits of births and deaths of worldly life.

> Gurudev in verse 7 of 'Atmopadesa Satakam' explains it.
> Wake no more, remain as knowledge and be wakeful.
> If not fit for that today, keep the body fixed
> In the service of the sages, devoid of rebirth
> Who live awakened to the eternal spirit of Aum.

After sleep does not wake up to worldly life, for accomplishing this one has to always keep the awareness that everything, including himself, is Brahman. If one feels himself that he is not qualified now to be in such a state, he can dedicate the body and mind to serve an enlightened master who lives beyond births and deaths.

The dream and faithfulness are experiences that wake up from behind ignorance. To get rid of them, one should attain the experience of absolute truth. If all imaginations are removed, the experience of oneness will come to prevail. But this is not an easy task. At the same time, unless this is accomplished, one will suffer the miseries of repeated birth and death. The first way to accomplish it is to keep contacts and interaction with noblemen and read noble books written by great masters.

In this poem, Pranava means Brahman. The Upanishads endorse this meaning of Pranava (Aum) as Brahman or universe. An ascetic should serve those who have realized Brahman, live as Jeevanmukta with body and mind. The names Jeevanmukta, *Sthithaprajna*, *Brahmanagunatheetha*, *Athivarnasrami*, *Avadootha* are all synonyms of an ascetic. The meaning of the word *muni* is one with the habit of deep thinking and who always sees the Brahman everywhere. As the worldly responsibilities reduce, the ascetic gets lower and lower bodily movements. Depending upon the amount of movement, the ascetics are classified into four, namely, *Brahmavit*, *Brahmavidwara*, *Brahmavidwarya* and *Brahmavidwarishta*. That *Brahmanishta*, who engages in worldly activities, continues to live doing activities is the Brahmavit. That Brahmanishta, who has left all worldly activities and continues to live simply because the body has not fallen, continues to move always on earth is the Brahmavidwara. That Brahmanishta who engages in bodily matters only when others inform him about it, is the Brahmavidwarya, and that Brahmanishta who hesitates to take up the awareness of body even when others wake up and inform him and remains as the form of Absolute Brahman is the Brahmavidwarishta. All these four categories of ascetics do not leave the Brahman even for a moment. Arjuna asked Lord Krishna to explain the real characteristics of an ascetic ('Gita, Sankhya Yogam', 2–54):

Sthitaprajnasya ka bhasha
Samadhisthasya kesava,
Sthitadhee kim prabhashetha
Kimaseetha vrajathe Kim?

Oh, Kesava (Krishna)! What are the characteristics of a sage who possesses ever calm wisdom and who is steeped in samadhi (ecstasy)? How does this man of steady wisdom speak, sit and walk?

Verse 55 (Gita)

Pṛajāpati yatā kāmānsaṛvānpāṛtha manōgatān
Atmanyēvātmanā tuṣta stitapṛajñastadōcyatē.
The blessed Lord replied:

O Partha (Arjuna)! When a man completely relinquishes all desires of the mind and is entirely contented in the Self, by the self, he is then considered to be one settled in wisdom.

(Original text in Sanskrit)

Bhuja kimupadhānatām kimu na kumbhinī mañcatām
Vṛajēd vṛajinahāriṇī swapadapātinī mēdinī
Munēraparasampadā kimiha muktarāgasya ta
Twamasyadhigamādayam sakalabhōgyamatyaśnutē.

Muni pṛavadatām vara kwacana vāgyamī paṇditō
Vimūda iva paryaṭan kwacana samstitō a pyustita
Sarīramadhigamya cañcalamanēhasā khaṇditam
Bhajatyaniśamātmana padamakhandabhōdham param

Ayācitamalipsayā niyatidattamannam muni-
Stanō stitayaitya anwadan padhi śayānakō a vyākula
Sadātmadṛuganaśwaram swaparamātmanōraikyata
Sphurannirupamam padam nijamupaiti sacitsukham

Asatsaditi vādato bahiracintyamagrāhyama-
Nwaṛkhaṛvamamalam param stimitanimnamatyunnatam
Parangmukha istata parisameti turyam padam

Munissadasatōṛ dwayādupari gantumabhyudyata

Swavēśmani vanē tadhā puḷinabhūmiṣu pṛāntarē
Kwa vā vastu yōginō vasati mānasam bṛahmaṇi.
Idam marumarīcikāsadṛuṡamātmadṛuṣtyā khilam
Nirīkṣya ramatē muniṛ nirupamē parabṛahmamaṇi.

Meaning and commentary

Verse 1

Does it not befall the hand as the pillow for sleep; the earth
Becomes the cot, the earth becomes so sacred to remove
All sins by the touch of the feet what use of other things to a
Detached Ascetic uttering Tat Twam Asi and realize ultimate bliss.

Is it not the hand becomes a pillow for sleeping? Is it not the earth becomes the cot, is it not possible the earth becoming so sacred that it can remove the entire collection of sins where one's feet touched? What use is there in this world for an ascetic with other wealth who has no relation to anything in this world? As a result of his adopting the principle of Tat Twam Asi, the ascetic experiences the eternal bliss that excels the entire pleasures available in this world and other worlds.

Sree Narayana Gurudev experienced these qualities of ascetics himself and wrote these poems, and he explained the asceticism very beautifully in this work. Detachment from others is the main characteristic of an ascetic. Detachment is that which comes when one realizes that this world is transient and full of miseries that gradually lead to hatred towards worldly pleasures.

Verse 2

Ascetic at times act as an expert in explaining Brahma Vidya
At times keeps silence at times wander as a blockhead

Sometimes in deep meditation, sometimes awake does something
Sometimes in body disfigured and moving to experience the Absolute.

The ascetic at times behaves like an expert who explains spiritual philosophy. At some other times keeps silence and remains as one with a balanced mind. At some other time, he wanders around as a blockhead; at some other time, he sits in deep meditation, and at some other time sits wakeful and does normal activities. While remaining inside the body, which is constantly moving and evolving continues to experience the indivisible consciousness.

Verse 3

The ascetic being unattached takes only fated food
For survival without worries lie on the roadside
Self-seeking found through the unification of the self and
The Absolute rest in unequalled, eternal in being, mind and bliss.

The ascetic as he has no desires for anything, never asks anybody for anything but eats only food got by virtue of fate. He eats little enough food to maintain the body. He sleeps on the roadside without any worries. He always is an *Athmanishta* finding the eternal unique full of body, mind and bliss arrives at the unity of absolute consciousness, and human spirit relaxed.

Verse 4

One pledged to attain absolute reality beyond real and unreal
Is ascetic one as not interested to see this and that reach Turiya,
Cannot differentiate real and unreal viewing from outside not
Reachable to organs of sense and action, subtle but all-pervading.

An ascetic is one who has taken rigid determination to attain the real truth which is beyond the self with the entity and the inert without entity. Such an ascetic without taking any interest to look and listen to reach the state of Turiya goes beyond the states of wakefulness, dream and deep sleep. The experience of Turiya separating the state of entity and non-entity inexperience and by logical arguments cannot identify looking from outside the organs of activities, and the senses cannot catch them. The experience of Turiya is very subtle, but it is not small. It is a great experience that spreads throughout. The truth of Turiya is an experience without the touch of inert things and is unsullied.

Verse 5

Let the Yogi be in own house or forest or sand bed
Or nearby, his mind always remains in Brahman.
He sees the universe like water in the desert as a manifestation
Of supreme soul merged unequalled Brahman, rest in peace.

Let the Sannyasin remain either in his house, forest or sand bed or elsewhere his mind always remains steadily on Brahman seeing this entire universe like water in the desert, the ascetic sees it as the Brahman, dissolves in eternal bliss and rests in peace.

26

SLOKATRAYI

The blissful awareness is the truth of the universe. Everything we see as the universe (Dharma) is only virtual things seen on the creator (*Dharmi*) by virtue of ignorance. So long as we see the visual things only without thinking of the creator, they will be seen to be transient, and those appear and disappear now and then, then what is the way of finding creator—the Dharmi. According to non-duality and uniqueness (i.e., when it is there, there cannot be a second to it), the only way is to become one with it.

The first verse rejects the concept of conclusion; learning and appearance cannot exist in Dharmi since it is invisible and indescribable.

(Original text in Sanskrit)

Asti dhaṛmītyanumiti
Kadham bhavati vāgapi?
Asannikṛuṣtatwādasmin
Pṛatyakṣamanumānavat.

Na vidyatē fsti dhaṛmīti
Pṛatyakṣamanumānavat.
Mānābhāvādasau nēti
Bōdha ēvāvaśiṣyatē.

Asannikṛuṣtatwādasya
Pṛatyakṣam dhaṛmadhaṛmiṇō
Asṛuṣtasāhacaṛyāca
Dhaṛmiṇyanumiti kuta?

Meaning and commentary

Verse 1

How is it possible, to have the inference that there is
A creator and the sound, since the observational faith is
Equally impossible as the faith through inference to have
Interaction of senses with the unattributed Brahman (Dharmi).

The Dharma which appears as the universe has a Dharmi which is Absolute Brahman. How is it possible to know the unattributed Brahman through inference? It is impossible to, even with the inference through what is heard about it. It is impossible to the sense organs to interact with such a Dharmi, which is attributeless. Therefore the knowledge that there is Dharmi is equally impossible as that is obtained through inference.

The universe is nature (virtual effects), and Brahman is the cause. Whatever is that which evolves and disappears is nature. Whatever is that which does not evolve and perish, but always acts as support to nature, is the Brahman. In the universe its manifested effect, nature, is visible, Brahman is invisible. The existence of nature is known through four testimonies, namely, observable (*Pratyaksham*) through sense organs, inference (*Anumanam*), comparison (*Upamanam*), and hearing (*Sabdam*).

Knowledge through sense organs is known as direct vision. Knowledge through guess about the existence depending on an everlasting phenomenon is the inference. Knowing through comparison with something is known as Upamanam, and the knowledge through hearing from some other person who had experienced is known as Sabdam. The sense organs cannot reach the

Brahman the cause of the universe. Hence all the four testimonies to get the knowledge Brahman become irrelevant. Brahman can be reached only through transcendental methods. It never becomes subject to observation because it is unique, without a second. It can only be experienced.

Verse 2

There is no evidence of vision (Pratyaksha pramanam)
That supports faith through inference that the Dharmi
Is a reality, since there is no evidence through experience
That there is no Dharmi (cause) that remains.

There is convincing physical evidence to infer that there is the Brahman (Dharmi). Since there is no visual evidence to prove its existence, only the experience that there is no Brahman remains.

One's own self is the ultimate reality. It is the ultimate reality or self that whether there is or not its existence is experienced. But the blockhead cannot identify it. He takes the external things which come to visual observation as the real things—only things which become subject to any of the five sense organs. Consciousness (ultimate reality) cannot be linked with the senses. One who links the external visual things with logical approach cannot find the ultimate reality, the Brahman; to him, it is easy to decide that there is no absolute reality or Brahman.

Verse 3

Because the knowledge of this Dharmi is not possible
Through senses and the conclusion about Dharmi as
Rules of circumstances and inference are not possible in Dharmi
How is it possible to get a visual experience of existence?

Since the senses cannot interact with the Dharmi (the Absolute), how is it possible to have an awareness of it through vision (observation)?

Since the interaction between the Dharma (effect) and Dharmi (cause) is never established, how is it possible to get the knowledge through inference?

We have seen in verse 2 that it is impossible to approach or interact with the Brahman through the sense organs, as Brahman is attributeless and hence without any observable or measurable properties. The only way is to approach by transcendental methods which are not that easy. One has to meditate and do penance with utmost concentration, forsaking all worldly longings, closing all the sense organs and reach the state of Turiya. Then he becomes unique without a second and experiences that he is Brahman himself.

27

VEDANTA SUTRAM (VEDANTA SUTRAS)

Sree Narayana Gurudev used to teach Vedanta at Aruvippuram and Sivagiri. These sutras are believed to be written by Gurudev as part of the teaching. This is a noble work that makes a review of the entire Vedanta with a different vision. This makes Gurudev one of the very few saints who wrote sutras. Composing sutras requires deep thinking and selection of appropriate words that can contain a wide spectrum of meanings.

These sutras, like Brahmasutras, follow strictly the rules of composing sutras.

There are certain common features for all sutras. They are,

Alpākṣharamasannigdham
Sāravadhwiŝathōmugham
Asthōbham anavadyancha
Sūtram sūtra vidō Vibhu: (Sanskrit)

(It is) 'With minimum words, beyond doubt, meaning full, multifaceted, unhindered and is unblemished'.

We have to understand the meanings of the overcrowded ideas expressed in a minimum number of words. In the case of 'Vedanta Sutras', there were only a few who could combine words in a simple way, without the loss of real meaning. It is very difficult to conceive the ideas in the lines as many of the inevitable words are left out. In fact, in many sutras, subjects and predicates, which are very important for getting the meaning, are missing. Therefore, the readers of 'Vedanta Sutras' had no other means other than depending on Bhashyas (Commentaries).

In excellence, 'Vedanta Sutras' are on par with the Brahmasutras of Maharshi Badarayana (Vyasa).

(Original text in Sanskrit)

Meaning and commentary

1. *Atha yadātmanō jijñāsu*

After that, due to what reason he has become eager to learn about the Brahman?

In this sutra, Gurudev indicates the necessity of obtaining the eligibility for the study of Brahman—the universe. A question then arises as to what kind of eligibility? The answer is evidently available from Gurudev's work, 'Brahmavidyapanchakam'. The question also refers to the eagerness of the disciple as to who am I and also indirectly to another question, after all, what is this universe. The next sutra gives the answer to this.

2. *Tadidam bṛahmaivāham.*

This universe is Brahman itself.

The word 'Tat' means the gist of the doctrine. Idam in Vedanta language means 'this universe'. So the meaning of *Brahmaiva* becomes it is only the universe. In short, the sutra tells, the universe is that Brahman. The master advises and the disciple concludes that it is Idam (this universe) seen as different name forms. Brahmaiva means it is only the Brahman.

3. *Aham bṛahmaivā*

I am the Brahman himself.

Aham (the single-word sutra) discloses that the spirit (Atman) also is Brahman. The feeling 'I' is the result of the reflection of Brahman in the Maya-created mind, like the virtual image of one's face seen in the mirror or like the reflected image of the Sun on the water surface, reflected in the inner self. But the original face and the Sun remain as separated from their reflected images. The fact is that the face and the Sun are not two separate systems separating their respective objects (face or the Sun) from their virtual images. It is in this way Brahman reflects on the inner spirit. When the mirror and the water surface are removed, only the objects remain, and the images will disappear in their own original on the objects, the face or the Sun. Similarly, when the spirit or the inner self of one is removed by yoga training, the feeling of self 'I', 'I' will dissolve into Brahman, which is eternal and undivided. Gurudev declared these facts from his own experience.

The Upanishad doctrines, 'Prajnanam Brahma': (knowledge is Brahman), 'Aham Brahmasmi' (I am the Brahman), 'Tat Twam Asi' (Thou Art It), Ayam Atma Brahma (Atman is Brahman) give the same argument.

4. *Kim tasya lakṣmaṇam*

What are its characteristics?

Here 'its' means, of the Brahman. In Vedanta 'that' means the Brahman and 'this' means the universe. The characteristics of Brahman are Sat (real entity), that is to say the experience of existence. Chit is the awareness (or mind) through which it is experienced. Ananda is pure knowledge (absolute knowledge), which is nothing but the bliss. When such knowledge gets mixed with inert things, then absolute knowledge or bliss is not experienced fully. In bliss all the three, real entity absolute, knowledge and bliss, become one showing that all three are one—the characteristics of Saguna Brahman.

5. *Asya ca*

Asya means the universe.

In the Vedic language, Brahman is knowledge (wisdom), and the universe is inert (ignorance). Therefore, these two are light and darkness. Vedanta gives a meaning contrary to this. The universe is inert in another sense, *anitya*—transient, and it is a form of grief. Inert is the opposite of knowledge again, anitya is opposite to real entity; grief is the opposite of happiness; thus, the characteristic of Brahman Satchidananda is considered as '*anyatajadadukham Jagat*'. Anyata is Maya or illusion or unreal.

6. *Kati ganana yēti*

How many types of Brahman and the universe?

Even the universe is unique and non-dual. Due to distinguishing properties, it is seen separated as jeevatman. Therefore, Brahman can be considered as two—jeevatman (human soul) and paramatman (supreme soul). The same Brahman due to distinguishable properties appears as the visual universe.

7. *Tat Jyōti*

That is the brilliance.

That means the Brahman, Jyoti, means the brilliance—Brahman as brilliance is not something shining like the Sun or the stars. But it is the self-experience of a real entity. It is this Brahman in the form of brilliance that makes all other things shine, Kathopanishad says while it shines by itself.

Na tatra suryo bhati na chandratarakam
Nema vidyuto bhanti kuto yamagni:
Tameva bhanṭamanubhati sarvam
Tasya bhasa sarvamitam vibhati.

The stars and the Sun do not cause the Brahman to shine while the lightning and fire depend on other agents for their burning or ignition.

8. *Tēnēdam Prajwalitam*

This causes to shine by that.

Idam means the universe seen in different name forms. By the Brahman, the universe seems to be caused to shine. The inert universe does not shine in the absence of knowledge, the Brahman. The universe is the observed and Brahman is the observer. Once the observer is absent, there is no observed.

9. *Tadidam Sadasaditi*

It is that Brahman taking the form of the universe is manifested as 'there is' (existent), and as 'there is not' (non-existent).

That (Tat) indicates the Brahman and This (Idam) indicates the universe. The universe is the Vivartha of Brahman (Vivartha is a virtual image in the ordinary sense). The universe experienced as if existent and non-existent is the answer to the question as to when Brahman is observed as the universe, how the universe is experienced. Gurudev refers to this in 'Advaita Deepika' (Poem 6) as:

The ambivalent feelings 'there is' and 'there is not'
The real and unreal are dispositions of Maya
Once searched the unreal is non-existent
In the piece of coir, there is no snake but only coir.

Remember it is from the eternal Absolute Brahman the universe is manifested as if existent and non-existent.

10. ***Bhuyōf Satassadasadidi***

Again and again from the absolute entity, the universe appears as if existing and not existing.

The universe appears as existent and as non-existent again and again from the absolute entity. This experience is the experience of the universe. Even the experience of non-existence depends upon existence. No experience begins from the absolute void. In short, even for the experience of non-existence, there should be an absolute entity behind.

11. ***Satcabdādayōfsadabhāvarščēti***

'There is' and its synonyms, by 'there is not' and its synonyms; the virtual universe known.

Sachabda means 'there is' and its synonyms. You know the observed things by the synonyms of there is (it exists) is known as experience, etc. are used to indicate the presence of an object like saying the pot is there, the pot exists, the pot is seen as, the pot is known as, etc. These kind of things, known by the word there is and their synonyms, form the imaginary universe *satabhavaščheti*, and indicate that the universe can be understood by this way of using suitable synonyms. By the word, there is not or with its synonyms, the non-existent universe.

12. ***Pūṛvam sadidam***

This universe before became separated thus in name forms; it was only the absolute consciousnesses.

This universe, before becoming corpulent with many name forms, was unique without a second. Adi Sankara classifies the difference in name forms as self-difference, similar kind difference, and dissimilar kind difference. The differentiation imagined in the body itself is known as self-difference. For example, one, in happiness, one in grief, etc. it is like one's legs, etc.; in trees, there are different components like leaves, flowers, fruits, etc. but all in the same body of the tree. The difference between two individuals belonging to the same clan is the similar kind difference. Examples like the mango tree, coconut tree, jack tree, etc. are a similar difference. The difference between two individuals belonging to two separate clans is known as the dissimilar kind difference. Examples are the tree and an animal. Other than these differences, there cannot be another one. This sutra evokes the hymns (6, 2, 1) of Chandogyopanishad. '*Sadeva somyedamagra asidekamevadwiteeyamē.*'

13. *Anusṛutyacakṣurādayaścaikam cēti*

Following the real entity existed, in the beginning, the 'I', etc. and the life in their reflected image formed.

Among the visuals in name forms in the universe, the existent is the only real entity, like in gold ornaments of different forms, the only real entity is the gold. Like that, the real entity among things in different name forms in the universe is the consciousness. *Chakshuradaya* indicates the five sense organs; the eye, nose, tongue, ear and skin, along with the five organs of action, the five spirits; wisdom in mind, all adding up to seventeen principles that combine to form the subtle body. Without the subtle body, life cannot exist, and without life, the subtle body does not exist. The subtle body is the instrument of life. The terms *eakamcha* indicates life. In short, the unique real entity (consciousness), the subtle body and life simultaneously develop and become mutually related to form the absolute reality.

14. ***Ñātṛu ñānayōranyōnya***

Viṣayaviṣayitwāt midhunatwamiti

Understand that the sense organ and the object made subject to it that is one who observes and that which is observed have the state of entanglement or couple.

Iti indicates when the spirit and subtle body have formed the knower (observer) Atman and its object subjected to it (observed). The spirit—the observer and its subjects such as sound, etc.—as observed appear to have separated though in experience they appear as entangled or a couple.

The observer and the observed continue to exist as inseparable twins.

The observer without observed and the observed without observer never exist as separate things.

15. ***Ēvam jñānajñēya vibhāga ēkaikam***

How the universe takes the observer–observed form existing as twins, like that the knowledge and the known though separated exist as twins.

The coexistence of the separated knower and known as couple or twins can be seen everywhere. But it should be noted that when the knower and the known are separated, the third component also comes as an inevitable part. It is the knowledge or say, knower, knowledge and known. These three are the well-known triputi in Vedanta. They are the same as jnatya, jnana and jneya. In the division of knower and known, the knowledge is inherent in the known. Similarly, in the division of knowledge and known, the known is understood in the knowledge. This is why there is no mention of triputi in the sutra in the discussion of the knower–known relation.

(Ref. observer–observed relation.)

16. *Rudratwamāsiditi*

This universe existed in the form of Rudratwa before separating into the observer–observed and knower–known.

Rudra is the destroyer of everything. Rudratwam is, therefore, the state of destruction of everything. This is the same as the illegible or invisible state (Avyakta) in Vedic philosophy. The universe is the visual name form appearing and repeatedly disappearing where the knowledge, known form separate and vanish in this illegible state. The change of name forms is the creation, the feeling of their existence is the state of being and the coming back to the illegible state, and dissolving in it is the total dissolution (*Pralaya*); again, the change of name form is the creation. In this way, the processes of creation, being and dissolution are repeatedly happening in the illegible.

See Gita, Poem 28, 'Sankhya Yogam'

The beginning of creatures is veiled, the middle is manifested, and the end again is imperceptible, O Bharata (Arjuna). Why, then, lament this truth? This is the same process as described in physics as the big bang, the existence and big crunch cycle.

Oh! Arjuna the universe begins from indistinctness, in the middle, it is manifested as if it exists again it merges to darkness or void at the end, then why should you lament on it? Here Krishna narrates how the supreme soul, is transforming to the state Saguna Braḥman (supreme soul with attributes) from the state of Nirguna Braḥman (supreme soul without attributes) and back again to Nirguna Braḥman after its manifestation in the middle period. In the state 'everything is me' (Aham Braḥmasmi) there is not a second one in the universe but only the unique supreme soul. These lines indicate that in the above situation, Arjuna cannot see or know anything because what is present there is only the supreme soul. Hence to Arjuna, who is second to the unique supreme soul, is indiscernible. Though Arjuna thought that He (Braḥman-Krishna) was not there, Krishna makes Arjuna understand that He (Braḥman) is very much there in the state of being. There is an indication in these lines about the fact that even if Arjuna could see anything, it is only Lord Krishna (Braḥman) in the state of Saguna Braḥman.

It is because the state of destruction of all name forms in the sutra it is referred to as Rudratwam. This invisible state in Brahman is the illusion created by Maya. The hiding power of Maya creates the illusion of visible things, and hence, the visible universe also is an illusory experience. The example—snake superimposed on coir.

17. ***Ithi bṛahmaivāham***

Only the Brahman is existent.

Once thought the only existent is the Brahman. The snake in the coir and water in the desert are correspondingly the coir and the desert only. Therefore, whatever is the experience of the universe it is all the Brahman and the Brahman only.

18. ***Aham tat***

That I am (Thou Art It).

Aham here refers to the jeevatman, which is seeing all living things, and Tat is the famous doctrine Aham Tat. This sutra contains the spirit of the doctrine Aham Brahmasmi in Brahadaranyakopanishad.

19. ***Idam Bṛahmaivā***

This inert universe is also Brahman.

Idam refers to the universe, and it says that the universe is also the Brahman, 'this' statement contains the spirit of the line in Chandogyopanishad; 'Everything seen around is Brahman himself.' Human life (spirit) is Brahman; the inert universe also is Brahman, so is the life experience 'I' that contains the entire universe?

20. ***Ahamasmi***

I am that.

Like what is established through the Sutra 'Aham Tat' (Thou Art It), the unity of life and universe is mentioned here, the feeling that spirit, Brahman and the universe are entirely different things is only the illusion due to ignorance.

Here Gurudev establishes the basic doctrine of Advaita philosophy.

21. ***Atheethagaminorasatwam yata***

The non-entity of the past and future will be manifested if deeply thought.

In this poem and in the following one, Gurudev removes the doubt regarding how is it possible that the transient universe and the eternal Brahman can be united.

Once deeply analysed, there is no meaning in the concept of present, past and future. In a universal view, it becomes meaningless. In short, in a many-universes concept, the Brahman is considered to pervade the entire universes. Therefore, the local space-time consideration as here and now has no meaning.

The past of one universe is the present of another universe. Again, the past of one universe is the future of another in the many-worlds (universes) concept, as space and time are associated in a physical sense. (See *The Great Universe*, G.K. Sasidharan)

In a logical way, the past is non-existent because it is already lost. Similarly, the future is to come, but at present, it is not existent.

22. ***Yadethadatwichatha***

If there is any doubt about the fact that 'everything is Brahman', find it through scientific analysis.

The following arguments are given as evidence (inert universe).

When viewed on a universal basis, our concept of past, present and future becomes a myth. This can be understood from the following examples. Imagine an event that took place on Earth 3000 years ago; say, the Kurukshetra war. Let our example be the scene of Lord Krishna pronouncing Gita—the great doctrines—to Arjuna on the first day of the war. For the people now on Earth, it is a past event. Whereas for an observer on a world 3000 light years away (say, the Crab Nebula at 1050 parsec in constellation Taurus M1, NGC-1952), the scene can be seen as a present event. Now, for a person observing from a world at 6000 light years away [say, the Omega Nebula at 1.8 kilo parsec in constellation Sagittarius, M17, NGC-6618], the Kurukshetra incident is yet to happen in 3000 years. For him, it is a future event. To a person observing from the Andromeda galaxy [M31], Kurukshetra war is yet to happen after 2.2 million years. The reason evidently is—as mentioned above—that light from the places of events should bring the information to the eyes of the respective observers. For the people (if there are) in Proxima, which is at a distance of 4.25 light years, the Manmohan Singh government is yet to complete its term (as on 2 July 2018).

It was mentioned earlier that the worlds at the visible limit of the universe are moving with the velocity of light. Since any point anywhere in the universe can be taken as the centre of the universe, its border will change accordingly. To a person observing from the visible limit of the universe, as it is equivalent to the observation of the observer at a speed of light, our world will appear as one with the present only, i.e., eternal. This expresses the truth of the great cosmic rule that nothing is created or destroyed as mentioned in Bhagavad Gita.

When observed from inside the universe, as our speed of movements is negligible compared to the velocity of light, we feel the sense of past, present and future. On the whole, it is like a person visiting different stalls in an exhibition ground one after the other and seeing exhibits and another person seeing the entire stalls by standing on the top of a tower located at the centre of the exhibition ground. Here, the former can be imagined as a local observer and the latter as a universal observer.

In the real sense, the universe that we see is the past universe. Note that past events and connected things are non-existent (quantum physics) and hence are not real (Maya doctrine). Since all the objects in the universe are at different distances from us, the 'now' ('this instant') of such bodies will be different from our 'now' or 'this instant'. Besides, this phenomenon will exist forever until the observer, and the observed object become 'one'.(Here comes the relevance of 'Advaita'—'It is all me'.) It is evident from the above that there is no such thing as a 'universal now' applicable to the entire universe. Even if it is there, that won't have differentiation in time viz. past, present and future. In short, there is no unified 'now' or 'this instant' that you can share with the galaxies, the stars, the Sun, the moon or even a person sitting in front of you until everything in the universe becomes one, the Absolute.

(Ref. *Sree Narayana Gurudev the Maharshi Who Made Advaita a Science*, G.K. Sasidharan)

Another fact we infer from the above is that when the 'now' or 'this instant' in a frame of space-time changes, the past and future also change correspondingly. 'Now' (present) is that which separates the past and future. When the 'now' changes, the 'here' also changes accordingly since space and time are inseparable. Therefore, the concept of 'here and now' also is a myth. What we understand from all these is that the events considered as past, present and future ones are only the perceptions of the mind of the observer, and that also according to his own frame of reference in space-time, and it is all human creation (illusion), which Brahman has nothing to do with.

23. *Parimanam Thata*

The visual universe evolved from that.

The word Parimanam is suggested to denote all visual things in the universe, which are measurable. 'That' indicates all such things are formed from the all-pervading Brahman.

The universe is a transient phenomenon which comes into being, exists and dissolves. But to undergo such changes, there should be a cause behind it. Spirituality and physical sciences are trying to find out this primordial cause. In physics, there are scientists who even argue that being spontaneous, there need not be a cause for the creation. But recent developments in physics, especially in quantum theory and string theory, do not accept this descending approach in total. But Vedanta takes the stand that the entire process of creation, existence and dissolution is due to a primary desire—the cause. Gurudev, while praying to the god (Brahman) in 'Daivadasakam', says,

Nīyallō sṛiṣtiyum sṛaṣtā-
Vāyatum sṛiṣtijālavum
Nīyallō daivamē, sṛiṣti
Kkulla sāmgṛiyāyatum.

Oh! God! You are the creation (the universe)
The creator and the multitude of creatures
Oh! God you are
Instrumental in the creation.

Though these lines are written in simple language and style, it contains the entire spirit of Advaita philosophy. We have seen in our earlier discussions the role of primordial life force (consciousness) as the instrument for creation, the content of the entire matter and energy of the universe being kept void forever, the act of creation of the universe and the inflation in a colossal way in the process of early evolution of the universe.

In this poem, Gurudev takes the instrument as the cause. This gives the gist of the Advaita arguments about the cause.

24. *Sadasatōranyōnyakāryakāraṇatwāt*

Since being and non-being had a mutual cause and effect relation, it becomes evident that they are only illusions.

In the Sutra 'Sat' (being) indicates the jeevatman (life self) and Asat (non-being) inert. It is this life self and the inert things that united and created all the visual things in the universe (since the presence of inert things are manifested only due to the observation by living things). For all living things, there are three different types of bodies, namely, the inner body (astral body) the subtle body and the corpulent body. The awareness, when reflected on the inner body makes the state of deep sleep or Sushupti, when it is reflected in the subtle body, it makes the state of the dream (Swapna). When reflected on the corpulent body, it is the state of wakefulness (Jagrat). Anyway, without reflecting on any of the above bodies, awareness of life form with or without awareness is impossible. This is the reason why it is said that there are mutual cause-and effect-relations between the being and non-being.

25. *Aham mameti vijnatha*

What is known as 'I','Mine', etc. is the experience of the universe.

The experience 'I','I' in communion with the inert bodies is the experience of life. The experience of 'I', 'I' is impossible without contact with inert things. Without the subtle sound, the experience of 'I' is also impossible. The sound is a subtle, inert thing. It means the self-experience of 'I', that is, the experience of self 'I', itself is the experience of awareness that reflects on sound. Being and non-being mutual dependence from where the life gets formed begins with the experience of 'I', 'I'. Following that the experience of 'I' joining with inner body, subtle body and corpulent body attain the level of Individual. The individual form attained the individual soul gets affinity or attachment with external inert things is the worldly relation. Note that for this to happen, the mutual dependence of being and non-being is essential.

26. *Matho nanya*

There is nothing other than me.

Everything visual is mutually dependent. This gives the awareness that everything, including 'Me', is Brahman. This experience leads to the relevance of the above sutra. Though not in the same sense, it has resemblance with the universal Law of Gravitation where everybody in the universe is attracted by every other body, or everybody is influenced by all other bodies of the universe.

27. *Thadwat Thasmat*

It can be concluded that everything seen attached to it comes up from it.

All feelings of illusion anywhere are experienced along with the basic component. If the basic factor is not there, there is no experience. The water in the desert is seen associated with the desert. In the desert, there is no water. Therefore, the water seen in the desert is coming up from the desert. Similarly, the visual universe is seen coming up from the Brahman.

28. *Digdrisyayo samakalinathwat*

The observer and the observed have contemporariness.

As the observer and the observed are contemporary, it underlines the authority of Advaita as true. Experience of the universe can be divided into two—the observer and the observed. Both are interdependent and experienced simultaneously.

The relation between the observer (drik) and the observed (*drisya*) had been a very famous topic of discussion in spirituality, especially Advaita Vedanta and modern physics. Gurudev is supposed to be the Vedanti who established the facts in a manner that fits exactly with the Copenhagen interpretation in modern physics.

(See Cosmology Brings Science Closer to Spirituality)

Gurudev gave elaborate details through his works about observer–observed relation, which are discussed and pointed out in this book on many occasions, examples are 'Chijjada Chintanam', and 'Darsanamala', etc. See the notes on observer–observed relation in physics along with objective and subjective realities.

29. *Sukhaikatwat*

Since everyone seeks the only thing – the happiness, it can be inferred that the ultimate truth is bliss, the unique non-dual thing.

The Brahman is believed to be the embodiment of bliss and bliss is the Absolute happiness which is unique. This is the state of experience when one reaches salvation.

30. *Vyapakataya disamastitwat*

Filling the inside and outside and going beyond (all-pervading) Akash.

Vyapakata indicates that 'filling the inside and outside and going beyond it (all-pervading)' and '*disa*' refers to Akash (quintessence) though it is mentioned as direction. Astitwat means seen as filling or seen as existing. In short, the Akash (quintessence—Brahman) pervades the entire universe.

If the Akash is contained in everything, there cannot be anything left as another. Simple logic can prove that nothing can be created from the mere void. (See Gita, Sloka 16, 'Sankhya Yogam')

Na satho vidyathe bhavo
Na bhavo vidyathe sata:

Upayorapi drishtanthou
Sthanayosthathwa darshibhi:(Sanskrit)

Of the unreal, there is no existence. Of the real, there is no non-existence.

31. ***Anumahadava yataratara tamyasya bhavat***

There is no relevance in differentiating the size of the constituents of the universe as small and big; it is an absolutely impossible concept and hence can confirm that Advaita is the absolute truth.

We have seen that all constituents, even the atom is not independent, but are interdependent. They are only bubbles in the ocean of the five elements, and these elements, in turn, are only illusory.

As stated above in the sutra, the differentiation of constituents of the universe confirms that Advaita is the ultimate non-dual truth.

32. *Asatho vyapakatwat*

The non-pervading nature of non-being also proves that 'being alone is existent'.

In the experience of the universe, non-being is inert, and the consciousness that stands reflected on it is the 'being'. Through yoga practice, the experience of inert can be removed. When the imaginations are completely stopped, the inert feeling will vanish; this is the non-pervading nature of non-being.

33. *Aatmanyath Kinchinnasti*

There is nothing other than the consciousnesses.

There are not many things in the universe which are seen before the creations. The only thing that existed was the consciousness unique and without a second. Here, in the statement, Gurudev gives the gist of the doctrines of Chandogyopanishad, Aitareyoopanishad.

34. *Tasmat tasya satwacha*

Since its existence takes place from itself, it becomes proved that it (consciousness) alone is the truth (reality).

The primordial cause, the consciousness, cannot be formed from something else. Consciousness is that which is not formed from anything else existing as eternal and infinite that stands by itself. Those things which appear and disappear are all untrue. Everything from Akash exists in consciousness.

The things we see (drisya—the observed) around us are not of a real entity. In the absence of the observer (drik), the observed will cease to exist. What we observe as the universe is nothing other than the perception, the cause. The universe is nothing but a mirage in the desert of perception. What really exists in effect (the manifested universe) is only the cause, like what is contained in the waves is only water. The first line '*Neralla drisymithu drikkine neekki nokkil*' clearly says that it is the observer who makes the collapse; the same argument as in quantum mechanics.

Reality

Sree Narayana Gurudev, being an Advaiti, does not believe in a reality dependent on any beliefs, perception, etc. (objective reality). Gurudev's logical interpretations are in tune with the arguments of the Copenhagen interpretation of quantum physics (subjective reality).

The reality in philosophy is the state of things as they actually exist rather than as they may appear or might be imagined. Reality includes everything that is and has been whether or not observable or comprehensible. A broad definition includes everything that has existed, exists, or will exist in one's sight and thought. The idea that there is a reality not dependent on any belief is called realism.

George Berkeley had a view that objects of perception are actually ideas in the mind. He went to the extent of saying nothing exists except the mind and ideas. This may tempt us to say that reality is a 'mental construct'. It is a view opposed to realism. A traditional realist position in the ontology (the study of being) is that apart from the human mind, time and space have an independent existence. The idealists deny or doubt the existence of objects independent of mind. Some anti-realists believe that objects outside the mind do exist, but they doubt the independent existence of time and space. The German philosopher Immanuel Kant held the belief that time and space are not entities in themselves; rather, they are elements of a systematic framework we use to structure our experience. The idealist, J.M.E. McTaggart, argued that time is an illusion.

Realism in physics does not equate to realism in metaphysics. The latter claims that the world, in some sense, is mind-independent, even if the result of a possible measurement does not require that they are the creations of the observer. Note that it is contrary to Vedic metaphysics and also to the consciousness collapse interpretation of quantum mechanics and Sree Narayana Gurudev's approach in this respect.

Classical physics is based on the belief that there exists a real external world in which the properties of the constituents are definite and independent of the observer who perceives them. Objects have physical properties such as length, speed and mass that have well-defined values. Both observer and observed are parts of a world that has an objective existence.

From very old times, Indian philosophers held the view that the concept of what we see around us (space) and past, present and future (time), are the only delusion of man and are not real. Why do we say that the substance of materials we see around us is the only delusion? The universe is a multidimensional phenomenon. It is a riddle created by many worlds such as one-dimensional world, two-dimensional world, three-dimensional world, four-dimensional world, or even 10, 11 or 26-dimensional world. A straight line without thickness (with length only) can be imagined as a one-dimensional world. It is a world of imaginary objects having no bulk or size, and is capable of moving only back and forth, not even crossing one another.

One-dimensional world cannot create a shadow; even if it can, that will only be a dimensionless point or a point of the void. A world with length and breadth without thickness is called a two-dimensional world. Ordinary shadow is a good example of this. A shadow of this shadow world will be a straight line without thickness. This means the shadow of a two-dimensional world is a one-dimensional world. Again, the shadow of this one-dimensional world is a dimensionless point.

The world in our imagination and that which is familiar to us is a three-dimensional world with length, breadth and height (thickness). As seen above, the shadow of this familiar world is a two-dimensional world. According to the inferences in modern scientific theories, the real universe is a four-dimensional world where quantities such as length, breadth, width and time unite. No substance in the universe can exist without one of these. Evidently, the three-dimensional world, where we live, is only the shadow of the real four-dimensional world. In other words, whatever we see in the universe is, in fact, the shadow of the real one. The indivisibility and inevitability of the aforesaid four-dimensional space-time have been confirmed by many theories and experiments in physics. The experiment by Michelson and Morley, Maxwell's electromagnetic equations, Einstein's special theory of relativity and the general theory of relativity, and Minkowski's space-time continuum are milestones in the road to the 'ultimate'. (See *The Great Universe*, G.K. Sasidharan). I feel that one has to examine the question of 'reality' with these facts in mind.

Local realism is a feature of classical mechanics, of general relativity and of electrodynamics. But quantum mechanics totally rejects this argument in the light of the theory of distant quantum entanglement, an interpretation rejected by Einstein in the EPR paradox, but subsequently qualified apparently by Bell's equations. Stephen Hawking in his book *The Grand Design* says, 'It would be easy to call the world the aliens live in as the "real" one and the synthetic world a "false" one. But if—like us—the beings in the simulated world could not look into their universe from the outside and there is no reason to doubt their own pictures of reality. This is a modern version of the idea that we are all figments of someone else's dream.' He continues,'There is no picture or theory-independent concept of reality.' He comes to the conclusion that 'there seems to be no single mathematical theory that can describe every aspect of the universe; instead, there seems to be the network of theories called M theory. Each theory in the M theory network is good at describing phenomena within a certain range. In that view, the universe must not have just a single existence or history, but rather every possible version of the universe exists simultaneously in what is called a quantum superposition.'

In fact, a particle has neither a definite position nor a definite velocity unless and until these quantities are measured by an observer. Hawking says that both observer and observed are parts of a world that has an objective existence. He argues that the brain builds a mental picture or model. A model or a pattern is a solid preliminary representation of something to be followed in construction, an imitation of something or something resembling another. Model-dependent realism corresponds to the way one perceives the objects. In the act of vision, the brain receives a series of signals down to the optic nerves, and the brain builds a mental model.

Model-dependent realism depends upon the way one perceives the objects. While looking, one's brain receives a series of signals through the optic nerves. The raw data that comes to the brain is like a badly pixilated picture with a hole in it. The hole is evidently due to the blind spot where the optic nerve attaches to the retina. The human brain processes the incomplete data, mixing the input from both eyes, filling the gaps. It reads a two-dimensional array data from the retina and creates from it a three-dimensional picture or model. This is a model depending on the individual, strictly speaking, depending upon the physical and biological characteristics of the observer and the properties of the surroundings. For example, a person standing on the surface of the planet Venus will feel as if he is standing at the bottom of a huge cup (by terrestrial standards) irrespective of where he stands. It is because of the very high density of the atmosphere of Venus. On Earth, a fish in the lake sees a straight coconut tree as a bent tree. It is due to refraction of light while passing through a denser medium (water) to a rarer medium (air). In both these examples, the Venusians and the fish believe that what they experience is real according to their models (of the universe). About the reality of time, metaphysical theories differ in their ascriptions of reality to the past, present and future separately.

The 'presentism' views the past and future as unreal and an ever-changing present only as real. The Block universe theory, which is otherwise known as eternalism, holds that the past, present and future are all real, but the passage of time is an illusion. In reality, Stephen Hawking, in his book *The Grand Design,* remarked, 'Of the big bang model and the Genesis model, of the universe the former is more useful than the latter as far as observations are concerned. But neither model is more real than the other.'

Quantum mechanics and the phenomenon of entanglement defy many of our perceptions about reality. Among them, more important is that it does not approve the hegemony of speed of light. In quantum mechanics, one particle (one location) inexplicably shares the information with its entangled partner (another location) instantaneously without being carried by electromagnetic waves at the speed of light, even if the locations are light years apart. Until the entanglement (observation or measurement) is made, no information exists. In short, in the wonderful world of quantum physics, all possible information exists.

In the current, generally acceptable version and also in quantum cosmology, objects do not have existence or any inherent properties, and their existence becomes real only when mind interacts with them through observation or measurement. This means that reality is the creation of interaction. Until interaction, all possibilities are probable superpositions of wave functions, and the wave functions collapse to create an observable form of reality, and that makes the other probabilities disappear.

Many cosmologists believe that some hidden variables are involved in the phenomenon of entanglement. According to quantum cosmology, the universe, in the beginning, was a huge quantum superposition of infinite possible states until the first primordial mind (The 'ONE' in 'Nasadeeya Suktam', Rig Veda) effected observation, causing collapse into one reality getting rid of all other states. Each one of these actions gives rise to another universe, thereby creating an infinite number of universes. On the basis of this, some scientists argue that creation of the universe from a singularity demands that everything created later, including stars, planets, plants, animals and humans are entangled with each other as the super primordial entanglement is not broken but has only spread to a larger extent. It is a very encouraging explanation to the advocates of paranormal (beyond scientific investigation) phenomena such as telepathy, who claimed that the cells of our brain are entangled with everything else in the universe, making it possible to decode information received from any other object or part of the universe. In view of the multiverse concept it goes without question that Gurudev's arguments in the light of Vedic philosophy the visible universe is only the superposition of infinite possibilities over absolute reality.

Vittonnutān vividhamāy vilasunnitinka-
Larddhantaram cerutumilla visēṣamayi;
Rajju swarūpamariyātiruḷal vivartta-
Sarpam ninakkilitu rajjuvilninnu vērō? (Sloka 12, 'Advaita Deepika')

It is the same primordial seed that is manifested as different kinds of things in the universe. There is nothing other than that seed. For example, in darkness, a piece of coir creates the feeling that it is a snake. One need not say such an imaginary snake is nothing but the piece of coir once observed under the light.

Though written many years before the advent of quantum physics, Sree Narayana Gurudev gave the argument about the superposition of infinite possibilities (including stars, planets, plants, animals and humans) in the universe as those once collapsed (observed), will reduce to one and the only thing—the primordial seed, which he described as the '*Karu*' in 'Atmopadesa Satakam', the 'Dignified Eye' in 'Sivasthavam','drik' in 'Daivadasakam', etc.(See also 'Creation of theUniverse')

The question of various kinds of reality does not arise in Advaita philosophy because it holds that there is only one reality, and that is an absolute reality. This absolute reality is the NirgunaBrahman, the Brahman (the universe) without attributes. (See 'Chijjada Chintanam')

28

CHIJJADA CHINTANAM I

Objects come into being only when they are observed. When everything around you becomes vanished, your entity also becomes vanished. Then, how can it be possible for one to think of any kind of reality other than the consciousness? Now let us see how Sree Narayana Gurudev discusses this metaphysical phenomenon in 'Chijjada Chintanam'.

Chijjada Chintanam is a metaphysical topic which relates to the observer–observed interaction. We have seen what quantum physics tells about the relation in its latest conclusions.

Sree Narayana Gurudev wrote 'Chijjada Chintanam' in both verse and prose. Here, we discuss the prose version. A deep analysis of the work will make us wonder how Gurudev could foresee the discoveries in physics and cosmology more than a century ago. Though difficult to understand in a light reading, 'Chijjada Chintanam' is definitely one of the masterpieces among Gurudev's philosophical works. It is more scientific than spiritual. One can see in these lines how discerningly Gurudev brought forward his arguments based on spiritual metaphysics which became true in view of the latest conclusions in quantum cosmology.

'Chijjada Chintanam' has to be analysed on the basis of the debate between (EPR paradox interpretation) the team headed by Albert Einstein–Podolsky–Rosen and the Copenhagen interpretation of the team headed by Niels Bohr. Gurudev's argument contradicts

Einstein's claim that there is 'no instantaneous spooky action at a distance' and 'the object exists even when it is not observed', and what Einstein said, 'the moon is there even when not being observed'. Gurudev's argument in this regard—though stated a century ago—was in favour of the Copenhagen argument that 'an object does not exist when it is not observed'.

(Original text in Malayalam)

Anu muthal aana vare ullavayokke ilakinadakkunnathum pullu muthal bhooruha paryantham nilayil nilkkunnathumakunnu. Ennu venda nammude kannu, mookku, muthalaya indriyangalil ninnum Brhmam vare okkeyum chithum,manninnu thottu moolathiraskarani vare kanappedunnathokkeyum jadavum akunnu. Ee irupirivukalumayi soothrathil korthittirikkunna manikal pole ella vakayum adangikkidakkunnu. Ee iru pirivukalilumulla pandangalokkeyum ariyikkunnathinu purappedunna namabhedham onnu, ivakalil ninnum athmikamayum bhouthikamayum velippedunna sabdhabhedam onnu. Ithu random cheviyilum thanasrayichirikkunna pandam innathennulla soochayodu koodi varunna sparsabhedham twakkilum suryan, chandran, agni muthalaya jyothissukal ennalla, ivakalekond sobhikkunna sakala padharthangaleyum eanthikond nilkkunna varnabhedham kanninum mundingapazham muthalaya rasa vargangale ullil adakkikondu varunna rasabhedham navilum thanirunnunnilaki varunnathu innathil ninnanennu aa gandha dravyathe ariyikkunna thantrathodu koodi varunna gandhabhedam mookilumayi adangiyirunnariyappedunnu ennullath spashtamakunnu. Ennal ee sabdhathi vishayam anjum srothram muthalaya indriyangalil ninnu appozhappol thalli veliyil vannirunnu kanunnatho athalla bhouthikamayi veliyil nilkkumbol athil indriyangal vannu patti ariyunnatho ennu nokkiyal, bhouthikamayi veliyil nilkkumbolindriyangal vannupatti ariyappedunnuvenkil ithoru asambhavam thanne. Enganeyennal nammal kanappedunna ee kudam undayittippol uddesam oruvarshathil athikamayirikkunnumennu thonnunnu. Ennal kanunna kshanathil udhicha vilangikondirikkunna ee kudam kanunnathinu munpil illayirunnu ennallathe undayirunnu ennullath suddha asambandham thanne. Aganeyalla nam kandilla enneyullu kudam undayirunnu enkil ith ee kudathil kanunna pazhakkathil ninnum thalli varunnathil oru vyavaharamanu ithu nilkkatte, nammal kanappedunna kudam nam illatha dikkil illayirunnu ennallathe undayirunnuvennu paranju kooda. Athalla undayirunnuvenkil avide appol kandathiloralum koodi vendiyirikkunnu. Athengane kanunna dikkil kandavanundennallathe kanatha dikkil kandavanundayirunnu ennu parayunnath. Angane kandavanilla enkil kanappedunnathumilla. Appol ee kudam ithinu munpil illayirunnu vennum ippol ee kshanathil udhichu vilangunnuvennum velivakunnu. Ingane kudam thanne illathirikkumbol kudathil ninnum thalli varunna ee kudam undayitt oruvarshathiladhikamayirikkunnu ennulla vyavaharam engane nilanilkkunnu. Athalla innappol nirmithamaya innayinna lakshanangalodu koodiyirikkunna oru kudam inna dikkilirikkunnu enningane nam orapthanil ninnum grahichukondu vannu. Itha ippol aa adayalangalodu koodiya ee kudathe kanunnu. Athukondanu anuu thottinnu vareyulla alaveduthunokkiyathil eppol ee kudam undayitt oru samvalsarathilathikam ayirikkunnu vennu parayunnathenkil athum ee kudathil ninnum ippol thallivarunnathallathe melprakaram ithinu munpil illayirunnu ennuthanne parayanam. Athalla nam thanne pandorikkal kandirunna kudamanu ith, annu kandittulla adyalangal ellam itha ithil kanunnu. Aa kudam thanne ee kudam athukondanu ee kudam undayittippol oru samvalsarathil adhikamayirikkunnuvenuu parayunnuvenkil ippol nammodu koodiyirikkunna ee kudam appol ithupole nammodu koodi irunnirunnu ennum idayil nasichu aa sudhasoonyathil ninnum ingane nammodu koodi pongiyirikkunnu ennu vyavaharam neridunnu. Appol nam illathirunna soonyathinte appuramulla kathayenam iviede prasangikkunnath bhramam kondu thanneyennu varunnu. Allenkil nammude poorva janmathilulla kadhayude njapakam namukkippol undayirikkanam. Athillallo. Ennal athupole thanne ithum alochichu nokkumbol ariyam. Athalla sushuptiyil ninnu unarnnuvarumbol aa sushupthiyude poorvavasthayilulla njapakam undayirikkunnathu poleyenkil ath vandhyayude puthran illennu parayumbol, alla avan sasavishanam pole ullavananennu parayumbole theerunnu.

Ingane onnumalla yenkil pinne enganeyanu ee kudathil iprakaram bhoothakala vyavaharam undayirikkunnath ennu chodhichal ee varthamanakshanathil kudamundayi eevidhathilayirikkunnathinu avakasam illalloyennulla ooham ullilninnum thalliveliyil vannu kudathil veenu ; ithil poorva kaaleenamaya vyavaharathe thoduthu ingane asambandhamayi vyavahrikkunnathallathe vere onnum alla. Ath enganeyennal swapnathil nam oru vrikshathe kandu chennu aduthu ninnu kondu ha! Ha! Ee vriksham undayittippol oru nooru samvalsarathil adhikamayirikkunnu ennu uddhesikkunnuvenkilum ippol nokkiyal innalathe swapnathilulla vrikshathil kanda nooru samvalsarathinte pazhakkam asambandhamennum vriksham appol swapnadrishtiyil ninnum veliyil thalli vannirunnu kandathennum swapnam bhouthikamayi veliyil undayirirunnathallennum velivakunnu. Athupole ee kudavum ippol kannil ninnum veliyil thalliyirunnu kanunnathallathe bhouthikamayi veliyilirikkunnathalla ennu visadamakunnu. Ini ithupole thanne mattulla vishayangalum athathu indriyingalil ninnum appozhappol veliyil thallivarunnu ennullathu parayanamennillallo. Ha! Ha! Kollam sari, ippol sareeradhi sakala prapanchavum ullilninnum veliyil thalli varunnu ennullath nallavannam anubhavmayi enkilum ithinum oru samsayam koodiyirikkunnu.

Athenthennal thejomayangalayirikkunna indriyangalil ninnu thamomayangalaya vishayangal varunnuvenkil sooryankal ninnum irul pongi varunnu ennulla virodha neridunnu athukond angane paranju kooda. Pinne indriyangalodu koodi varunnathinu valla nyayavumundo ennu nokkiyal athum kanunnilla. Enthennal anganeyenkil irulum velichavun koodi oru dikkilirunnu oru samayam pongi varunnu ennu parayanam. Ath orikkalum nadappullathumalla. Ayyo! Ithenthonnu indrajalamanu ee prapancham. Veliyil kanunnathumalla indriyangalil ninnu thallivarunnathumalla, indriyangalodo koodi varunnathumalla pinne enganeyaniprakaram nirhethukamayi kanappedunnathennu chodhichal athu avicharadasayil kaanal jalam pole thonnunnathallathe vicharichu nokkumbol ithellam suddha chittayi thanne vilangunnu. Ath enganeyennal oru kayattin kandathil kalpithamayirikkuna nagam velicham varumbol adhistanamaya aa kayattil thanne maryum appol munpil nagam enningane idhamvrithiyal grahikkappettirunna kalpanagathil ninnu vittu kannu aa kayattil thanne pattininnu vilangunnathu pole avichara dasayil kanappedunna ee sareeradhi prapancham muzhuvanum iprakaram nishkaranamayi akhandachinmathramayirikkunna brahmathil irikkunnathinu orikkalum avakasamilla enningane chinthichundakunn bodhothayathil ithokkeyum adhishtanamya brahmathil thanne marayunnu. Appol ithu munpil kandirunna kalppitha prapanchathil ninnum vitt niradharamayirikkunna idhamvrithi oordhwa mukhiyayi jeevabodhathodukoode akhandachithil layichu chithu mathramayi varunnu. Pinneyum poorva vasanakal peruth pandathepole prapancham thonnum ithum melprakaram apadachoodam chinthichu chithathilodukki chithayi nilkkanam. Ingane cheythu cheythu varumbol asudhavasana kshayichu adharamillathe sudhavasanayil thanmathrayil thanne adangi ee randu vasanakalilum bandhichirunna ahankariyum kettu poornamayi nilkkum. Ee sthanam chithum alla jadavum alla sathuma alla asathum alla sukhadhukhadikalaya dwnthangal onnumalla ingane anirvachaneeyamayirikkunna ithil ninnu srishtyadhikal nadannum kondirikkunnath thanne ascharyam.ithinte mahathmyam alpabodhikalaya athmakkal enthariyunnu? Ha! Jaya jaya nadesa! Nadesa! Nadesa!

Gurudev says:

'All things from atom to elephant are moving things; from grass to the tree are non-moving things. Not only that, all things from our sense organs such as eyes, nose, etc. to Brahman are conscious or living and those from sand to the veil of illusion that covers the Brahman are inert. All these things belonging to the live and inert categories are stringed together like beads. To manifest everything in these two divisions, come the identity of names as one, spiritually and physically manifested sound like another. Both these go to the ear. That which comes indicating the material on which one feels the sense of touch is in the skin. The sense of colour that carries brilliant objects like the Sun, Moon and fires beside everything that shines reflecting their light is in the eye. The taste contained in eatables like grapes is in the tongue and odour or smell that indicates the source from which it comes is in the nose.' (Every sense organ is an instrument for measurement according to quantum physics.)

'It is evident, if you look on to whether these five different subjects—pertaining to the five senses of the body—are coming out then and there from the sense organs like the ear, or whether the sense organs reach the objects that remain outside and experience them, it is impossible that the senses reach on objects when they remain physically outside. It is like this:

'This pot which I see now seems to have completed one year after its production. But this pot which rises and shines at this moment of observation, did not exist before. Instead, the argument that it existed before is utter nonsense. If the argument is that it was existing, but we have not seen it, it is only a discourse that comes out from its having become old.

'Let it be there, what else I can say about the pot which I see now was not there, where I was not present. Instead, I should not say it was there. On the other hand, if it were there, there has to be another person also who has seen it then. Except claiming that he has seen the pot when placed in front of him, how can it be possible for me to claim that I had seen it when the pot was not there in front of me? Therefore, if the observer is not there, the observed also is not there. This makes it clear that the pot was not existent before and came manifested at this moment only.' (Actually, it is when the two wave functions of the observed object and the observer collapse, the object gets an entity.)

'In a condition where the very existence itself of the pot is ruled out, how can the argument prevail that this pot was existing for the last one year after its production. If not, suppose that I learn from a trusted friend that a pot with a specific mark produced at a particular time exists at a particular place, and we see it now with the same mark, and it is because on measuring its size from that day to the present day, the pot has completed one year after coming into being, that too, only means its manifestation is coming out only now, and it was not existing before.

'Not that, if this pot is the same pot I myself saw some time ago, all the marks seen on that pot is seen on this pot, and this pot is the same old pot; if you say, that is why this pot has completed more than one year in its existence, then it faces a discourse. This pot which is with me now has been with me then in the same manner, and in between, it perished into the absolute vacuum, and from that vacuum, it came up now. In that case, it becomes evident that what I state here as the story beyond the state of the void [vacuum] during which I was not present is only something due to the illusion. Otherwise, I would have knowledge of my previous birth. I don't have it. This will also be known once pondered. Lest, if it is like one has knowledge of the past who wakes up from deep sleep [Sushupti]. It is similar to the statements like the son of an impotent woman is not there, or he is there like the horns of a rabbit.

'If, things are not like this,' supposing somebody asks then, how is then the discourse of the past faces the pot, it is nothing other than a guessing that there is no reason why this pot came into being at this present moment and remain as it is, comes out from inside, fall on the pot, join discourse of the past and continue discourse in an inconsistent way. It is like this: We see a tree in a dream. Standing by its side exclaims Ha! This tree has completed more than a hundred years after its coming into being. If we look at it now, we come to know that the state of being old for more than hundred years of the tree appeared in the last night's dream is nonsense that the tree was manifested from the state of a dream then, and was not present physically outside. Similarly, this pot we see now is only manifested from the eye and not existing outside. One need not say all these objects are manifested from the sense organs then and there only.

'Ha! It is all right. Even though we could experience the entire universe consisting of everything, including our body, is coming out from the inside. Still, there comes a doubt about it. If the objects related to darkness are coming out from shining sense organs, there arises a question as to how darkness is rising out of the Sun. Therefore, we cannot say so. If we look at whether there is any reason for coming along with the sense organs, we do not see any such things. Because, in that case, we will have to say both darkness and light come up together at the same time. That is never possible.

'Alas! What magic is this universe? Not that seen outside, not that evolves from the sense organs, not that comes with sense organs, how then all these things are seen without a cause. When thought, all these are not mere illusions like a mirage, but something shines as absolute soul. It is like a snake being superposed on a piece of coir when brought to light that the snake disappears into the coir. Then the eye leaving the illusory snake that has been imagined as the real snake will stick on to the coir. It is like, in the enlightenment from long thinking one feels that there is no reason for the entire universe including ourselves seen casually rest in Brahman which is unbroken.

'Consciousness is without any reason. All these disappear into the Brahman, which is the base, the prime cause. Then the entire things are seen in the illusory universe leave from it, and this baseless phenomenon as high looking with live consciousness blend and become one with the unbroken soul, and becomes the soul ultimately only.

'Again, because of previous instinct, the universe will be seen as a colossal thing as before. This also, on thinking throughout from head to foot, should remain dissolved into the soul and remain as the soul itself. When it is repeatedly done so, the impure instinct decays, becomes baseless and gets contained in the minute pure instinct. Then the arrogance that was tied up with both the instincts will decay and remain absolute. This condition is neither that of the soul nor of the inert. It is neither consciousness nor ignorance [void]. They are not dualities of happiness and affliction. It is really wonderful that from this indefinable thing the creations are going on. How can the blockhead souls understand its greatness?'

This subjective reality-oriented approach of observer–observed relation is used by Gurudev in many of his works, showing his stern belief in the partnership phenomenon of the observer and observed. For example, in 'Advaita Deepika' (Sloka 2),'Vedanta Sutras' (Sutras 9, 10 and 18), 'Bhana Darsanam', 'Darsanamala' (Poem 8), 'Yoga Darsanam', 'Darsanamala' (Poem 7), etc. (See also 'The Role of the Observer').

Niels Bohr, Heisenberg and others brought forward an interpretation of quantum mechanics, which is the most discussed interpretation among scientists. According to it, though quantum mechanics gives a description of an objective reality, it deals with only probabilities of measuring various objects of energy quanta, the entities that fit neither the classical idea of particles nor the classical idea of waves. According to this interpretation, the act of selection or measurement causes the set of possibilities to assume only one of the possible values immediately. This feature is known as wave function collapse. There are many interpretations by different scientists. All of them generally accept certain basic principles. They are:

1. The description of nature is probabilistic with the probability of a given outcome.
2. The state of a quantum system is represented by a wave function ψ.
   When the measurement is made, it 'instantaneously' collapses into an Eigenstate.
3. It is impossible to know the values of all properties of the system at the same time.
4. Matter exhibits a wave-particle duality.
5. Measuring devices being classical, they measure only classical properties like position and momentum.
6. Quantum description of a large system makes a close approximation of the classical description. The wave function ψ, according to the Copenhagen interpretation, is nothing more than a theoretical concept. It considers wave function collapse as a fundamental apriori (proposing the probable result of a known cause) principle.

The Copenhagen interpretation argues that changing one characteristic of one member of the pair (entangled pair) will not only make determinate the same characteristic of the other member, but will also make indeterminate the second characteristic of the other member. The change, from a condition wherein both the particles share the same wave function, to a condition wherein one characteristic of one particle is made determinate and its complex conjugate is made indeterminate, is something that happens as the result of measurement of the first feature of one of the pair and that is reflected 'instantaneously' in the other member of the pair.

The Copenhagen interpretation generally does not give the outcome of any measurement with certainty. It indicates the probabilities of outcome with indeterminism of observable quantities constrained by the uncertainty principle. The question is whether there is some deeper reality hidden beneath quantum mechanics that will be explained by a more fundamental theory which predicts the outcome of each measurement with certainty. In case properties of every subatomic particle were known, a deterministic physics could have been framed like classical physics.

The probabilistic nature of quantum mechanics comes out of the act of selection or measurement. It is the most difficult aspect of quantum systems to understand. It was mainly based on this problem the famous Bohr–Einstein debate took place. They attempted to clarify these fundamental principles by way of thought experiments. Very extensive studies were carried out to solve the question of what constitutes a measurement, including a new interpretation of quantum mechanics to get rid of the concept of wave function collapse. The concept there is, when a quantum system interacts with a measuring system, their respective wave functions get entangled so that the original quantum system loses its original identity as an independent entity.

The electron which we believed to be a particle earlier may have a wave function spread out over a whole room. But if you have many detectors all over the room, only one of them will detect the electron. In quantum mechanics, we cannot give a good reason why an electron is found in only one detector and not in all others though dispersed over the entire room. This problem gave rise to a lot of discoveries in physics during the last seven decades.

Many extensive studies have been made about measurement. Many interpretations came up. Feynman's path integral formulation, in which quantum mechanical amplitude is considered as a sum over history between the initial and final states, is an alternative formulation of quantum mechanics. It is really a quantum mechanical counterpart of 'action principle' in classical mechanics (see sum over histories).

In 1935 Albert Einstein, collaborating with Boris Podolsky and Nathan Rosen, published the paper EPR Paradox. It is a criticism levelled against quantum mechanics. They argued that quantum mechanics is incomplete. There exist the so-called 'hidden variables'. Hidden variable means that there are microscopic properties that we are unable to observe directly by means of testing, perhaps due to the present technological limitations. This limitation may not be there in future when instruments become much more precise. As we are unable to observe them at the present state of precision of the measuring instruments, they are believed to be hidden. Once we come to know more about these hidden variables, they might explain the otherwise mysterious behaviour of particles. According to Heisenberg's uncertainty principle, these variables are not just unobservable. They simply do not exist outside the context of observation. But this deviates from our day-to-day concept of reality.

EPR continues to argue that according to quantum mechanics, a single system has its own wave function. If such a system can be transformed into two individual systems, in doing so, it does not create two wave functions; instead, each of them will share the single wave function. Does the question then arise as to what happens to this wave function when one or the other of the pair is measured? EPR claims that measuring one feature of the system (say, the momentum of one of the pair of particles) will reveal the same feature of the other particle. It believes that as the two systems are physically separated, the action on one particle cannot affect the other particle, and it is therefore impossible that any indeterminacy could be induced to the system which is not measured directly.

The EPR paper concludes that quantum mechanics is incomplete, because it portrays a pair system in a way that after one measurement each has one determinate characteristic. In reality, it argues one could measure the first system to get the real value for the position of the second and could have measured the first system to get the real value of momentum of the second; the result is that the second system must have both a real position and a real momentum. That is, they would both be determinate, not only one of them as pointed out by quantum mechanics.

Werner Heisenberg, Eugene Wigner and Henry Stapp introduced a speculative suggestion that selection (measurement) is something that is to do with consciousness or mind. This argument was followed by a series of proposals propounding consciousness getting more and more involved in trying to solve the intricate problem of quantum physics. Forty years ago, Wigner suggested that it is the consciousness of the observer that makes the selection. In Stapp's opinion, since a quantum brain has many alternative things that can happen, consciousness selects one of them to produce a result. There were many ideas put forward by different scientists to solve the problem. Some took quantum physics as a way of learning about spirituality—a way back to spirituality. Subsequently, there came a great number of possible suggestions that can help solve the problem. The basic perplexity is that when physicists think about nature, they have only two things in mind—waves or particles. Unfortunately, the objects that quantum physics deals with are not just waves or particles. This requires a new understanding of nature.

Albert Einstein, in response to various interpretations, once remarked,'Quantum mechanics is worthy of regard. But an inner voice tells me that this is not yet the right track. The theory yields much, but it hardly brings us closer to the old one's secrets. I, in any case, am not convinced that He [God] does play dice.'

Based on 'locality' and 'realism', the EPR paradox criticized quantum mechanics as incomplete and maintained the hope that a more complex theory might one day be discovered. Locality meant 'no instantaneous spooky action at a distance', and realism meant the object exists even when it is not observed. In 1964 John Stewart Bell put forward an analogy to the EPR paradox based on the spin measurements of entangled electrons. Using the same argument as that of EPR, he said, 'A choice measurement setting here should not affect the outcome of measurement there and vice versa.' He revealed specific cases where this would be inconsistent with predictions of quantum mechanics, giving a mathematical formulation of locality and realism. Many experiments which were done following Bell's example using entanglement of photons instead of electrons proved that the predictions of quantum mechanics are correct.

According to Bell's theorem, the concept of local realism (favoured by Einstein) provides only predictions that disagree with those of quantum theory. Many experiments which agree with predictions of quantum theory show correlations. These experimental results have been taken by many as disproving the concept of local realism. If Bell's conditions are correct, then the results that are in agreement with quantum mechanics will appear to evidence superluminal effects in contradiction to the principle of locality.

In the graph connecting the angle between detectors and quantum correlation, if local hidden variables existed, they would have agreed with a linear dependence of the correlation curve. According to Bell's inequality, the local hidden variables did not agree with dependence predicted by quantum theory. It was found that experimental results agreed only with the curve predicted by quantum mechanics. Bell's theorem is generally regarded as supported by a lot of evidence and hence, is considered a fundamental principle in quantum mechanics.

Bell's theorem put an end to local realism. If Bell's theorem is correct, either quantum mechanics or local realism has to be abandoned as they are contradictory to one another. Bell said, 'No local deterministic hidden variable theory can reproduce all the experimental predictions of quantum mechanics.'

The basic scenario an interpretation must address is when a quantum system is in a combination of states known as a superposition. A particle can be at both locations, A and B, or in Schrödinger's thought experiment, the quantum cat can be alive and dead at the same time. The problem is that when we observe or measure a superposition, we get only one result: the measuring instrument reports either 'A' or 'B', not both; the cat would appear either alive or dead. The Copenhagen interpretation has long been the accepted line for quantum physicists. The Schrödinger equation describes how a wave function evolves smoothly and continuously over time, until the point when our big, clunky measuring apparatus intervenes. The wave function enables us to predict, say, there's a 70 per cent probability we'll detect the particle at location A. After we detect it at A or B, we have to represent the particle with a new wave function that conforms to the result of the measurement.

29

CHIJJADA CHINTANAM II

'Chijjada Chintanam' is the thought of differentiating consciousness and inert things. This is a topic that has been elaborately discussed in many works of Vedanta. Gurudev in this work gives a very simple, yet at the same time very elucidative, presentation covering the entire spirit of Vedanta in ten verses in pure Malayalam. In its aesthetic sense, it is exemplary; written with all the ingredients of good poetry.

The words chit (consciousness) and *jata* (inert) are synonyms to many pairs of words like observer-observed, knower-known, Atman-body, eternal-transient, truth-illusion, real-virtual, etc. The seekers of truth ultimately find that there are only two fundamental categories in their existence in the world. These two are the chit and jata (consciousness and inert). What exists in all stages of existence is the consciousness as it is all-pervading and eternal. What does not is the inert. In the worldly experience of existence, it is all a mix of both witness aspects (vivartha) of consciousness and inert.

Those things which are produced and perish are inert, and that which is never created nor destroyed is consciousness—birth, growth, decay, destruction, evolution, etc. are characteristics of inert. Not subject to any of these, without being subject to evolution is the consciousness. In short, inert is that which undergoes evolution continuously, whereas consciousness is that which is beyond beginning, end and evolution.

The primordial vibration though subtle was inert. The inert subtle force of vibration in the consciousness creates the impression of a vacuum. This is the quintessence—the fifth element. Since it is one of the components of the universe, it is an inert thing. This is what probably they refer to as inflation—the vacuum that led to chaotic inflation. The consciousness hidden behind the all-pervading quintessence throughout experiences it. This first inert stage is called 'Avyakta'. The universe from its aggregate form—space, prana, etc. to matter—is inert. In the individual form, the throbbing, ego, etc. to the inert body, are inert things. Chit is that which exists beyond all these inert and evolutionary stages irrespective of whether it is the universe or the individual, without any change. Chit (consciousness) is real, and inert is unreal. As inert is transient and subject to evolution and takes changing forms whereas consciousness is not subject to evolution and is eternal that never undergoes any change, they are two different aspects and hence not inseparable, rather they are two absolutely separate things.

(Original text in Malayalam)

Orukōṭi divākararottuyarum
Paṭi pāroṭu nīranalādika/um
Keṭumāṛu ki/aṛnnu varunnoru nin
Vaṭivennuminnumirunnu vi/aṅṅiṭēṇam

Iṭaṇēyirukaṇmunayennilati
Nnaṭiyannabhilāṣamumāpatiyē
Jadaminnitu koṇṭu jayikkumiti
Nniṭayillayirippatilonnilumē.

Nilamoṭu neruppu nirannoẓukum
Jalamāśuganambaramañcilumē
Alayāteyaṭikkaṭi na/kuka nin
Nilayinnitu tanne namukku mati.

Mati toṭṭu maṇam mutalañcumuṇaṟ-
Nnaruḷōḷavumuḷḷatu cinmayamām
Kṣiti toṭṭiruḷōḷamahō! Jadamā-
Mitu raṇṭilumāyamarunnakhilam.

Akhilaṟkkumatiññane tanne matam
Sukhasādyamitennu śūkādikaḷum
Pakarunnu parambarayāy palatum
Bhagavānude māyayahō! Valutē.

Valutum ceṟutum naṭumadyavumā-
Yalayaṟṟuyarunna citambaramē!
Malamāyayilāṇu mayaṅṅi manam
Nilaviṭṭu nivaṟnnalayātaruḷē

Aruḷē! Tirumēniyaṇaññiṭumī-
Yiruḷē! Veḷiyē,yidayē potuvē!
Karaḷē! Karaḷinkalirikkumarum
Poruḷē! Puri mūnnumericcavanē!

Erikayyēntiyiṟaṅṅi varum
Tirumēni citambaramennaruḷum
Pūri tannilirunnu puram pori ce-
Ytaruḷum tanneyoratbhutamām!

Putumāmkani putamṟutē guḷamē!
Madhuvē! Madhurakkaniyē! Rasamē
Vidhimadhavarādi tiraññiṭumen
Patiyē! Padapankajamē gatiyē!

Gati nīyaṭiyannu gajatteyuri-
Ccatukoṇṭuda cāṟtiya cinmayamē!
Caticeyyumiruṭṭoru jāti viṭu-
Nnatininnaṭiyannaruḷēkaṇamē!

Meaning and commentary

Verse 1

Like the rising simultaneously of a billion
Suns come up to extinguish the glory of all
Elements such as earth water and fire should
Shine your godly form always not departing.

Like a billion Suns rising together such that earth, water, glory, all five elements vanish come ablaze the absolute consciousness in Lord's form, be made always shining without disappearing.

Verse 2

Oh, Shiva! Husband of Parvathi! Bless me shedding
Both your eyes on this servant who has intense
Longing to see the absolute reality which alone wins
Over inert things as none of them can remain in truth.

Oh! Husband of Goddess Parvathi! Shed mercy on me by both your eyes, this devotee longs to see your absolute form and experience happiness on seeing your real form. As your form shines the illusion of inert will become removed, thereby the journey in the inert body will become gratified. The absolute consciousness can never exist in any form of inert things.

Verse 3

Let not mind always reach and long for none of the mixed
Inert things to the earth, fire, steadily flowing water, sky and such
Five elements, in every step, bless me to experience the existence of
The Absolute by that alone, my life becomes fulfilled.

Oh! Lord! Bless me to see the existence of absolute truth and to get filled with bliss in every step of my journey in the inert body without the mind being coveted and attached to inert things which are a mix of the five elements, earth, water, air, space and fire. Our life will become blessed by that alone.

Verse 4

Knowing from wisdom smell and such five elements to the
Ego, what remains without change is the absolute truth
Wonderful! From earth to ignorance all things seen are inert
The secret of existence is contained in this absolute truth and inert things.

It is only the absolute consciousness that remains unchanged in all experience from wisdom, smell, taste, etc. to the awareness, of 'I', 'I'. Everything from earth to ignorance is all inert. The entire secret of existence is contained in this inert and absolute consciousness.

Verse 5

All those who found the real truth of existence have
This opinion, the seekers of truth like Suka traditionally
Advise disciples that it is attained without any difficulty
Oh! The Ultimate! This is all Maya! It is wonderful!

All those who found the actual truth, have the same opinion as said above. The seekers of truth like the monk Suka have explained traditionally through disciples that the above state can be easily attained, always experiencing the absolute truth leaving all ignorance of inert by separating the Absolute and inert. Anyway, it is difficult to overcome Maya the power of Absolute. Wonderful!

Verse 6

Oh! The all-pervading truth that rises and multiplies
As micro-macro and mega forms, protect us without
Being trapped and wandering in the forest of inert things
Created by the veil of Maya that hides the reality.

Oh! Lord! The one who multiply into many different forms as subtle, corpulent and medium, without any movement and who is spread widely as space! The absolute truth! Protect us! Without being trapped in the feeling of deep forests of worldly life and wandering with the swooned mind, Lord! Bless shedding mercy on me!

Verse 7

Oh, merciful! The veil that hides your real form, space
That forms from it, which shines as a middle stage, the embodiment
Of the great rule, the seat of life that shines as absolute wisdom
That burnt to ashes the three cities of Tripuras, I adore you.

Oh! Lord! The embodiment of mercy! The veil that comes to cover your form! The space that formed from it! That shines as the middle stage in the evolution of inert things! One who exists as the ego that all evolutionary changes are me. One who seems like the seat of spirit! One who 'glitter as I, I' in heart and shine as the absolute consciousness! One who burnt the three bodies, cause, subtle and corpulent! I see you everywhere in all the forms mentioned above and bow.

Verse 8

Taking the form of light, one shining as the Absolute
In the realization of life and as all-pervading soul
Removing all-cause and micro-macro bodies and shining
As the embodiment of bliss is really wonderful!

Taking the form of light, the body form shining through the attainment of self-realization, existing in the state of widely known undivided consciousness itself alienating the cause, subtle, corpulent bodies brightening the embodiment of bliss, is really wonderful!

Verse 9

Oh! Ripe mango fruit! Fresh nectar, sweet jaggery,
Honey, sweet fruit and essence! Oh, my Lord!
Whom Brahma Vishnu and others long for seeing,
Your lotus-like feet, which is my only refuge.

Oh! Fresh seasoned ripe mango! New nectar (ambrosia)! Jaggery, honey, fruit full of sweetness, joy, my Lord whom gods Brahma, Vishnu, etc. wish to bow their heads! Only your pair of lotus feet is my shelter.

Verse 10

One who dressed in the skin of elephant you are the only
Refuge for this devotee wandering in worldly sufferings
Lord! Bless this servant to remove the cheating
Veil of Maya that creates worldly sufferings.

Oh! Lord! The embodiment of consciousness, who exists wearing the dress of leather, the stripped-off skin from the elephant you are the refuge to this devotee who wanders in miseries of worldly life. Bless the devotee to remove somehow the veil of Maya that causes the miseries of worldly life and hides the absolute consciousness.

30

DHARMAM

This poem was written by Sree Narayana Gurudev after he composed 'Vishnuashtakam'. Gurudev wrote this poem in a notebook of Sri Sivalingadasa Swamikal, the first direct disciple of Gurudev.

Dharma is the basic cause of the universe.

Dhaṛma ēva param daivam
Dhaṛma ēva mahādhanam
Dhaṛmassaṛvatṛa vijayī
Bhavatu śṛēyasē nṛuṇām. (Sanskrit)

Dharma is the primordial cause of the (Nirguna Brahman) universe.

Dharma is the biggest of all wealth.

Dharma attains success everywhere.

Let such Dharma become useful to men for their salvation.

Dharma is the unique primordial cause of the universe—the Brahman. Dharma is the greatest wealth of all wealth. Dharma achieves success everywhere. Let such Dharma be helpful to men for attaining salvation.

Line 1

Even great scholars are unable to give a clear definition of Dharma. Gurudev in the first line itself gives a clear definition of Dharma as the primordial cause of the universe. The meaning of the word Dharma is, whatever is put on (worn) is Dharma. Vedanta says that it is the Brahman that wears the universe. The universe is the temple (residing place) of Dharma. This means the universe is the virtually manifested (Vivartha) body of Brahman. (Ref. Chapter1, Hymn1, Bhagavad Gita)

Line 2

The greatest wealth is Dharma. The purpose of wealth is to enjoy greater worldly pleasures. The realization of divine bliss is the experience of the greatest pleasure. The worldly pleasures with ordinary wealth are only transient, whereas the realization of Brahman is an eternal bliss—the greatest pleasure. In that sense, the attainment of eternal bliss—Dharma (Brahman) is the greatest wealth.

Line 3

It is an inviolable universal law. Whoever approaches the absolute truth along the virtuous path, he succeeds physically and spiritually; on the other hand, one who approaches the absolute truth through an unrighteous path fails, losing everything. In Mahabharata, Vyasa states, '*Dharmi rakshati rakshita*': this means, if Dharma is maintained, that in turn maintains you.

Line 4

The word *Sreyas* means the realization of Brahman or attainment of salvation. Gurudev in this line, clearly declares that Dharma is the attainment of salvation. Whatever is hidden in the cave (heart) inside is the consciousness, the phenomenon that removes the veil hiding it and manifests is the Dharma. It is the secret of Dharma.

31

CHIDAMBARASHTAKAM

Sree Narayana Gurudev wrote this prayer song sometime between 1887 and 1897. The exact time is not available. Gurudev travelled widely in and around Kerala after consecration at Aruvippuram. He consecrated a number of idols of Shiva, Subramanya and Devi in various temples in south India. This poem might have been written on the occasion of any of these consecrations.

This poem beautifully reflects Gurudev's skill as a great poet, and it is capable of taking the devotees deep into meditation and relief from worldly grief. The musical harmony and rhythm of the poem make it excellent work.

(Original text in Sanskrit)

Bṛahmamukhāmaravanditalingam
Janmajarāmaranāntakalingam
kaṛmmanivāraṇakauśalalingam
tanmṛidu pātu cidambaraliangam.

Kalpakamūlapṛatiṣtitalingam
Daṛppakanāśayudhiṣtiralingam
Kupṛakṛutipṛakarāntakalingam
Tanmṛitu pātu cidambaralingam

Skandagaṇēśwara kalpitalingam
Kinnara cāranagāyakalingam
Pannagabhūṣaṇa pāvanalingam
Tanmṛitu pātu cidambaralingam.

Sāmbasadāśivaśankaralingam
Kāmyavarapṛadakōmaḷalingam
Sāmyavihīnasumānasalingam
Tanmṛitu pātu cidambaralingam.

kalimalakānanapāvakalingam
salilatarangavibhūṣaṇalingam
palitapṛatangapṛadīpakalingam
Tanmṛitu pātu cidambaralingam.

Aṣtatanupṛatibhāsuralingam
Viṣtapanādha vikaswaralingam
Śiṣtajanāvanaśīlitalingam
Tanmṛitu pātu cidambaralingam.

Antakamaṛddanabanduralingam
Kṛuntita kāmakaḷebaralingam
Jantuhṛidistitajīvakalingam
Tanmṛitu pātu cidambaralingam.
Puṣtadhiyassucidambaralingam
Dṛuṣtamitam manasānupaṭanti
Aṣtakamētadavāngmanasīyam
Aṣtatanum pṛati yānti narāstē

Meaning and commentary

Verse 1

One with the idol adored by gods like Brahma
One with the idol that ends birth, ageing and death

One with the idol apt to abolish instincts of previous births
Let Lord Shiva at Chidambaram! Protect us.

Brahma (not Brahman) is the Lord of virtual creation, but he is only a small reflected phenomenon of the real all-pervading Brahman. Even Brahma is carrying out the process of creation, always with Brahman the Absolute as the witness. Brahma is secondary and is a creation of Maya. He is transient, whereas real Brahman is eternal. We know the word 'Śiva' is a synonym of the word Brahman. Hence Gurudev remarks that all gods including Brahma adore Shiva.

Verse 2

One whose idol founded beneath the celestial tree
One who stood strong in fight burning the Cupid
One with the idol who smashed the wicked demons
Let merciful Shiva at Chidambaram! Protect us.

This says that the idol of Shiva is founded at the foot of the celestial 'Kalpaka Tree'. This celestial tree is an astonishing phenomenon. It delivers everything requested to it. In spite of its existence in heaven, the gods have founded Shiva's idol beneath the celestial tree. This shows that Shiva, the Brahman himself, if pleased gives everything on the devotee's request.

Verse 3

One who gave birth to Subramanya and Ganapathi
One with the idol adored by songsters kinnaras and Charanas
One with the sacred idol wearing snakes as ornaments
Let Lord Shiva at Chidambaram! Protect us.

Lord Subramanya (Skanda) and Ganapathi are the sons of Lord Shiva. Subramanya is the commander of the army of gods in heaven, and Ganapathi is the head of the army of hindrance makers. Therefore, Subramanya and Ganapathi can be considered as symbols of intelligence and ego. We know Brahman is the source of intelligence and ego. *The kinnaras* and *charanas* can be taken as some type of songsters who go around the world singing in praise of Shiva.

Verse 4

One with Goddess always remains as an idol of bliss to others
One with beautiful body blessing devotees giving boons
One who shines in the hearts of good folks
Let that Lord Shiva at Chidambaram! Protect us!

One who always remains with Goddess Parvathi as the idol of blessings to devotees giving them boons and one who shines in the hearts of noble men let that Lord Shiva protect us.

Lord Shiva is one who has shared one half of his body with the Goddess and remains as a combined form of half man and half woman. Brahman (Purusha), the cause of the universe, always depends on nature (Prakriti) for visual existence. There are doctrines saying that both the souls (Purusha) and nature (Prakriti) are eternal without a beginning.

Verse 5

One who shines as the fire that burns the forest of strife-time
One who wears the waves of Ganga beautifully on the head
One with the idol that brightens the world like the setting reddish Sun
Let that Lord Shiva at Chidambaram! Protect us.

One who shines as the fire that burnt the forest of evils of strife period (of desire and anger), one who wears the waves of beautiful river Ganges on the head, one with the idol that brightens the world like the reddish setting Sun, blessings of merciful Lord at Chidambaram be showered on us!

Meditation with or without attributes will remove the evils of strife period of desire and anger gradually. Therefore Lord Shiva, either with attributes or without attributes, is one who burns to ashes the forest of strife period. The idol of Shiva shines like the setting Sun in the heart of the devotee in a reddish colour.

Verse 6

The one who shines with eight bodies visible
One who pervades the universe as its Master
One with the habit of protecting noble people
Let the merciful Shiva at Chidambaram! Protect us.

The universe is considered as the eight bodies of Lord Shiva. The five elements, earth, water, fire, air and space, the Sun, the Moon, and the soul, are the eight bodies. He is Vishtapatināta because he is spread in all these eight bodies and makes them act. Let the Lord at Chidambaram the one with the idol that possesses the habit of protecting the nobles! Protect us!

Verse 7

One of the beautiful idol who killed Yama
One with the idol who burnt the Cupid
One stays in hearts of creatures make us live
Let Lord Shiva at Chidambaram! Protect us.

Markandeya, the son of Mukundamuni with the awareness that he is short-lived, once meditated Shiva intensely. His fate was to live for only sixteen years. At the age of sixteen, when Yama the Lord of time came to take Markandeya, Lord Shiva prevented and killed him. Thereafter Shiva is known as the killer of the killer (Yama).

This indicates that one, who searches the real truth, goes beyond the limits of time and attains eternal bliss.

Verse 8

Those wise who keep Lord Shiva at Chidambaram
In hearts and see him through imagination and
Utter his prayer of these eight poems daily
They attain the eight-bodied Shiva.

These poems are meant to reveal the greatness of Brahman. Brahman, Shiva and universe are synonyms. Throughout the poem, Shiva is either taken as Brahman or a symbol of Brahman. Either considering Shiva as Saguna Brahman (attributed) or as Nirguna Brahman (unattributed) as felt in mind, these poems are to be chanted every day. The way to self-realization requires concentration. Even if it is difficult to maintain concentration, the devotee gets self-happiness through the chanting and can attain the merger with the Nirguna Brahman the Absolute—Lord Shiva gradually.

32

GADYAPRARDHANA

This prayer in prose was composed by Sree Narayana Gurudev for thinking and chanting, while he was staying at Kolatukara temple in connection with the consecration of the idol in the temple. It is published in the book written by Sri Kottukoikkal Velayudhan, a journalist and a household disciple who accompanied most of Gurudev's visits.

(Original text in Malayalam)

Kanappedunnathokkeyum sthoolam, sookshmam, karanam ennee moonnu roopangalodukoodiyathum paramathmavil ninnunmundayi athilthanne layikkunnathumakunnu. Athinal paramathmavallathe veronnumilla. Sakala papangaleyum nasippikkunna—veruthukalayunna—paramathmavinte yathoru swaroopam ente buddiye thelichu nalla vazhiye kondupokumo, dyanikkendathaya paramathmavinte aa divyaswaroopathe njan dyanikkunnu. Allayo paramapithave! Iprakaram idavidathe enikk angaye dyanikkunnathinum angayude paramanandam labhikkunnathinum angayude anugraham undakename. Allayo daivame! Kannu kondu kanunnathonnum nithyamalla. Sareeravum neerkumilapole nilayattathakunnu. Ellam swapnathulyamennallathe onnum parayuvanilla. Nam sareeramalla, arivakunnu. Sareeramundakunnathinu munpilum arivaya nam undayirunnu. Ini ithokkeyum illathepoyalum nam iprakaram prakasichukonduthanneyirikkum. Jananam, maranam, dharidryam,rogam, bhayam ithonnum namme theendukayilla. Iprakaram upadesikkappedunna thiruvakkukaleyum ee thiruvakkukalude upadeshtavaya paramathmavineyum njan oonilum urakkathilum idavidathe ellayppozhum chinthikkumarakename, nee ente sakala papangaleyum kavarnneduthukond enikku ninte paramanandham nalkename. Ente lokavasam kashtappadu koodathe kazhinju koodunnathinum oduvil ninte paramapadham prapikkunnathinum ninte anugraham ennil undakename.

'Whatever is visible in the form of corpulent, subtle and cause, belong to three forms and created from the ultimate soul, the Brahman and dissolves in it. Therefore, there is nothing else other than Brahman. Whichever shape of the Brahman brightens my wisdom, and take along the auspicious way I adore that divine form that burns—roasts all sins. Oh! The ultimate soul, let me have your blessings to meditate you uninterruptedly and get your blessings. Oh! God! Whatever is seen by the eye is not real. The body which is transient like a bubble of water is not with any entity. Nothing else can be told about it other than everything is like a dream. I am not the body. I am knowledge. I, the knowledge was there even before the creation of the body. Hereafter, if all these vanish, I will continue to shine like this. Birth, death, poverty, disease, fear, none of these will touch me. The holy doctrines thus advised and the Brahman who is the adviser of these holy words be remembered by me in wakefulness and sleep incessantly. Oh! Lord! By forcibly taking all my sins to give me your bliss. Oh! Lord! Shower your blessings to carry on my worldly life without sufferings and to attain your supreme feet ultimately.'

33

KALINATAKAM

The date of writing this poem is not known definitely due to non-availability of evidence. But some are of the opinion that it was written in the middle of the period 1887 and 1897. This poem is written in a way that it can be sung in tune suitable for musical concerts and dance performance on stage. It clearly manifests Gurudev's proficiency in vocabulary.

It describes in the following lines a drama of Goddess Kali. Kali is a symbol of Brahma power Maya. The meaning of the word Kali is 'lady with black colour'. It is really the Brahman himself appearing as the Goddess Kali wearing a black veil. Gurudev gives a beautiful limb-by-limb explanation for the adoration of the Goddess. Those who read and analyse these verses can see that human life also is only a good drama. (There are about 120 lines in this poem. The following are the most outstanding from the cosmological point of view. The remaining is mostly an adoration part.)

(Original text in Malayalam)

Namō nādabindwātmikē! nāśahīnē!
Namō nāradādīddya pādāravindē!
Namō nānmaṛaykkum manippūm viḷakkē!
Namō nānmukhādipriyāmbā Namaste!

Samastapṛapancam sṛujicum bharicum
Muda samharicum rasicum ramicum
Kaḷicum puḷacum mahaghoraghoram
Viḷicum mamānandadēsē vasicum

Teḷiññum maṛaññum tuḷumbum pṛapancam
Tuḷaññuḷḷileḷḷoḷamuḷḷayirunnum
Tiriññum piriññum mahānandadhārām
Coriññum padāmbhōjabhaktaṛkku nityam

Varunnōru tumbaṅaḷellamaṛiññum
Karinjīṭumaṛavirātankabījam
Kuṛaññōrunēram ninakkunna bhaktaṛ-
Kkaṛiññīla maṛṛuḷḷa kaivalyarūpam

Niṛaññaṅṅanē viśwamellāmoruppō-
Laṛam ceṛṛumillāte vāṇum cirannāḷ
Kaẓiññālumillōru nāśam; kuṛaññō-
Nnaṛiññīṭarāyinnihō! Ghōrarūpam
Maṛaññīṭumō; viśwamellāmitennōṛ-
Taṛiññīṭuvān saktarāruḷḷu lōkē?

Meaning and commentary

Oh! Mother, one who takes manifested form first from the point, sound, etc., the first state of Pranava in the order of evolution of the universe. One who never perish! I prostrate you, one who is worshipped by great ascetics like Narada bowing their head at your lotus feet, Oh! Mother! I prostrate you! One who shines like the diamond lamp for the shining of the four Vedas, I adore you! Oh! Mother! Who is dear to gods like Brahmadeva, I adore you, Oh! Mother! I bow.

Oh, Mother! You create the entire universe, maintain and happily dissolve, amuse and enjoy, play and prolifically roar loudly, make others fear and always stay in my heart, the place of self-happiness.

This universe as subject to senses, as hue and cry, filled throughout and overflowed if looked introvert into inside seen as existing in the form of mind like subtle seed of sesame and to such introverts shedding shower of happiness whatever changes the universe undergo, to those who seek shelter knowing their day-to-day afflictions and remove the grief completely then and there and to those devotees who worship concentrating even for a short while need not worship any other for getting a way to salvation.

Oh! Mother, you pervade inside and outside of everything in the entire universe without leaving a little. Oh! The embodiment of divine power! You do not undergo any change as time passes as you are eternal. It is wonderful! Who is capable of knowing all these? Will this frightening universe ever vanish? If at all vanish who is there capable of knowing when?

34

INDRIYA VAIRAGYAM

This work is believed to be done in 1897. Control over the five senses and the mind (abstinence) are the two main factors in the search for truth. Sree Narayana Gurudev, even at the time of his young days, could obtain these two qualities to a great extent. For this, he left his house and family and went to the forest and mountains like Marutwamala for doing penance and to lead the life of an ascetic.

This poem is meant for those who wish to become seekers of truth. For obtaining control over the five senses, one who seeks truth should get control over the mind and control over the senses simultaneously. In 'Atmopadesa Satakam' (Poem 1), Gurudev mentions closing all the five sense organs to see the Karu (the Brahman). Here, Gurudev explains how to attain such a state capable of realizing the absolute truth. The control over senses is obtained by closing all five sense organs, and control over mind through the concentrated chanting of hymns.

(Original text in Malayalam)

Nādam kaṭannu naṭuvevilasunna ninmey
Cētassilāy varika janmamaṛunnatinnāy
Bōdham kaḷanju puṛamē cuẓalum cevikko-
Rātankanillaṭiyanuṇṭi, tu tīṛkka śambhō!

Kāṇunna kaṇṇinorudandavumilla kaṇṭen-
Pŗānanveṭinjiṭukilentinu pinneyellām
Kāṇum niŗam taramitokkeyaẕinjeẕum nin-
Cēṇuŗŗa cenkaẕalu tannu jayikka śambhō!

Twakkinnu dukhamorunēravumillatōŗkkil
Dukham namukku tuṭarunnu durantamayyō!
Vekkam taṇuppu veyiloṭu viḷaṅiṭum nin-
Pōkkalppolinjiṭùvatinnaruḷīṭu śambhō!

Taṇṇīrumannavumaŗinjutarunna ninmey
Veṇṇīŗaṇinjuvilasunnatinentu bandham?
Maṇṇinnu toṭṭu matiyantamirunnu minnum
Kaṇṇinnu kaṣṭamitu ninte vibhūti śambhō!

Nāvinneẕunnanarakakkaṭalilkkiṭannu
Jīvantaḷaŗnnu śivamē! Karacēŗtiṭēṇam
Gōvindanum nayanapankajamiṭṭu kūppi
Mēvunnu, ninmahimayāraŗiyunnu śambhō!

Nīrum niranna nilavum kanalōṭu kāŗŗum
Cērum cidambaramatinkalirunniṭum nī
Pāril kiṭannalayumen paritāpamellā-
Māriṅu ninnoṭaŗiyippatinunṭu śambhō!

Nālinnu ninte tirunāmameṭuturacu
Mēvunnatinneḷutilonnaruḷīṭanē nī
Jīvan viṭumbozhatilninnu teḷinjiṭum pin
Nāvinnu bhūṣaṇamitenni namukku vēṇṭa.

Kayyonnu ceyyumatupōle naṭanniṭum kā-
Layyō!malatoṭu jalam veḷiyil patikkum
Poyyē puṇaŗnniṭumatiṅane ninnu yudham
Ceyyumbōẕeṅane śivā tirumey ninappū?

Cinticiṭunnu śivamē! Ceṟupaitalāmen
Cintakku cētamitukoṇṭorutellumillē
śandhiciṭunna bhagavānoṭu tanne collā-
Tentiṅu ninnuẓaṟiyāloru śādhyamayyō!

Ayyō! Kiṭannalayumippulayaṟkku nīyen-
Meyyō koṭutu vilayāy vilasunnu mēlil
Kayyonnu tannu karēṟṟaṇamenneyinnī-
Poyyinkal ninnu putumēni puṇaṟnniṭānāy.

Meaning and commentary

Verse 1

Your body hidden by the interference of sound
Let come to mind to break births and deaths
Ear (sense) that wander outside veiling the mind
Have no grief, but I have. End it, Oh! Blessed One!

Oh! Lord! The embodiment of bliss! Since the subjects of sense organs interfere with the vision, your holy form is lost from my mind. It should be made to shine in my mind to break the worldly longings like repeated births and deaths. Hiding the consciousness, the sense organs that wander outside do not have any grief (as they are inert). But this devotee who goes after sense organs is suffering from worldly miseries. Oh! Lord! Save me from it.

Verse 2

The eye that sees has no miseries if my life ends
Seeing all these illusory things what use in having
Seen colour, shape and all, give your self-shining feet
Oh!Lord! One free from all these Be Victorious!

Oh! Lord! The embodiment of bliss! The sense organs that see all these as many have no grief. Being inert instruments, they never get afflicted. If I happen to end my life fascinated by all these virtual scenes, what use is there in being a human with wisdom, etc. remove all these colours and forms shown by the sense organs completely, bless me showing your self-shining feet, Lord! Be victorious!

Verse 3

Once thought the skin has no grief at any time
To us, the miseries continue, pitiable!
Oh! God! Who shines everywhere bless me
The cold and heat be alleviated in you immediately.

Once thought, the skin that gives the sense of touch being inert never grieves. But the ever-increasing affliction happens to my awareness. Oh! All-pervading Lord! The embodiment of Bliss! The heat and cold together be alleviated in you, Lord! Bless me.

Verse 4

Why is your body shines smeared with ashes as if poor?
Who always knowingly deliver water and food?
The ultimate eye that shines from inert bodies to wisdom
It is difficult to understand your show of prosperity.

Oh! Lord who gives water and food to the world without fail, what is the reason why your body is smeared with ashes as if you are a poor man. Even to those who experience the presence of Brahman that he himself is that ultimate truth, after realizing the Brahman that pervades everything from pure inert things to absolute knowledge is incapable of understanding the secret of your blissful appearance in full.

Verse 5

Being in the sea of hell that comes out of the tongue
Life becomes exhausted. Oh! Blissful Lord! Put me
Ashore giving self-happiness, even Lord Vishnu looks
Upon you in salutation, who knows your greatness?

The prana (life) unable to get ashore becomes exhausted immersing in the sea of unending desires coming one after the other to the sense organs. Oh! The embodiment of bliss, take me to the shore and save me giving self-happiness. Even Lord Vishnu looks upon you with respect and adoration. Oh! Lord! Who can know your greatness?

Verse 6

In the sky of consciousness spread in water
Earth fire and air where you live Oh! Shiva!
Who is there to inform you about my sufferings?
That I experience wandering on earth?

Oh! The embodiment of bliss you exist densely in the sky of consciousness spread everywhere, in water, earth, fire and air. Oh! Lord! Who is there to inform you about the struggle of this devotee always with worldly subjects, who is there to inform you about my suffering?

Verse 7

Oh! Lord! To spell your holy name from remembrance and chant
Give my tongue an easy invocation once done when the life
Departs from the body your holy form becomes clear, chanting of
Your name is the adornment of tongue nothing else I want.

Oh! Lord! Be kind enough to teach my tongue an easy chant, which is always in a hurry to taste worldly desires that can help meditation remembering your divine song. After getting properly trained to chant the prayer songs, if chanted when Atman (life) begins to liberate from the inert body, the figure of the Lord should become manifest. The prayer song of God is an adornment to the tongue. This devotee does not want anything else.

Verse 8

The hand always does something likewise the leg moves
Pity! The anus discharge faeces genital organ semen and urine
Embrace inert bodies when performing organs struggle with their
Inert subjects Lord! How can your holy name be remembered?

The hand will go on doing something; similarly, the leg also will go on moving. What a pity! The anus purge motion and genital organs excrete semen and urine, embrace the inert bodies. When the organs of activities always struggle with inert phenomena, oh! Lord! How is it possible to remember your divine figure?

Verse 9

Auspicious Lord! I always think of you but
Being a child in divine thought my worldly desires
Do not reduce a bit, what is the use of getting
Perplexed without praying to the Lord, really a pity!

Oh! Lord! The embodiment of bliss! While in the middle of sensual pleasures, I used to think of you also. Still, there is no lessening in my worldly pleasures in the path of truth. What use is there in getting perplexed without praying to the God who is to be always remembered in mind, really it is pitiable!

Verse 10

Oh! Lord! It is a pity that my entire body is given

To the sense organs and pretend to be unaware of it
Give me a helping hand to reach the shore from
This illusory ocean to embrace the absolute truth.

It is a pity. Oh! All powerful Lord! Leaving my body to the sense organs that wander without being satisfied with anything, Lord! You remain as if a person who is not aware of anything. Oh! Lord! Kindly raise this devotee, giving your helping hand to save from this virtual world to experience the self-happiness bringing closer to the absolute truth.

35

JANANI NAVARATNA MANJARI

This was written by Sree Narayana Gurudev on his birthday in 1912 (1087 ME) on the occasion of the consecration of the idol of Goddess Sarada at Sivagiri. Though it appears as a prayer song to the deity, this is a unique literary creation of Advaita philosophy. These verses manifest the talent of Gurudev as a great poet in presenting the serious contents in a very simple, aesthetic manner. The nine verses are offered to the mother Sarada as a bunch of nine diamonds, like a bunch of flowers. The title of the poem is given in that sense.

One cannot find the absolute reality by merely studying the universe from outside. The study of the absolute reality should begin from the inside, that is, from the mind. In other words, the path in search of finding the secret of the universe should be directed towards the inside. It should be directed towards wisdom linked with a transcendental approach. Without knowing the secrets of the self, it is absolutely difficult or futile to investigate the secret of the universe.

It is due to the Maya power of the unchanging undivided Absolute that the visual things in the universe come up one by one. It separates into two, namely, ignorance and wisdom. The Goddess Sarada is considered the symbol of wisdom that leads ultimately to the level of realization of the absolute consciousness.

(Original text in Malayalam)

Onnāyamāmatiyil ninnāyiram tṛipuṭi-
Vannāśu tanmati maṛa-
Nnannādiyil pṛiyamuyaṛnnāṭalām kaṭali-
Lonnāyi vīṇuvalayum
Ennāśayam gatipeṛum nādabhūmiyila-
Maṛnnāvirābha paṭarum
Cinnābhiyil tṛipuṭiyennāṇaṛum paṭi
Kalaṛnnāṛiṭunnu jananī!

Illātamāyayiṭumullāsamonnumaṛi-
Vallātayillanilanum
Kallāzhiyum Kanalumallāte śūnyamatu
Mellāmorādiyaṛivām,
Tallāghavam paṛakilillāraṇam kṛiyakal
Mallāṭukilla matiyī-
Sallābhamonnu matiyellāvarum tirayu-
Mullāghabōdhajananī!

Uṇṭāyi māṛumaṛivuṇṭāyi munnamitu
Kaṇṭāṭumaṅamakavum
Koṇṭāyiramtaramiruṇṭāśayam pṛaticu-
Ruṇṭāmahassil maṛayum
Kaṇṭālumīnilayiluṇṭākayillaṛiva-
Khaṇṭānubhūtiyilezhum
Taṇṭāril vīnumadhuvuṇṭāramikkumoru
Vaṇṭānusūri sukṛuti.

Ārāyukil tirakal nīrayiṭunnu, phani
Nārāyiṭunnu, kuṭavum
Pārāyiṭunnatinu nērāyiṭunnalaka-
Mōrāykiluṇṭakhilavum
Vērāya ninkazhalilārādhaṇam taraṇa-
Mārālitinnoru varam

Nērāyi vanniṭukavēṛārumilla gati
Hē! Rājayōgajananī!

Mēlāyamūlamatiyālāvṛutam janani!
Nīlāsyamāṭiviṭumī-
Kīlālavāyvanala kōlāhalam bhuvana-
Mālāpamātṛamakhilam;
Kālādiyāya mṛitunūlāle neyyumoru
Līlāpaṭambhavatimey-
Mēlāke mūṭumatinālārumuḷḷataṛi
Vīlāgamāntanilayē!

Mīnāyatum bhavathi mānāyatum janani!
Nī nāgavum nagakhagam-
Tānāyatum dhara nadīnāriyum naranu-
Mā nākavum narakavum-
Nī nāmarūpamatil nānāvidhapṛakṛiti
Mānāyi ninnaṛiyu mī
Njānāyatum bhavati hē nādarūpiniya-
Hō! Nāṭakam nikhilavum.

Enpāpameyvatinorampāyiṭunnaṛivu-
Nin pādatārileẓume-
Nnanpāṇumauṛviyorirumpāmmanam dhanura-
Hambhāviyānuvijayī
Ambā! Tarunnu vijayam pāpapankilama-
Hambhānamākumatināl
Vanbhāramārnatanuvum bhānamāmulaka-
Vum bhānamākumakhilam.

Satāyininnupari citāyi raṇṭu-
Moru mutāyi mūnumaṛiyum
Hṛitāyi ninnatinu vitāyi viṇṇoṭuma-
Rutāyi dṛiṣti mutalāy

Kotāyiṭum viṣayavistāramannamati-
Natāvumāyi vilasum
Siddānubhūtiyilumetāteyāmatima-
Hatāyiṭum janani nī

Bhūvādi bhūtamatināvāsamilla veṛu-
Mābhāsa māmitaṛivi-
Nnābhāviśeṣamitināvāsamiṅulaki-
Lāpāditam bhavatiyāl
Nāvādi tanviṣayitāvāsamaṟṟabhava-
Dāvāsamākevilasum
Dyōvāṇatinte mahimāvāraṛinju jana
Nī! Vāzhtuvānumarutē.

Meaning and commentary

Verse 1

From the unique wisdom when
The Tripudies come up forgetting
The Self, getting desire on inert
Worldly things, I suffer immersed
Fully in the sea of miseries
Oh! Mother when is all tripudies
Disappear and merge into the absolute
Consciousness and subside giving peace.

When thousands of tripudies—knower, known and knowledge or jnatya, jneya, jnana separated and came up, the supreme reality started creation. Then the Atman forgetting that it is the idol of non-dual (unique) consciousness, the real self, developed longing towards inert things and that resulted in immersing fully in the sea of miseries. Oh! Mother! When am I going to get the opportunity of joining the divine voice (Aum) which shows the Absolute, merge and all tripudies subside and become one with you?

Verse 2

Non-existent in reality nothing visual in the universe that
Maya creates is not different from the Absolute Truth.
Air, earth, water, fire and space are not different from this
They are only the Absolute if it is realized
Haughtiness, rivalry and horror of war will vanish
Will not suffer involved in the after-effects of deeds.
Oh! Mother! Who renders knowledge making capable of
destroying all sins
I want the only achievement of truth that everyone desires.

The visual scenes which are not real in fact in the universe created by Maya are not at all different from the embodiment of knowledge, the primordial cause. The five elements, space, air, fire, water and earth, are also not different things separated from the Absolute, how great will be the peace and happiness of that once the truth is realized! All envy and rivalry vanish, will become detached from the wisdom and after-effects of deeds that have been done earlier. All living things move towards achieving that truth. Oh! Mother! Who gives the knowledge making capable of removing all sins, to me that knowledge of truth alone is enough.

Verse 3

Visuals in the universe are not existent though seen as existent
Seeing the transient scenes go after them with the body and mind
tempted
By thousands of imaginations, the imaginations shrink getting into
Narrow ideas dissolve into the self as instincts, even witnessing of
Creation and dissolution fail to get the awareness of the cause
behind it.
Considering the self and the Absolute as one, the black beetle that
Falls into the lotus mind and enjoy the experience of
The Absolute knowledge and eternal bliss is the virtuous soul.

All known visual things are transient. They appear and disappear. Seeing these things which are not existent before seeing and after seeing for some time as existent and then become vanished and non-existent, the mind and body go after them, and thousands of imaginations creep up. Such imaginations shrink getting into narrow ideas and at last dissolve into the self in the form of instincts. It is only these instincts that come up as virtual visual things repeatedly. Even after seeing the repeated creation and dissolution, one cannot get the awareness of the eternal truth behind it. It is only he who concentrates in the lotus mind and experiences the feeling of everything as one the Absolute enjoys the honey of self-happiness. It is the only virtuous soul.

Verse 4

Once thought, the waves are only water, the snake imagined on coir
Is only coir, the pot made of sand is nothing but sand.
The experience of the visual universe also is similar to this.
To one who does not try to understand this, the entire things
Will be seen as real, Oh! Mother! The ultimate cause of everything!
Give me refuge at your feet, for that, bless me at once!
I do not have any other support. Oh! Mother! One who can directly
Show the ultimate truth through the noble way of attaining salvation!

One who thinks deeply can easily understand that the waves seen on the surface of the water are nothing other than water. Similarly, in darkness, a piece of coir imagined to be a snake by mistake can be found as only coir when brought to light. So also, in potteries like pots, there is nothing other than sand. This is the same as the case of the universe. Though appear as full of diverse things, it is nothing other than the ultimate reality. To an ignorant, these things will be seen as different things. Oh! Mother! Who makes me believe that there are many things around me, bless me, giving refuge at your feet to experience the ultimate reality—mother! One who can remove all illusions from the mind and show the real truth.

Verse 5

This universe is filled with the all-pervading Brahman
Oh! Mother! Water, air, fire and earth, mixed up and
Appear as hue and cry formed depending on the frequency
Of your steps in dance, this universe seen as many is only names
Whereas Oh! Mother! You cover your body with the
Soft cloth weaved with the thread of space, time
And cause and always exists in Brahman
Therefore, nobody understands the real truth.

The Brahman pervades the entire universe. This universe which is seen as full of hue and cry produced by the mixing of the five elements, water, air, fire, earth and space, produced in tune with the frequency of steps in your dance are only named forms. Oh! Mother! You dance on the stage covering your body with the soft cloth weaved with threads of space, time and cause and always exists in the realm of Brahman. Therefore, everybody fails to understand what the real truth is.

Verse 6

Oh! Mother! You are the one who appears as fish, as deer,
As snake, as mountain and as birds, everything is seen
Your own transformed form, you are the earth, the river,
The woman and man, heaven and hell, what
Exists as an ego with different attributes depending on many
Name forms come one after other is all your Maya power.
Oh! Mother one who is known for sourceless sound (Nada Brahman, Aum)
It is all your drama. Wonderful!

Everything seen around us, formed as fish, deer, snake, mountain, birds, etc. are all nothing but Maya power. Similarly, the earth, river, woman and man, heaven and hell are also only Maya. The ego that experiences everything knowingly enticed by enumerable temptations like love and hatred going around many name forms is also the creation of this mysterious force. Oh! Mother! One who originates from the sourceless sound you are the doer of all such things. The entire universe is a drama you act.

Verse 7

The self-awareness is the arrow that destroys sins, my adoration
At your feet is the bowstring, the mind
As hard as iron is the bow, the ego that throb 'I',
'I' is the winning archer, Oh! Mother, you are the donor
Of victory my egoistic form is spoilt with my sins, because
Of that, I get the feeling of my heavy body as existent
So also, is this universe is felt to be existent.
Therefore, everything formed of corpulent and subtle is felt to be existent.

The self-awareness is the arrow that destroys all my sins. Oh! Mother! My adoration at your lotus feet is the bowstring. My mind as hard as iron is the bow. Ego is the fight-winning archer. Oh! Mother! You are the one who bestows the victory. My egoistic form is spoilt by sin, and that is why I feel my heavy body as existing, and it is in the same manner the universe is felt as existent. In short, the entire collections of subtle and corpulent materials are felt to be existent because of this.

Verse 8

Shining outside as the ultimate, inside as joining with
Mind forming bliss then joining consciousness, mind
And bliss shine subject of experience remaining in the heart

Created in the subtle form inside and corpulent outside by
Space, wind, etc. elements shining as the consumer of
The food of the inert visuals and in a state of bliss
Which even seers could not find. Oh! Mother! Your
Form is so great that even seers cannot understand you.

Shining outside as the ultimate Brahman, once gone inside as knowledge combining both the ultimate and mind forming one as bliss then joining the ultimate, mind and bliss as one is produced in the heart which experiences all this knowledge then becoming the five elements such as space and air the senses like eye, etc. and shines as the eater of food of inert external things. Oh! Mother! Your form is so great that it is beyond the reach of even seers.

Verse 9

None of the elements from the earth exists
Their existence is merely a feeling; they are only different
Illuminations of knowledge Oh! Mother! It is only you who cause
The knowledge to appear as different visible things in this world,
The five elements are incapable of experiencing or describing you
By words and the seat of such mother
Is the self-shining ultimate reality the Brahman, who knows
Is it greatness? Oh! Mother! It is beyond description.

The material things like earth are not existent, and the feeling that they are existent is only a mere imagination. All these are only different illuminations of knowledge in this universe. Oh! Mother! It is only you who shows the knowledge as different visible things in this world. The five senses are not capable of either experiencing or describing you by words. The seat of such mother is the embodiment all-pervading, self-shining Brahman, who knows its greatness? Oh! Mother, it is beyond the limits of description.

AUM